FIELD BOOK OF INSECTS

PUTNAM'S
NATURE FIELD BOOKS

Companion books to this one

Mathews	American Wild Flowers
	American Trees and Shrubs
	Wild Birds and Their Music
Durand	Wild Flowers in Homes and **Gardens**
	My Wild Flower Garden
	Common Ferns
Lutz	Insects
Loomis	Rocks and Minerals
Eliot	Birds of the Pacific Coast
Armstrong	Western Wild Flowers
Alexander	Birds of the Ocean
Anthony	North American Mammals
Thomas	Common Mushrooms
Sturgis	Birds of the Panama Canal Zone
Miner	Seashore Life
Breder	Marine Fishes of Atlantic Coast
Morgan	Ponds and Streams
Longyear	Rocky Mountain Trees and Shrubs
Olcott } Putnam }	Field Book of the Skies
Beebe } Tee-Van }	The Shore Fishes of Bermuda

Each in One Volume
fully illustrated
including many
C o l o r e d
Plates

Plate I

Papilio cresphontes

FIELD BOOK OF INSECTS

OF THE UNITED STATES AND CANADA,
AIMING TO ANSWER COMMON QUESTIONS

By FRANK E. LUTZ, Ph.D.

CURATOR, DEPARTMENT OF INSECT LIFE
AMERICAN MUSEUM OF NATURAL HISTORY

*Third Edition, Rewritten to Include Much
Additional Material
With about 800 Illustrations, Many in Color*

G. P. PUTNAM'S SONS
NEW YORK

Fourth Impression

The study of entomology is one of the most fascinating of pursuits. It takes its votaries into the treasure-houses of Nature, and explains some of the wonderful series of links which form the great chain of creation. It lays open before us another world, of which we have been hitherto unconscious, and shows us that the tiniest insect, so small perhaps that the unaided eye can scarcely see it, has its work to do in the world, and does it.

REV. J. G. WOOD.

TO MY
ENTOMOLOGICAL COLLEAGUES
AT THE
AMERICAN MUSEUM OF NATURAL HISTORY
AND TO
YOU

PREFACE

During the sixteen years since the first edition of this book was published we have had some additions to our knowledge about insects and a great many confusing changes in names. In bringing you "up to date" the shifting from the old names to the new has been made as painless as possible and occasional warnings of future changes have been offered.

Our Southern and Western friends properly objected to the former editions' slighting of their insects. Even in this one there is a strong Northeastern flavor—perhaps somewhat in proportion to the distribution of human population—but an attempt has been made to include all of the principal families, most of the subfamilies, and many of the genera of English-speaking North America.

By adopting various typographic tricks and by severely condensing technical matter it has been possible to increase very materially the amount of included information and, nevertheless, keep the number of pages within bounds. It reminds me of a telegraphic night-letter with space left for "Love," which in this case means "I hope that you will find the book helpful."

As before, I owe everything to others who know more about their specialties than I do: J. Bequaert about wasps; W. S. Creighton, ants; C. H. Curran, flies; H. B. Hungerford, bugs; A. J. Mutchler, beetles; J. A. G. Rehn, the old Orthoptera; H. F. Schwarz, bees; and F. E. Watson, butterflies and moths. These and others have been most kind.

Quite probably I shall never revise the Field Book of Insects again. In offering this revision to you I wish you all "Good Hunting."

FRANK E. LUTZ.

December 1934.

CONTENTS

INTRODUCTION

When the publishers of this series spoke about a Field Book of Insects to be a companion to the excellent books already published we began to deal with the arithmetic of large numbers. There are, for example, approximately 15,000 species of insects to be found within fifty miles of New York City. More than 2,000 of these are either moths or butterflies. A book to enable the student to recognize all the insects of even this limited region would have to be as large as one for the birds of the whole world. However, only a few of these thousands are usually noticed by the layman or, outside of his specialty, by the average amateur; and often the interest is not so much in knowing the specific name as in learning the general group to which the insect belongs and what it does. This constitutes a general knowledge of insects. To go further, in most groups, one must become a specialist. This book refers, by specific name, to many different kinds of insects inhabiting the United States and nearly 600 of these are illustrated by one or more figures. If the selections were wisely made, the non-specialist should be able, by its aid, to recognize, at least in a general way, most of the insects that attract his attention and to find the answer to most of his questions. It is not intended to be a manual of economic entomology although most of our relatively few injurious insects are included. It is intended to be an introduction to commonly observed species and to the larger groups (genera and particularly families) of insects. Although the species mentioned are, for the most part, inhabitants of northeastern United States, many of them have a wide distribution in this country and some of them even in other continents. I hope, therefore, especially since generalities are more important than concrete illustrations, that this little book may be useful to laymen "wherever dispersed." You can provide your own concrete illustrations, once you have the general idea. I have been guided in the choice of subject matter by what the public seem to want to

know, judging by the letters received and personal inquiries made at an institution whose motto is "For the
people, for education, for science." Really, the title might
be *Answers to Common Questions about Insects.*

Certain families or groups of species were selected in
each of the important orders for more detailed attention
on the theory that it is well to "know a little about many
things and much about a few." In beetles, for example,
a general survey is given of the order and the Long-
horns receive an "unfair" amount of space; in the True
Flies it is the Syrphidæ and the various House Flies; in
Hymenoptera it is the Bumblebees; and in Lepidoptera it
is the Butterflies (exclusive of Skippers) and the Saturnid Moths. I have found that such a combination of
general and special study has been very profitable and I
hope that you may find it equally so. The groups given
more detailed treatment were selected partly on the basis
of general interest and partly because their study did not
involve technicalities that would be likely to discourage
the amateur.

All of us are immensely indebted to those who have
gone before us. The mass of knowledge about insects,
great in reality but small in comparison with our ignorance, has been accumulated, bit by bit, by the laboring
man in his Sunday strolls and by the highly trained in-
vestigator. Much of this has been told over and over.
None of us can hope to prove all of the statements. I
have drawn freely on books and papers, too numerous to
mention, for facts which I did not previously know, some
of which I have already forgotten. This book is frankly
a compilation.

At the American Museum of Natural History we were
once severely criticized by an excitable school-marm
because we had labeled a number of exhibition specimens
with their scientific names but had neglected to give
English names to them. I once tried an interesting ex-
periment on a very young child with whom I was rather
intimately associated (She was my own). The first move
was to tell her that the name of a certain burly bee she
saw in the garden was *Bombus*. About a week later there
were near-tears because a neighbor insisted it was a
Bumblebee. Matters were smoothed over by explaining

that *Bombus* was the real name for such bees and Bumble-bee was a nickname. There are thousands of kinds of native-born, United States insects that have been really-named but not nicknamed.

I have made an effort in this book to record the real names correctly and have given the nicknames when I knew them; when I did not, I usually have left you the pleasure of inventing new ones. Often real names are no longer or harder than the "common" names. An insect is considered to be scientifically christened when some student who has found a kind that he thinks has never been named publishes a description of it and gives it a properly formed name. If somebody had previously named the same kind, the prior name usually holds. There is a complicated code governing the matter, and the confusing changes of scientific names are caused by the discovery and rectification of violations of this code. The shaking-down process is painful but we hope for ultimate stability. Many nicknames call an insect what it is not. Thus: a "Fish-moth" is not a moth and a "Fire-fly" is not a fly. I have tried to make this point by keeping the last part of the name separate only when it is correct for the group to which the insect belongs. Thus: "Clothes Moth" but "Fish-moth"; "Fire-fly" but "Horse Fly"; "June-bug" but "Lace Bug." Some names, such as "Bedbug," are so old and common that each has become one word.

Clearly some system of filing is necessary in order to keep track of the hundreds of thousands of insect names. A business man keeps his reference cards or letters in groups and sub-groups. As his business grows he not only adds new groups but he breaks up the old groups into finer divisions. It is the same with the classification ("taxonomy") of insects. Formerly nine major groups ("orders") were enough for insects, the "class" of animals with six legs. Some recent works divide insects into several classes and nearly forty orders. Not to make it too complicated, we will follow a moderate course and consider all insects as belonging to one class, divided into two subclasses and about thirty orders. Flies, in the strict sense, have no more than two wings and belong to the two-winged order (Diptera) ; the order to which butter-

flies and moths belong is Lepidoptera; that to which beetles belong is Coleoptera; and so on.

Orders are divided into suborders and these into
families. Lady-bird beetles belong to the family Coccinelidæ, while carpet beetles are Dermestidæ. Sometimes several families are combined into a superfamily
and sometimes a family is split into several subfamilies.
Family names end in "dæ" and subfamily names in
"næ." (In this book superfamily names end in "oidea."
Some authors group related orders into "superorders"
and use that ending for them.)

The next division that need concern us is genus; and
then species. The names of these divisions are the ones
ordinarily used. The generic name should always be
written with a capital and the specific with a small initial
letter. They are usually printed in italics. Bumblebees
are *Bombus;* a common species is *Bombus pennsylvanicus.*
There may be subgenera and subspecies. Some species have
varieties. For example, one of our beautiful butterflies is
Papilio glaucus variety *turnus.* There is no generally
accepted distinction between "subspecies" and "variety."

This system is more than a pure matter of convenience.
It aims to point out relationships. The species of a given
genus are supposed to be more closely related to each
other than they are to the species of other genera of the
same family; and the different genera of a given family
are believed to be more closely related to each other than
to those of other families of the same order.

Thus early be it said that insects do not grow after
they have wings. Small, winged flies do not grow to be
large, winged flies even though the same kitchen window
frequently contains all sizes. There are two main sorts of
life histories, called respectively Incomplete and Complete
Metamorphosis. Insects having the first kind (grasshoppers for example) look, when they leave the eggs,
more or less like miniatures of the adults except that
they have no wings even if the adults do have. Immature
insects having incomplete metamorphosis are called
nymphs. Young insects of the second sort may be as
different from the adult as a caterpillar is from a butterfly, and they go through a relatively quiet resting (pupal)
stage before they get wings. Young insects having com-

plete metamorphosis are called larvæ until they molt to become pupæ. The term is sometimes used for the young of other insects also.

Young insects may be said to grow by leaps and bounds, not gradually. They are largely covered by a shell-like skin that will not stretch. All the flesh is inside of this shell, and when the quantity of this flesh gets too large the shell splits, the insect emerges, swells out, and its new skin in turn hardens. This process is repeated several times before adult life is reached. The number of molts is usually very definite for each species and sometimes an insect, so starved that it has not largely increased its flesh, will, nevertheless, carry on its accustomed molts. In the case of winged insects having incomplete metamorphosis, the developing wings show as pads several stages before the adult. In those having complete metamorphosis, even the full-grown larvæ have no external indication of wings. Their wing-pads appear externally after the molt which results in the pupa. When the pupa molts, out steps the usually winged adult.

Mention has been made of the hard skins of insects. It is their skeleton and their muscles are attached to it. In man, the blood is sent to the lungs for a load of oxygen which it then carries to the tissues. Insects do things more directly: air is conducted to all parts of the body by means of a system of tubes called tracheæ. This system usually has a number of outside openings (spiracles) placed along each side of the body, but there is none on the head. Insects do not breathe through their mouths. Blood completely fills the body cavity and is kept in motion by means of a "heart" which is merely a pulsating tube open at both ends. The central nervous system is a double, longitudinal series of ganglia connected, one with another, by cords. There is no brain, strictly speaking, for the ganglia in the thorax seem to be about as important as those in the head. Nerves run from each ganglion to nearby parts of the body. Most insects seem to smell by means of their antennæ and some to hear with the same organs, but the location of "ears" is various and not always known; also there seem to be organs of smell on the feet and elsewhere.

All insects are divided into three parts: head, thorax

and abdomen. In some larvæ these parts are not distinctly marked off, but usually there will be no difficulty in recognizing the head. The thorax bears the wings, if any, and the true legs, if any. No insect ever has more than three pairs of true legs, and no other creature that the amateur is likely to notice and confuse with insects has as few as three pairs of legs. The part of the thorax which bears the front legs is called the prothorax. The middle legs and front wings, if any, are on the mesothorax; and the hind legs and hind wings, if any, on the metathorax. The top is called the notum and the under side the sternum. We have, then, "pronotum," "prosternum," and so on. The sides are the "pleuræ." The abdomen is the part of the body back of the thorax. In many larvæ, such as ordinary caterpillars, the abdomen may have leg-like, fleshy props or claspers; and in many adult insects there are appendages of one sort or another at the hind end of the abdomen. The "cerci" are a pair of such appendages.

The principal parts of the legs, going from the thorax outwards, are coxa, trochanter, femur, tibia and tarsus. The tarsus is usually made up of several "joints" (meaning segments, not articulations) and usually ends in one or more claws. The first joint of the tarsus is sometimes much larger than its companions and is called metatarsus or basitarsus. The big joints of the leg are the tibia and femur. The trochanter is small and sometimes two-jointed. The coxa usually looks like a small part of the thorax.

Wing "veins" or "nerves" neither contain blood nor have anything to do with the nervous system. They are thickenings that, for the most part, follow the course of tracheæ. The wing-venation is so important in the classification of insects that there is considerable truth in the saying that the names of insects are written on their wings. However, the writing is in a difficult code made more confusing by the lack of any generally accepted system of naming either the veins themselves or the spaces ("cells") between them. The classification of Lepidoptera into major groups largely depends on wing-veins but for several reasons they are not discussed here.

An insect's jaws usually chew, if they do chew, sideways, not up and down; but, see *Curculio*. The mouth-parts are subject to a great deal of modification and in some groups, instead of biting, they pierce and suck. Typically, there are two sets of jaws: mandibles and maxillæ. The latter are usually the more delicate and are furnished with a pair of feeler-like structures called palps. The lower lip (labium) also has a pair of palps. These two sets of palps are supposed to be tasting organs.

The eyes are of two sorts: compound and simple. The pair usually noticed are the compound eyes and are compact clusters of single eyes (ommatidia). Some insects, such as certain "silver-fish," have not more than 12 ommatidia to each eye; and some dragon-flies have 28,000 or more. The simple eyes (ocelli), if present, are situated between, and usually a little higher than, the compound eyes. There are usually three.

The antennæ ("feelers") are of various shapes and degrees of complication. At least some of the sense of smell is connected with them.

Finally, the outside of an insect's body is usually more or less covered with hairs. In butterflies and moths these hairs are largely scale-like. The "skin" is usually hard except at the articulations of joints or segments. These hard parts are often said to be "chitinized" but there is chitin in the soft parts as well.

This is about all the anatomy one needs to start with. More will be explained as occasion arises. See the index for references to definitions.

COLLECTING AND PRESERVING INSECTS

The following directions are, with slight changes, those in the American Museum's leaflet on *How to Collect and Preserve Insects*.

An entomologist is frequently amused at being asked by well-meaning friends if he found anything when he went out. Insect hunting is a sport in which there are no blanks if you know the game. Frequently the most unpromising times and places are the best, for others have been discouraged by the outlook and you get what they have missed. We can never truly say that we know an insect's haunts until we can tell where to look for it every hour of every day in the year. Many insects are great hiders and should be looked for under bark; in rotten wood; under stones, dead leaves, etc.; among the roots of plants; in stems and flowers—in short, everywhere and at all times.

The great essentials for insect collecting—eyes, fingers and an inquiring mind—were given each of us at birth and need only to be improved by use. Very few insects sting to such an extent that collecting with unaided fingers is uncomfortable and even the swiftest fliers can be caught by hand when they are young or asleep. However, certain tools are handy. They can either be made at home or purchased rather cheaply from dealers.

Mention of insect collecting immediately suggests a net. For the capture of adult butterflies, moths and other delicate, flying creatures this should be of the lightest possible material. Fine Brussels net or bobbinet is used for the larger sizes (1 to 2 ft. in diameter) and silk veiling for the pocket sizes. The depth of this net should be at least twice the diameter of its rim so that, when an insect is caught, a twist will fold the bag against the rim and leave the insect imprisoned in the lower end of the bag. The beginner is apt to choose too long a handle and can then take only long, slow strokes. Three feet is usually long enough for a handle.

The sweeping net should be made of stout, white muslin, or light duck, on a strong rim well fastened to a handle of such a length that the user can just touch the ground with the rim of the net without stooping. It is used to sweep blindly through grass, bunches of flowers light bushes, etc., in a fairly certain expectation of getting something. Many of the specimens will be damaged by the rough handling, but it is the quickest way to get large numbers of specimens and the only way to get certain things quickly. The tendency seems to be to make the handle of the sweep net too short, some on the market being only 6 in. long. These do not tire the arm so much as nets with longer handles, but you either miss the insects living near the ground or you get a very tired back. After sweeping for a few minutes one can, if desired, quickly twist up the bag and moisten the bottom of it with chloroform, ether, or carbon tetrachloride. In a short time even the liveliest grasshopper will be asleep and can be picked out and either saved or rejected. The rejected specimens will all shortly revive and walk, hop, or fly away.

The third net of the complete outfit is the water net. The bag should be of some strong material through which water will run readily. The rim should be strong and may be either circular in outline or flattened at the side opposite the handle. The advantage of the flattening is that the bottom of ponds can be skimmed, but the circular rim does fairly well, as the stirring of the water stirs up even the insects at the bottom and they are caught in the return swish of the net. A great deal of mud and weeds will also be caught, but devices to prevent this, such as covering the mouth of the net with a coarse wire screen, do not work well in collecting insects. After clearing the net of mud as much as possible by washing it through the net, dump the rest on the bank, preferably in the sun. Some insects will probably be seen at once; others will appear as the mass dries out. After you think that you have found everything, wait a while and look out for very small beetles. Many collectors miss them.

Some of the nets that are for sale have folding rims and jointed handles. Opinion differs as to the best. When, as is often the case, lightness and ease of transportation are desired, it is well to have but one handle and frame, with interchangeable bags. A fisherman's landing net has a frame consisting of two pieces of flexible steel that lie close together when not in use. It is what I use. The two-jointed handle is better than the three-jointed one, as one of the joints of the former is just right except for high flying or deep diving quarry. In these cases add the second.

A sieve is handy for getting the small insects hiding under accumulations of dead leaves, in moss, trash, etc. Two sieves with meshes of different sizes are handier. A good plan is to have a strong bag about a foot and a half square by two feet deep. About nine inches from the top sew strips across the corners so that a piece of half-inch mesh wire screen can rest on them. Sift through this until there is quite a bit of fine material in the bottom of the bag. Then retire to a comfortable place protected from the wind and spread a small sheet of white muslin or canvas. Now resift, using a mesh about four or five to an inch. The flat-bottomed sieves, six or eight inches in diameter, that are used for making French fried potatoes are excellent. Sift a very thin layer onto the white cloth and examine carefully the coarse stuff for relatively large things before it is thrown away. Be patient with the small stuff. Insects have a habit of "playing possum" and have plenty of patience themselves. They do not seem to like tobacco smoke. If you do, blow some on the litter. It will hasten matters—at least, smokers think so.

This is a good place to mention collecting forceps, as they are almost necessary in picking up very small insects as well as insects concerning whose ability and inclination to sting there may be some suspicion. The best forceps for handling very delicate insects do not seem to be on the market. They are made of strips of German silver and have small but rounded points. However, small steel ones do very well. Steel forceps about a foot long are handy for picking caddice cases, etc., out of water, but they are of little use in general work. Dealers also carry forceps having gauze-covered frames at the tips. They are meant for holding stinging insects while they are being examined, but they, also, are of very little use to the general collector.

A strong knife for cutting off galls, stripping bark, splitting infested branches, etc., is essential. A trowel is useful in following insect burrows or digging for root-borers. The entrenching tool used in the army is a fair combination of trowel, hatchet, and large knife.

There are two chief methods of night-collecting in general use: "sugaring" and at light. Another, while not so productive of specimens, is more interesting. It consists in simply prowling around with a lamp, examining the centers of flowers, the underside of leaves, tree-trunks, etc., to find out what the nocturnal insects are doing and also where and how the day-flying insects are passing the night.

There are about as many recipes for making the sugar mixture as there are for "mother's biscuits." Baking molasses usually forms the basis. Some additions may

PLATE 2

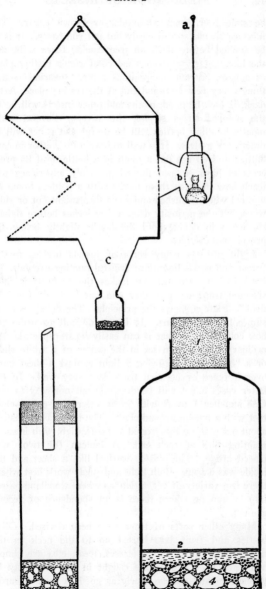

II

be stale beer, rum, asafœtida, or brown sugar. The mixture should spread easily but not run badly. It is to be applied before dusk on tree trunks, fence rails, and the like. Starting from some comfortable resting place as a base, lay out a circuitous route, "sugaring" something every few feet, and end at the resting place. After dark, if luck be good, moths and other insects will be on the sugared strips sipping the sweets. Several wide-mouthed killing bottles will be useful, but a net will be practically useless. It is well to have a little ether in each bottle; and do not put a moth in a bottle until its predecessors have stopped fluttering. Only experience will teach how to catch these moths with a bottle. Some fly upward when disturbed and some fly straight out or sideways, but the majority drop a few inches before flying; so, when in doubt, hold the bottle slightly below the prospective captive.

Light attracts many sorts of insects besides moths. Street and porch lights are fruitful hunting grounds. A lamp by an open window makes the room it is in a splendid trap; or a smaller one can be made for "the field." Plate 2 shows the principle. The details vary to suit collectors' whims. It is not difficult to make the box collapsible so that it can easily be transported. An ordinary barn-lantern set in the center of a white sheet or a "bull's eye" throwing a light against a sheet hung over a fence or between trees does very well. In the latter cases a net will be desirable but not easy to use. One summer I used, with great success, a cheese-cloth tent with a muslin ground-cloth. The tent was A-shaped, about 9 x 6 ft. on the ground and 6 ft. high, with inward-pointing flies at each end. A lantern (or two) was placed inside. The outside worked like a sheet and the inside was a trap. Both light and sugar work best where there is a variety of vegetation, as where woodland passes into swamp or where there is an abundance of second growth.

Many other sorts of traps have been devised. Olive bottles and fruit jars buried up to the neck in the ground and baited with molasses, meat, etc., are simple and effective. The insects caught in this way may be washed off and will be nearly as good as new. Boards, daubed on the under side with molasses or covering meat, are not bad. Girdled branches and cut limbs, hung up, attract wood-boring insects which can then be collected by beating them into an upturned umbrella by sharply rapping the limbs with a stout stick. In fact, an umbrella is a very useful piece of apparatus. Branches, both living and dead, are full of insects. The inverted umbrella catches what are knocked off but does not hold them for long. The collector must act quickly. Some collectors put a quill in the cork of a collecting tube as shown in Pl. 2. If the outer end of the quill be put over the insect, it will crawl up through the quill and into the bottle from which exit is difficult. If the umbrella be white, or at least lined with white, the insects can be more easily seen but so can the umbrella— not by the insects particularly, but by inquisitive humans —and the non-committal black does very well.

Beating will knock down many larvæ. Directions for preserving them are given on p. 20. Some, at least, should be reared and here ingenuity is of more value than volumes of instructions. The beginner will doubtless be inclined to give his charges more light and air than is necessary and not enough moisture. Pasteboard shoe-boxes are excellent for large caterpillars. Tin boxes keep the food longer and are easily cleaned, but must be watched carefully or the food will mold. If the foodplant can be potted, a good contrivance is to slip a lantern globe over it, sinking the bottom far enough into the ground to prevent the escape of larvæ in that direction and covering the top with cheese-cloth. Even if the plant cannot be grown, twigs can be kept fresh for some time by keeping their cut ends in a small bottle of water sunk in the ground and used inside a lantern globe. (See Pl. 3.) The twigs will be held in place and larvæ prevented from drowning if cotton be loosely stuffed in the neck of the bottle around the twigs. It is well to throw a thin layer of dirt over the cotton so that fallen larvæ can easily get back to their food. Another device is shown, in section, in Pl. 3. It is made of plaster of Paris and a glass cover. Water put in *b* keeps the block moist. It is useful chiefly for ground-inhabiting larvæ or for galls. However, for the latter, fruit jars with moist sand or a moist sponge in the bottom do just as well or better. Do not forget the larvæ living in hollow stems, dead wood and under bark.

When caterpillars are about to molt, especially when they are about to change to pupæ, they stop eating and act as though they are sick. If you are in doubt as to how a species pupates, it is well to give the caterpillar potting soil covered with dead leaves and some twigs of their food-plant, not merely fresh leaves. A desirable, but not necessary, refinement of technique is to bake the soil in order to kill bacteria and fungi. Species which "should" pupate underground will often get along fairly well even if they have no earth—much better than if they be covered with earth after pupation takes place, as this would pack them and that is injurious.

Up to this point but little mention has been made of killing insects and that little was really not necessary. Insects can be studied alive with great pleasure and profit. However, there are so many kinds and the differences between species are often so minute that it is well to kill and preserve at least samples. Fortunately, this can be done with less trouble and less injury to the "balance of Nature" than is the case with most animals or even plants. Furthermore, the collection can be made very attractive and instructive without taking up much space.

The best all-around killing agent for adult insects is cyanide. Sodium cyanide should be broken into pieces varying in size from that of a small pea to that of a hickory nut, according to the size of the bottle to be used. Do not inhale the dust or get any into your mouth. It is deadly. Olive bottles make good medium-sized bottles, while fruit jars are better for large-sized moths and butterflies. Tubes, even as small as ¼ in. in diameter by about 2 in. long, are not too small for some things. Avoid bottles with strongly constricted necks. Avoid, also, bottles made of thin glass. There are many ways of keeping the cyanide in position and the bottle in good condition. The most general way is to pour a thin layer of plaster of Paris over a layer (from ¼ to ⅓ in. deep) of cyanide. However, since such a bottle will quickly get too moist from the specimens and the decomposition of the cyanide, some further device is almost always used. The pieces of cyanide may be wrapped in soft absorbent paper or imbedded in dry sawdust before the plaster is poured on. Another way is to imbed it in dry plaster before pouring on the wet. A piece of blotting paper should be fitted tightly over the plaster after it has "set." See Pl. 2. Some do not use plaster but imbed the cyanide in cotton and cover this with a piece of blotting paper or a thin porous cork. It is always well to have a few narrow strips of loose absorbent paper in the bottle. They prevent injury to the insects by shaking and help to keep the bottle dry, as they can be frequently changed. Ordinarily a bottle should be allowed to ripen for several days before using. Collectors of delicate moths and butterflies frequently put a few drops of ether or chloroform in their cyanide bottles before starting out. This is to quiet the insects at once, for the cyanide sometimes kills slowly. Experience will teach the collector that some insects die very slowly and revive after apparent death. Too long an exposure to cyanide fumes changes the color of some insects.

It may be difficult for those not connected with scientific institutions to get cyanide of potassium and there is a fear that cyanide bottles are dangerous in the hands of children. Cotton, saturated with carbon tetrachloride (sold also both as a fire-extinguishing and as a cleaning fluid) may be kept in an olive bottle or something of the sort; and specimens are killed by putting them into this bottle for a few minutes. Ether or chloroform may be used in the same way. Each of these three tend to make the specimens stiff and brittle.

Practically all beetles and dragon flies, together with dull-colored, hairless insects of other orders, can be killed in alcohol and kept there indefinitely. Fifty percent is strong enough for killing and 70% for preserving. Higher grades make them brittle. No fly, bee, butterfly, moth, or any green insect, other than those previously mentioned, should be put into alcohol. In an emergency, kerosene, gasoline, or benzine, put on the thorax, will kill and give satisfactory specimens. Butterflies and moths may be killed by carefully but firmly pinching the thorax between the thumb and finger, one on each side. In fact, many collectors of these insects pinch their captures before taking them out of the net. This prevents their injuring themselves by thrashing about.

The stock method of mounting is on pins. The almost universally adopted pin is 1½ in. long and has a very small head. It varies in thickness from extremely slender to as thick as an ordinary pin. The useful sizes are from No. 0 to No. 3. They are either plain "white" or black. Much is to be said for each, with the voting probably in favor of black. At any rate, they should snap back when bent a reasonable amount. A pin that bends easily and stays bent is apt to produce profanity. Beetles are usually pinned through the right wing-cover. All other insects, when pinned, are pinned through the thorax. In the case of flies it is well to pin a trifle to the right of the middle line, as the bristles on the back are important in taxonomy and one side of the body should be perfect. True bugs should be pinned through the triangular portion of the thorax which is between the wings.

Very small insects are usually mounted on the tip of small paper triangles, a medium-sized pin being stuck through the broad end of the triangle. The triangle may be cut out with scissors or a sharp knife to a suitable size and shape. The best way is to cut tough, rather stiff paper into strips about 0.4 inch wide and then snip off triangles from them by making transverse cuts. It is well to pin up a quantity of these triangles in odd moments and keep them on hand. When ready to mount, put a small bit of white shellac dissolved in alcohol or of some good elastic glue on the tip of a triangle and touch it to the under side of the thorax. Some difficulty will be experienced in keeping the insect straight on the point, especially if the adhesive be too thin. The triangles for ants should be fairly broad at the "point," and the front end of the abdomen as well as the thorax should be supported. We are now using a method that, at least for small flies, seems to be better. It consists of simply putting a ring of glue around the pin and, before the glue has set, touching the side of the insect with it. This leaves most of the insect quite visible.

The height of the insects on the pin is important for the final appearance of the collection. A strip of cardboard whose width is ¼ to ⅓ the length of the pin makes a convenient gauge. With one edge held at the head of the pin push the insect up until it touches the other edge. Or a block of wood containing a hole whose depth is ¼ to ⅓ the length of the pin may be used. Devices for regulating the height by sticking the *point* of the pin into a gauge are not satisfactory because of the varying thickness of the specimens.

Mounting insects in balsam on glass slides will probably not be taken up by the general collector unless he be already accustomed to making balsam mounts. It is, however, a satisfactory method of getting extremely small forms ready for study. They may also be put between bits of celluloid, the mount then being pinned with the rest of the collection.

Mounted butterflies and moths usually have all four wings expanded to their utmost and more or less in line with the creature's body. This makes a nice-looking collection and is the best that can be done with most butterflies. However, many moths have natural rest positions which are not only interesting but save space. It is well, therefore, to expand the wings of the left side so that the markings on both front and hind wings show, but to leave the right wings in the natural rest position. The reason for expanding the left side, rather than the right, and for putting the triangles, etc., on the left side is that most people are right-handed. This arrangement makes it easy to use the pinning forceps with the right hand. For the same reason, when the wings on one side of grasshoppers, wasps, etc., are to be spread, the left wings should be selected for the purpose. Pinning forceps are strong forceps with broad, roughened ends and are useful for pushing the pins into the cork of the storage boxes.

The most common form of spreading board is illustrated in Pl. 3. The sides are made of soft wood. In the bottom of the central channel is a piece of cork or of balsa wood. After pinning the insect, push the pin into this central cork until the back of the insect is nearly flush with the board. Then draw the wings to the desired position by means of forceps or of a fine needle caught in the strong front margin of the wings. Never use the fingers on moths or butterflies, as this will rub off the scales which cover the wings and give color to them. The wings may be kept in position by means of fine pins, or bits of heavy glass, or strips of tracing cloth held in place by pins placed outside of the wings. A combination of the last two methods, glass on paper, is best. It is well to have a number of boards with grooves of different widths for use with different-sized insects. The same plate shows a setting board for spreading caddice flies and other insects when it is desired to have the legs spread as well. The holes running down the center are just large enough to accommodate that part of the pin which is above the insect. The wings are spread as before, except that now the under side of the insect is visible and the legs are accessible.

Should insects get dry and stiff before they are spread, they must be relaxed. This is done by putting them in a covered jar or tin box containing water or moist blotting paper. A few drops of carbolic acid added to the water will prevent mold. Twenty-four hours will usually be sufficient to relax even the driest, but more time may sometimes be necessary. If the insect has neither scales nor hairs, it can be relaxed quickly by immersing it in warm water.

It will be noticed that both of the setting boards illustrated here give the wings a slight upward tilt. If they keep this position, it will not be objectionable, but they are not likely to do so, since the weight of the wings will probably drop them to at least the horizontal. Large insects dry more slowly than small ones and it will probably be necessary to allow them to remain on the boards for about two weeks. They should certainly remain until thoroughly dried. No further preservation is then necessary, as a rule, for the fairly hard-bodied, adult insects. Some grasshoppers have large abdomens full of fat and decomposing food. These should first be opened by a cut along the belly, the

PLATE 3

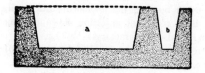

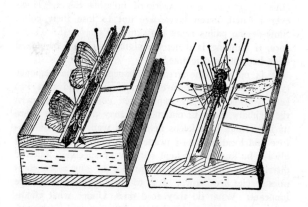

viscera taken out and the abdomen stuffed with cotton. I have been told that injecting large specimens with formalin is also satisfactory.

Broken insects may be repaired by the use of shellac thin glue, or dissolved celluloid.

Caterpillars may be prepared as follows: Make a small opening on the under side near the hind end and cut the intestine loose from the outer body wall. Then, laying the caterpillar on a piece of clean blotting paper, squeeze the viscera through this opening by gently rolling the caterpillar with a lead pencil, beginning near the hind end and gradually working toward the front. After getting rid of most of the viscera, insert a straw and fasten the first segment of the larva to the end of the straw by means of a fine needle. Draw the hind segment up the straw until the larva is natural length and fasten it in the same manner. Then, inflate the larva by gently blowing through the straw. Since the front end of the straw may get plugged up, it is well to make a small hole in the side of the straw before it is inserted. This hole had best come about midway between the larva's head and tail. Since inflation must be kept up until the larva's skin is dried, gentle heat is usually used. A tin can, with holes punched in it for ventilation and heated by an alcohol lamp, makes a good oven, or one can be purchased. Dealers also sell bellows, tubing, clips, etc., to make the work of inflating easier. However inflated, green larvæ are apt to lose their color. Slow-drying paints relax the skin and distort it. Therefore, if painting is done, the pigments should be mixed with benzine or the like.

It is only by the greatest chance that the beginner gets a new or even rare species on ground that has been worked over by experienced collectors, but even the primary class in entomology may add to our store of knowledge if it keeps field notes well. Date of capture and locality are of prime importance. They should always be known and kept with every specimen, but the distribution and time of appearance of our more common species are known. It is of their habits that we are ignorant. What do they feed on? Under what conditions are they to be found when young and when old, e willing to look over collections which are not too miscellaneous for the privilege of retaining duplicates f the species they identify. If the species is undescribed, hey usually wish to describe it and keep a set, one pecimen of which is designated a "type" of that species. A very large majority of entomologists are kind, helpful individuals; I merely wish to say that laymen are often unwittingly unreasonable in their requests.

KEYS.—Such keys as are given here are, for the most part, simplified versions of keys in special, more technical, books and papers. They have been simplified in two ways: by leaving out forms that are not very likely to attract the notice of beginners or whose separation involves too great technicalities and by using, as far as possible, easily appreciated characters even though they may not be, otherwise, the best ones to use. The result of the first simplification is that forms will be found which do not fit anything in the key although they may come close to it. An attempt has been made to word the keys so that forms which were not intended to be included will not fit anywhere, thus avoiding a misidentification. This attempt has not always been completely successful. Working a key backward, from the name to the start, usually gives so good a description of the form in question that it is not further described in the text.

To use a key start at 1 and decide which of the two (or more) alternatives best agrees with the specimen; then go to the number indicated at the right. Continue this process until a name without a following number is reached. *Do not take too much for granted.* If a thing is said in one alternative to be black, it is not necessarily not black in the other unless this is definitely stated. If you reach a point where neither alternative fits, go back to the place where you had most doubt concerning a choice and take the other alternative; perhaps the statements were not sufficiently clear and you made a wrong choice. If nothing works, it would be kind of you to conclude that you have a species which was not included in the key, although the fact of the matter is that it is next to impossible to draw up a relatively simple key that will not sometimes stick in the lock.

day and night, winter and summer? What do they do and how do they do it? Some system of keeping notes is imperative if your collection is to be worth while.

The pin label should be small but legible. It should give the locality and date of capture; possibly also a number referring to your notebook. Certain firms make a business of printing these labels from small type, or the collector can make up a sheet by means of an ordinary typewriter (black ink is best) and have a block made from this, greatly reduced in size. From this block any number of impressions can be made. If dates are not printed, they should be filled in before cutting the labels apart. Field numbers can be written on the back of these labels or put on a separate label. The collector's name can also be put on a separate label. Similar labels should all be the same height on the pin throughout the collection. This is accomplished by sticking the pin first through the label, then into a hole of a given depth or cork of given thickness, thus pushing the labels up to a uniform height.

Since members of a family of beetles (Dermestidæ) are given to eating dried insects, the storage boxes should have tight-fitting lids. Except for that, almost anything will do. Cigar boxes are not bad if carefully watched, but better boxes can be purchased at reasonable prices from dealers. Glass-topped drawers are nice but not necessary. Whatever sort of box is used, the bottom, inside, should be covered with something which is soft enough to allow a pin to enter easily but which will hold the pin when it is once in. The compressed cork of the dealers is best. Balsa wood is good. Sliced cornstalk is used by some beginners but two layers of the corrugated paper, such as bottles are packed in, are better than cornpith. The layers should be placed so that the corrugations run at right angles to each other.

Camphor balls or flaked naphthalene will help to keep Dermestids out. If camphor balls are used, first heat the head of an ordinary pin and, while hot, push the head into the ball. When cool, it will be solid and the ball can be pinned into the box. If Dermestids do get in, they may be killed by pouring into the box about a teaspoonful of carbon bisulphide or carbon tetrachloride and closing the lid down tightly. Remember that the bisulphide is very inflammable.

It frequently happens that the collector cannot attend to his catch at once, or possibly for months. Of course, those things that are collected in alcohol may remain there. Butterflies should be put into triangular envelopes. The manner of making these is shown in Pl. 4. Never put more than one specimen in an envelope. Other insects can be packed between layers of cotton and cheese-cloth, with naphthalene flakes put in to keep out ants, etc., or they can be put in sawdust. In the latter case it is well to sprinkle carbolic acid on the sawdust to prevent mold. An excellent method of packing insects (except butterflies and moths) that are to be dried is to make tubes of unglazed paper around a lead pencil after writing the data on that part of the paper which will be outside. One end is closed by folding in the paper there, and then the tube is nearly filled with freshly killed insects. Finally, the other end is closed by folding in the paper. These tubes and the triangular envelopes can be packed in a cigar box and, if sprinkled with naphthalene to keep out ants and Dermestids, will keep indefinitely. Never pack moist insects in a tin box and never close even a wooden box tightly if there are many moist insects in it. Mold will result if you do.

IDENTIFICATION

For this work a magnifying glass of some sort is usually necessary except for the larger Lepidoptera, and even with these it is useful when mouth-parts and the like are to be examined. If you collect at all extensively, you will get many species that are not mentioned here in sufficient detail to enable you to fix on their names. Separate these into their orders and, if possible, families and even genera. Then await your chance to consult more technical books or identified collections. Possibly you can arrange to have some specialist identify them for you, but this deprives you of the pleasure and benefit of doing it yourself. Furthermore, specialists usually have more than they can do, although they frequently

PLATE 4

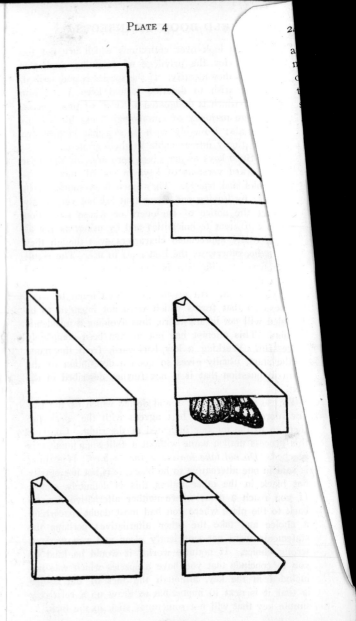

THE CONTROL OF INJURIOUS INSECTS

This section may seem out of place in a Field Book, but the garden is a part of the "field" as far as insects are concerned. I once made an at-first-sight rash statement to the effect that at least five hundred species of insects are naturally in my back yard near New York City and now I have proved it. Some of these insects are not welcome. Although the American Museum has no department of economic entomology, many of the inquiries that are made there about insects concern methods of control.

If the injury is serious, write to your State Entomologist or to the Bureau of Entomology of the U. S. Department of Agriculture. They, especially the State Entomologist, should know about serious outbreaks. They are fitted by training and constant work along these lines to give good advice and, if the occasion demands it, personal supervision. Furthermore, you have a right to do this; you help to pay the salaries.

Few insects are injurious in all the stages of their life-history, and the fight against injurious insects should start before the injury begins. Mosquitoes and flies should be killed before they can fly; the first meal of leaf-feeders should be their last, even if they get that. All of this requires a knowledge of the life-histories so that we may know the best time to fight. Fall or winter plowing may uncover pupæ which are hibernating in the ground and kill them. If the insect passes the winter in the egg stage, spraying, provided spraying will kill the larvæ, should be done just as the eggs hatch. Therefore, we should know when that will be. This your State Entomologist can tell you for your particular locality and I can not.

Predacious and parasitic insects are now "the one best bet" in economic entomology. Why cover our vegetation with poison year after year if we can set insect friends to killing insect enemies? This, again, is work for the professional economic entomologist, although I have tried to help you to distinguish friends from enemies.

If possible, prevent breeding. This applies especially

to such enemies as mosquitoes and flies. Why live in a wire-and-wood cage when draining swamps, putting fish in ponds, and similar preventive measures will control mosquitoes, and general cleaning up will do away with flies? Many insect enemies of cultivated plants breed on weeds. Either treat the "weeds" as cultivated plants or get rid of them.

Insecticides may be roughly divided into four classes: stomach poisons, contact insecticides, repellents and gases. Stomach poisons (arsenic and the like) are used to control chewing insects. To control sucking insects, such as plant lice, contact poisons (e.g., kerosene emulsion) are used. Since there are many such poisons and frequent improvements are being made, the best advice that I can give you is to write to your State Entomologist and to the U. S. Department of Agriculture for their latest bulletins.

CHIEFLY ABOUT SPIDERS

Animals having no backbone but jointed legs are called Arthropoda. Some of these have two pairs of antennæ ("feelers") and at least five pairs of legs; these are Crustacea and include lobsters, crabs, crayfish, sow-bugs, and the like. Some have no apparent antennæ; one class of these lives in the sea (the "king" or "horseshoe crab") and another is, for the most part, terrestrial, breathing air. The latter class is called Arachnida and includes spiders and their relatives. Finally, disregarding minor groups, there are three classes the members of which have one pair of antennæ. Two of them have more than three pairs of jointed legs and no wings: the Diplopoda, or millipedes, have two pairs of legs on each of some, at least, of what appear to be body segments; the Chilopoda, or centipedes, have only one pair of legs to a single segment. The third class is Hexapoda, or insects. When adult, insects never have more than three pairs of legs but usually have wings.

Some of the relatives of spiders have the abdomen distinctly segmented. If there is a tail-like hind end, it is a scorpion of some sort; if not, it is, in northeastern United States, either one of the small pseudoscorpions or else a "harvestman," also called "grandfather-gray-beard," "daddy-long-legs," etc.,—the creature some of us used to deprive of most of its legs in order that it should point the way to our cows or to our home. Mites and spiders have unsegmented abdomens; mites have no constriction of the body between the abdomen and the leg-bearing portion, but spiders do. Ticks are a sub-order of mites. When very young ("seed ticks") they have only three pairs of legs. The distinctions between the various kinds are rather technical. If interested, write to the U. S. Dept. of Agriculture for their latest bulletins.

Many of the not-yet-acquainted consider spiders to be insects and for that reason they are mentioned here—but briefly, because they have no more claim to be con-

27

sidered insects than have lobsters, except that they approach insects in the matter of interesting habits. Among other even more important differences, they have four pairs of legs; also the head and thorax are merged in one piece (cephalothorax). Palpi are frequently so developed as to look like a fifth pair of legs. The eyes are simple, usually eight in number, and differing in size and arrangement in different sorts of spiders. The bite of practically all spiders is poisonous— that is the way they kill their food—but there is so little poison and so few spiders are strong enough to bite through the human skin, even if they would try, that most spiders are not dangerous. At the hind end of the abdomen are small appendages, the spinnerets, from which come the fluids that harden on exposure to air and form silk. The silk of insects usually comes from their mouths.

Spider's silk has been used by man for cross-threads in telescopes and in other ways. Spiders originally used silk only to wrap up their masses of eggs (See *Lycosa*, Pl. 6). Then they took to lining their retreats with silk; later they built platforms outside of their retreats and from these developed the snares which have been the wonder and admiration of all ages, humanly speaking. These snares, even those that are orb-shaped, differ greatly among themselves. Most of the orb-snares are made by members of a single family, Argiopidæ (or Epeiridæ), and a large proportion of our spiders make no snare, catching their prey by stealth, fleetness of foot or length of jump. Silk is used by certain young spiders for "ballooning." They stand on some elevation, spin a thread into the air and, when the wind catches it, sail away. This is the explanation of "showers of gossamer."

This is not the place to go minutely into the subject, but spiders may be divided into two sorts: what are called, in this country, tarantulas and the, strictly speaking, spiders. The large, hairy, much-feared tarantulas live in the South and some of them build interesting trap-door nests. The following families are true spiders.

The Dictynidæ belong to a group having special attachments on their spinning machine by which they

PLATE 5

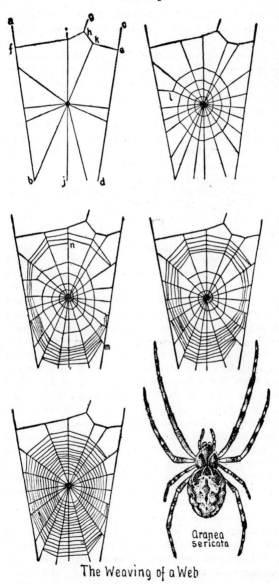

The Weaving of a Web

Aranea sericata

make hackled bands in their webs. Most of the sheet-webs on the sides of houses, especially at windows, are made by *Dictyna sublata*. The Theridiidæ have a well-developed comb on the hind legs to aid in throwing liquid silk over the prey they wish to entangle. *Theridion tepidariorum* is a common house spider, the one that makes the tangled web in the corners of rooms where "no beaux will go." *Latrodectus mactans,* the Black-widow, a jet-black spider marked with red or yellow, living under stones or pieces of wood, also belongs to this family and is the only spider of northeastern United States concerning which there is good evidence of its seriously biting human beings.

The Argiopidæ are the chief orb weavers. They usually have relatively large abdomens. The maker and the making of a fairly typical web are shown in Pl. 5, which is based upon an exhibit in the American Museum of Natural History. This spider is very common about buildings and has had a variety of names of which *Aranea sericata* is believed to be better usage than the more commonly employed *Epeira sclopetaria.* After the outer framework and the inner spokes of the web are finished the spider puts on the "primary spiral," shown as ending at *l.* All of these threads consist of smooth, tough silk that is not sticky. From this point on the spider uses the sticky threads that constitute the real snare. The details of spinning the web vary but the putting in of the first sticky threads is very irregularly done. In the figure given here it may be followed from *m* to *n.* From *n* she continued in a regular spiral until the primary spiral of smooth silk was reached. She then cut away the outer portion of the primary spiral, so that she might have more room for the snare. This process of cutting away the primary spiral and putting in the sticky spiral is shown, in the fourth figure, about half finished. Finally, there is the complete web with nearly all of the primary spiral removed.

Each species has its own distinct way of making webs and so many species of this family are commonly noticed (especially the females when they are swollen with eggs), both because of their beautiful colors and of their in-teresting webs, and some of the species are so variable,

PLATE 6

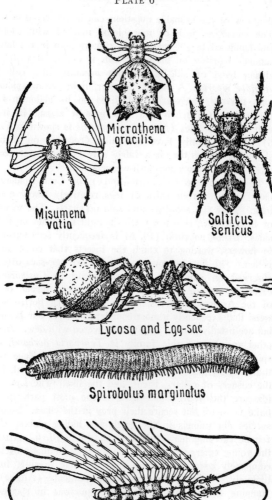

Micrathena
gracilis

Misumena
vatia

Salticus
senicus

Lycosa and Egg-sac

Spirobolus marginatus

E.L.B.

Scutigera forceps

that few of the probable questions can be answered here. The spider an inch or more long, marked with spots and bands of bright orange and usually seen in the late summer hanging on an orb which is decorated with a zigzag band of silk is *Miranda aurantia,* also called *Argiope riparia.* A slightly smaller, light yellow spider with narrow transverse black lines on its abdomen is *Metargiope trifasciata* and also puts a zigzag in its web. Some species (*Micrathena gracilis* is shown in Pl. 6) of this family have spine-like processes on their abdomens but *Aranea* is a fairly safe generic name for most of the conspicuous orb-weavers.

The Thomisidæ (or Misumenidæ), or Crab Spiders, have the two front pairs of legs relatively heavy and long. They run sideways and spin no snare. The white or light yellow, sometimes with a light red band on the sides, *Misumena vatia* (Pl. 6) is frequently seen sitting in flowers, waiting to catch the insects that come for pollen. The flat, lustrous, parchment-like egg-sacs often observed on stones in pastures belong to *Castaneira descripta,* one of the Clubionidæ. *Agelena nævia,* one of the Agelenidæ, is responsible for the flat horizontal webs that frequently almost completely carpet our lawns but are usually noticed only when covered with dew. Another member of this family is *Tegenaria derhami,* a spider that lives with man from the Frigid Zone to the Tropics, making a flat sheet, often dust-covered, in the corners of cellars, barns, and the like. The Lycosidæ are the Wolf Spiders. For the most part, they build no snare but secure their prey in the chase. Some species dig tunnels in the earth for hiding places. A female carrying her egg sac is shown in Pl. 6. After the young emerge they will ride on their mother's back, completely covering it, until they are able to shift for themselves. Finally we come to the Salticidæ (Attidæ), Jumping Spiders, of small size, numerous in species, and replete with interest because of their beauty, their mating habits, their occasional mimicry of ants and other things concerning which you are referred, first of all, to Nature. If you see a small spider springing about, sometimes sideways or backwards, on a fence rail or the sunny side of a building, it is probably a Salticid

(possibly *Salticus scenicus;* Pl. 6) and will repay a
bit of watching.

DIPLOPODA

The large, commonly observed *Spirobolus* (Pl. 6) is
a typical Millipede. There are a number of smaller
species in our gardens. These creatures feed on
vegetable matter and do not "bite." When disturbed,
they curl up into a spiral and sometimes exude a defensive fluid.

CHILOPODA

The bite of all Centipedes is poisonous and that of
large species may be serious. The only common sort in
the North is *Scutigera forceps* (Pl. 6). It lives in
houses, feeding upon flies, roaches and other insects.
Dr. Felt says "its presence in a house should be wel-
comed, since it is capable of inflicting no injury aside
from a somewhat poisonous bite, the latter being extremely rare." I confess that any found in our house
get stepped on.

INSECTS

For certain distinctive characteristics of insects see p. 27 and the sections on anatomy in the Introduction.

I know of no wholly satisfactory "key" (p. 24) to the orders of insects. Highly technical characters are required and the student who understands these technicalities usually needs no key. *Classification of Insects: A Key to the Known Families of Insects and Other Terrestrial Arthropods* by Brues and Melander is excellent and has been freely drawn upon in preparing this book. However, the beginner can usually get along without a key to orders by leafing through a book until he either finds what he wants or still has an interesting question for future solving. Below is given a list of North American orders with brief, often technical, descriptions of adults. It, together with the following hints, may be a little helpful.

If the insect is wingless.—If inactive but not worm-like, it is probably a pupa of one of the Endopterygota (Orders 23 to 33) or of Thysanoptera (12); see also 21 (scale insects) and 32. If a legless larva, try 29 to 33. If a larva has jointed legs on the thorax and fleshy, leg-like props on the underside of the abdomen, it may be either a larval Lepidoptera (5 or less pairs of "props") or, if it has more than 5 pairs of "props," it may be the larva of either Hymenoptera (one ocellus on each side of the head) or Mecoptera (several ocelli on each side). If otherwise, there are too many possibilities to outline here. If the underside of abdomen has appendages, see 1 to 4. Almost every order contains at least some species with wingless adults; and no immature insect ever has wings. The mouthparts may help. The following have sucking mouthparts, if any: 12, 20 to 22, and 28 to 30. Others have chewing mouthparts, if any, although some Hymenoptera combine chewing and sucking.

If two pairs of wings.—If the wings are largely covered with microscopic scales concealing the wing membrane it is almost certainly Lepidoptera but Trichoptera have scale-like hairs. If the front wings are distinctly thicker or more pigmented than the hind ones, try 9 to 11, 13, 14, 22, 32 and especially 31. Sucking mouthparts indicate either 12, 21, 22, 28, 29 and, not strictly, 33.

34

If only one pair of wings.—Probably Diptera but see also 5 and 21 (male scale insects). A few species in other, usually 4-winged orders have one pair so reduced as to be practically absent. Also, you may be mistaken; the front and hind wings of some Hymenoptera are somewhat firmly held together by microscopic hooks.

Subclass APTERYGOTA.—Wingless. Underside of abdomen with appendages. Mouthparts vestigial, usually barely, if at all, visible without dissection. No pupal stage. Metamorphosis so slight as to be practically absent.

1.—PROTURA. Slender and very small. Neither antennæ nor eyes. The basal three abdominal segments with ventral appendages. No cerci, but a short anal tube. Prothorax short.

2.—THYSANURA. Antennæ threadlike, many-jointed. Eleven abdominal segments, with ventral appendages on at least the seventh. Prothorax not short. Body tapering behind and usually covered with minute scales. Tips of mouthparts visible. End of abdomen with 3 thread like appendages. See p. 40.

3.—ENTOTROPHI (called also other names and treated as a suborder of Thysanura). Antennæ threadlike, many-jointed. No eyes. Eleven abdominal segments, with ventral appendages on at least the seventh. Prothorax not short. Body not scaly. Mouthparts, except palpi, concealed. End of abdomen with a pair of appendages but no median one. See p. 40.

4.—COLLEMBOLA. Not more than 6 abdominal segments. Antennæ 4- to 6-jointed. Body sometimes with scales or hairs. Eyes, if present, composed of a few separated facets. A ventral tube at base of abdomen; and near the tip of abdomen an appendage that is usually forked. See p. 40.

Subclass PTERYGOTA.—Winged (when adult); or, if wingless, either presumably descended from winged ancestors or closely related to winged insects.

Division Exopterygota.—Usually incomplete metamorphosis, lacking a true pupal stage. The wings develop externally, hence the name.

5.—PLECTOPTERA. Delicate. Abdomen tipped with 3 (or 2) many-jointed filaments. Four, rarely only 2, wings with numerous crossveins. Hind wings distinctly smaller than front ones. Compound eyes and 3 ocelli. Antennæ with two large basal joints and a bristle-like apical part. Chewing mouthparts usually vestigial. Prothorax small. Legs weak. Tarsi usually 4- or 5-jointed. Aquatic young usually with abdominal gills and 3 caudal filaments. See p. 43.

6.—PLECOPTERA. Usually at least moderately large. Anal area of hind wing relatively large, pleated; usually a notch in the wing-margin where the anal area begins.

Crossveins usually rather numerous. Head broad, flat. Chewing mouthparts sometimes vestigial. Antennæ long, threadlike. Three ocelli. Prothorax large, free. Tarsi 3-jointed. A pair of many-jointed, usually long, cerci. See p. 44.

7.—ODONATA. Usually rather large. Abdomen long and slender. Head relatively large, very movable. Eyes large. Three ocelli. Antennæ small, 4- to 7-jointed. Chewing mouthparts. Prothorax free; other thoracic segments fused. Legs relatively short, usually spined. Tarsi 3-jointed. Four similar, membranous, not-folded wings; network of veins. Male sexual apparatus on lower side of second abdominal segment. See p. 44.

8.—GRYLLOBLATTODEA. Wingless. Head nearly horizontal. Chewing mouthparts. No ocelli. Tarsi 5-jointed. Body elongate; not flat. Cerci 8- or 9-jointed. Adult female with a sword-shaped ovipositor at tip of abdomen. See p. 52.

9.—ORTHOPTERA (as limited here). Chewing mouthparts with conspicuous mandibles. Body not flattened; thoracic segments not very long and slender. Usually the hind legs, particularly the femora, are enlarged; if not, the front ones very broad and used for digging. Prothorax large. Front wings usually thicker or tougher and more pigmented than the hind ones, which, if functional, are larger than the front ones. Sometimes even adults are wingless. Antennæ usually many-jointed. Some males have sound-producing organs on the front wings. Some females have a long ovipositor. Wing-pads, if present, of immature specimens with the hind pair overlapping the front pair. See p. 52.

10.—PHASMATODEA. Body usually slender and cylindrical. Chewing mouthparts. Prothorax short. Hind femora at most not decidedly larger than front ones. Tarsi 5-jointed. Even the adults of many species wingless. If winged, the front wings usually much shorter than the hind ones. See p. 63.

11.—DERMAPTERA. Elongate body. Chewing mouthparts. Unjointed (except in some young) cerci usually like a pair of pincers on the tip of the abdomen. If winged, the front wings much shorter than the hind and more leathery or even hard. Tarsi 3-jointed; with claws. Antennæ threadlike, with 10 or more joints. See p. 64.

12.—THYSANOPTERA. Small. Some species jump. Wings, if any, very narrow but with long marginal hairs. Tarsi 1- or 2-jointed; tipped with 1 or 2 claws and a protrusible, bladderlike pad. Sucking, more or less asymmetrical mouthparts. Antennæ 6- to 9-jointed. Compound eyes and usually 3 ocelli. Last abdominal segment tubular in some species. The pre-adult stage practically a pupa. See p. 66.

13.—MANTODEA. Front legs enlarged and fitted for grasping insect prey. Body elongate. Chewing mouthparts. Head freely movable. Usually 3 ocelli. Antennæ many-jointed. Prothorax long, movable. Front wings, if present, smaller than the hind and usually stouter and more pigmented. Tarsi usually 5-jointed. Cerci usually jointed. See p. 67.

14.—BLATTARIÆ. Flat of body and fleet of foot. Head usually bent under, face down. Chewing mouthparts. Usually compound eyes and 2 ocelli. Antennæ many-jointed. Prothorax large, movable. Front wings, if present, usually parchment-like but with many veins. Hind wings, if present, with the large hind part folding fan-like. Tibiæ usually spined. Tarsi 5-jointed. Jointed cerci. See p. 67.

15.—ISOPTERA. "Social." Usually small. Prothorax smaller than the head; movable. Without one or more slim segments between thorax and main part of abdomen. Chewing mouthparts. Two, if any, ocelli. Antennæ threadlike. Tarsi usually 4-jointed, with well-developed claws. Only fertile castes winged. Their wings narrow and deciduous; few veins and no crossveins. Cerci short. See p. 69.

16.—EMBIODEA. Rare. Southern. Slender. Small. Head large. No ocelli. Antennæ many-jointed. Chewing mouthparts. Thorax relatively long; divisions subequal. Tarsi 3-jointed, the basal joint swollen. Females wingless. Male wings, if any, pubescent. Tip of male abdomen usually asymmetrical. See p. 70.

17.—CORRODENTIA. Usually very small. Head relatively large and having a Y-shaped suture on its top. Antennæ slender; with 9 to many joints. Chewing mouthparts. Usually 3 ocelli. Thoracic segments usually distinct. Wings, if present, usually held roof-like over the body; the front ones the larger; few veins, some usually strongly curved. Tarsi 2- or 3-jointed; the first joint long. No cerci. See p. 72.

18.—ZORAPTERA. Rare. Southern. Gregarious, or social. Body flat. Antennæ 9 jointed; the second joint small. Winged forms eyed; wingless not. Chewing mouthparts. Abdomen not much longer than the thorax. Hind femora stout. Tarsi 2-jointed; first joint short. Wings, if any, narrow; few veins. If wings were present on an individual and were lost, a stub remains. Cerci short, 1-jointed, bristle-tipped. See p. 72.

19.—MALLOPHAGA. Small. Wingless. Live on birds or, rarely, mammals. Body distinctly flat. Chewing mouthparts. Antennæ 3- to 5 jointed. Legs short. Tarsi 1- or 2-jointed. No cerci. See p. 72.

20.—ANOPLURA. Small. Wingless. Live on mammals. Body rather flat. Eyes reduced or absent. Sucking mouthparts. Thoracic segments fused. Legs stout. One-jointed tarsi bent like claws. No cerci. See p. 73

21.—HOMOPTERA. Includes a great variety of insects ranging from small to large. All have sucking mouthparts, if any; the jointed beak starting from the hind edge of the head and projecting backwards. The basal part of the front wings not distinctly less membranous than the apical part. Wings, if any, usually sloping over the sides of the body. Tarsi 1- to 3-jointed. No cerci. At least male scale insects have a pupal stage. See p. 73.

22.—HETEROPTERA. Sucking mouthparts; the jointed beak usually starting from near the front end of the head and usually pointing downwards. Antennæ with few joints; those of aquatic species short. Prothorax large; free. Wings, if any, overlapping on the abdomen; the front pair usually less membranous at the base than at the apical end. Tarsi 3- or, rarely, 2-jointed or less. No cerci. See p. 85.

Division Endopterygota.—There is a pupal stage during which the insect changes from larva to adult. The larval stages do not show developing wings externally.

23.—MEGALOPTERA. Soft-bodied. Usually at least moderately large. Chewing mouthparts. Antennæ sometimes pectinate. Prothorax rather large, quadrate. Costal cell of wings with many cross-veins. Anal area of hind wing not of unusual size; folded fan-like. Larvæ aquatic, with lateral abdominal gills. See p. 105.

24.—RAPHIDIODEA. Slender; with elongate, cylindrical prothorax. Head large. Chewing mouthparts. Long, threadlike antennæ. Front and hind wings much alike. Ends of wing-veins tending to fork near margin. Costal cell with cross-veins. Front legs attached at the rear of the prothorax. Tarsi 5-jointed. No cerci. Females with a long ovipositor. See p. 106.

25.—NEUROPTERA (limited sense). Slender. Eyes large. Chewing mouthparts. Prominent prothorax movable. Abdomen rather long and narrow. Wings relatively large but flight slow. Wings at rest usually held roof-like; anal area not large. Numerous branching longitudinal wing-veins. No cerci. See p. 108.

26.—MECOPTERA. Usually rather small. Head usually prolonged into a beak but with small chewing mouthparts. Eyes large. Antennæ thread-like, many-jointed. Wings, if present, usually long and narrow. Legs slender; coxæ large; tarsi 5-jointed. Abdomen usually slender; that of some males swollen at the bent-up tip. Cerci small. See p. 110.

27.—TRICHOPTERA. Up to medium size. Slender-bodied. Eyes relatively large. Chewing mouthparts, if any. Thread-like antennæ often very long. Prothorax small. Wings more or less hairy; numerous longitudinal, few cross veins. Tibiæ with spurs. Tarsi 5-jointed. See p. 112.

28.—LEPIDOPTERA. The butterflies and moths. Antennæ various. Coiled, sucking mouthparts, if any.

Wings, if present, usually entirely covered with scales. See p. 114.

29.—DIPTERA. Only one (the front) pair of wings, if any. Small knobbed "balancers" (halteres) where the hind wings would be. Antennæ variable. Sucking mouthparts. Tarsi usually 5-jointed. See p. 224.

30.—SIPHONAPTERA. Fleas. Small. Wingless. Flat vertically. Jumping. Live on warm-blooded animals. Head small. Antennæ short, thick. Eyes simple or wanting. Sucking mouthparts. Thorax small. Stout legs. Large coxæ. Tarsi 5-jointed; with strong claws. Cerci 1-jointed. See p. 274.

31.—COLEOPTERA. Beetles. Usually hard-bodied. Front wings, if present, at least parchment-like; usually hard. Head usually prominent. Chewing mouthparts, sometimes at the end a beak-like projection of the head. Antennæ various but usually about 11-jointed. Prothorax free. Tarsi usually 5- or 4-jointed. No cerci. See p. 275.

32.—STREPSIPTERA. Small. Parasitic on other insects. Adult males winged; front wings reduced to mere clubs; hind ones rather large but almost veinless. Larva-like females wingless and confined to their host. Male antennæ with one or more of the 3 to 7 joints having a long lateral process. Mouthparts much reduced. See p. 388.

33.—HYMENOPTERA. Ants, bees, wasps. If winged, the front wings somewhat larger than the hind. Chewing mouthparts but they may be formed for lapping or sucking also. Antennæ various; some with few joints, others many, but in higher forms usually 12 in female and 13 in male. Ocelli usually present. Prothorax not free. Tarsi usually 5-jointed. Abdomen usually having (not counting what is really the first segment but is so joined to the thorax as to appear to be a part of it and not of the abdomen) 6 visible segments in females and 7 in males; often fastened to the thorax by a narrow "waist." No cerci. Ovipositor sometimes very long, in many cases functioning as a sting. See p. 389.

APTERYGOTA

See p. 35. Following the majority, we still call these the most primitive insects, although some students think that they are degenerate descendants of more typical forms. They were, not long ago, all put in a single order: Aptera. Recently some authors have not only classified them in a number of orders but have even arranged the orders in classes each on a par with all other insects. A middle road is followed here.

Users of this book are not likely to notice specimens of PROTURA. THYSANURA, as here restricted, contains two distinct families: LEPISMATIDÆ (body flattened; eyes, if any, consisting of separated facets and not extending over the front; coxæ without a process) and MACHILIDÆ (body convex; eyes large, usually touching above, and each with numerous small facets; middle and hind coxæ with processes). Two rather common species of Lepismatidæ are (Pl. 7) *Lepisma saccharina* and *domestica,* the latter now being put in *Thermobia.* Common names for them are Silver-fish, Fish-moth, and Firebrat, the latter because they are fond of warm places. If such a creature is eating your wallpaper, starched clothes, photographs or other belongings, your sorrow may be mitigated by your interest in seeing the most primitive insect you are likely to observe without special effort. Further damage may be prevented by fumigation or by liberal use of fresh Pyrethrum powder, but see p. 25.

ENTOTROPHI are also not likely to be noticed by the users of this book although one of the genera, *Heterojapyx,* contains the largest Apterygota, about 2 in. long.

COLLEMBOLA are commonly seen. Frequently the surface of a still pool is covered by a mass of these tiny dark insects springing about without making an apparent dent in the surface film. Sometimes similar creatures are seen under rubbish or, during bright spring days, even on snow. These Spring-tails are grotesque creatures which

PLATE 7

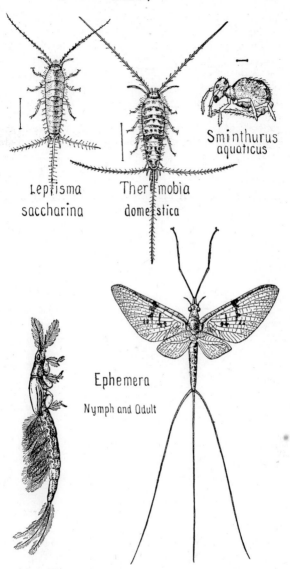

Lepisma
saccharina

Thermobia
domestica

Sminthurus
aquaticus

Ephemera

Nymph and Adult

keep the "tail" curved under when at rest, and jump by straightening out. See *Sminthurus aquaticus,* Pl. 7. *Anurida maritima* occurs on the seashore between tide marks. The wide distribution of some of these minute forms is remarkable. *Sminthurus hortensis,* for example, occurs in Europe, North America, Tierra del Fuego, and Japan. They have no Malpighian tubes (roughly corresponding to kidneys). Waste material accumulates in the fat-body and remains there until death but, in addition, the lining of the intestine accumulates excretory material and sloughs off. There are two suborders: SYMPHY-PLEONA has the abdominal segment fused but the abdomen has a large basal part and a small apical one; ARTHROPLEONA has distinct abdominal segments.

PTERYGOTA

Although the name of this subclass refers to wings, no immature insect ever has wings and even the adults of many Pterygota do not now get them. See p. 35.

PLECTOPTERA

See p. 35. The May-flies (See *Ephemera,* Pl. 7) were formerly considered to be one family, EPHEMERIDÆ. The many species are now grouped in several families but the distinctions are difficult and not generally accepted. A few of the species have but one pair of wings, the front. Although many adult May-flies live but a day—or a night—their lives from egg to adult are, insectly speaking, not short, some taking three years. Some females go under the water to oviposit but most merely drop one or two packages, each of which may contain several hundred eggs.

The larvæ usually have gills (absent in newly hatched) along each side of the abdomen and three tail-filaments. Some swim rather freely; others burrow in mud; and others—the sorts usually seen—crawl about on the under side of submerged stones. They molt frequently, some over twenty times. As is the case in other orders having incomplete metamorphosis, these young stages are often called nymphs, although this term is sometimes restricted to the stages having quite evident wing-pads. Full-grown May-fly nymphs crawl out of the water or float to the surface, frequently in crowds. The skin splits down the back of each and the freed creatures make short flights. But molting is not over yet. Nature loves exceptions, possibly "lest one good custom should corrupt the world," and these insects, unlike others, molt after they have obtained functional wings.

Thousands of adults may join in a joyous dance that may lead to an heirless death if near human habitations, for May-flies yield to the attraction of bright lights. Their mouthparts are vestigial and useless. Fish eagerly eat insects which fall on the water; and a favorite dry-fly, "gray-drake," of fishermen is made in imitation of these.

PLECOPTERA

All observant trout fishermen have noticed on the stones in rapid streams hordes of flat larvæ (nymphs) clinging tightly or scuttling from place to place. They usually belong to this order (Pl. 11) as may be told by the two tail filaments, two tarsal claws, and the thread-like gills, if any, at the bases of the legs. They never have gills along the sides of the abdomen, although there may be gills at the bases of the tail filaments. The thoracic gills are not large and the smaller species have none at all but depend upon the thinness of the skin on their under side for the transfer of oxygen. Since the breathing apparatus is so poorly developed, they are largely confined to well-aerated water. They feed chiefly on vegetable matter and are eagerly eaten by trout, making excellent wet bait. Especially during the first warm days of spring, the full-grown nymphs crawl out on stones or logs and the adults leave the nymphal skin, which, complete even to the lining of the main tracheæ and of the fore-gut, is hooked to the molting place. The adults are gray or greenish, usually with two tail filaments and, in some cases, with degenerate gills at the bases of the legs, curious reminiscences of their former life. Often adults appear in large numbers, especially from large, swift streams. A single female may lay as many as 6,000 eggs, dropping them either promiscuously into the water or done up in a loose packet. There are now considered to be four families in our fauna separated by differences in wing-venation. Common names for them are Stone-flies and Salmon-flies. Some adults emerge so early in the spring that they are called Snow-flies.

ODONATA

The Dragon- and Damsel-flies have been called Devil's Darning-needles and accused of sewing up the ears of bad boys; Snake-doctors and Snake-feeders on the theory that they administer to the needs of reptiles; and Horse-stingers on the equally mistaken notion that they sting.

PLATE 8

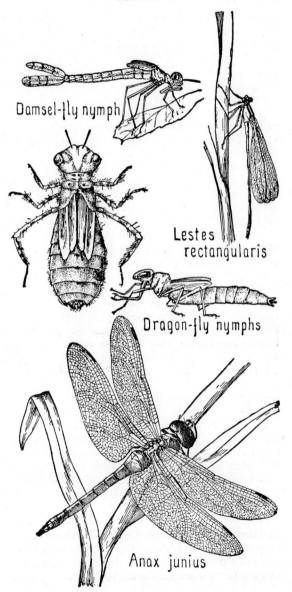

Damsel-fly nymph

Lestes rectangularis

Dragon-fly nymphs

Anax junius

All of them live in water until they get wings. They are predacious from hatching to death but the aquatic young catch their prey in a very different manner from that practised by the aerial adults. The flying "dragon" darts back and forth with swift, well-controlled motions, scooping up insects in a "basket" formed by its extended legs and the front of its thorax. The young, however, are sluggish and lie in wait for unwary aquatic animals. When their chance comes a curious thing happens. Jaws seem to shoot out from the mouth and snap up the victim. Really, it is a jointed lower lip which is extended, and the "jaws" are hooks on its end (Pl. 8).

Odonata have incomplete metamorphosis but the pre-adult stage, although active and showing wing cases, does not at all resemble the adult, differing in little except size and wing-pads from its appearance when newly hatched. When full-grown these nymphs crawl out of the water; their skin splits; and the flying adult crawls out, leaving the discarded skin behind.

There are two suborders: ZYGOPTERA (Wings at rest held together over the abdomen. Front and hind wings nearly alike; with narrow bases. Adult eyes widely separated. Nymphs with three tail-like gills) and ANISOPTERA (Wings held out from body. Hind wings broader near the base than the front wings. Adult eyes not farther apart than the diameter of one of them. Nymphs without external gills). See Pl. 8.

ZYGOPTERA

These are Damsel-flies. They are not as strong fliers as the "dragons" and they are more frequently seen flying tandem. A male often grasps with the pincers on the end of his body a female and, flying in front of her, accompanies her on egg-laying excursions, even going under the water with her if she descends to place eggs inside the stems or leaves of submerged plants. The males are of real assistance on such occasions. The legs of Odonata are so poorly fitted for walking that it is difficult for them to crawl up through the water's "film," and after the joint efforts of both sexes get the male through he pulls the female out by flying.

Two or more families are recognized. According to some authors *Hetærina* and *Calopteryx* (or *Agrion*) are AGRIONIDÆ (Adults often with bright metallic colors. The first antennal segment of nymphs as long as the rest of the antenna; the two lateral gills 3-sided) and our other genera, including *Lestes,* are CŒNAGRIONIDÆ (Metallic colors rare. The first antennal segment of nymphs relatively shorter; lateral gills flat). Unfortunately, generic distinctions involve technicalities beyond the scope of this book.

The male Ruby-spot, *Hetærina americana,* is more jeweled than his mate (Pl. 78). The young cling to plants in running water or along the edges of large ponds.

The Black-wing, *Calopteryx maculata,* is blackest in the male. Pl. 78 shows a female. The young have a light band on each leg and gill-plate.

Lestes (Pl. 8) is a large, widely distributed genus usually abundant in marshes and about shallow pools that contain standing vegetation. *L. unguiculatus* places its eggs in aerial parts of plants growing in pools that usually dry up in midsummer. The young, instead of hatching as soon as they are developed, stay inside the egg-shell until the plants die at the end of the season and drop into the then well-filled pool. Development goes on so rapidly that the adult stage is reached before the pool dries up next summer. Probably, however, some of the species lay their eggs under water.

ANISOPTERA

The lower intestine of a Dragon-fly nymph is thin-walled and acts as a gill, absorbing air from the water that is drawn in and expelled through the anus. These nymphs are stout-bodied in comparison with those of Damsel-flies and, while the latter swim by sculling, using their gills as oars, the young dragons shoot themselves forward by forcibly expelling water from the rectum. This may be seen by placing one of them in a saucer with just enough water to cover the hind end of its body. The adults are, perhaps, the strongest fliers of all insects. Eggs are either merely dropped into the water or placed on or in aquatic plants.

This suborder may be divided into two families. In the basal half of each wing may be seen a triangle formed by adjacent veins. Still nearer the base is what appears to be a cross vein ("arculus") from near the middle of which two main veins go toward the tip of the wing, the hindmost of these two veins touching one corner of the triangle in question. The ÆSCHNIDÆ have the distance between this triangle and the arculus about the same in both front and hind wings. The LIBELLULIDÆ have the triangle in a hind wing not the same distance from the arculus that it is in a front wing. The nymphs of Æschnidæ usually have a flat labium and two teeth on the margin of the mentum (part of the labium). The labium of the Libellulidæ nymphs is a more or less spoon-shaped mask for the under side of the head and the mentum does not have two large teeth. If you wish to consider these families as superfamilies, Æschnoidea and Libelluloidea, then move what is given here as subfamilies up to family rank. Æschnidæ may be divided into three or four subfamilies. Adult Æschninæ have the eyes touching for a considerable distance. The eyes of Cordulegastrinæ touch at a single point. Those of Gomphinæ are separated on top of the head by a distance as great as half of that between the antennæ.

Gomphinæ are usually clear-winged and have bodies striped with black and green or yellow. They do not seem to fly as much in pure sportiveness as do some of their relatives. The females, especially in June, skim the surface of ponds and streams, striking the tips of their abdomens into the water. At each dip gelatin-covered eggs are deposited; the gelatin dissolves; the eggs drop to the muddy bottom; and there, covered with silt, the wide, flat young later on lie in wait for their food.

Needham calls the subfamily Æschninæ "the largest, fleetest, and most voracious of our dragon flies." Many of them hunt well into twilight. The young are clean, slender-bodied, active climbers among green plants along the borders of ponds and streams. The following are two of the common species.

Anax junius (Pl. 8) is found in Asia, throughout the Western Hemisphere from Alaska to Costa Rica, and in various Pacific Islands. The clear wings are at least

PLATE 9

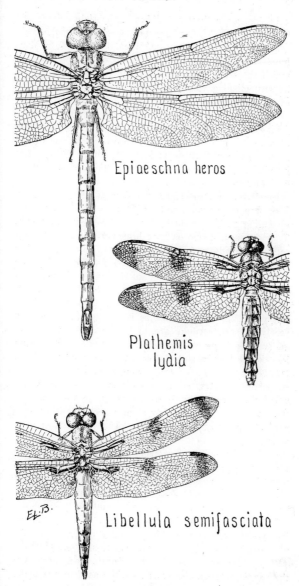

Epiaeschna heros

Plathemis
lydia

E.L.B.

Libellula semifasciata

2 in. long; the thorax and head are bright green; and in front of the eyes is a round, black spot surrounded, first, by a yellow ring, and, then, by a ring of dark blue. The dry shell of a full-grown nymph, out of which the adult came during the night, is frequently to be seen clinging to the stems of plants which grow out of or near water.

Epiæschna heros (Pl. 9) might be confused with *A. junius* except that it is larger and has a T-shaped, instead of a round, spot in front of its eyes. It is one of the largest of our dragons and one which frequently gets into buildings, especially during migrations of large numbers to some place not known to us.

Libellulidæ include some of our most common species. They are collectively called Skimmers from their habit of sailing back and forth close to the ground or water. They frequently rest on bare branches or tall grass and seem ever ready to dart after a fly or to drive off another Dragon poaching on their preserves. The females do not place their eggs in plants but either drop them loosely or hang them in gelatinous strings on aquatic vegetation.

The Water-prince, *Epicordulia princeps* (Pl. 10), will test your skill with the net, as it is a splendid flyer and rarely at rest. Adults are to be found from May to midsummer along muddy, reed-grown banks. The young live on the bottom among detritus or on submerged logs. Not being good climbers, the nymphs usually seek a broad supporting surface, even some distance from the water, when they are ready to split down the back and free the adults. The females fly alone when depositing their eggs and make their dips some distance apart in open water.

The Amber-wing, *Perithemis domitia,* is one of the smallest of our true dragon-flies and may be easily recognized by reference to Pl. 78. It flies rather slowly and clumsily in May and June, frequently resting, and hiding completely if a cloud but cover the sun.

Individuals of *Libellula* are common and conspicuous. The young are elongate, tapering, and provided with hairs which collect a concealing covering of silt. *L. pulchella* (Pl. 78) frequents ponds; the female does not have the spaces between the spots so white as does the male.

PLATE 10

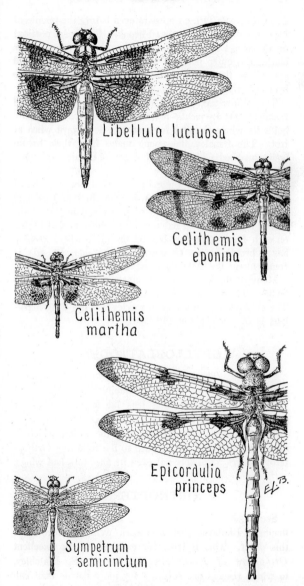

Libellula luctuosa

Celithemis
eponina

Celithemis
martha

Epicordulia
princeps

Sympetrum
semicinctum

L. semifasciata (Pl. 9) appears even before the middle of
May, usually about woodland brooks. The basal portions
of the wings of *L. luctuosa* (Pl. 10) are brownish or
black; the outer portions are clear except that the old
males have the middle chalky white and the females have
brownish tips.

The White-tail, *Plathemis lydia* (Pl. 9, also called
trimaculata) frequents ponds and ditches. It usually
holds its wings slanting forward and downward when at
rest. The females and young males have their brown
bodies marked with yellow, but the old males are pow-
dered with white.

Celithemis includes three of our most beautiful small
species. *C. eponina* (Pl. 10) is adult in late June and
early July along the borders of ponds and in the neighboring fields. *C. elisa* has a small rounded spot of brown
on each front wing just beyond the place where *eponina*
has a brown band. *C. martha* (or *ornata,* Pl. 10) is
found along the Atlantic coast from Maine to Florida.

Many of the large genus *Sympetrum* have brilliant red
bodies. They frequently fly far from their marshy home.
The only one of our common species that has wing-markings is *S. semicinctum* (Pl. 10).

GRYLLOBLATTODEA

See p. 36. The wingless *Grylloblatta campodeiformis*
occurs under stones in the mountains from Alberta to
California. It has running legs lke a roach (*Blatta*)
and the female has an ovipositor like a cricket (*Gryllus*).
Other characters also suggest that the order, which is
also found in Japan, is ancestral to the following Orthop-
teroid orders. Possibly not even its ancestors had wings.

ORTHOPTERA

See p. 36. Even quite recently the Phasmatodea, Dermaptera, Blattariæ and Mantodea were classified with
this order. This is true, for example, in the excellent
Orthoptera of North America by W. S. Blatchley,
to which readers are referred for more details than can

PLATE II

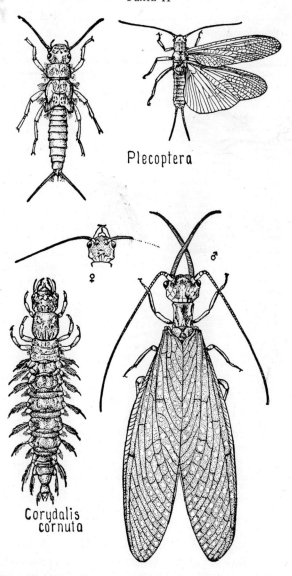

Plecoptera

Corydalis
cornuta

be given here. As here limited, the principal North American families are as follows:

1.—Antennæ usually nearly as long as the body or longer. "Ears," if any, on the front tibiæ. Ovipositor usually long. Tarsi 4-jointed or less.—Suborder TETTIGONIODEA (or Locustodea)...........................2.

Antennæ shorter. "Ears," if any, near the base of the abdomen. No long ovipositor. Tarsi 3-jointed or less.—Suborder ACRIDODEA. ....7.

2.—At least the hind tarsi 4-jointed. Ovipositor typically sword-shaped. ....3.

Tarsi 3-jointed or less. Ovipositor, if any, needle-shaped ....5.

3.—Tarsi distinctly compressed (higher than wide). Even adults usually wingless.—STENOPELMATIDÆ (p. 54).

Tarsi more or less depressed (wider than high)....4.

4.—No "ears" on front tibiæ.—GRYLLACRIDÆ. The wingless *Camptonotus carolinensis* of our Southeast is our only species. It rolls leaves and fastens them with silk for daytime retreats, feeding on aphids at night.

"Ears" on front tibiæ.—TETTIGONIIDÆ (p. 55).

5.—Antennæ 12-jointed or less; not tapering at tip. Hind femora very thick. No "ears."—TRIDACTYLIDÆ. Our two species are small. The hind tarsi of *Tridactylus apicalis* are 1-jointed and *Ellipes minuta* has no hind tarsi. They burrow in loose earth.

Antennæ with more joints; tapering at tip.........6.

6.—Front tibiæ much enlarged. Ovipositor not protruding.—GRYLLOTALPIDÆ. These are the Mole Crickets, rarely seen above-ground except at the mating season, when they are sometimes attracted to lights. We have two genera: *Gryllotalpa* (each front tibia with four "fingers") and *Scapteriscus* (2-fingered). Pl. 12 shows *G. borealis*, which may also have short hind wings. They feed on roots, earthworms and larvæ. Clusters of eggs are laid in underground chambers and tended by the females.

Front tibiæ not enlarged. Ovipositor projecting except for *Anurogryllus* of our South.—GRYLLIDÆ (p. 58).

7.—No pad between tarsal claws. Pronotum extended over most or all of the abdomen. Front wings vestigial. Antennæ longer than the front femora.—ACRYDIIDÆ (p. 60).

Usually a pad between tarsal claws. Pronotum of our genera, even if extending backwards, usually covering little of the abdomen.—ACRIDIDÆ (p. 60).

STENOPELMATIDÆ

We have two of the subfamilies: the Western Stenopelmatinæ (pulvilli, or pads, beneath tarsal claws; base of hind femora produced above) and Rhaphidophorinæ (Also called Ceuthophilinæ. No pulvilli; base of hind femora produced below). *Stenopelmatus,* variously called Niños de la Tierra, Sand-crickets, Jerusalem-crickets and Baby-faces, is the type genus of Stenopelmatinæ but *Cyphoderris* has wings. Our principal genus of Rhaphidophorinæ is *Ceuthophilus* (Pl. 12), called Cave-crickets or Camel-crickets. None of these things are crickets. All are nocturnal and usually to be found under boards or stones.

TETTIGONIIDÆ

These are the Long-horned Grasshoppers, including the famous but rarely seen Katydid. Unfortunately, one of the names for the family is Locustidæ and it contains no locusts, strictly speaking. Like the crickets, the males make sounds by rubbing their front wings together. We have the following subfamilies.

1.—First and second joints of tarsi longitudinally grooved at the sides...2.
    Not so. Hind tibiæ with an apical spine on each side above.—Phaneropterinæ.
2.—No terminal spines on front tibiæ above.........3.
    Front tibiæ with a terminal spine above on the outer side. Pronotum extending to the abdomen. Except in some Western and Southern genera the hind wings are absent or rudimentary and the front ones are short.—Decticinæ. These Shield-bearers are rarely seen. *Atlanticus* is our principal genus in the East. In the West the numbers of *Anabrus simplex,* the Mormon-cricket, frequently increase suddenly and so greatly that it becomes a destructive pest. Then the numbers suddenly decrease. It, and not the Rocky Mountain Locust, seems to have been the species that threatened to wipe out the early Mormon settlement in Utah, incidentally giving the gulls a feast and winning for them a monument in Salt Lake City.
3.—The margins of the grooves in which the antennæ lie raised. Front wings of our genera broad; concave within; longer than the hind wings.—Pseudophyllinæ.
    The margins of the antennal grooves not decidedly raised ....4.
4.—All the femora without spines beneath; rarely the hind ones with lateral spines. Vertex of head a rounded tubercle with concave sides.—Conocephalinæ (Xiphidiinæ).

Femora usually spined beneath. Vertex typically a long, usually sharp cone but in *Homorocoryphus* of Florida it is a short, blunt knob.—Copiphorinæ (Conocephalinæ).

Phaneropterinæ might be called False Katydids. The males "sing" chiefly at night. Eggs are usually glued in double rows on twigs or are placed in the edges of leaves. Pl. 79 shows *Amblycorypha oblongifolia* in pink. It is usually green but it and many other green insects have brown or pink "sports." Note the curved ovipositor, rather characteristic of the females of this subfamily. In *Microcentrum* the hind femora do not reach beyond the basal two-thirds of the front wings. In both of these genera the front wings are distinctly wider at the middle than at the apex. This is not so in *Scudderia,* another common genus.

Pseudophyllinæ includes the True Katydid, *Pterophylla camellifolia.* They probably rarely fly but soar like a flying squirrel. Pl. 79 shows a male. At the base of the wings is the organ with which he argues whether "Katy did" or "Katy didn't." Katy, unlike most female insects, can faintly make her own sounds but she apparently rarely does so unless much disturbed. Eggs are laid in soft bark or the like.

Copiphorinæ, the Cone-headed Grasshoppers, includes *Neoconocephalus,* a large genus which used to be called *Conocephalus.* They, too, "sing" most actively by night.

Conocephalinæ, the Meadow Grasshoppers, are much given to singing by day. "The poetry of earth is never dead. When all the birds are faint with the hot sun and hide in cooling trees a voice will run from hedge to hedge about the new-mown mead. That is the grasshoppers." There are two common genera: *Orchelimum* (usually an inch long; front wings usually extending beyond the abdomen; females with stout, somewhat curved ovipositors) and *Conocephalus* (Pl. 12; usually smaller; front wings shorter; ovipositor slender and straight), formerly called *Xiphidium.*

PLATE 12

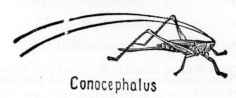

Conocephalus

Ceuthophilus

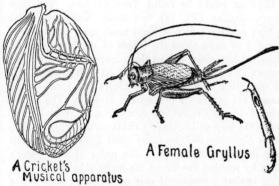

A Cricket's
Musical apparatus

A Female Gryllus

Gryllotalpa borealis

GRYLLIDÆ

Our Crickets include six subfamilies:

1.—Tarsi flattened sideways; the second joint minute..2.
    Tarsi flattened vertically; the second joint distinct, heart-shaped. ....4.
2.—Body nearly spherical; wingless. Pronotum covering the eyes. Hind legs much swollen.—Myrmecophilinæ, small creatures found in ant nests.
    Not so. ....3.
3.—Hind tibiæ spined but without fine notches. Body stout; usually dark-colored.—Gryllinæ.
    Hind tibiæ spined but with notches between the spines. Body and legs slender.—Œcanthinæ.
    Hind tibiæ with two rows of fine notches but no spines. Wings not well developed. Body with fine translucent scales.—Mogoplistinæ. Mostly Southern.
4.—Hind tibiæ not notched; two rows of spines and 5 apical spurs.—Trigonidiinæ. *Anaxipha* belongs here.
    Hind tibiæ notched; spined; 6 apical spurs.—Eneopterinæ.

Gryllinæ might be called True Crickets. The type genus, *Gryllus* (Pl. 12) has stout, immovable tibial spines; ocelli not in a straight row; space between antennæ 2 or more times the length of the basal joint of antennæ; hind tibiæ at least three-fourths as long as hind femora and with 5 or more spines on each margin. All of our black ones, common outdoors but rarely so in houses, are practically one species, *assimilis*. The straw-colored House Cricket, *G. domesticus,* is from Europe and is the hero of Dickens' "Cricket on the Hearth." The genus *Nemobius* includes many small, brown species with long movable tibial spines. The males of both genera chirp by rubbing the file on the under side of one front wing against a roughened spot on the upper side of the other. Eggs are laid singly in the ground. *Nemobius* is chiefly vegetarian; *Gryllus,* omnivorous. They, especially *Gryllus,* make good pets. A lantern globe set on soil in a flower pot is a satisfactory cage. Feed them lettuce, moist bread and, to lessen cannibalism, some bone meal. If you wish to incubate the eggs, water the soil about as you would for plants. Most crickets pass the winter as eggs but some as almost-mature nymphs.

Œcanthinæ are the usually pale green Tree Crickets.

PLATE 13

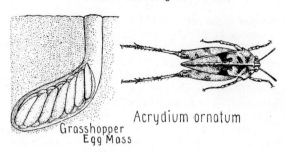

Grasshopper
Egg Mass

Acrydium ornatum

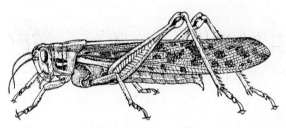

Schistocerca americana

Truxalis brevicornis

Spharagemon bolii

Œcanthus is the principal genus. A broad-winged male is shown on Pl. 79. Among other characters distinguishing species are the shape and arrangement of the black dots on the two basal antennal joints. As is the case with other Orthoptera, species differ in the males' song but the *tempo* depends largely on whether it is day or night, sunshiny or cloudy, warm or cold. *Œ. niveus* has been called the Temperature Cricket because if we divide the number of chirps per minute by 4 and add 40 the result is approximately the temperature Fahrenheit. In this genus the male seems to have gone largely to music— he has broad front wings but a relatively small body. The female, whose wings are wrapped closely to her body, lays her eggs in plant stems. *Neoxabea* (*Xabea* of the former editions) has no spines on the hind tibiæ but two very small apical spurs.

ACRYDIIDÆ

These are the Grouse or Pigmy Locusts. The subfamily Acrydiinæ (Pl. 13, *Acrydium ornatum*) is characterized by having less than 16 joints in each antenna; Batrachidinæ have more. There are numerous species, some of which are quite variable. They are given to hibernating as adults. Those who think that *"Acrydium"* is essentially the same word as *"Acrida"* and, hence, preoccupied use "Tetrigidæ" as the family name.

ACRIDIDÆ

By remembering that the antennæ are always much shorter than the body, one usually does not confuse this family of Short-horned Grasshoppers with anything except Acrydiidæ. The migratory Rocky Mountain Locust (*Melanoplus spretus*), that occasionally has been so destructive in our West, and the Biblical locusts that were eaten with wild honey belong here. Some species make a rasping sound by rubbing their hind legs against their front wings (tegmina); others rattle their hind wings against the tegmina while flying. These sounds may be amorous serenades and Nature's serenades without attentive ears would be even more curious than the ears for which the grasshoppers perform. In this family there is an auditory organ on each side of the first abdominal segment, just above and back of the places where the large hind femora start. Notice the clear round spot on the next grasshopper you catch. Perhaps you have noticed in the fall of the year females along the path with their abdomens sunk to the base in a small hole which they had made by pushing aside the earth. They were laying a cluster of eggs (Pl. 13) in each hole.

Our species represent the following subfamilies:

1.—No spine or tubercle between the bases of the front legs. . . . .**2.**

Such tubercle present. Face nearly or quite vertical except in Leptysmi. Pronotum with the dorsal surface flattened; not strongly crested or roughened. Hind wings usually (not so in *Romalea,* for example) without contrasting colors.—Cyrtacanthacrinæ (Acridiinæ or Podisminæ). See p. 62.

2.—Antennæ longer than the front femora. . . . .**3.**

Not so.—Eumastacinæ. Southwestern.

3.—Face oblique, usually meeting the vertex at an acute angle; small depressions absent or usually invisible from above. Median ridge of the pronotum neither especially high (except for a few Western genera) nor cut by more than one groove. Hind wings without contrasting colors. —Acridinæ (Tryxalinæ or Truxalinæ), p. 61.

Face nearly or quite vertical; rounded at its junction with the vertex; small depressions on it and visible from above. Pronotal ridge often crested and usually cut by more than one groove. Hind wings usually with contrasting colors.—Œdipodinæ, p. 62.

ACRIDINÆ

I wish that these might still be called Truxalinæ. They typically have receding chins (*Truxalis,* Pl. 13). Males make rather faint sounds by rubbing their hind legs against their front wings. Our genera have been grouped in the following "tribes":

1.—Antennæ stout, rather sword-shaped. Face very oblique.—Truxalini, including the genus *Truxalis,* also spelled *Tryxalis.*

Antennæ more thread-like. . . . .**2.**

2.—No small depressions on vertex of head visible from above. Face usually distinctly oblique. . . . .**3.**

Small depressions on vertex of head. Face usually

nearly vertical. (Both of these indicating intergradation with the Œdipodinæ)..................................**4.**

3.—A distinct median ridge on disk of vertex. Antennæ usually somewhat flattened but not strongly tapering.— Amblytropidi. *Syrbula admirabilis* is a pretty species with more than 16 small spines on the outer margin of a hind tibia. The male's note is a weak lisp. *Chloealtis conspersa* is brownish; the lateral ridges of the pronotum closer together near the middle than at the ends; the hind edge of the pronotum square-cut; about 12 spines on the outer margin of each hind tibia, the apical spurs all of about the same size. It has a different song in sun than in shade. Small masses of eggs are laid in stumps and logs.

No such ridge on vertex. Antennæ usually not longer than head plus thorax.—Orphuli. *Dichromorpha viridis* has a brown male and a usually green female. The front wings of both are distinctly shorter than the abdomen.

4.—Median ridge of pronotum not high and not cut at or in front of its middle.—Chorthippi.

Median ridge of pronotum high and cu at or in front of its middle.—Mecostethi.

ŒDIPODINÆ

These Gay-winged Locusts include species whose males make a clattering noise when they fly and sometimes hover in the air above a female, rattling and showing off their colored hind wings. When at rest on the ground with the hind wings covered, they are difficult to see. We have two tribes:

Hippisci (median ridge of pronotum either entire or cut by only one notch except in Western forms such as *Xanthippus*).—The pronotal ridge of *Arphia* is quite a crest, which is at most feebly notched. *Dissosteira carolina* is shown on Pl. 79. The color of its front wings is variable. The hind wings of *Spharagemon bolli* (Pl. 13) are pale greenish-yellow at the base.

Trimerotropi (two notches in pronotal ridge, the front one sometimes small).—The sand-colored species, with pale yellow and black hind wings, so common on the shores of the Atlantic and of the Great Lakes is *Trimerotropis maritima.*

CYRTACANTHACRINÆ

It is certainly unfortunate that we must use that name instead of others, such as Acridiinæ, Podisminæ, or Locustinæ, that have been used. It is an immense group with many common species. Some of these have been divided among the following tribes:

1.—Hind wings red with a black border. Front wings shorter than the abdomen. An apical spine on each side of each hind tibia.—Romali. *Romalea microptera* occurs in the Southeast. Its large size (2 to 3 in.) and clumsiness justify the common name, Lubber Locust. (The almost wingless Lubber of the Southwest is *Brachypeplus magnus*.)

Hind wings nearly or quite transparent. No apical spine on outer side of hind tibia. .2.

2.—Face very oblique. Top of head much extended in front of eyes. Antennæ somewhat sword-shaped, the basal half flat. Front and middle legs short.—Leptysmi. They strongly suggest Acridinæ. The head of *Leptysma marginicollis* is as long as the pronotum; that of *Stenacris vitreipennis,* shorter. Both are Southern.

Not so. . . . . .3.

3.—Lobes of mesosternum longer than broad; their inner margin straight. Length of body usually 2 in. or more.—Schistocerci. *Schistocerca* is a typically American genus. *S. americana* (Pl. 13) is one of the largest in size and strongest in flight of our grasshoppers. A relatively small one, *damnifica,* has a name that appeals to him who chases these Bird Locusts in the hot sun.

Lobes of mesosternum at least as wide as long; their inner margins usually rounded. Body not usually more than 2 in. long.—Melanopli.

There are numerous genera of Melanopli and some of them, especially the type genus, *Melanoplus,* contain many species. Apparently the Rocky Mountain Locust (*M. spretus*) is merely a migratory form of *M. mexicanus,* formerly *atlanis,* which closely resembles the common *M. femur-rubrum.* It has been shown for the Migratory Locust of the Old World that the migratory form arises when the non-migratory one becomes so numerous as to be crowded. There are slight color and structural differences between the two.

PHASMATODEA

See p. 36. In the Tropics, where the Walking Sticks are most abundant, many of the species have wings but our northern representatives are wingless—sticks without leaves (Pl. 80).

1.—Middle and hind tibiæ each with a triangular area on the under side at the apex.—The suborder or superfamily PHASMATOIDEA. We have the family PHASMATIDÆ in which the tarsi of *Anisomorpha* are 5-jointed and those of the Western *Timema* are 3-jointed. Both are Southern.

These tibiæ without that triangular area.—BAC-TERIOIDEA. *Aplopus meyeri* of southern Florida belongs to BACTERIIDÆ ("median segment"—the first abdominal—much longer than wide). Some of our genera of BACUNCULIDÆ (median segment not relatively so long) may be separated as follows. ....2.

2.—Antennæ not more than half as long as front femora. —The Western *Parabacillus*, sometimes put in a separate subfamily, Pachymorphinæ.

Antennæ relatively longer (true of the Phasmatidæ also).—Bacunculinæ. The head of the large Southern *Megaphasma dentricus* is scarcely longer than broad. In *Diapheromera* the hind femora of both sexes have a subapical spine on the under side and the male's middle femora are distinctly thicker than the hind ones. The common Eastern species is *D. femorata*. In *Manomera* (middle femora with a distinct subapical spine) and *Heteronemia* (not so) the hind femora are not spined below.

These curious insects, which may be either brown or green, look so like twigs that they are rarely seen except when unusually abundant. They feed on leaves. The shot-like eggs are dropped singly and promiscuously to the ground, where they lie over winter or possibly sometimes longer. I once found *Diapheromera* so abundant in Pennsylvania that the trees in a small area were all but stripped of leaves and the dropping eggs sounded like rain. Parthenogenesis may be rather common; no males of *Manomera* have been found in the East.

DERMAPTERA

See p. 36. This name alludes to the skin- or leatherlike front wings of Earwigs. Another name, Euplexoptera, refers to the skill with which they fold their hind wings. Of the nickname Grant Allen says: "It is called earwig, gossips will tell you, because it creeps into the ears of incautious sleepers in the open air and so worms its way to the brain." But it doesn't.

These insects are easily confused with Staphylinid beetles because the front wings of neither cover the body;

PLATE 14

Labia minor

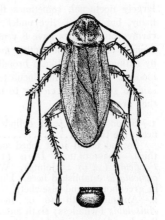

Periplaneta americana

Blattella
germanica

P. australasiae

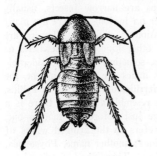

Blatta orientalis

but earwigs have pincers on behind (Pl. 14). They are largely nocturnal, sometimes flying to lights. By day many, but not all, live under rubbish and seem to be carnivorous. Males have 8 ventral abdominal segments, females only 6. The mother guards her cluster of eggs by sitting on them like a brooding hen but, being "cold-blooded," she does not incubate them. The young are said to stick rather closely to mother for a while after they are hatched.

1.—Second tarsal joint cylindrical; not prolonged beneath the third. ....**2.**

Second tarsal joint lobed and prolonged beneath the third.—FORFICULIDÆ. *Doru* (12-jointed antennæ) and *Forficula* (14 or 15 joints). We have the European *F. auricularia* established here. Unfortunately it eats plants in greenhouses and elsewhere.

2.—Antennæ with 16 or more joints.—LABIDURIDÆ. *Anisolabis* (wingless; sixth antennal joint slightly longer than broad) *maritima* (antennæ 24-jointed) is common on our Atlantic shore. The possibly introduced *Labidura bidens* is winged when adult.

Antennæ less than 16-jointed.—LABIIDÆ. *Labia* (fourth antennal joint as long as third) *minor* is another introduced European species now well established. *Vostox* (sixth antennal joint much shorter than the first) is put in the subfamily Spongiphorinæ.

THYSANOPTERA

See p. 36. The Thrips are narrow insects, usually black, and usually not over 0.1 in. long. There are many kinds but their classification is difficult. Flowers are frequently full of them; other kinds live elsewhere, as under bark and on leaves, sometimes doing considerable damage. In some species males are rare or absent, the eggs developing without fertilization much as in aphids, for example. The young resemble adults but there is a quiet, very pupa-like stage just before the mature one. The name of the order refers to the fringed wings of those species that have wings; another name, Physopoda, to their peculiar bladder feet. There are two suborders:

Front wings, if any, with veins. Terminal segment of female conical; of male bluntly rounded.—TEREBRANTIA.

Wings, if any, almost or quite veinless. Terminal abdominal segment of both sexes tubular.—TUBULIFERA.

MANTODEA

See p. 37. One of the favorite attitudes (Pl. 80) of these insects is supposed to be devout and has given them the name Praying Mantids. I hate to go against custom but the pose does not seem to me devout and I know that the Mantis is seeking what it may devour. See those big eyes and especially the spines on the jaw-like front legs. Please do not accuse me of punning when I suggest that they be called Preying Mantids. Other names are Devil's Rearhorses and Soothsayers. In the South they are believed to poison stock and are called Mulekillers. They are harmless except to other insects and they can turn their heads better than most insects to look over their shoulders.

We have a single family, MANTIDÆ, including a number of species in the South and West. In the Northeast *Tenodera* (or *Paratenodera*) *sinensis* claims the stage. It is rarely less than 3 in. long. The broad, green, front margin of the front wings is sharply separated from the much larger brown portion. The egg-mass is shaped like a short, broad cornucopia of dried foam. Introduced about 1896 from Asia to the vicinity of Philadelphia, it has now (1933) spread or been spread to Ohio and southern New England. Some of us like to keep specimens as interesting pets, feeding them on flies and grasshoppers. In 1933 another Asiatic species, *T. angustipennis,* somewhat smaller and making a rather cylindrical egg-mass was reported in Delaware and Maryland. Another immigrant is the European *Mantis religiosa,* now established in central New York. Including the wings, it is rarely over 2.5 in. long. A native species, *Stagmomantis carolina* (Front wings of female shorter than the abdomen. Width of face below the antennæ more than twice its height. Pl. 80 shows it and, a trifle small, its egg-mass), occurs as far north as southern New Jersey.

BLATTARIÆ

See p. 37. The Roaches are widely known, at least by reputation. There are over 1000 different kinds. I like the spirit in which Sutherland views these none too well-liked creatures: "If the test of nobility is antiquity of family, then the cockroach that hides behind the kitchen sink is the true aristocrat. He does not date back merely to the three brothers that came over in 1640 or to William the Conqueror. Wherever there have been great epoch-making movements of people he has been with them heart and soul, without possessing any particular religious convictions or political ambitions. It is not so much that he approves of their motives as that he likes what they have to eat. Since ever a ship turned a foamy furrow in the sea he has been a passenger, not a paying one certainly, but still a passenger. But man himself is but a creature of the last twenty minutes or so compared with the cockroach, for, from its crevice by the kitchen sink, it can point its antennæ to the coal in the hod and say: 'When that was being made my family was already well-established'."

Except for the extreme South and West the following key to certain families may suffice:

At least the hind femora with several distinct marginal spines beneath.—BLATTIDÆ (Large. Seventh ventral abdominal segment of female divided) and PSEUDOMOPIDÆ (Or Blattellidæ; incorrectly called Phyllodromiidæ. Smaller. That segment not divided).

Middle and hind femora without marginal spines beneath, although there may be bristles or apical spines. Seventh abdominal segment not enclosing terminal ones. A terminal tarsal pad.—PANCHLORIDÆ. One genus, *Panchlora* (Pl. 79), includes rather pretty, green roaches that come to us from the Tropics in bunches of bananas. The eggs of at least some species hatch in the female's body. *Pycnoscelus* is native in the Southeast.

BLATTIDÆ.—The front wings of both sexes of *Periplaneta* extend beyond the abdomen. They do not in *Blatta* (terminal tarsal pad, if present, not half the length of the claws) and *Eurycotis* (this pad relatively longer). In fact, the wings of the female *B. orientalis* (Pl. 14) are mere pads, although the male is better equipped. This rather common arrangement among insects does not seem quite fair as it means that the lady must walk when she wishes to establish her family in a new place. A nickname for the Oriental Roach is Black-beetle! Like most roaches directly associated with man, it is now cosmopolitan. *E. floridana* is said to be "one of the most ill-smelling insects" in America. *Periplaneta* is occasionally brought to our attention by the large, trim *P. americana* (Pl. 14, which shows an egg-capsule also) from our South or by *P. australasiæ,* not so elongate and wearing yellow shoulder-stripes lengthwise of its front wings. There are several other species.

PSEUDOMOPIDÆ.—*Blattella* is represented by New York City's famous Croton Bug. Linnæus called this species *germanica* many years ago but probably did not mean to insinuate anything disagreeable, although some scientific christenings have carried thinly veiled humor or spite. As a matter of fact, this household guest probably accompanied our ancestors when they moved from Asia to Europe. It got the name Croton Bug in America because it first attracted general attention in New York about the time the Croton aqueduct was built. Perhaps the most interesting thing about it is the way the mother carries around her package of eggs sticking out of the hind end of her body (Pl. 14). Those who go afield find numerous species of *Ischnoptera, Parcoblatta,* and other genera under loose bark. These roaches are independent country folk that never live in towns.

By the way, in addition to eating our food, clothing, etc., roaches help us kill our bedbugs, if we have any. Contrary to general opinion, it usually takes roaches a year or more to reach breeding age.

ISOPTERA

See p. 37. The Termites, often called White-ants, are not ants at all but might almost be called Social Roaches. Furthermore, the winged forms are dark, not white. Their principal home is in the Tropics. In our Northeast the only, but common, native species is *Reticulitermes* (formerly *Termes*) *flavipes* (Pl. 15). It nests in and under old logs and stumps, more rarely in decaying wood of houses when the wood touches earth. It was here before 1492. Like other Rhinotermitidæ and some Termitidæ, it lives in the ground and will not go far above ground to reach wood. Hodotermitidæ (Termopsinæ of some authors) live in moist wood and Calotermitidæ (also spelled with a K) live in dry wood without access to earth. It is the latter, native in our South and West, that are difficult to combat where established. If you think that you have them in your house, send samples to the Bureau of Entomology, U. S. Dept. of Agriculture, or to your State Entomologist, and ask for advice.

Termite colonies differ greatly from ant colonies. Workers and soldiers are modified males as well as females and, since there is no pupal stage, the young resemble adults. Only the typical, sexual males and females ("first reproductive caste") have wings and even they lose them. After the marriage flight the male ("king") lives on with the "queen." Furthermore, some individuals ("second and third reproductive castes") may lay eggs even though they never get fully developed wings. It is all too complicated to be discussed here.

An interesting physiological point is that the wood which they eat is apparently digested for them, in some cases at least, by single-celled animals, Protozoa, which live in their intestines.

The following key refers chiefly to "soldiers."

1.—Fontanel (A depression on the forehead where the median ocellus would be. In some species it secretes a defensive fluid) present. Eyes poorly, if at all developed. Clypeus of winged forms divided by a median line. ...2.

Fontanel absent. Eyes present. Mandibles often with very strong teeth. Clypeus of winged forms not divided. . . . . .3.

2.—Pronotum saddle-shaped; with distinct lobes in front. Head either with a snout-like projection (nasute) or with toothed mandibles.—Termitidæ.

Pronotum flat; without separated lobes in front. Head not nasute. Mandibles not toothed.—Rhinotermitidæ.

3.—Antennæ more than 21-jointed. Compound eyes usually black.—Hodotermitidæ.

Antennæ less than 21-jointed. Compound eyes usually white.—Calotermitidæ.

EMBIODEA

See p. 37. These are so rarely seen that they have not been nicknamed. So far as known they are active, often gregarious, and usually live in silken nests on or in

PLATE 15

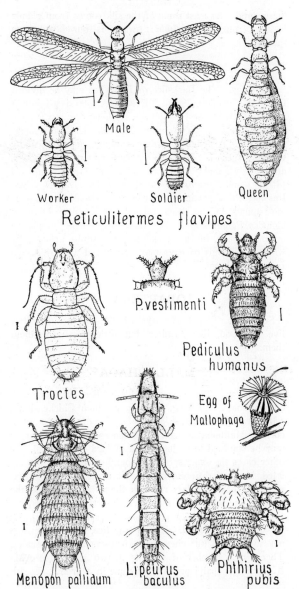

Male

Worker

Soldier

Queen

Reticulitermes flavipes

P. vestimenti

Troctes

Pediculus
humanus

Egg of
Mallophaga

Menopon pallidum

Lipeurus
baculus

Phthirius
pubis

the ground. At least some of the silk comes from glands
in the front legs. *Embia texana* is our best-known
species.

CORRODENTIA

See p. 37. The Bark-lice or Book-lice may be divided
into two superfamilies: TRIMERA (tarsi 3-jointed)
and DIMERA (tarsi 2-jointed). Among the first are the
families TROCTIDÆ (no suture between meso- and metathorax) and ATROPIDÆ (these parts not fused) with usually
wingless species. They are rather common in old books,
dusty shelves and behind wall-paper. *Troctes divinatorius*
(Pl. 15) and *Atropos pulsatoria* are called Death-watches.
Possibly these particular species do not make faint ticking sounds but at least related species do. Diamera
includes PSOCIDÆ and other familes frequently found on
or under bark, in fungi, and so on. Adults are usually
winged. Clumps of eggs may be covered with silk spun
from the labium.

ZORAPTERA

See p. 37. To date *Zorotypus* is the only genus. They
live in wood, like termites, but little is known about
them.

MALLOPHAGA

See p. 37. These are called Bird-lice but some live
on mammals. Plate 15 shows a common Chicken-louse
(*Menopon pallidum*), *Lipeurus baculus* of pigeons and a
curious Mallophagan egg. A given species of this order
may be confined to a single kind of bird or mammal. In
other cases the same species is found on different, but related, birds of different geographic areas, indicating that
evolution has been less rapid in the parasite than in the
hosts. The winglessness of these insects is a "degenera-
tion" such as usually accompanies parasitic habits—or
the other way 'round. Unlike true lice, these insects do
not suck blood but chew hair, feathers and skin-scales.
There are a number of families in two suborders: AM-
BLYCERA (palpi present; antennæ in a groove beneath

the head) and ISCHNOCERA (no palpi; antennæ not concealed).

ANOPLURA

See p. 37. This order of True Lice is also called Siphunculata. Members of three families may be temporary—very temporary—visitors in even good homes. If they have eyes they are *Pediculus* of PEDICULIDÆ or *Phthirius pubis (inguinalis)* of PHTHIRIIDÆ (Pl. 15). If not or very indistinctly so, they are HÆMATOPINIDÆ from rats or dogs. The Head-Louse of man is *Pediculus humanus,* also called *capitis.* His Body Louse, Cootie, Gray-back and other names, is, according to some authorities, a different species, *P. vestimenti. Phthirius* is the not common Crab Louse of man.

HOMOPTERA

See p. 38. This group contains such a variety of insects that it is almost certain to be broken into several orders. Furthermore, the families as given here have already been split by some authorities. The present arrangement is too conservative to last long and the following key is not without faults.

1.—Active, free-living species. Beak plainly arising from the head. Tarsi 3-jointed. Antennæ very short; with a small, terminal bristle.—Suborder AUCHENOR-RHYNCHA. ....2.
    Males usually active; females often inactive. Beak appearing to arise between the front legs; sometimes absent in males. Tarsi less than 3-jointed. Antennæ, if developed, without a conspicuous terminal bristle.—Suborder STERNORRHYNCA. ....6.

2.—Our species usually at least 0.5 in. long. Three ocelli on top of head. Antennæ with a short basal joint; terminal, hair-like process about 5-jointed. Front femora thickened and usually spined beneath. Hind legs not fitted for jumping.—CICADIDÆ, p. 74.
    Our species less than 0.5 in. long. Usually not more than 2 ocelli. ....3.

3.—Antennæ arising from below the eyes. Ocelli placed beneath or near the eyes, usually in cavities in the cheeks. Pronotum not usually greatly developed.—Superfamily FULGOROIDEA, p. 78.

Antennæ arising from in front of and between the eyes. Ocelli, if any, not usually below the eyes. ......4.

4.—Pronotum enlarged, usually extending back over the abdomen.—MEMBRACIDÆ, p. 77.

Pronotum not so enlarged. ....5.

5.—Hind tibiæ with 1 or 2 stout teeth and, at its apex, with a cluster of small ones.—Superfamily CERCOPOIDEA, p. 78.

Hind tibiæ ridged and with one or more rows of spines.—Superfamily JASSOIDEA, p. 79.

6.—Tarsi usually 2-jointed. Four wings, if any. ....7.

Tarsi usually 1-jointed. Females wingless, often legless, and usually covered with a waxy substance, powdery or scale-like. Males 2-winged or wingless; mouth-parts not developed.—Superfamily COCCOIDEA, p. 84.

7.—Jumping insects with thickened hind femora. Antennæ with from 5 but usually 10 joints. Front wings somewhat thicker than the hind ones.—CHERMIDÆ, p. 79.

Hind femora not thickened. Antennæ 3- to 6-jointed. ....8.

8.—Wings, if any, transparent, though sometimes colored. Basal joint of tarsus sometimes very small. Process between the tarsal claws absent or nearly so. Body not covered with "powder" but sometimes with waxy "wool."—Superfamily APHIDOIDEA, p. 80.

Wings usually whitish. They and body of adult covered with fine powder, the scale-like immature individuals not so but often with marginal waxy plates. Tarsal joints approximately equal in size. Usually a distinct process between the tarsal claws.—ALEYRODIDÆ, p. 83.

CICADIDÆ

See p. 73. These are called Cicadas, Harvest-flies, and "Locusts." The eggs are laid in twigs. The newly-hatched young drops to the ground and, burrowing into it, feeds by sucking the juices of roots. It lives in this way for some time (the duration depending on the species), its appearance changing but slightly. Finally, it digs out by means of its enlarged front feet, crawls on a tree-trunk or some such thing, splits down the back and liberates the adult. The adult male "sings," often very loudly and shrilly, by vibrating membranes stretched over a pair of sound-chambers situated, one at each side, near the base of the abdomen.

The Periodical Cicada or Seventeen-year Locust—Thirteen-year Locust in the South—is *Magicicada*

PLATE 16

Magicicada septendecim

A Cicadid nymph

Cicadid
egg-scars

Tibicen
sayi

Cicada
hieroglyphica

(formerly *Tibicina*) *septendecim*. The adult has the same general shape (Pl. 16) as its relatives but its "music boxes" at the base of the abdomen have no cover and its eyes and the principal veins of the wings are red. There is nothing mystical in this color or in the W on the wings, although the sudden appearance of the adults in large numbers has been supposed to foretell war. For about sixteen years, in the North, the young suck at the roots of plants. Toward the end of this period scale-like rudiments of wings appear. In the spring of the 17th year the nymph makes its way to the surface of the ground by a smooth, firm tunnel. Sometimes, especially if the soil be moist and leaf-covered, it constructs a "chimney" over the exit-hole. Then, from late May to early July, it and the other members of its brood crawl out singly or in droves and, fastening on some support, molt to become adults that have a week or so of aerial life to recompense them for the long period of preparation. There are a score or more of different broods, each of which has a rather definite, often restricted, distribution and time of emergence. Suppose there are three such broods in your neighborhood. One of them (that is, the adults) may have appeared in 1911; its next appearance was in 1928. Another might be 1916, 1933 and so on; while the third might be 1919, 1936, and so on. As a matter of fact, these are actual broods, although they may not be the ones of your neighborhood. However, the example shows that we may have Seventeen-year Cicadas oftener than every seventeen years, to say nothing of the possibility in the various broods of laggards or extra-spry individuals that do not appear on schedule time.

There are numerous other species of this family, the differentiation being based largely on the form of the male genital plates, although there are size- and color-differences and an attentive ear can detect differences in their "music." Of the genus *Cicada* (as here limited, *Tettigia*), the small *hieroglyphica* (Pl. 16), with an almost transparent abdomen, may be found in pine barrens, and is our only species. Pl. 16 also shows a common species of *Tibicen* (music boxes covered) that is fairly typical of its genus, the common one in our region. The somewhat similar *Okanagana* (head, including eyes, considerably narrower than the base of the mesonotum) is more common in the West than in the East.

MEMBRACIDÆ

See p. 74. The Tree-hoppers have been aptly called Insect Brownies. If you doubt the aptness see Pl. 81 or, better, look at a number of species, full in the face, through a low-power lens. The prothorax is variously modified and in some of the Tropical species the modifications are very extraordinary. They are called Tree-hoppers because most of the species live on trees and low bushes, hopping vigorously when disturbed. All of the species suck plant juices. Eggs are usually laid in the tissues of the food-plants. The young differ in being more normally shaped. Many of these young and some of the adults excrete "honey dew," much as Aphids do, and are eagerly attended by ants for this fluid and for sap from the punctured bark.

The following subfamilies are the most important here. Centrotinæ has the pronotum produced posteriorly but not concealing the scutellum (the somewhat triangular piece just behind the mesonotum). *Microcentrus caryæ* on hickory is our common species. Hoplophorioninæ has the hind tarsi much shorter than the others. *Platycotis vittata* is our principal species. Membracinæ has one or more pairs of tibiæ broad and flat. Among other genera, *Campylenchia* has the lateral ridges of the "horn" close to the upper margin (*C. latipes* lives on grasses and has no yellow markings on its back) and *Enchenopa* has them about midway between the upper and lower margins. (The back of *E. binotata* is marked with yellow. It lives chiefly on woody plants and covers its eggs with froth.) Smiliinæ has normal tibiæ. Among the genera in which the pronotum does not cover the front wings *Ceresa* can usually be recognized by the horn on each shoulder as shown in *bubalus,* Pl. 81. There are numerous species. As shown for *belfragei,* the pronotum of *Archasia* is high and thin. Typical pronotal crests of *Thelia, Telamona* and *Entylia* are also shown on Pl. 81.

FULGOROIDEA

See p. 73. This is the old family Fulgoridæ now raised to superfamily rank and the numerous species are grouped on technical characters in a number of families. The prothorax of the Membracids is over-developed but the Fulgorids have gone to head. *Fulgora lanternaria* (Pl. 81), of the American Tropics, is an extreme type and one of the insects which is commonly sent to the Museum as a great rarity. It is shown here partly because it illustrates the truth that weird-looking things are not always rare; and also because it and some of its relatives have given the common name of Lantern-flies to the family. There were circumstantial stories concerning the luminosity of Fulgorid heads and categorical denials. The Noes have it but, at any rate, the name sticks. Pl. 81 shows also *Scolops sulcipes,* which is fairly common in our region on grass and other plants, especially where the ground is somewhat moist. Other species, such as *Acanalonia bivittata* (Pl. 81; pink specimens are not uncommon), have a more normal head and frequently look like small moths. Such species are often covered with an easily rubbed "meal" and in the Tropics there are species which bear so many and such large filaments of a waxy substance that other insects live in the excretion. The eggs, as far as I know, are laid in plant-tissue.

CERCOPOIDEA

See p. 74. The principal family is CERCOPIDÆ. In Cercopinæ the front margin of the pronotum is straight; in Aphrophorinæ it is rounded or angular. These Frog-hoppers or Spittle Insects get their common names by being broad, squat, hopping creatures whose young live in masses of white froth (Pl. 81) sucking sap. "The spittle is a viscid fluid expelled from the alimentary canal of the insects and beaten up into a froth by the whisking about of the body. What advantage it is to the young insects is hard even to conjecture; it certainly is not known" (Kellogg). Possibly it is a protection against drying out; and it is said to harden into a protective shell when the insect molts.

JASSOIDEA

See p. 74. These are the Leaf-hoppers. In the South, the species that attack cotton have been named Sharp-shooters and Dodgers. All of our numerous species are small and occur on vegetation of various kinds, especially grasses. Doubtless the small amount of sap taken by each of thousands of individuals amounts to a great deal per acre of grassland, vineyard, and orchard. Pl. 81 shows *Graphocephala coccinea*.

Certain of the families may be recognized as follows:

1.—Ocelli either on the disc or margin of the vertex, not on front. ....2.
    Ocelli on front, below margin of vertex. Head very short, sometimes very broad.—BYTHOSCOPIDÆ.
2.—Ocelli on disk of vertex, usually distinctly not on the margin. ....3.
    Ocelli, if any, on margin of vertex or between vertex and front.—JASSIDÆ.
3.—Body usually elongate, cylindrical. Head often angulate.—CICADELLIDÆ.
    Body usually flattened, broadly oval. Head acutely angled between crown and face. Face relatively narrow. Lateral sutures of front obsolete beyond antennæ.—GYPONIDÆ.

CHERMIDÆ

See p. 74. Another name is Psyllidæ. The Jumping Plant-lice are usually described as resembling miniature Cicadas. The antennæ are long and the wings are transparent. Some of the species, especially of the genus *Pachypsylla,* produce galls (p. 443), while others feed in exposed situations on the leaves. Probably the most injurious species is the Pear Psylla, *Psylla pyricola.* It was introduced from Europe about 1832. "Usually the first indication of the pest is the presence of large quantities of honey-dew, secreted by the nymphs, with which the foliage becomes covered, and which attracts numerous ants. ["Weeping trees" are caused by a number of different Homoptera.] A blackish fungus grows on the honey-dew and is always a good indication of the presence of the psylla. The adult is about one-tenth inch long, of a reddish crimson color with brownish-black markings, bronzy eyes and dark wing-veins. The egg is about one-eighteenth inch long, hardly perceptible without a lens, and orange-yellow in color. It is pear-shaped with the small end drawn out into a long thread" (Sanderson).

APHIDOIDEA

See p. 74. In his memoir on insects affecting park and woodland trees Dr. Felt has a section which he entitles "The Battle of the Weak or Interesting Facts about Aphids." The title is striking and true. These creatures (Pl. 17) are called Plant-lice, Green-flies, Blight (from the damage they do) and other things also. They are among the most injurious, the most interesting, and the most puzzling of insects. It would be difficult to improve on some of the many general accounts of their life cycle. As Dr. Felt has just been mentioned, his summary may be quoted: "Many of the species pass the winter in what we know as the winter egg, which is usually deposited in crevices of the bark or at the base of buds or branches, where it remains during the winter. The young hatch therefrom, in some cases at least, at about the time the foliage begins to develop and in other instances not till well toward midsummer, establish themselves at some favorable situation and begin to draw nourishment from the unfolding tissues. These young are all females and in the language of science are known as 'stem mothers.' They usually begin to produce young in a few days after hatching from the egg and these are also females and in turn produce others. This method of reproduction is what is known as agamic or asexual and differs from the ordinary in that males have no part in the process. A number of generations may be produced in this way, the adults being wingless, and after a time, usually at the end of a certain number of generations, winged females develop. These latter forsake the original, usually by this time crowded, food-plant and either fly to similar ones in the neighborhood or, as in the case of some species, betake themselves to entirely different plants, where another series of wingless agamic or asexual generations are brought forth. This may continue for some time and after a certain number

PLATE 17

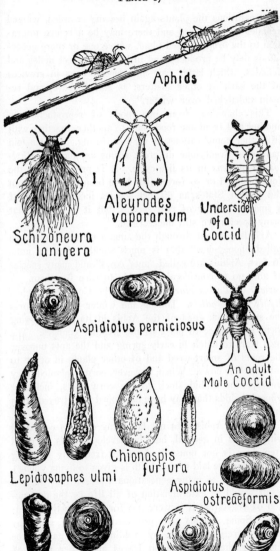

Aphids

Schizoneura lanigera

Aleyrodes vaporarium

Underside of a Coccid

Aspidiotus perniciosus

An adult Male Coccid

Lepidosaphes ulmi

Chionaspis furfura

Aspidiotus ostreaeformis

Aspidiotus ancylus

Aspidiotus forbesi

of generations the plants again become crowded, winged females are produced and there may be a return migration to the original food plant, where one or more generations may be produced and ultimately perfect males and females, which latter pair and deposit eggs in crevices of the bark of other shelters, as stated above, and remain unhatched over winter."

This changing from one mode of reproduction to another and from one food plant to another, together with still other complications, is very confusing. Lichtenstein has noted twenty-one different forms assumed by *Phylloxera quercus* in its life-cycle. It is probable that the four hundred or so forms that have been described from the United States as distinct species include phases of a smaller number of real species, but it is certain that many species are still undescribed.

Aphids pass out through the anus a sweetish substance called "honey-dew" that is much sought after by ants. In fact, Aphids are called "ants' cows" and many species of ants go to considerable trouble to care for them. A variety of *Lasius niger* attends to the Corn-root Aphis, *Aphis maidi-radicis*. During the winter this ant stores the small black eggs of the Aphis in its nests, moving them from place to place as the weather changes. The eggs start to hatch in early spring and the ants uncover the roots of smart-weed and of other plants in order to pasture their cows. When, however, corn is planted, they transfer the Aphid stock to the corn roots, including winged Aphids that may have developed and strayed from the herd.

A female Aphis does not lay many eggs as compared with insects in general, but the development is so rapid (ten days is not unusual, the eggs frequently hatching before they are laid so that birth is given to living young) and there are so many generations a season that the end result would be extermination of all life by the destruction of vegetation if it were not for counteracting agencies. Some Aphids are protected by ants, some by waxy secretions, some by foldings and galls produced by their presence on leaves and other parts of plants, but all are injured by damp weather, by fungi and by insect enemies. Among the latter are Coccinelidæ,

Syrphidæ, and Chrysopidæ, which, together with less important enemies, devour them from the outside. But we should not overlook the Chalcididæ, which feed internally. Look at the Aphid colonies on a rose bush and you are almost certain to see the dried shells of individuals which have been parasitized by these, our friends, a small hole in each showing where the Hymenopteron had emerged.

Classification is based on technical characters and is still much confused, changes of names being frequent. In the following "parthenogenetic" or "agamic" means capable of reproducing without mating; "oviparous," laying eggs; "viviparous," holding the eggs until they hatch inside the female's body, also called "ovivivparous."

APHIDIDÆ.—Parthenogenetic females are viviparous; sexual females oviparous. They and usually the males are able to suck sap. Cornicles (the pair of dorsal appendages formerly supposed to excrete honey-dew, now believed to furnish only a waxy fluid) rarely absent. The subfamily Hormaphidinæ contains the gall-makers *Hormaphis* and *Hamamelistes* (p. 446).

ERIOSOMATIDÆ.—Parthenogenetic females are viviparous; sexual females oviparous. The former are able to suck sap, but the latter and males lack mouthparts and wings. Cornicles much reduced. Some of these Aphids are very conspicuous because of the white, waxy excretion that covers them. For examples, the Woolly Apple Aphis (*Eriosoma*, formerly *Schizoneura, lanegera*, Pl. 17) and the Alder Blight (*Prociphilus tessellatus*) that is fed on by the caterpillar of the butterfly *Feniseca*. Others are gall-makers (*Colopha* and *Pemphigus*, p. 446).

ADELGIDÆ.—Both sexual and parthenogenetic females oviparous and able to feed; the latter secrete a waxy "wool." No cornicles. Infest only Conifers.

PHYLLOXERIDÆ.—Both sexual and parthenogenetic females oviparous. The former and males have no beak; the latter feed but without defecating. No cornicles. *Phylloxera* (p. 446) secretes a waxy powder.

ALEYRODIDÆ

See p. 74. This is the White-fly family. *Aleyrodes* (or *Trialeurodes* or *Asterochiton*) *vaporariorum* (Pl. 17) is the species most often found on house-plants. The young somewhat resemble scale-insects and the pre-adult stage is a pupa similar to those of Endopterygota. As

seen through a lens, they are rather pretty, usually shiny
black with white, wax-like rods and tufts. Each egg is
mounted on a small, curved stem.

COCCOIDEA

See p. 74. These are the True Scale Insects, Bark-
lice, or Mealybugs. The sexes of the same species differ
almost as much in the adult stage as do the members of
different orders. The males undergo a complete metamorphosis, but possess only a single pair of wings, the
hind wings being represented by a pair of club-like
halteres as is the case in the Diptera, or Flies. Each of
these halteres is furnished with a hooked bristle, which
fits in a pocket on the upper wing on the same side. The
males possess no mouth. The females and young are
always wingless and have either a scale-like or a gall-
like form, covered with larger or smaller scales of wax,
which may be in the form of powder, of large tufts or
plates, of a continuous layer, or of a thin scale. All scale
insects suck plant juices and are injurious to the plants
upon which they feed, but, as far as man is concerned,
the harm which certain species do is slightly offset
by the benefits derived from others. The statement that
the manna which fed the Children of Israel was honey-
dew secreted by a scale insect is open to considerable
doubt but shellac is derived from the scale of *Tachardia*
in India and the insect itself contains a red substance
called "lake." Other species furnish wax. Before the
present extensive use of aniline dyes, coloring matter was
derived from a number of different species of Coccidæ,
especially from the Cochineal Insect of Mexico.

Parthenogenesis and viviparity occur, but these phe-
nomena are not so general as among the Aphidoidea. A
single female Coccid may give birth to a very great many
young, but these do not reach maturity as quickly as do
the plant-lice. The males of many species of scale
insects are unknown, probably because their small size
and short life have caused them to be overlooked, rather
than because they are rare or absent. Classification is
based on technical, microscopic characters and the speci-

mens must be specially prepared. The following are some of the recognized families.

MONOPHLEBIDÆ.—*Icerya purchasi,* introduced from Australia to California, did much damage until it was checked by introducing its natural Lady Beetle enemy, *Rodolia cardinalis.* The natives of St. Vincent, Lesser Antilles, make necklaces of the covering of *Margarodes,* calling them "ground pearls."

COCCIDÆ.—Contains the Cochineal Insect, *Coccus cacti,* and many others.

ORTHEZIIDÆ.—The white plates covering the body are usually arranged in a symmetrical pattern.

ERIOCOCCIDÆ.—These are the Mealybugs, so called because they seem "dusted with flour." No real scale is formed and the female is active throughout her life. The males spend their late nymphal life in a cocoon. *Pseudococcus* is a common genus on house-plants.

LECANIIDÆ.—The females have two lobes at the hind end of the body and a pair of plates at the base of the cleft. Some are practically naked (e.g. *Lecanium hesperidum* on house-plants); others excrete a great deal of wax or have a cottony egg-sac (e.g. *Pulvinaria* on maple and other plants).

KERMESIDÆ.—*Kermes* on oak has large gall-like females.

DIASPIDIDÆ.—A large family with a number of subfamilies. The shape of the pygidium (fused terminal abdominal segments) and of the scale, which includes cast skins, are diagnostic of species. Professor Comstock called the pernicious San José scale *Aspidiotus perniciosus* but it is now put in the genus or subgenus *Comstockaspis.* Pl. 17 shows this and other common species, including *Lepidosaphes ulmi,* the principal one of several "oyster scales" on our trees and shrubs.

HETEROPTERA

See p. 38. These are the True Bugs. Nymphs may usually be distinguished from wingless adults such as occur in certain families by the fact that most nymphs have two (or three) pairs of pimple-like odor-glands near the middle of the back of the abdomen. The "scutellum" is a usually triangular area just behind the mesonotum. When the basal part ("corium") of the front wings is thickened, the apical unthickened part is called the "membrane." The triangular area, when present, at the tip of the corium is called the "cuneus." The "clavus" is an oblong basal part along the inner edge of the front wings. The following key is necessarily rather difficult and does not take account of all exceptions. One troublesome thing about Heteroptera is the tendency of the adults of many species to have short winged forms; others are wingless.

1.—Antennæ shorter than the head and, except for Ochteridæ, hidden in cavities. No terminal pad between tarsal claws. Living in or near water.—Suborder CRYPTOCERATA. ....2.

Antennæ usually at least as long as the head (not so in the blind families TERMITAPHIDIDÆ in termite nests and POLYCTENIDÆ parasitic on bats) and usually free but may (Phymatidæ) fit in grooves on the prothorax. Tarsi with or without terminal pads.—Suborder GYMNOCERATA ....9.

2.—Front tarsi 1-jointed, spatulate, with a leaf-like claw. Hind legs used in swimming, their tarsi with bristle-like claws. Middle legs long. Body flattened above. Head protruding above the pronotum. Beak 1- (or 2-) jointed. —CORIXIDÆ, p. 92.

Not so..3.

3.—Ocelli present. Proboscis 4-jointed. Small species living on shores. ....4.

No ocelli. Aquatic. ....5.

4.—Antennæ hidden. Front legs stout, formed for grasping. Broad, squat, roughened bugs with prominent eyes.—GELASTOCORIDÆ; also called Galgulidæ and Nerthridæ. These predacious Toad Bugs frequent muddy banks. *Gelastocoris* (= *Galgulus*) is our principal genus (Pl. 18); the front tarsi have 2 claws. *Mononyx* of the West and *Nerthra* of the Southeast have but 1 claw on each of these.

Antennæ not hidden. Front legs slender, as long as middle ones, formed for running.—OCHTERIDÆ. Resembles the preceding in form and habits; apparently closely related to Saldidæ also. *Ochterus* is our only genus.

5.—Body convex above. Front wings convex; the membrane without veins. Front and middle legs fitted for grasping; hind ones for swimming. Hind tarsi without conspicuous claws. Front coxæ fastened at the hind margin of the prosternum. ....6.

Hind tarsi with distinct claws. Front legs fitted for grasping. Front coxæ fastened near the front margin of the prosternum. ....7.

6.—Hind tibiæ and tarsi hairy. Abdomen with a median ridge below. Eyes large. Beak 4-jointed.—NOTONECTIDÆ, p. 93.

Not so.—PLEIDÆ, considered by some to be a part of Notonectidæ but by others to belong to Homoptera.

Plea striola is only about 0.06 in. long. It is carnivorous and creeps about on aquatic plants.

7.—"Membrane" of wings without veins. Hind tibiæ slender, with small spines.—NAUCORIDÆ. They resemble Gelastocoridæ but do not have prominent eyes and they crawl about on submerged plants. *Pelocoris femoratus* occurs in the East. It is about 0.4 in. long; pronotum shiny brownish yellow, marked with numerous dark spots: front wings dark brown with a light shoulder-area.

Membrane with net-like veins. Beak with very small labial palpi. Rather large insects. . . . . .8.

8.—Hind legs tibiæ flattened and fringed. Tip of abdomen with two short, flat, retractile appendages.—BELOSTOMATIDÆ, p. 92.

Hind legs not flattened. Abdominal appendages long and slender.—NEPIDÆ, p. 93.

9.—Claws of at least the front tarsi placed back of the tarsal tip, which is more or less cleft. Hind coxæ distinct. Front wings of fairly uniform texture throughout. Under side of body pubescent.—Superfamily GERROIDEA . . . . .10.

Claws apical. Last tarsal joints not cleft. . . . . . . .11.

10.—Hind femora extending well beyond the abdomen. Bases of hind legs close together and not near the front pair. Proboscis with 4 joints, the first short.—GERRIDÆ, p. 95.

Hind femora not (except for some *Microvelia*) extending much beyond the apex of the abdomen. Middle legs about equidistant from front and hind ones. Proboscis 3-jointed.—VELIIDÆ, p. 95.

11.—Body very narrow. Head horizontal, as long as the thorax and widened toward the apex. Legs slender. Antennæ 4-jointed. Often wingless.—HYDROMETRIDÆ, p. 96.

Body rarely very narrow (but see, e.g., Ploiariidæ). Head shorter than the thorax including the scutellum. .12.

12.—Each antenna 4-jointed, not counting the head's antennæ-bearing tubercles, if any (but see Hebridæ, 30). Antennæ visible from above. Head not shield-like. . .13.

Antennæ 5-jointed. . . . . .36.

13.—Wings vestigial or lacking. Body broad and flat. Clypeus triangular, broader apically. No ocelli. Beak 3-jointed. Sucks blood of vertebrates.—CIMICIDÆ, p. 97.

Not so. . . . . .14.

14.—Front wings usually so veined as to appear lace-like. Body rather flat and with a net-like surface; rather delicate. Tarsi 2-jointed.—Superfamily TINGIDOIDEA. 15.

Wings and body not lace- or net-like. Ocelli usually, but by no means always, present. . . . . .16.

15.—Side lobes of the head not prominent. No ocelli. Pronotum extending over the scutellum and sometimes over the head.—TINGIDIDÆ, p. 101.

Head appearing split in front. Ocelli present. Pronotum not covering the scutellum.—PIESMIDÆ, of which *Piesma* may be our only genus.

16.—Front wings usually with a cuneus and embolium (i.e., the outer or costal part of the corium sharply delimited by a suture). Veins of membrane few. Front legs not fitted for grasping prey. Except in some Miridæ, no pad between the tarsal claws. ....**17.**

Front wings without a cuneus. Front legs more or less fitted for grasping prey. Head cylindrical. Beak usually 3-jointed, the first joint stout and usually curved; rarely with an extra, very short, basal joint. Pronotum with a transverse groove. Prosternum usually with a median roughened groove in which the beak fits. ....**22.**

Neither of these. ....**27.**

17.—Antennæ whip-like; the first two joints very short; the third thickened at the base; the last two long and very slender, hairy. Ocelli present. Beak 3-jointed. Usually very small species.—Superfamily DIPSOCOROIDEA. "Jumping Ground Bugs," usually found in moist places and under dead leaves. There are two families: DIPSOCORIDÆ, head extended horizontally or slightly bent down; and SCHIZOPTERIDÆ, head bent between the prominent front coxal cavities.

Third antennal joint not thickened at the base; the second joint rarely shorter than the third.—Superfamily MIROIDEA. According to some authors these and Cimicidæ are combined in the Superfamily Cimicoidea. **18·**

18.—Ocelli present. ....**19.**

No ocelli. Beak 4-jointed. ....**21.**

19.—Tarsi 3-jointed. ....**20.**

Tarsi 2-jointed. Beak 3-jointed; if 4-jointed, the third joint very small.—MICROPHYSIDÆ. Rare with us. *Mallochiola* reported from Washington, D. C.

20.—Beak 3-jointed. Third and fourth antennal joints usually very slender and with numerous long hairs.—ANTHOCORIDÆ. Found under bark and dead leaves, fungi, flowers, and even bird-nests. Predacious.

Beak 4-jointed. Antennal tip without numerous long hairs; the second joint more than half the antennal length.—ISOMETOPIDÆ. "Jumping Tree Bugs" usually found among lichens on bark.

21.—First joint of beak longer than broad, usually extending beyond the hind margin of the head.—MIRIDÆ (also called Capsidæ), p. 96.

First joint of beak scarcely longer than broad and not extending beyond the middle of the eyes.—TERMATOPHYLIDÆ. *Hesperophylum heidemanni*, about 0.2 in. long may be our only species.

22.—Front legs more or less fitted for grasping prey. Head cylindrical. Beak usually 3-jointed, the first joint stout and usually curved; rarely with an extra, very short, basal joint. Prosternum usually with a median, roughened groove in which the beak fits. Pronotum with a transverse groove.—Superfamily REDUVIOIDEA. 23.

Not so. ....27.

23.—Pronotum with 3 lobes. Head narrowed at the base and also behind the eyes. Front wings membranous. Front tibiæ swollen. Front tarsi 1-jointed; hind ones 2-jointed.—HENICOCEPHALIDÆ. A small family. *Systelloderus biceps,* our principal species, has been reported as doing aerial dancing in swarms.

Not so. ....**24.**

24.—Antennæ short; the last joint thickened. Front femora very stout; the front tibiæ short and folding against the femora. Tarsi 2-jointed.—PHYMATIDÆ, p. 100.

Antennæ "elbowed," thread-like, often very thin at the tip. ....**25.**

25.—Prosternum with a median, cross-striated groove in which the proboscis can fit and may, by rasping, cause a stridulation. Beak 3-jointed. ....26.

Prosternum without a stridulation groove. Beak usually 4-jointed. Legs slender; the front pair distinctly "raptorial." Tarsi 3-jointed.—NABIDÆ. "Damsel Bugs." They are usually yellowish or black; rather flattened; predacious; and found on flowers. *Nabis* is our principal genus.

26.—Front coxæ very long, as is the body also. Middle and hind legs long and thin; the front ones well fitted for grasping prey.—PLOIARIIDÆ (also called Emesidæ), ᵖ. 100.

Front coxæ short. Body rather robust. Front legs usually not very greatly modified for grasping prey.— REDUVIIDÆ, p. 98.

27.—No pad between the tarsal claws. ....**28.**

A pad between the tarsal claws. ....**31.**

28.—Body flat, not covered with pile; abdomen broader than the wings. No ocelli. Beak 4-jointed or with the basal joint so small as to be practically 3-jointed. Tarsi 2-jointed.—Superfamily ARADOIDEA, p. 103.

Not so. ....**29.**

29.—Membrane of front wings, when present, without veins and clavus scarcely differing in texture from it. Found on aquatic plants or on or in water. ....**30.**

Membrane with 3 to 5 long, closed cells. The clavus more or less distinct from membrane and like the corium. Eyes large, prominent.—SALDIDÆ, p. 94.

30.—Antennæ long and slender. Body narrow. Tarsi 3-jointed but the basal joint minute. Corium somewhat membranous, with raised veins.—MESOVELIIDÆ. These are small, predacious, often wingless even when adult. They are usually found on floating vegetation.

First two joints of antennæ thicker than the others. Body stout, clothed with velvety pile, rarely over 0.08 in.

long.—Part of HEBRIDÆ, also called Næogæidæ. Usually found on still water. Only a few species are known.

31.—Membrane of front wings with numerous longitudinal veins which often unite. Antennæ placed well up on the sides of the head. Ocelli present.—Superfamily COREOIDEA ....**32.**

Membrane usually with few veins; if many branching veins are present there are no ocelli.............**34.**

32.—Fourth segment of the abdomen constricted in the middle line above. Openings of metathoracic stink-glands usually absent; if not, they are behind the coxal cavities.—CORIZIDÆ. Usually small and pale. Often abundant on various plants in open places.

Basal margin of both the fourth and fifth abdominal segment above usually concavely curved. Metathoracic gland openings usually distinct. ....**33.**

33.—Head much narrower and shorter than the prothorax. Cheeks usually reaching behind the insertion of the antennæ.—COREIDÆ, p. 103.

Head nearly as broad and long as the prothorax. Cheeks scarcely extending back of the antennæ— ALYDIDÆ (or Coriscidæ, possibly only a subfamily of Coreidæ). Species of the largely predacious *Alydus* (or *Coriscus*) are usually fully 0.5 in. long, slender and have a row of spines on the hind femora.

34.—Ocelli present. ....**35.**

Ocelli absent. Membrane of front wings with 2 large basal cells which give off 7 or 8 branching veins. Stout and of moderate size.—PYRRHOCORIDÆ, p. 101.

35.—Antennæ elbowed; the first joint long and club-shaped, the last joint spindle-shaped. Head narrowed in front of the eyes. Femora club-shaped.—NEIDIDÆ, p. 103.

Not so.—LYGÆIDÆ, p. 102.

36.—Front wings with clavus and membrane of about the same texture.—See Hebridæ, **30.**

Front wings with the clavus heavier than the membrane. First antennal joint thickened; the second joint. Head rather broad, the side margins acute in front of the eyes and thickened above the base of the antennæ. Ocelli present. Scutellum large.—Superfamily SCUTELLEROIDEA, p. 104, also called Pentatomoidea. ....**37.**

37.—Scutellum very large, V-shaped and convex, covering most of the abdomen. Opaque part of the corium much narrowed toward the apex. ....**38.**

Scutellum (Except *Stiretrus* in Pentatomidæ. In this case the colors are bright and contrasting; tip of scutellum twice, or more, the width of corium; frena about a fourth its length) rather triangular, narrowed behind. Opaque part of the corium broad apically. ..**40.**

38.—Tibiæ with 2 or more rows of distinct spines.— CORIMELÆNIDÆ. "Negro Bugs." Chiefly on grasses and other low plants.

PLATE 18

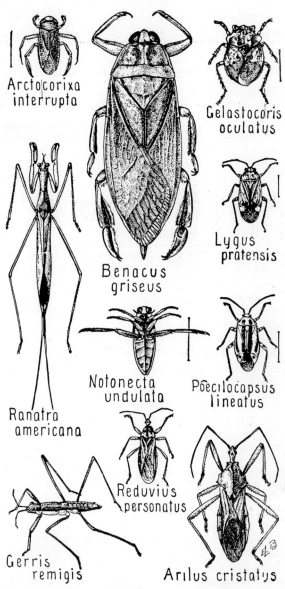

Arctocorixa
interrupta

Gelastocoris
oculatus

Benacus
griseus

Lygus
pratensis

Ranatra
americana

Notonecta
undulata

Poecilocapsus
lineatus

Reduvius
personatus

Gerris
remigis

Arilus cristatus

Tibiæ without strong spines. ....39.

39.—Prothorax with a pair of prominent teeth or lobes at the front and another pair near the back, each of the latter pair being just in front of the "humeral angle" (near a wing-base). Eyes protruding.—PODOPIDÆ. "Terrestrial Turtle Bugs." Found chiefly on the ground in moist places.

Not so. Hind wings with a heavy, spur-like vein ("hornus").—SCUTELLERIDÆ. "Shield Bugs." Found chiefly on trees and shrubs near water.

40.—Tibiæ distinctly spiny. Front legs fitted for digging. Veins of membrane of front wings radiating from the base.—CYDNIDÆ. "Burrowing Bugs." Found chiefly near water, under stones or even in ant nests.

Tibiæ with, at most, weak spines. Front legs not modified. Membrane veins starting from a vein which is nearly parallel with the edges of the corium.—PENTATOMIDÆ. "Stink Bugs." See p. 104.

CORIXIDÆ

See p. 86. The Water-boatmen (Most boatmen are that kind) swim "right side up." Compare Notonectidæ. Most species are slightly heavier than water and rest on the bottom or on aquatic plants. When they come up for air they float in a horizontal position, taking air directly into the thoracic spiracles and renewing the supply of air which is carried by hairs when they dive. Males make sounds by rubbing the front legs against the face. Apparently they are vegetarian, possibly also predacious. Sometimes great numbers are attracted to lights. The eggs are fastened on, not in, submerged objects. Certain Tropical species are so abundant that they and their eggs are gathered for food of man and bird. The tip of male abdomens is not symmetrical. See Pl. 18 for a species of *Arctocorixa*.

BELOSTOMATIDÆ

See p. 87. This family contains the Giant Water Bugs; also called Electric-light Bugs because adults were formerly frequent about electric lights. Some of the Tropical species are the largest of Hemiptera, being about four inches long. The broad, flat hind legs and the flat body, with a keel in the middle underneath, well fit them for aquatic locomotion. The sharp-hooked front legs

and the short, powerful beak make their predatory habits
not to be despised by even fair-sized fish. They lurk on
muddy bottoms, often slightly covering themselves with
mud or leaves, ready to dart out after the unwary.

1.—Mesothorax with a strong midventral keel. Membrane of front wing reduced. Western.—*Abedus.*
    Not so. ....2.
2.—Front femora not grooved. Basal segment of beak
shorter than the second. Hind tibiæ broader than middle ones.—*Benacus griseus* (Pl. 18), about 2 in. long,
lays its eggs on aquatic plants.
    Front femora with a groove into which the tibiæ
fit. ....3.
3.—Basal segment of beak shorter than the second. Body
elongate-oval, 1.5 in. or more long.—*Lethocerus.* Eggs
probably laid under stones, etc., near water.
    Basal segment of beak longer than the second. Body
broadly oval, rarely over 1 in. long.—*Belostoma.* Eggs
are laid on the backs of males. It is said that the males
do not take kindly to this but usually can not help themselves. At least some *Abedus* have the same habit.

NEPIDÆ

See p. 87. The long "tail" of Water-scorpions is not
fully developed until the molt which gives them wings.
It is an air-tube for breathing purposes and is perfectly
harmless; all the sting these creatures have is at the other
end, their beak. The body of *Nepa apiculata* is oval,
flat, and thin; that of *Ranatra* (Pl. 18) is linear and
cylindrical. The Southern and Western genus, *Curicta,*
is intermediate in shape. All are aquatic and predacious.
They are sluggish creatures, crawling but not swimming,
often remaining motionless for hours on the muddy, leaf-
covered bottom of their favorite haunts and rarely, if
at all, coming to lights. Their eggs, which are placed
in or on submerged objects, are furnished with filaments at one end, seven in *Nepa* and two in *Ranatra.*
Species of *Ranatra* squeak by rubbing their front coxæ
against the body.

NOTONECTIDÆ

See p. 86. The Back-swimmers are shaped somewhat
like an overturned boat, but they overturn themselves

when they are in the water. They are lighter than water and normally rest at the surface, floating head-down, with the tip of the abdomen piercing the surface-film, their long hind legs extended like sweeps ready to send them swiftly to safety or food. They do not breathe through their tail but from it the air passes through hair-covered channels to spiracles on their thorax. Small aquatic animals are easy prey, and the suctorial beak will pierce even the careless collector's fingers. Possibly the pearly color of their backs, which, as they swim, is seen against the sky, and the dark of their under (upper) side helps them to approach their victims and avoid becoming victims. The adults fly well and are frequently attracted to lights. Some males stridulate by rubbing legs or face. The eggs are placed in the submerged stems of aquatic plants. The principal genus, *Notonecta* (Pl. 18) has pubescent front wings and the last antennal joint is much shorter than the one next to it; neither is true of our other genus, *Buenoa*. In the latter genus there are definite body-cells containing hæmoglobin.

SALDIDÆ

See p. 89. Uhler, one of the master Hemipterists, wrote: "In the present family we have types which, like *Galgulus* [See key p. 86], make holes for themselves, and live for a part of the time beneath the ground. Like the members of that genus too, a majority of them inhabit damp soils, and are often found in countless numbers on the salt or brackish marshes of our sea coasts [also along streams and ponds]. Their manner strongly recalls that of the tiger-beetles that inhabit the same places. When approached, or in any way disturbed, they leap from the ground, arise a few feet into the air, by means of their wings, and alight a short distance away, taking care to slip quickly into the shade of some protecting tuft of grass or clod, where the soil agrees with the color of their bodies." They feed chiefly upon the juices of drowned insects. Their size is never large and their color is black, sometimes marked with white or yellow.

VELIIDÆ

See p. 87. The Broad-shouldered Water-striders' motion on water is more like running than is that of Gerridæ; they also spend more time on land. Furthermore, they are more given to going into the water than are their relatives and they may sometimes be seen running, back downwards, on the under side of the surface film. Adults of a given species may be long-winged, short-winged, or wingless.

GERRIDÆ

See p. 87. Common names of these insects are Pondskaters and Water-striders. A child to whom I was showing some on a quiet brook misunderstood the latter name and unintentionally coined a much better one: Water-sliders. Watch them for yourself. They may be seen sliding about on the surface of ponds or of the less rapid parts of streams, often jumping up and landing again, making dimples in the water's surface without breaking it. They go about on the two hinder pairs of legs, pushing with the middle pair, steering with the last, and holding the front pair up so as to be ready to grasp their food, which consists of either living or dead insects and the like. Why are they able to run on the surface of water? Because their hairy legs are not wetted and so, with the slight pressure of the insect's little weight, they dimple but do not break the surface film. A greased needle will float for the same reason. Both winged and wingless adults of the same species occur. Eggs are laid at or just beneath the surface of the water on almost any solid object. Adults occasionally go under water. They hibernate and sometimes come out in warm winter days to stretch their legs. If you desire to bring home alive for your aquarium species of this and related families, use a box in which there is some damp moss; they frequently drown if carried in a pail containing water.

Our more common subfamily, Gerrinæ, has the inner margin of the eyes wavy behind the middle and the body rather long and narrow. *Limnoporus rufoscutel-*

latus (antennæ half as long as the body) and species of *Gerris* (Pl. 18) are often abundant. The subfamily Halobatinæ (inner margin of eyes convexly rounded; body rather short and broad) includes the interesting *Halobates,* species of which live on the ocean, often far from land.

HYDROMETRIDÆ

See p. 87. Our only genus of Marsh-measurers or -treaders is *Hydrometra. H. martini* is not rare on water and projecting plants but it is not often seen. It is very thin and not quite 0.5 in. long. Quoting Uhler again, "They delight to remain at rest, with perhaps a single claw hooked to some projecting object. When disturbed they move very slowly, and seem disposed to save themselves rather by concealment among rubbish and tangled growths than by active movements. The young forms are so very slender that they can only be detected with great difficulty in the places to which they resort."

MIRIDÆ

See p. 88. This is one of the largest families of true bugs. It and related families are very bewildering to students who would attempt to classify the species. Most of them are leaf-feeders but some are predacious. The eggs of many, at least, have two filaments at one end. These project from the plant-stems in which they are laid.

The ground-color of the very common Tarnished Plant Bug, *Lygus pratensis* (Pl. 18), ranges from dull to yellowish brown, and its markings are also variable. Typically, the head is yellowish with three narrow, reddish stripes and the following markings also are yellowish: margin of pronotum, several longitudinal lines on it, a V on the scutellum, the legs, and a spot at the apex of the thickened part of each front wing. This insect is very destructive of a large range of vegetation from strawberries to fruit-trees. Adults hibernate in rubbish and appear in early spring. The punctures, made for the purpose of sucking juices, seem to have a poisonous effect on buds and leaves. Probably the eggs are laid in plant-tissues.

The Four-lined Leaf Bug, *Pœcilocapsus lineatus* (Pl. 18), is dark green (yellow after death), with the head, forepart of the pronotum, and under side of body, orange-red. There are four, more or less continuous, black, longitudinal lines on the pronotum and front wings. While particularly injurious to currants and the like, it attacks many different plants. "The presence of the pest is indicated by the appearance of the peculiar brown depressed spots on the tender terminal leaves in early summer. As the attack continues, whole leaves turn brown, curl up, and become brittle, and are torn or broken by the wind. The young shoot is checked and frequently droops and dies. The buds of dahlias and roses are often blasted." The vermilion nymphs hatch from overwintered eggs placed in slits, cut lengthwise into the stems of the plants, each containing six or more eggs. The adult stage is reached about the middle of June.

CIMICIDÆ

See p. 87. Most of us have had experience with one member of this family, although many of us do not like to talk about it. Perhaps no other insect has been given so many euphemistic names, but the one which is most generally understood is plain Bedbug. In fact, that is a translation of (Or, is it the other way around?) its specific name, *lectularius*. It belongs to the genus *Cimex*. A description of its appearance and smell is unnecessary, especially in a Field Book; it is never found afield, under bark and the like; those (Aradidæ) are quite different creatures. It is also confused with another Cimicid that closely resembles it and is often found in the nests of swallows; that is *Œciacus vicarius* and rarely bothers man. Before the days of fumigation the bedbug was much given to going down to the sea in ships and almost certainly it came to America with our best families in the *Mayflower*.

The number of generations a year of *lectularius* depends on the temperature and food-supply; there are, normally, only one or two and it is not true that "they become grandfathers in a night." Kerosene in all the bedroom cracks and crannies will do the trick but, especially in the spring, the treatment should be repeated in order to kill those which were unhatched at the time of the first application and may have been protected by the egg-shell.

REDUVIIDÆ

See p. 89. Some of the very numerous species of Assassin Bugs are rather striking creatures; nearly all are fairly large and some are gayly colored. They are predacious, feeding chiefly on the juices of other insects.

As a "Kissing Bug" *Reduvius personatus* (Pl. 18) received considerable newspaper space some years ago. Another and better common name is Masked Bedbug Hunter. It often enters houses, where it and its young feed on bedbugs, if any. Especially the young have many sticky hairs to which dust and other small particles adhere, making the mask. Many Reduviids have these sticky hairs and should not be put in a collecting bottle together with delicate insects. When *personatus* bites humans, as it rarely does, a very painful wound is caused, so that the newspaper stories have some basis in fact.

A Southern species of similar habits, but much more given to sucking human blood, is *Triatoma sanguisuga*. In the South it is called the Big Bedbug. It is about an inch long; black, marked with red on the sides of prothorax, at the base of the apex of the front wings, and at the sides of the abdomen; the head is long, narrow, cylindrical, and thickest behind the eyes. It is said that the effect of its bite may last for nearly a year, and it is probable that many attacks attributed to spiders are really the work of this insect. Out-of-doors, it feeds on insects, including grasshoppers and potato beetles.

Another species which has been accused of being a Kissing Bug is *Melanolestes picipes*. It is black; about 0.6 in. long; the head well drawn out in front of the eyes, behind which is a transverse, impressed line; the prothorax is more or less bell-shaped and divided into two lobes; the legs are short, the femora stout, and each tibia has a large pad at its apex. In nature it is often found hiding under stones and boards.

PLATE 19

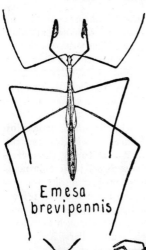

Emesa
brevipennis

Phymata erosa

Corythuca
arcuata

Blissus
leucopterus

Lygaeus
Kalmii

Myodocha
serripes

Anasa
tristis

Podisus
maculiventris

Murgantia
histrionica

Euschistus
variolarius

Mormidea
lugens

Apiomerus crassipes is about 0.6 in. long; rather broad; black, the pronotum, scutellum and abdomen margined with red. It is usually found on pine trees, feeding on plant-lice and young caterpillars, often holding them down with the front feet as a dog does his bone.

Arilus cristatus (Pl. 18) varies from less than an inch to 1.5 in. in length; the middle of the pronotum has a longitudinal elevation something like a chicken's comb; general color grayish black, slightly bronzed. It is called the Wheel Bug. The nymphs are red, with black marks. They are our friends, if we do not handle them carelessly, as they use their beaks with good effect on many kinds of caterpillars and other injurious insects.

Sinea diadema is about 0.5 in. long; brownish; front femora, head and pronotum largely covered with short spines. It is often found on the flowers, such as goldenrod. Although it eats injurious caterpillars, it does not hesitate to attack stinging insects and so it is not especially welcome near bee-hives.

PLOIARIIDÆ

See p. 89. Thread-legged Bugs used to be classified as Reduviidæ. They occur under loose bark, in tufts of grass, vacant buildings and similar places, feeding upon other insects and spiders. The front legs (Pl. 19; *Emesa,* or *Emesaya, brevipennis*) are much like those of Mantids and are used in the same way for catching prey. The shape of the body suggests a delicate Walking Stick. Heteroptera, however, have beaks instead of jaws. Its slow swaying motions reminds one of Crane Flies. Truly, "this is an extremely curious insect, built in the most intangible manner."

PHYMATIDÆ

See p. 89. The two genera of Ambush Bugs may be separated as follows: Scutellum short, head with a bifid prolongation above the insertion of the antennæ, *Phymata;* and scutellum very long, extending to the tip of the abdomen, head without such prolongation, *Macrocephalus.* We have but a few species. *Phymata erosa*

(Pl. 19) is the one most likely to be collected. Like most of the others, it conceals itself in flowers, where it captures various insects, including large butterflies and even bees. The front legs are short but very powerful, and apparently its beak is quite deadly. The generic name means "tumor" and was probably suggested by the projections from the body. This species is greenish-yellow, marked with a broad black band across the expanded part of the abdomen. The female is about 0.4 in. long; the male somewhat less.

TINGIDIDÆ

See p. 87. The adult Lace Bugs are small, delicate and, under a lens, beautiful insects. In most of the species the front wings and other parts, including expansions of the prothorax, are like fine lace. Furthermore, they lack the unpleasant odors of many Hemiptera. On the other hand, they suck the sap of plants, sometimes doing definite damage. They are usually found on the under sides of leaves. The eggs are often placed near the leaf-veins. At least some species hibernate as adults. Pl. 19 shows *Corythuca arcuata,* which is common on oaks and other trees.

PYRRHOCORIDÆ

See p. 90. The Cotton-stainers are also called Red Bugs but they are not the creatures (mites) that get in human skin and cause red sores. Our Northern species is *Euryophthalmus succinctus.* It is about 0.5 in. long and rather stout; brownish black above, with red on the margins of the prothorax, outer margin of front wings, trochanters, and bases of femora; a fine bluish pubescence underneath. The young are brilliant steel-blue, with reddish legs, and a bright red spot at the base of the abdomen. Some authorities say it is a plant-feeder and others that it feeds mainly on insects and was "found to be very useful in California by eating the destructive cottony cushion scale, at one time threatening to destroy entirely the orange groves of that state." Perhaps it does both. The real Cotton-stainer of the South is *Dysdercus suturellus.*

LYGÆIDÆ

See p. 90. The Chinch Bug family contains at least 200 species in America, north of Mexico. Plant sap is their chief, if not sole, food. Most of us have heard of the Chinch Bug, *Blissus leucopterus* (Pl. 19), and all of us have helped pay for it. This pest has cost the United States over half a billion dollars. The worst injury has been to small grains and corn in the Mississippi Valley but frequent injury is done in the East, especially to timothy meadows which have stood for several years. It also attacks lawns. It is black and white except for the red legs and bases of the antennæ. Most of the adults occurring between the Rockies and the Alleghanies have normally long wings; in the South, East, and along the Lakes to northern Illinois, short-winged individuals are usually the more common. The young are yellowish or bright red, marked with brownish. Adults hibernate in clumps of grass or under rubbish. In early spring the females lay their yellowish-white eggs (up to 500 each) on the roots or at the bases of stalks, usually of grasses and grain. Even the long-winged adults do not fly much but usually walk from field to field. The first annual generation matures in early summer. The next matures in August and September.

Oncopeltus fasciatus is about 0.6 in. long; red and black, the black above being a spot covering most of the pronotum and scutellum, a broad band across the middle of the closed wings, and the membranes. *Lygæus kalmii* (Pl. 19)—and other species—has the same colors but the black on the pronotum is at the front, the wings are black next to the scutellum, and the middle band does not go all the way across; it is about 0.5 in. long.

Myodocha serripes (Pl. 19) "is rendered very comical by the swinging of the long antennæ with their thickened apical joint, while running over the ground among stones and rubbish of its favorite haunts. Meadows and rich soils in thin woods furnish it with needed shelter, and there it may be found throughout the entire year, half concealed by bits of twigs and dead leaves, or stowed away beneath the loose fragments of rock which lie scattered over the ground" (Uhler). The long, slender neck is quite distinctive.

NEIDIDÆ

See p. 90. Apparently we have a very few species of Stilt Bugs. *Jalysus spinosus* is widely distributed and not really rare. It is about 0.3 in. long, with a very slender, pale body, and long, slender legs. It is rather sluggish and usually found in the undergrowth of oak woods. At first sight it suggests a tawny Crane Fly.

ARADOIDEA

See p. 89. These Flat Bugs are responsible for the notion that bedbugs live also under bark and that they then may have wings. They are dark brown or black; and the reddish, wingless young do look like bedbugs. They probably feed on fungus. A good way to collect them is to knock dead sticks together over a white sheet. This jars off the insects and they can be seen more readily. *Aradus* is our principal genus of ARADIDÆ (head narrowed behind the eyes, the latter projecting beyond the cheeks). We have more genera but fewer species in the Southern family, DYSODIIDÆ, also called Meziridæ (head wider just behind the eyes than in front of them).

COREIDÆ

See p. 90. The Squash Bug family is a very extensive one. Most of the species have an unpleasant odor, and there is a tendency to have the edges of the abdomen raised so that the wings lie in a depression.

The Squash Bug, *Anasa tristis* (Pl. 19) is known to most gardeners who have grown any of the squash family. Its chief claim to scientific fame is that it was used prominently in the development of our present knowledge concerning the germinal relations of sex. The pronotum and the thickened parts of the front wings are speckled brown, the side-margins of the pronotum are yellowish; the hind femora do not bear a row of spines. Adults spend the winter, as well as the summer nights, under rubbish. The oval, pale-yellow to dark eggs are laid in irregular clusters, usually on the under side of leaves. The young are rather gregarious and gay with their crimson legs, head, and front part of thorax, but these change to black as they grow. In the North the adult stage is reached about August.

The following rough notes may be helpful in the Northeast. A brownish species about 0.4 in. long, without a row of spines on the hind femora, but with a leaf-like expansion on each antenna, is probably *Chariesterus antennator*. The following are usually more than 0.6 in. long and have spines on the hind femora: *Archimerus* and *Euthochtha galeator* (antenna-bearing tubercles spined on the outer side) have more or less cylindrical hind tibiæ; *Acanthocephala* and *Leptoglossus* (head greatly extended beyond the antennal bases) have leaf-like expansions of the hind tibiæ.

SCUTELLEROIDEA

The name Stink Bugs has been fastened on this super-family, possibly because some of the species are responsible for giving raspberries a bad, smelly taste once in a while. Another name is Shield Bugs, on account of the large scutellum. See p. 90 for a key to and notes about the several families.

PENTATOMIDÆ has been divided into subfamilies as follows.

Asopinæ have the first joint of the beak largely free and relatively short and thick; there is a spine on the basal abdominal segment. A common genus is *Podisus* (Pl. 19), in which the pronotum is sometimes extended into a sharp spine on each side. The Northern subfamily Acanthosomatinæ has but two joints in each tarsus.

The following subfamilies have 3-jointed tarsi.

Graphosomatinæ have a broad scutellum, which is blunt at the apex and extends back to near the tip of the abdomen. *Podops* is our only genus and *cinctipes* (over 0.25 in. long; 2nd to 4th antennal joints darker) is our common species.

The principal subfamily, Pentatominæ, has the scutellum smaller and more or less narrowed apically. The following belong here.

Brochymena (*quadripustulata* is a common species with us) has a shallow groove on the under side of the abdomen and the beak extends back of the posterior coxæ. The species are broad, rough, brown, 0.5 in. long, and live on trees. They look like bits of bark and are best obtained by beating.

A medium-sized brown species with an angle on each side of the pronotum, behind, is usually a *Euschistus* (Pl. 19). The first segment of the beak is not much thicker than the second, and all the tibiæ are grooved. *Chlorochroa uhleri* is a bright green bug about 0.5 in. long, with yellow side-margins and a yellow tip to the scutellum. Bright green bugs larger than this are usually *Acrosternum*. *Mormidea lugens* is shown on Pl. 19.

The popular interest in *Murgantia histrionica* (Pl. 19) is indicated by its long list of nicknames, among which are Harlequin Cabbage-bug, Calico-back, Terrapin Bug and Fire Bug. It is shining black or deep blue, profusely marked with red. It feeds on cabbage and related plants, wild and cultivated. The white eggs, which are placed in a double row, look like small barrels because of their two black bands and a white spot. Adults hibernate.

MEGALOPTERA

See p. 38. This "pigeon-hole" in the classification of insects is the former Neuropterous family Sialidæ. As an order, it now has two families of its own: SIALIDÆ (in a limited sense) and CORYDALIDÆ. Before telling about the only species concerning which I have actually been asked by laymen, I will slip in a few words about some of its relatives. Species of *Sialis* (the principal genus of Sialidæ) are called Alder-flies or Orl-flies. They differ from other members of the order in having no ocelli and their fourth tarsal joints are bilobed. Their larvæ are aquatic; carnivorous; each of the first seven segments of their abdomen bears a pair of five-jointed filaments (gills); and a single (but longer and unjointed) appendage forms a kind of tail. The larvæ live buried in the bottom of streams but they crawl out and bury themselves in above-water earth to pupate—all Megaloptera have complete metamorphosis and so do pupate. The Corydalidæ differ from the Sialidæ by having three ocelli and simple fourth tarsal joints when adult, and two hooked fleshy projections, instead of a single "tail," on the hind end of the abdomen of the larva. The family is divided into genera, two of which concern us: *Chauliodes,* in which the adults have the hind corners of the head rounded, and the larvæ have no hair-like tufts at the bases of the lateral filaments of the abdomen; and *Corydalis,* in which the adults have the hind corners of the head sharply angled and the larvæ have hair-like tufts at the bases of the lateral filaments. The species of *Chauliodes* are called Fish-flies. The adults are grayish or brownish, with whitish spots or bands, and have feathered antennæ. The larvæ are aquatic, but do not favor swift streams. Pupation takes place out of the water in rotten logs or in the earth. Now we come to the creature laymen ask about.

I cannot give all the nicknames of *Corydalis cornuta* and have no preference. Some of those that I have heard are Dobson-fly, for the adult, and, for the larva, Hellgrammite, Dobson, Crawler, Hell-devil, Hell-diver, Conniption-bug, and Arnly. Others have been published, but when I read this short list to a ten-year-old she said, "It must be an awful-looking thing." Whatever its appearance (Pl. 11), the larvæ make irresistible bait for bass. Many of us have turned over stones in streams looking for them with that end in view. In the May or June that the larvæ are full-grown, a matter of probably three years after hatching, they crawl out on the bank and pupate under stones, the adults emerging several weeks later. Now, the male is not as terrible as he looks. Those long jaws are to embrace the female when mating. The female's jaws are short, stubby and much more likely to pinch. Two or three thousand eggs are laid in a whitish, rounded mass on a leaf or some other object that overhangs a stream.

RAPHIDIODEA

See p. 38. These Snake-flies apparently do not occur in our East. The prothorax is long "like the neck of a camel" and the ordinary-looking front pair of legs is

PLATE 20

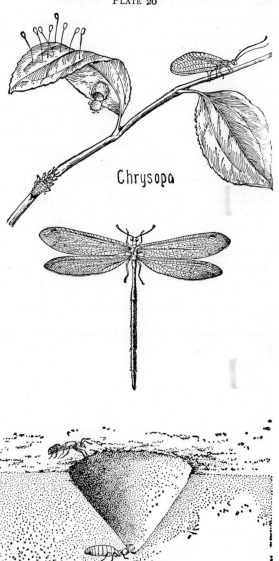

Chrysopa

Myrmeleonid

attached to its base. The larvæ, usually found under bark, are carnivorous and beneficial to man. The pupæ are not enclosed in cocoons and may crawl around a bit before the adult emerges. Of our single family, RAPHI-DIIDÆ, *Raphidia* has 3 ocelli; *Inocellia,* none.

NEUROPTERA

See p. 38. This order, in the limited sense used here, is not only largely terrestrial but, in some cases, inhabits the dryest deserts.

1.—Veins and usually cross-veins abundant; radial sector (the hindmost of the two main divisions of the radius, which is the 3rd of the principal veins of the typical wing) with several branches or forkings. Wings not covered with a whitish powder. ....**2.**

Veins and cross-veins few in number; radial sector at most only forked. Wings covered with a whitish powder. Very small, slender, rare insects.—CONIOP-TERYGIDÆ. The larvæ feed on other small animals such as plant-lice, scale-insects and the "red-spider" (a mite).

2.—Look as though they are fairly large moths that run. Antennæ thread-like, tapering, with 40 or more joints. Male with "pincers" on end of abdomen.—ITHONIDÆ (*Oliarces* on the Pacific Coast).

Not so. ....**3.**

3.—Antennæ long, slender, with a pronounced "club" at the end. Eyes usually divided into two parts by a groove (not so in *Neuroptynx*). The hind margin of the wings indented in *Colobopterus;* not so in *Ululodes.*—ASCA-LAPHIDÆ. Put with Myrmeleontidæ and several exotic families in the superfamily MYRMELEONTOIDEA. The larvæ do not make pits but capture their prey lying in ambush on the surface of the ground.

Antennæ weakly clubbed, or flattened at the tip. Body and wings pubescent. The hypostigmatic cell (the one just behind the stigma, a thickened spot on the front margin of a wing) elongated.—MYRMELEONTIDÆ.

Antennæ not enlarged toward the end; thread-like or like a string of beads, rarely comb-like.—Superfamily HEMEROBIOIDEA. ....**4.**

4.—Front legs fitted for grasping prey; their coxæ elongate; their femora thick and spined; their tibiæ curved to meet the femora. Prothorax elongate. Antennæ short. Wings rather narrow.—MANTISPIDÆ. See *Mantispa,* Pl. 21. The adults are predacious. Not much is known of the habits of the larvæ of our species but, like those of other countries, some probably live in the egg-sacs of *Lycosa* spiders, others in wasp nests, and so on.

Not so.—Other families of Hemerobioidea separated by difficult wing-vein characters.

MYRMELEONTIDÆ

Another spelling of the family name is Myrmeleonidæ. Translating the name of the type genus, *Myrmeleon,* we get the "common" name, Ant-lion, but probably no four-footed lion has ever dug a trap in which to catch its prey. The trap of an ant-lion larva is ingenious. It is a pit made in sand or loose soil. The larva lies hidden at the bottom as shown in the diagrammatic cross-section on Pl. 20. When an ant or some other insect steps over the edge, it tumbles into the waiting jaws below, often being assisted in its downfall by a shower of sand thrown up by the hidden "lion." A favorite place for the pits of some species is the ground below shed-roofs. Pupation takes place underground in a spherical silken cocoon. The delicate gauzy-winged adults are frequently attracted to lights.

The larvæ of some other genera of this family are more lion-like, merely hiding at the surface of the ground and pouncing upon unwary victims.

HEMEROBIOIDEA

Our best-known family is CHRYSOPIDÆ, the Aphis-lions, also called Golden-eyes, of which *Chrysopa* (Pl. 20) is the principal genus. The species of *Chrysopa* all look pretty much alike. They come every year on my honey-suckle and I bring more from the fields and turn them loose in my garden. I have never considered, carefully, the moral side of such an action but I am sure the owners of the "fields" would tell me I was welcome if I showed them the *Chrysopa*—they wouldn't know what a splendid help these insects are in keeping down Aphids (plant-lice). One Sunday afternoon I tried to see how many such pests a single *Chrysopa* would eat; I have forgotten what the count was when I stopped but I know that I got tired before the Aphis-lion did and I turned it loose on the honeysuckle to keep up the good work. The larva spins a delicate silken cocoon in which to pupate; the cocoon opens like a box when the adult is ready to emerge. The odor of the adult is not always as delicate as the appearance; they are sometimes common about lights and you can easily determine this yourself.

In his *Book of Bugs* Harvey Sutherland says of the Aphis-lion: "Its mother, the golden-eyed lace-wing fly, is a dear, sweet thing, that you would think fit only to go on an Easter card, so pale and æsthetic are her light-green wings. But her children are such regular little 'divvels' that she dare not lay her eggs in one mass, for the first one out would eat up all the rest. So she spins a lot of stalks of stiff silk and sticks one egg on the end of each, thereby giving each young one a chance for its life." The captious would remark that a given egg and its stalk are arranged before another stalk is made, but the final effect is the same (Pl. 20). Incidentally, a hungry female will eat her own eggs.

The larvæ of HEMEROBIIDÆ are also Aphis-lions. Look for them on trees, especially conifers, but note that many of them cover themselves with empty aphid skins and other things. So, watch for a tiny moving pile of trash.

The small, rare *Dilar americanus* seems to be our only representative of DILARIDÆ. The male antennæ are comb-like.

Of SYMPHEROBIIDÆ we apparently have only *Sympherobius* and *Psectra diptera*. The male of *P. diptera* has the hind wings reduced to mere scales.

We have at least two species of *Polystœchotes* of the POLYSTŒCHOTIDÆ but we do not at present know how the larvæ live.

SISYRIDÆ larvæ go into the water for their food, fresh-water sponges. It may surprise some readers to be told that we have fresh-water sponges, but we do. The Sisyrid larva comes out of the water to spin the double-walled cocoon within which it pupates. The cocoon cover of *Climacia dictyona* is beautifully lace-like.

MECOPTERA

See p. 38. This is a small order of curious insects. A general characteristic is the prolongation of the head so that the mouth is at the end of a "trunk."

The BITTACIDÆ have much the appearance of Crane

PLATE 21

Bittacus
strigosus

Panorpa
nebulosa

Mantispa
brunnea

Net of
Hydropsyche

Halesus argus

Phylocentropus
lucidus

Molanna
cinerea

Platycentropus
maculipennis

Phryganea
interrupta

Helicopsyche
annulicornis

Caddice Cases

Flies. The single-clawed tarsi are fitted for grasping prey, the fifth joint folding back on the fourth. The scientific name *Apterobittacus apterus* doubly emphasizes the winglessness of that Californian species. *Bittacus* (Pl. 21) is winged. Its few species are given to hanging by their front legs and using the others to grab passing insects of small size.

The wings of BOREIDÆ are reduced to mere bristles (male) or scales (female). There are no ocelli. Although not more abundant then, our only genus, *Boreus,* is more often seen when snow is on the ground.

The principal family is PANORPIDÆ. The tarsi are two-clawed and thread-like. The adult male *Panorpa* (Pl. 21) has a pair of claspers on the swollen end of his abdomen. These hold the female while mating. The scorpion-like pose of these harmless creatures has given them the name Scorpion-flies. Their wings are usually yellow and black. The larvæ, as far as known, live on or just below the surface of the ground, especially if it be moist, and are carnivorous. The adults appear to be less so.

Merope tuber of the MEROPIDÆ is rare and little known.

TRICHOPTERA

See p. 38. These insects have an incidental interest in that, systems of classification notwithstanding, they are practically moths having aquatic larvæ and pupæ. However, they need no reflected glory to give them an appeal. The habits of the larvæ are sufficient. Many of them make portable cases (Pl. 21), each according to its kind.

The common name is Caddice- or Caddis-flies. The scientific name of the order means "hairy winged" but the hair is often difficult to see without a lens and sometimes it is almost as scale-like as on some Lepidoptera. The adults, looking like moths that hold their wings trimly against the body and having long antennæ, are frequently attracted to our porch lights. The following are the principal families in America:

RHYACOPHILIDÆ.—Larvæ are common on the under sides of stones in streams. Cases, if any, made of small pebbles. Unlike most Trichoptera, they make a parchment-like cocoon.

HYDROPTILIDÆ.—Adults are very small and hairy; the marginal fringe of wings longer than the wings are broad. The larval cases are usually made entirely of parchment-like silk, usually flat and much larger than the larvæ.

PHILOPOTAMIDÆ.—At least some species make "fishing-nets" and the larvæ live in them as well. The nets of *Chimarrha aterrima* resemble the fingers of a glove.

HYDROPSYCHIDÆ.—Most caddice larvæ seem to be vegetarians but those of *Hydropsyche* may be carnivorous. They live in swift currents, making a rather crude, but firmly fastened, hut of silk, strengthened with pebbles and debris. Not far from its door it makes a "fishing net" between small stones or on the top of some large stone where it is in the current's sweep. This net is always placed across-stream and its top is often framed with sticks. Now all *Hydropsyche* needs to do, when hungry, is to go out of its hut and eat whatever food the net has caught. On such excursions it keeps hold of a strand of silk which has one end fastened to the door so that it can pull itself back if the current should loosen its footing. Pupation takes place in the larval dwelling, but how about the adult? Most insects slowly work their way out of the pupal case and then rest for some time until their wings are dry and strong. This would never do for *Hydropsyche*, nor for many other species of Trichoptera, since fish would snap them up even if the current did not overpower them. It is said that the pupa leaves its protective case, swims to the surface, and instantly the adult shoots out of the pupal skin and flies away.

POLYCENTROPIDÆ and PSYCHOMYIDÆ.—The larvæ make silken galleries (sometimes in the banks of streams. *Phylocentropus,* Pl. 21) in which they live. Apparently none make portable cases.

CALAMOCERATIDÆ.—Mentioned merely to say that the larva of *Ganonema americana* hollows out a piece of dead twig for its case.

ODONTOCERIDÆ.—At least one *Psilotreta* makes a slightly curved cylinder of sand, closing the ends with pebbles and silk when pupating.

MOLANNIDÆ.—See the illustration of a typical *Molanna* (our principal genus) case, Pl. 21.

LEPTOCERIDÆ.—Larval cases various; usually somewhat cone-shaped and often of sand.

PHRYGANEIDÆ.—Most of the larvæ live in rather still water and, as is usual in such situations, they make portable cases of light vegetable matter. See, for example, *Phryganea,* Pl. 21. Since they are used to still, poorly aerated water, they make good aquarium pets. Species of *Neuronia* make cylindrical, not cone-shaped, cases with rather large pieces of leaves. If you have several of the same species and size in your aquarium and, after inducing one of them to leave its case by touching it in the rear, you remove the case, there will be more larvæ than cases and plenty of action. I shall not describe it here.

LIMNOPHILIDÆ.—Some larvæ in still, other in flowing water. *Platycentropus,* Pl. 21, is in a fairly typical "log-cabin" case.

SERICOSTOMATIDÆ.—Larvæ in streams and lakes. Cases various, including the "snail-shell" made with sand and silk by *Helicopsyche* (Pl. 21).

LEPIDOPTERA

See p. 38. Most students of insects start by collecting Butterflies and Moths; and some people act as if adult Lepidoptera were the only "bugs" worth looking at. It is true that most butterflies and many moths, when they are mature, are among the beautiful things of this earth, but still

> "And what's a butterfly? At best,
>   He's but a caterpillar, drest"

and, until you get the right viewpoint, the larvæ, or "caterpillars," are not so pretty. Compared with many other insects, Lepidoptera are uninteresting; most adults are not given to doing things much more exciting than flitting about, mating, and laying eggs in a relatively common-place way. However, it is only in comparison with some of the other insects that they are uninteresting—

> "How happy could I be with either,
>   Were t'other dear charmer away!"

A good hint for identifying a caterpillar is to note what it is eating and then look up that plant in the index, remembering, however, that some species have a varied menu. Another "hint" is to rear the caterpillar. This involves work but it will be both interesting and instructive. Descriptions usually refer to full-grown caterpillars and here we meet the difficulty that a young caterpillar of a given species may differ more from full-grown specimens of the same species than do those of different species. Specific differences are often technical and, furthermore, the larvæ of many common species are still little or not at all known.

A "caterpillar" with only one ocellus on each side of its head and no circles of hooklets on its abdominal legs is not a caterpillar (a Lepidopterous larva) but the larva of a Saw-fly. A caterpillar more than three inches long is certain to be one of the Sphingidæ if it has either a "horn" or an eye-like spot on its eleventh body segment; otherwise it is likely to be either a Saturniid or a Ceratocampid. A very hairy caterpillar, unless very small, is almost certainly one of the Arctiidæ. A caterpillar without legs on the sixth, seventh and eighth body segments that moves by "looping" belongs to the Geometridæ, but note that some Noctuidæ lack one or more pairs of legs from the middle of their body and also do a sort of a loop. Caterpillars with a slit in the top of the first segment from which, when disturbed, they protrude a yellowish or reddish V-shaped scent organ are, in Eastern United States, those of some Swallow-tail butterfly, *Papilio*.

The name Lepidoptera means "scaly-winged" and refers to the fact that the hairs covering the wings are flattened or scale-like. It is these scales that give color to the wing, as may be seen in Plate 1, which shows the wings of one side after the scales had been removed. We may accept two suborders: RHOPALOCERA and HETEROCERA. The "cera" in these names means "horn" and refers to the antennæ; the "Rhopalo" means "club," and the "Hetero" means "otherwise," in the same sense as when we say "Orthodoxy is my doxy and heterodoxy is another kind of doxy." Butterflies have club-shaped antennæ, a knob at the extreme end, and belong to the Rhopalocera. Moths are Heterocera: some of them, especially the males, have feathered antennæ; some have thread-like antennæ; some have a swelling in their antennæ near, but not at, the end; but a few rare Tropical species have orthodox butterfly clubs. The pupæ of butterflies are not usually protected by cocoons as are those of some moths and are sometimes called "chrysalids" (singular: "chrysalis"). Butterflies, as a rule, fly only by day when but few moths are stirring. Butterflies usually hold their wings erect when at rest, while moths hold them flat or fold them against the body.

RHOPALOCERA

Our Butterflies are now classified in the following families.

NYMPHALIDÆ.—In both sexes the front legs are so reduced as to be useless for walking and are often quite inconspicuous. Because of these brush-like front feet the family is sometimes called Brush-footed Butterflies. The eggs are rather globular and many have radiating ridges. The larvæ usually have at least a few branching spines. Usually the pupæ are angular and hang head-down; often they bear golden or silvery spots. See p. 117.

LIBYTHEIDÆ.—Females have six usable feet but the front legs of males are reduced. An important family characteristic is that the palpi are long and projecting, hence the name Snout Butterflies. See p. 130.

RIODINIDÆ.—Also called Erycinidæ. Legs as in Libytheidæ but palpi not prolonged into a snout. Their antennæ are relatively longer and more slender than in Lycænidæ and they are given to holding their wings out flat when at rest. The pupæ of at least some species have a silken support around their backs. See p. 131.

LYCÆNIDÆ.—Legs as in the two preceding families. Wings at rest held upright. The usually flattened eggs are often beautifully "sculptured." The larvæ are stout and somewhat slug-like. The pupæ have a girdle holding them close to the supporting surface. See p. 131.

PIERIDÆ.—Each sex has six usable feet. The hind wings are not tailed. Eggs cone- or spindle-shaped; with vertical ridges. The smooth, slender larvæ do not have osmateria (see Papilionidæ). The pupæ are rather elongate, often flattened laterally; the narrowed head-end is not forked. They have a girdle but it rarely holds them close to the supporting surface. See p. 134.

PAPILIONIDÆ.—Each sex has six good legs. The eggs are globular. The larvæ have osmateria (forked scent-organs which may be protruded from just back of the head). See p. 140.

HESPERIIDÆ.—Each sex has six good legs; usually the tibiæ have spurs. The eyes are usually overhung with curving "lashes" and the antennæ of many species are hooked at the tip. Eggs are rather hemispherical, smooth or sculptured. The larvæ are smooth and usually have a head, somewhat rough and hairy, which looks too big and seems to be supported by a too slender neck. The pupæ are usually in a loose, cocoon-like arrangement of leaves and silk. See p. 144.

NYMPHALIDÆ

The Monarch (Pl. 82) is technically called *Anosia plexippus* (also *Danais* or *Danaus archippus* or other combinations according to what technicality is followed). It is the species that gathers in large flocks at the end of summer. Together they move south, coming back in the spring as stragglers. The male has a small black patch on one of the veins on the upper side of each hind wing. This patch is a pocket containing scent-scales, a sachet bag. The adult is "mimicked" by *Basilarchia archippus*. The easily recognized larva feeds on milkweeds, fearless of birds because of its acrid taste. The pupa in its "green house with golden nails" is to be found hanging in the same plants or on some near shelter. *Anosia* (or *Danais*) *berenice*, the Queen, somewhat like *plexippus* but with the ground-color a rich brown, occurs in the South. These two are our only species of the Danainæ (or Euplœinæ, again depending on what technicality you prefer).

The front wings of the subfamily Heliconiinæ are at least twice as long as broad. Our only representative is the Zebra, *Heliconius charithonius*, of the Gulf States. It is brownish black striped with yellow. Its larva, white with dark spots and long black spines, feeds on leaves of passion-flowers. Members of this subfamily are supposed to be very distasteful to insectivorous vertebrates, and therefore to be models for numerous mimics.

The Nymphalinæ and the Heliconiinæ have minute scales on at least the upper side of the antennæ; the Monarch and its relatives do not. The following, until we come to Satyrinæ, are Nymphalinæ.

The Gulf Fritillary, *Dione vanillæ*, comes as far north as Virginia. Its wing expanse is about three inches; reddish brown above with black spots, of which a row along the margin of each hind wing are circles enclosing brown, and three near the middle of the front margin of the front wing are circular, each enclosing a white dot; below it is gloriously spangled with silver. The larva feeds on passion-flower leaves. It is brownish red, with dark longitudinal bands and long blackish spines.

The upper side of the Variegated Fritillary, *Euptoieta*

claudia, is shown in Pl. 83; the under side is not silver-spotted. The larva feeds on pansies, violets, mandrake, passion-flower, *Portulacca,* and other things. It is about 1.4 in. long; black head; body usually orange to brownish red. There are two bands of white spots on each side and an indistinct one on top; two long, finely spined horns or tubercles on the first segment and six rows of shorter ones behind these. The pupa is white and black, with slightly gilded tubercles.

The Regal Fritillary, *Argynnis idalia,* usually prefers swampy meadows. The male differs from the female (Pl. 83) in having the submarginal row of spots orange, instead of cream, and the black margin of the front wings less pronounced. Eggs are laid in the fall and the young larvæ live over winter. They feed on violets; are black and yellowish red; and have two rows of yellowish, black-tipped spines on the back, and black spines with orange bases on the sides. The pupa is brown, variously marked.

Note (Pl. 83) the broad yellowish band near the edge of the under side of the hind wings of the Great Spangled Fritillary, *Argynnis cybele.* The larva feeds on violets and hibernates while still young, usually having eaten nothing but its egg-shell. When full-grown, it is rather velvety black with black, sometimes orange-based, spines. The pupa is a mottled dark brown.

Argynnis aphrodite.—Note (Pl. 83) the absence of a broad yellowish submarginal band on under side of hind wing, but usually there is a narrow one and it is often difficult to tell *aphrodite* from *cybele;* they may hybridize. The life history, immature stages, and range, much like *cybele.*

The Mountain Silver-spot, *Argynnis atlantis,* is much like the preceding species but is smaller, and darker at the base of the wings both above and below. On the upper side there usually is present a narrow black border to all the wings and on the hind pair the black spots in the middle are connected to form a very narrow irregular band. Below, the submarginal band of yellow on the hind wings is paler. The males have a decided odor of sandal-wood. In early stages and life history

Plate 22

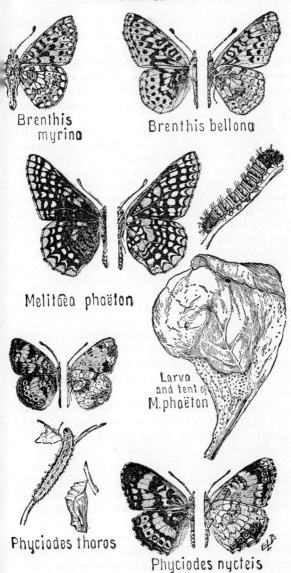

Brenthis
myrina

Brenthis bellona

Melitæa phaëton

Larva
and tent of
M. phaëton

Phyciodes tharos

Phyciodes nycteis

it is similar to *aphrodite* but, especially in the Southeast, it is more confined to mountainous regions.

There are many other species of this genus in the West, all rather difficult to identify correctly; and *Brenthis* is often united with it. *A. diana* of the Southeast is interesting because the male has the outer third of the upper side of the wings orange while the female is black with blue spots.

Although the upper side of the Silver-bordered Fritillary, *Brenthis myrina,* is tawny with black markings and resembles *B. bellona,* the species are easily distinguished by the fact that *myrina* is rich in silver spots on the under side of the wings (Pl. 22). The larva feeds on violets, and after hibernating gets to be about an inch long. It is dark olive brown with lighter markings and covered with fleshy spines. Pupa: dark with darker spots and somewhat curved forward. The pupæ of *Brenthis* have two rows of conical tubercles on their backs.

Brenthis bellona.—See Pl. 22 and the description of *myrina.* The Meadow Fritillary has no silver underneath. Its life-history is much like that of *myrina.* The larval spines of *myrina* are blackish; those of *bellona* are dull grayish yellow.

B. montinus is interesting because it is found only on, or near, the summits of the White Mountains. The under side of the hind wings is much darker than in *myrina* and the silver spots are not so large or so numerous.

The larvæ of *Argynnis* and *Brenthis* feed at night and hide by day. To find them locate patches of violets with irregular pieces eaten out of their leaves; then look carefully among the dead leaves near these plants.

Phyciodes nycteis.—See Pl. 22 and discussion concerning *Melitæa harrisi.* The wings of the Silver Crescent are tawny-orange, lighter on the under side, and marked with black; the hind wing, below, is largely silvery white; the usually imperfect "crescent" is along the margin. The larva, which feeds on sunflowers and other Compositæ, is brownish-black with a rather conspicuous orange stripe along each side; many rather short, black, hairy spines. Although the larva hibernates, it does not seem to construct a shelter. Probably it crawls into a "ready-made."

The variable Pearl Crescent, *Phyciodes tharos,* has two broods: those adults which come from over-wintered larvæ are (among other differences) brighter and with more distinct light markings on the under side (variety *marcia,* Pl. 22) than those which develop during the summer. By chilling the pupæ we can cause some of the summer brood to be *marcia.* The larva feeds on asters. It is black with yellow spots above, yellow side-stripes, and yellowish spines. The slightly angulated pupa has brownish creases on a light ground-color, and, on the middle of the abdomen, a slight transverse ridge.

Phyciodes batesi differs from *tharos* by having heavier black markings above and by the lack of conspicuous dark markings on the lower side of the hind wings, these being almost uniformly pale yellow. There are many other species in the West.

The adult Baltimore, *Melitæa phaëton* (Pl. 22), is found in swampy meadows during June and July. The wings are nearly black, marked with red and pale yellow. The larvæ, which feed chiefly on Scrophulariaceæ, are dark orange, ringed with black, and covered with short hairy spines. They hatch in late summer and are gregarious, spinning a silken tent in which they pass the winter; in the spring they scatter and become full-grown by June. The pupæ have rounded heads, sharp tubercles on their backs, and are whitish with dark and orange markings.

Melitæa harrisi resembles *Phyciodes nycteis* on the upper side, but the under side is darker and has a continuous row of silver spots along the outer margin of the hind wings. The larva feeds on the aster *Dœllingeria umbellata.* It is reddish with a black stripe down the middle and nine rows of black, branched spines. It lacks the Baltimore's black coloring at each extremity.

The species of *Polygonia* (also called *Grapta*) are the Angle-wings that "look as if Mother Nature had with her scissors snipped the edges of their wings, fashioning notches and points according to the vagaries of an idle mood." They are tawny, with darker markings above, and below there is a combination of brown and gray that corresponds closely with the color of dead leaves. The larvæ have rows of barbed spines on the body and a pair of spines on the head. The pupæ have forked heads and a prominent tubercle on the back of the thorax. All the species hibernate as adults, hidden in hollow logs and similar places.

By stretching your imagination a bit when looking at *Polygonia interrogationis* you may see a Question Mark made by the silver spots on the under side of the hind wings but they look to me like (. and I think Fabricius had some other question in his mind when he named the species *interrogationis.* It is also called Violet-tip, because of the violet Papilio-like tail. The summer form (*umbrosa*) has the dark markings on the upper side "clouded." Pl. 23 shows the typical winter form. The larva feeds chiefly on hop and elm. It is chestnut-colored with light dots in longitudinal rows; spines yellowish or reddish. Like other *Polygonia* larvæ, it frequently cocks its head when not feeding. The pupa, which is the color of dead leaves, is very angular and has a "Roman nose" on its thorax; in addition, the thorax bears one or more pairs of metallic silver or gold spots.

Harris, a pioneer American entomologist, named *Polygonia comma* from the silver mark on the under side of the hind wings (Pl. 23) ; and Edwards, one of our earliest and greatest Lepidopterists, named the lighter hibernating form, *harrisi,* in his honor, calling the darker summer form *dryas;* but, unfortunately, by the rules of the game *"harrisi"* is merely *"comma."* The larva feeds on hops, nettles, and related plants, slightly rolling the leaves for its protection while eating. Its color varies from brown to greenish white; spines whitish. "The angulated chrysalis closely resembles that of its allies of the same genus; it is pale wood-brown, tinged and streaked with pale green; the base of the tubercles along the back is of a metallic color, both in this species and in the Violet-tip (which it most resembles), and according to whether the color is silvery or golden, so will the price of hops (on which both are found) be high or low, according to the hop-growers; and so these chrysalids are termed Hop-merchants."

PLATE 23

Polygonia interrogationis

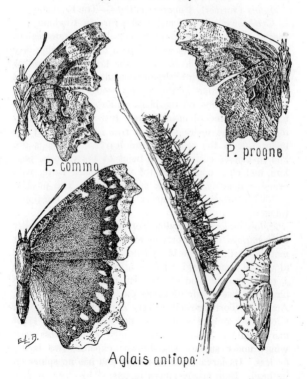

P. comma

P. progne

E.L.B.

Aglais antiopa

Polygonia progne (Pl. 23) is called Gray Comma. Its under side is grayish and its "comma" is tapering at the ends. The larva feeds on currant, gooseberry, etc. Its body is yellowish brown, variegated above with dark green; spines blackish. The pupa is a striking mixture of buff, olive-green, brown, salmon, and white.

The white-spined larva of *P. faunus* feeds on birch, willow, currant, and gooseberry. The adult's wings are deeply notched and the under side of the hind wings, each of which has a silver mark like *comma,* are strongly tinted with green along the outer third—the "leaf" is not quite dead! It is an inhabitant of mountains as far south as the Carolinas.

Aglais (formerly *Vanessa*) *antiopa.*—The English name is Camberwell Beauty and, while rare in England, this species (Pl. 23) is found throughout the temperate regions of the world and gets as far south as Guatemala. We call it Mourning Cloak. It is the largest of those of our butterflies which hibernate as adults; and he who has not seen it flitting in the leafless woods of very early spring or "resting on the black willows like a leaf still adhering" is indeed unfortunate. Just inside the yellow margin of the upper side is a row of blue spots; the under side is the color of dead leaves. The eggs are laid in masses encircling the twigs of the willows, poplars, and elms upon which the velvety-black larva, with orange-red spots and black spines, feeds. The pupa is yellowish brown, with darker markings and red-tipped tubercles.

Aglais j-album, Compton Tortoise, is slightly smaller than *antiopa,* tawny orange above with (among other markings) three large black patches and a spot of white along the front margin; below, ashy brown with a white J or L on the hind wings. Its larva feeds on white birch and has a pair of spines on its head. *A. milberti,* American Tortoise-shell, is very dark brown above with two tawny orange spots near the middle of the front margin and a broad band of similar color across each wing; under surface slate-brown; expanse, two inches or less. Its larva feeds on nettles and has no spines on its head. Both are Northern insects.

The Red Admiral, *Vanessa* (formerly *Pyrameis*)

atalanta, is found throughout most of the Northern Hemisphere. The upper surface is purplish black with markings as shown in Pl. 24, the lightly shaded areas being bright orange and the apical spots white; the under surface of the hind wings is marbled and marked with wavy lines of intricate pattern and also with a green-dusted submarginal series of obscure "eye-spots." The larva, which feeds on nettle and hop, is usually black, spotted with yellow; spines reddish but, like other larvæ of this genus, it has no spines on its head. The larva slightly rolls and lines a leaf for its protection. The pupa is ashy brown with golden spots and is to be looked for (but not always to be found) hanging in a leaf which the larva has rolled. Winter is passed in either the pupal or adult stage. The species is two-brooded.

Vanessa virginiensis (formerly *huntera*) is sometimes called Hunter's Butterfly or Painted Beauty. The upper surface is tawny orange and brownish black, except for the white spots shown in Pl. 24; the under side of each hind wing has *two* eye-like spots. The larva feeds on various "everlastings" and is velvety black with narrow cross-lines of yellow and a row of white spots on each side; anterior spines blackish, the others yellowish. At first it makes a cover, under which it feeds, of silk and the hairs of its food plant; later it fastens leaves together and often pupates in this nest. The pupa is difficult to describe. Find it. There are two broods a year. Pupa are to be found from June to March, although the adult usually emerges early and hibernates.

Vanessa cardui.—I like "Thistle Butterfly" better than "Painted Lady" since this lady "was born that way." The upper side is much like *virginiensis;* below, however, each hind wing (Pl. 24) has more than two, usually four, good eye-spots. The head of the larva is hairy on top; the body is greenish yellow, mottled with black, and the bristly spines are yellowish. It feeds on burdock, thistle, sunflower, hollyhock, and other plants, making a shelter much like that of *virginiensis.* The pupa is greenish or bluish white, marked with black and brown, and with tubercles that are often gold-tipped. This species is found throughout much of the habitable world with the possible exception of South America. It occasionally migrates in swarms.

The upper surface of the Buckeye, *Junonia cœnia* (Pl. 24), is dark brown with conspicuous peacock-like eyespots, small orange spots, a dull whitish band on each front wing and a narrow but conspicuous band of yellowish orange on each hind wing; the under surface is graybrown with much the same markings except that the eyespots of the hind wings are much reduced. The larva feeds on plantain, snapdragon, and *Gerardia*. It is dark gray, with yellow stripes and spots, and with purple spines, one pair of which is on the head. This Southern species gets as far north as New England.

The upper side of the Red-spotted Purple, *Basilarchia astyanax* (Pl. 24), is black and pale blue or green; the lower side is brown with a submarginal row of red spots, two red spots at the base of the fore wings, and four at the base of the hind wings. The curiously shaped larva is mottled with brown, olivaceous, and cream. It feeds on the leaves of a variety of woody plants, especially willow and wild cherry. When young, it is much given to eating each side of the outer end of a leaf and using the midrib, strengthened with silk, as a perch on which to rest. When about half grown, it rolls the uneaten portion together, lines it, fastens it to the twig with silk, and passes the winter in this snug retreat. Scudder describes the pupa as "grotesquely variegated with patches and streaks of pale salmon, dark olivaceous, inky plumbeous, and yellow-brown, the lighter tints prevailing." There are apparent intergrades between this species and *B. arthemis*.

Full-grown larvæ of the *Basilarchia* mentioned here have a pair of long, spiny, warty tubercles on the second segment and humps along the back, especially prominent on the fifth segment. The tubercles on the second segment of *astyanax* are not clubbed, the spiny warts being slender. Those of *arthemis* are conspicuously clubbed and short, the spiny warts being short and conical. Those of *archippus* are slightly clubbed and thickly covered with long, conical, spiny warts. All three feed on willow and poplar, but *arthemis* prefers birch and *astyanax* feeds on wild cherry, both being sometimes found on other plants.

PLATE 24

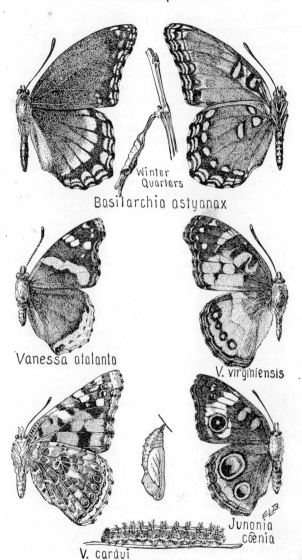

Winter
Quarters

Basilarchia astyanax

Vanessa atalanta

V. virginiensis

V. cardui

Junonia
cœnia

Plate 82 gives a sufficient description of the upper side of the Banded Purple, *Basilarchia arthemis.* The under side is dark brown with similar markings and some orange spots in addition. The larva feeds on birch, willow, poplar, etc. It is somewhat like *astyanax* (but has a saddle of pale buff) and has similar habits. Like some other young *Basilarchia,* it loosely fastens a small ball of leaf-scraps near its feeding place. This is supposed to distract an enemy's attention. This Canadian species reaches into northern United States in the high altitudes.

Plate 82 shows the Viceroy, *Basilarchia archippus,* also called *disippus,* in three of its stages. The larva, which feeds on willow and poplar, varies greatly in its coloration. The Monarch is believed to have a taste which birds do not like and, as that species has a very striking appearance, any species which resembles it would be likely to be unmolested by them. The Viceroy is said to "mimic" the Monarch for the sake of this protection but that implies more than we know, all of which is that the two look marvelously alike and that *archippus* has departed widely from the appearance of most of its relatives. Plate 82 was arranged to illustrate vividly this case of "mimicry," *arthemis* being taken as an example of the relatives of *Basilarchia.* Equally striking instances of the same phenomenon are known in Tropical butterflies.

Skipping a number of species that are not likely to be seen by many of the users of this book, we come to the subfamily Satyrinæ, the Nymphs and Satyrs, sometimes more descriptively called the Meadow-browns. Some of the veins of the front wings are greatly swollen at the base. Most of the larvæ of Satyrinæ have the last segment forked; and the pupæ are rounded.

The brown of Pearly Eye's wings, *Enodia* (formerly *Debis*) *portlandia* (Pl. 25), has been described as "clay," "soft," "Quaker drab" and "with pearly gray tints." The spots on the under surface are distinctly eyed and there are conspicuous pearly violet markings. The larva is yellowish green with red-tipped horns and caudal forks. It feeds on grasses and hibernates when about half grown.

PLATE 25

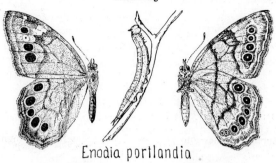

Enodia portlandia

Satyrodes
canthus

Neonympha eurytus

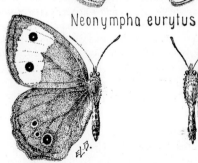

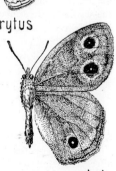

Cercyonis alope   variety nephele

Satyrodes canthus (or *eurydice*).—The color of the upper side of the Grass Nymph's wings (Pl. 25) is described as "mouse-brown"; below it is slaty brown and the eye-spots are larger than those on the upper surface. The tubercles on the head of the green larva are red, striped with brown, and the tails are also red. It feeds on coarse grasses and sedges and, unlike its near relatives, is active by day. It is rather local in its distribution, preferring moist meadows.

The Little Wood-satyr, *Neonympha eurytus* (Pl. 25), is dark brown above and lighter below, where the eye-spots are more distinctly ringed with yellow. It is a lover of shady forest-edges. The larva is greenish white, marked with brown, but there is no red and the anal forks are relatively short. It feeds on grasses.

Neonympha phocion is a Southern relative of *eurytus*. It has no spots above and the three (or four) spots on the under side of the hind wings are so narrowed that they might be called squint-eyed. Some recent authorities use the name *Euptychia* and others *Cissia* instead of *Neonympha*.

The dark brown Common Wood-nymph, *Cercyonis* (formerly *Satyrus*) *alope* (Pl. 25), has several varieties formerly considered to be distinct species. The variety in which the yellow bands on the fore wings are clouded with brown is called *nephele* and replaces *alope* in the North, New York City being in the tension zone. Together, they and other varieties of *alope* cover practically the whole of the United States and Canada. Along the Atlantic coast some individuals (called *maritima*) have the yellow band orange. The green larva has no "horns" on its head and is devoid of markings except for two pale stripes on each side. It feeds on grasses.

LIBYTHEIDÆ

See p. 116. Our only genus of Snout Butterflies is *Libythea* and our principal species is *backmani* (Pl. 84). The width of the egg is about half its height; the ridges alternately high and low. The larva feeds on hackberry (*Celtis*). It becomes nearly one inch long; slender except for the swollen front segments, which overhang the small head, especially when the larva assumes a Sphinx-like pose; dark green with longitudinal yellow lines; two black tubercles in a yellow ring on the second segment. The pupa is pointed at each end; two ridges in front, with a tubercle between them. The Southwestern *carinenta* has the yellowish on the wings paler.

RIODINIDÆ

See p. 116. The chief home of the Metal-marks is the American Tropics. All of our species are Southern or Western except the Northern Metal-mark, *Calephelis borealis* (Pl. 84), which ranges from South Carolina to New York and Michigan. A somewhat similar but smaller species, *C. virginiensis,* is found just south of it.

LYCÆNIDÆ

See p. 116. The Hair-streaks, Coppers, and Blues puzzle even the professional. Technical names are being shifted about so rapidly that whatever one you use is apt to be wrong according to some authority. Lycænid larvæ are short-legged and small-headed. On the back of their hind segments are one or more minute, extensible sacs from which exudes a secretion that is attractive to ants. Therefore, the larvæ may sometimes be found by noticing where ants congregate.

The larva of the Common or Gray Hair-streak, *Thecla* or *Strymon melinus,* feeds on the buds, flowers, and pods of Hairy Bush Clover (*Lespedeza*), also on the developing seeds of hop, beans, *Cynoglossum, Hypericum,* and other plants. It is a dull velvety green. Plate 84 shows the adult. In the Southeast there are two species whose upper sides somewhat resemble *melinus: T. wittfeldi,* which is larger and has conspicuous blue scales at the rear angles of its hind wings; and *T. favonius,* which has a red spot on each fore wing.

The larva of the Olive Hair-streak feeds on cedar, but not on smilax as some say. It is dark green, with three rows of whitish dashes on each side. The species is found in the East from Ontario to Texas, and several varieties have been described. I am still calling it *Thecla damon* (Pl. 84). Holland's latest edition calls it *T. gryneus.* Probably its generic name should be *Mitoura.*

T. halesus (Illinois southward) is iridescent bluish-green above on the thorax and basal half of the wings; below, the front wings are nearly plain; all of the wings have a crimson spot near the base and there are three rows of green spots on each hind wing. *T. m-album* (New Jersey and Wisconsin southward) is bluish on the inner half of the upper surface but, below, each front wing is crossed by two lines of white, one of which is continued on the hind wing and is M-shaped at the rear. The larvæ of at least *m-album* feed on oak; *halesus* possibly only on mistletoe.

Among the numerous species that have been put in *Thecla,* a name which *Strymon* may largely displace, the following have catch characters that are more or less safe in the Northeast.

Hind Wings with Long Tails.—*T. cecrops:* a red band across the lower surface of the wings just beyond the middle; New Jersey and Indiana southward. *T. calanus:* a double row of close, dark, blue-edged spots just beyond the middle; Quebec to Colorado and Texas; larva on oak, chestnut, and walnut. *T. liparops:* numerous, broken, white cross-lines on under surface; north of the Gulf States to Quebec and the Rockies; not common; larva on *Vaccinium* (other food records probably erroneous).

Hind Wings with Almost, or Quite, No Tail.—*T. titus:* a row of coral-red spots on under side of hind wings; Canada to Florida and the Rockies; larva on plum and wild cherry. Mr. Watson's directions for finding larvæ of *T. titus,* which get to be about .75 in. long and are bright green with each extremity bright rose color, are: "Look in June at small plants of Wild Cherry. First notice if the leaves are eaten in an irregular manner; then if there is an ants' nest at the base of the main stem. The next step will be to remove carefully the earth around this main stem to a depth of one or two inches. The larva will be found resting on the stem with ants in attendance. It crawls up to the top of the plant to feed at night." *T. niphon:* fringe of upper side of wings alternately brown and white, under side of wings rich, mottled brown, with distinct wavy white lines; larva on pines; Nova Scotia and North Atlantic States to Colorado. *T. augustus:* expanse less than one inch (smallest of the group), below uniform rusty brown except for darker basal area of the hind wings; larva on *Kalmia* and *Vaccinium;* North Atlantic States, northward and westward.

Feniseca tarquinius.—Scudder, the Master Lepidopterist, in whose works most of the statements concerning butterflies given in this and similar books are to be found, used "The Wanderer" as the nickname for this species (Pl. 84) but says in *Everyday Butterflies* that it is "a very local insect, and apparently never wanders more than a few rods from its birthplace." Holland, who has done so much to popularize the study of Lepidoptera, uses as the English name "The Harvester," but harvesting connotes vegetable products. I am taking the liberty of dubbing it The Carnivore because its larva alone, of all our butterflies, is regularly a meat-eater although its relatives, if pressed by hunger, will eat each other. The female lays her eggs, usually singly, in or near masses of Aphids (plant-lice), especially of the Woolly Aphis of the alder. The larva has mandibles with four sharp, claw-like teeth and the whole mouth is fitted for sucking the body fluids of the victims. If Aphids are the ant's cows, *tarquinius* is a Beef-eater. Possibly in order not to be seen by the ants, which might resent their ravages, the larvæ live in a silken web that they spin and cover with empty "hides." Possibly it is the strong meat diet that quickens the metamorphosis, for the larva reaches the pupal stage in three, instead of four or five, molts. Scudder points out a resemblance to a monkey's face in the markings of the chrysalis (enlarged in Pl. 84). This species, whose nearest relatives live chiefly in Asia and Africa, is found from Nova Scotia to the Gulf States and in the Mississippi Valley. The markings on the upper side of the adult are variable; the under side is paler and the hind wings have many small light-brown spots not appearing above.

There are other American Coppers—butterflies, I mean —but *Chrysophanus* (or *Heodes*) *hypophlæus* (Pl. 84) was once "really-named" *americanus,* hence the "common" name. The adult is a fearless, pugnacious, active, little beauty. The bright green larva feeds on sorrel (*Rumex, especially acetosella*). Pupation usually takes place under an over-hanging stone, in which condition one brood passes the winter.

The Bronze Copper, *Chrysophanus* (or *Heodes*) *thoe,* is about half again as large as *hypophlæus;* the female resembles that species on its upper side except that the dark base of the hind wing does not extend out so far; the male differs from both in having the upper surface of the front wing almost as dark as the base of the hind wing and with a violet reflection. The bright green larva feeds on *Rumex,* especially *crispus.* There are two annual broods, and winter is passed in the egg. Ranges from Maine to Pennsylvania and Colorado.

The delicate hair-like tails of the Eastern Tailed Blue, *Lycæna* (or *Everes*) *comyntas* (Pl. 84), will repay close examination; they have a white tip. The female is largely dark brown above. The brownish green larvæ feed on clover and other Legumes, those of one of the three annual broods hibernating.

The Common Blue or Spring Azure is here called *Lycæna ladon.* Its generic name probably should be *Lycænopsis* and its specific name *argiolus,* of which we have the variety *pseudargiolus* with several forms. It is all very complicated. Small, blue butterflies are pretty sure to be this species if they have no tails. It is a creature of many fashions, some of which are shown in Pl. 84. These forms are partly sexual, partly seasonal (There are three broods around New York), partly climatic, and probably partly something else. The whitish to greenish, sometimes tinted with rose, larvæ feed on the flowers of various plants including *Cornus, Cimicifuga, Actinomeris, Spiræa,* and *Ceanothus.* Ants attend the larvæ and, by touching them with their antennæ, induce the larvæ to excrete from abdominal glands a sweet fluid which the ants drink.

PIERIDÆ

See p. 116. This group used to be classed as a subfamily of Papilionidæ.

Pieris rapæ.—This undesirable immigrant, the Imported Cabbage Butterfly (Pl. 26), is the only butterfly that seriously injures our crops. It was accidentally introduced from Europe in 1860 at Quebec and in 1868 at New York. In twenty years it covered about half of the United States and Canada. Now no cabbage patch from Coast to Coast is too small or too isolated for *rapæ*. The well-known green larva feeds on a variety of Cruciferous plants but likes cabbage best. It is green, with three pale longitudinal stripes. There are usually three broods a season, winter being passed as pupæ from which adults emerge early in the spring before the native cabbage butterflies are stirring. These early spring adults are smaller and less heavily marked than the summer form, which is here illustrated. Some individuals (variety *immaculata*) are without the black spots on the upper side of the wings but the under side of the hind wings is yellowish as in the typical form.

The Checkered White, *Pieris protodice* (Pl. 26), is also called the Southern Cabbage Butterfly and used to be called the Common White but its numbers seem to have diminished. The larva feeds on crucifers and, when it gets a chance at cabbage, it eats merely the outside leaves, which are not worth much at any rate. It is green, striped with golden yellow and dotted with small, black "warts." The veins on the under side of the female's wings, especially the hind ones, are tinged with greenish yellow. Those adults which come from overwintered pupæ (var. *vernalis*) have so much greenish gray on the hind wings that the white is reduced to narrow triangular spots; spots on the upper side are much reduced, or even absent.

The larva of the Old-fashioned Cabbage Butterfly, *Pieris napi* (or *oleracea*), feeds on crucifers in or near woodlands. It is said to have been *the* Cabbage Butterfly when cabbage fields were usually near woods. Some call it the Mustard White; some, the Gray-veined White. It is naturally (not by human intervention) found in Europe and throughout the cooler parts of North America, but it varies greatly with region and season. Plate 26 shows the form you are most likely to see. The larva is green, minutely dotted with black except for a narrow streak down the back. From New York southward there is a species, *virginiensis,* that has been confused with *napi.*

In the Gulf States there is *Ascia monuste,* which has a wing expanse of from 1.75 to 2.3 inches. The male is whitish above, except for a narrow brown outer margin to the fore wings. The female has a broad brown outer margin on the fore wings, as well as a narrow brown outer margin on the hind wings, above. The larva is yellow, longitudinally striped with dull bluish and bright yellow bands and studded with shiny black warts, the larger ones being spiny.

Plate 26 shows the male Falcate Orange-tip, *Euchloë* (or *Anthocharis*) *genutia,* the orange tip being indicated by shading. The female has no such tip on the upper surface and neither sex has it below, the markings there being light greenish brown. The larva, which feeds on rock-cress (*Arabis*) and possibly other Cruciferæ, is bluish green, with pale dorsal and side stripes; but, if you look closely, you can see fine stripes of other colors, and it is dotted with minute black warts.

Probably you have noticed that there is sometimes a white individual among a flock of yellow butterflies, the Common Sulphurs, *Colias* (or *Eurymus*) *philodice,* that rises from a roadside pool as you pass. This is usually an albino *philodice* and, if so, almost certainly a female. However, even when white, the species can be distinguished from *Pieris* by the silvery-centered spots on the under side of the wings (Pl. 27). The common, but rarely noticed, green larva feeds upon clover leaves. It has a pale rose-colored stripe on each side.

Colias (or *Eurymus*) *eurytheme* is about as variable as *P. napi* but can usually be recognized by the strong orange tint of the yellow on the upper side and the marginal markings that suggest *philodice.* Its larva with two rose-colored bands on each side feeds on clover.

Most of us will agree with the Comstocks that the "face" of the Dog-face, *Zerene* (formerly *Meganostoma*) *cæsonia* (Pl. 27), is more like that of a duck than of a dog. However, it makes the species easily recognizable. Adults have been reported from New York (very rarely) and southern Wisconsin to the Gulf States. The larva feeds on false indigo (*Amorpha*) and (?) clover. It

PLATE 26

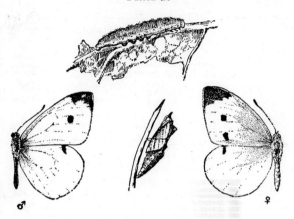

Pieris rapæ

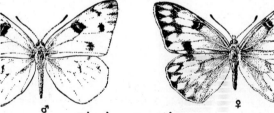

Pieris protodice

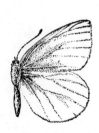

P. napi
oleracea

Euchloë genutia

Largely White Butterflies

is yellowish green, usually with narrow transverse bands of yellow or black or both, and dotted with small black warts.

Phœbis (or *Callidryas* or *Catopsilia*) *eubule.*—Nearly every year strong-flying individuals of this Southern species get even farther north than Long Island. It has a wing expanse of 2.5 inches. The male is plain yellow above; the female has a row of dark brown spots along the outer margin of the front wings and a somewhat similar spot in the center of these wings. The larva feeds on *Cassia* and other legumes.

The Little Sulphur, *Eurema* (formerly *Terias*) *lisa* (or *euterpe*), may be recognized by means of Pl. 27. The female is paler on the upper side than the male and the black border of the hind wing is much broken or nearly absent. The larva feeds on *Cassia*. It is grass-green, with a white line on each side. There are three broods, but we are not sure how our Northern winters are passed. My guess would be that they are passed in the South, after the fashion of the Monarch. In this connection it should be said that "clouds" of the autumn brood of adults have been noted as landing on Bermuda from the northwest, having covered six hundred miles of ocean. Albinic individuals are sometimes found.

Eurema nicippe is much like *lisa* but somewhat larger; the front wings of both sexes are tinged with orange, and the hind wings, especially of the female, have short, but rather broad, "rusty" cross-spots. The larval food and (?) life history are the same as *lisa*. The green larva has a broad yellow band, edged slightly with blue, on each side. In the Gulf States there are three rather common species (*elathea, delia* and *jucunda*) which cannot be differentiated in a few words. They may be known collectively by being something like *lisa* but with a conspicuous dark band along the hind margin of the front wings, upper surface. This generalization, however, includes *Nathalis iole,* which occurs from southern Indiana and Colorado to Florida and northern Mexico. Its small size (wing expanse of not over 1.25 inches) helps one to "spot" it.

Plate 27

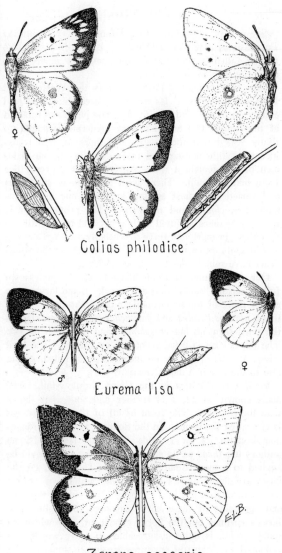

Colias philodice

Eurema lisa

Zerene caesonia

E.L.B.

PAPILIONIDÆ

See p. 116. There are two subfamilies (or families):
Parnassiinæ, that pupate in a loose cocoon-like structure
among fallen leaves; and Papilioninæ, that pupate more
after the fashion of Pieridæ.

Our only genus of Parnassiinæ is the Western and
Northern *Parnassius*. Its larvæ are "leech-like" and feed
chiefly on *Sedum* and *Saxifraga*. The pupæ are rounded
at the head. The adults are of moderate size and so
thinly scaled that their wings are more or less translucent. While mating, the male deposits on the abdomen of the female a waxy secretion that prevents her
from mating again. There seem to be many subspecies
and varieties of most species, including our only common ones, *clodius* and *smintheus*. The ground-color is
white, sometimes suffused with gray, and among all the
variations in markings there are usually two red or yellowish spots on each hind wing. In *smintheus* the wing-
veins have minute dark triangles at their tips.

Our only genus of Papilioninæ is *Papilio* unless we
follow certain "splits" that are urged. Some larvæ have
one or more of the segments near the front swollen. Of
these, *glaucus, troilus* and *palamedes* have "eye-spots" on
the third segment, but *cresphontes* and *marcellus* do not.
The pupal head is usually notched or forked. The hind
wings are often, but by no means always, tailed, giving
rise to the common name, Swallow-tails.

Papilio cresphontes is the Giant Swallow-tail. The
adult shown on Pl. 1 is smaller and somewhat duller
than the average. The form of all of the stages shown
is typical of the genus. In the South it is called Orange-
dog because its larva feeds on citrus leaves. Some
authors use *thoas* as its specific name, but this should be
applied to a more Southern species. The horns on the
larva are fleshy affairs that may be withdrawn or ex-
truded through a slit in the thorax. Not only is the sudden appearing of these horns supposed to frighten the
larva's enemies but the horns exhale an odor which, in
some species, is quite disagreeable—in other words, the
young of the beautiful creatures are insect skunks. The
meaning of the color on the right side of the adult, as

shown in Pl. 1, is explained on p. 115. The wings are more largely yellow below than above. The home of this species is the North American Subtropics, but it seems to be working northward (where the larva feeds on prickly ash and *Ptelea*) and has been taken in Canada. There are from two to four annual broods, depending upon location.

Papilio glaucus and var. *turnus.*—One of the rules about scientific names is that the first used for a species, if accompanied by a description, shall be *the* name. Now, Linnæus evidently intended to call the yellow Tiger Swallow-tail *turnus,* but, in his description, he first referred to the dark form of the female (Pl. 85), which is rare in the North but common in the South, as *glaucus.* Therefore, *glaucus* is the name of the species, but you may call it *turnus.* The larva feeds on orchard and other trees, especially wild cherry, but is never injurious. It has the luxurious habit of spinning a web on top of a leaf, drawing it so tightly that it forms a spring couch upon which to rest when not feeding. There is a pair of eye-like spots on the thorax, and, when the true head is drawn under so that these appear to be on the head, the thoracic "horns" are shot out, and the front part of the body is swayed back and forth, even you might hesitate to disturb its siesta.

Papilio troilus.—The Spice-bush Swallow-tail is sometimes called the Green-clouded Swallow-tail because of the color of the upper surface of the hind wings. The female does not have the green so pronounced but has hazy blue spots along the cloud's outer margin (Pl. 85 shows the male) ; below, at least the front margin of the green cloud is replaced by a row of orange spots. The larva feeds chiefly on sassafras and spice-bush (*Benzoin*). It makes a series of successively larger shelters for its resting time by folding a leaf at the midrib, fastening the fold by silk threads placed near the crease instead of at the edges. It keeps these shelters scrupulously clean. When it molts it eats the cast skin except that it throws out the inedible "skull."

Our common variety of *Papilio polyxenes* is *asterius,* which is also the common name. Plate 85 shows the female. The male is not so dark; his blue spots are not so pronounced; but his yellow spots on the inner row are much larger. The larva is wasteful; it eats our parsley and carrots, instead of sticking to Umbelliferous weeds, and does not eat its cast skins as do its near relatives. Otherwise it is a beautiful creature which, like many of its relatives, changes the color and cut of its dress at every molt and which will stick out its orange horns if you but threaten to poke it. The species is found throughout the Atlantic States and the Mississippi Valley. What have been considered races of it extend this distribution to most parts of North America and south to Cuba and Peru.

Pl. 85 shows the male Pipe-vine Swallow-tail, *Papilio philenor*. Some authorities use *Laertias* as the generic name. The female has a row of distinct spots on each fore wing, corresponding to those on the hind wings. The inner margins of the male's hind wings are folded over and contain scales that give off a faint odor, presumably for the sake of pleasing the female. It should be said that many male Lepidoptera have similar scent-scales placed in various parts of the wings, body and legs. The larva of *philenor* feeds on the Dutchman's pipe (*Aristolochia*), also on Wild Ginger (*Asarum canadense*), and differs from most of its relatives by having, even when mature, fleshy spines on several of the front and rear segments. Instead of depositing her eggs singly, the female lays them in little bunches; and the larvæ, when young, feed side by side at the edge of a leaf.

Papilio palamedes (wing-expanse, 4 to 4.5 inches) suggests a giant *polyxenes* in which the inner row of yellow spots on the upper surface of the hind wings is a continuous band and there are three yellow spots near the front between two rows on the front wings. Its normal range is from Virginia and Missouri to Florida and Texas, its larva feeding on Magnolia and Lauraceæ.

Papilio (or *Iphiclides*) *marcellus* (also called *ajax*) suggests *turnus,* but has tails twice as long, is white instead of yellow, has more black on the upper surface and, in addition, has a red spot or two near the middle of the inner (hind) margin of the hind wings. It is found almost everywhere that its larval food (Pawpaw) occurs in the eastern half of the United States.

We have other species of *Papilio,* especially in our West and Southwest. Some have no tails (e.g., *polydamas,* which also carries perfume, of Florida); some have two tails (e.g., *daunus* of the Western mountains); and the rare *pilumnus* of Arizona has three tails on each hind wing.

HESPERIIDÆ

See p. 116. I fear that Pl. 28 and the following notes will be exasperating to those attempting to start an acquaintance with this interesting but difficult family. One difficulty is that a given sex often resembles the same sex of a different species more closely than it does the opposite sex of its own species. Furthermore, the same sex often has two or more varieties. The technical names of the genera and subfamilies are being rapidly and widely changed at the present time. Possibly Hesperiinæ should be either Pyrginæ or Erynninæ; Pamphilinæ may be Hesperiinæ; and so on. It is too much for me and I leave them "as is." The subfamily Pyrrhopyginæ is represented in our Southwest by *Apyrrothrix.*

The family as a whole is a very large one. The adults are, for the most part, small and fly with rapid starts and stops, as is indicated by their nickname, Skippers. When resting, many of them (especially the Pamphilinæ) hold the front wings at an angle different from that of the hind pair.

Quite commonly Hesperid larvæ fold leaves or fasten several together with silk so that they may have a retreat when resting or molting. All species keep these nests quite clean and some have interesting little tricks about their homes. Scudder notes that *Thanaos icelus,* which folds over part of a leaf, fastens it at first with long strands of silk so that there is an "abundance of space for air, or, indeed, the entrance of nearly any enemy"; but, when the time comes for one of the several changes of clothes, the larva brings the edges of the leaf tightly together and fastens them securely. Many species make a new nest, out of a different leaf, at each molt, and the same keen observer noted that *Thanaos lucilius,* "when it leaves a nest to form a larger one always first bites off the strands which have kept the old flap in place." The appearance of Hesperid larvæ suggests those of moths and nearly all of the species show a further resemblance to moths in that they spin a sort of cocoon within which they pupate. This cocoon is never very thick or complete and is much like an ordinary larval shelter.

Reference has already been made to the fact that many male Lepidoptera are addicted to the use of perfume. Among the Hesperiidæ, the males of the subfamily Hesperiinæ tend to have the scent-scales (androconia) in a tiny fold along the front margin of the fore wings. In the subfamily Pamphilinæ these scales are near the middle of the upper surface of the fore wings in a conspicuous patch, which the Comstocks described as looking "to the naked eye like a scorched oblique streak or brand."

HESPERIINÆ

Epargyreus tityrus.—The light marks are yellowish except for the large silver spot on each hind wing. Pl. 28. Larva on locust (*Robinia*), etc. Its head reddish brown, with two bright orange-red spots; body yellowish green but first segment red and thoracic shield brown.

Eudamus proteus.—About the size of *E. tityrus* but each hind wing has a long tail; greenish on hind wings, especially of males. American Tropics to (rarely) New York. Larva on legumes is like *tityrus* but with orange longitudinal bands.

Achalarus lycidas suggests *tityrus* but has no tails; it has no silver spots beneath, but a white smear along outer margin of hind wings. Larva on tick-trefoil (*Desmodium*).

Thorybes bathyllus.—Adults have white faces. Pl. 28. Larva on bush-clover (*Lespedeza*) and other legumes. *T. pylades* is much like *bathyllus* but the spots are smaller and the face is brown. Larval food the same.

Hesperia tessellata.—Appears to be a white butterfly strongly marked with black. Pl. 28. Larva on *Sida*.

Thanaos juvenalis: general color blackish brown with black mottlings and white, semitransparent dots; larva on oak and legumes. Pl. 28. *T. horatius* is distinguished

PLATE 28

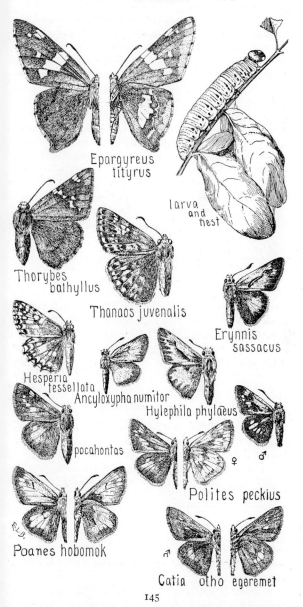

Epargyreus
tityrus

larva
and
nest

Thorybes
bathyllus

Thanaos juvenalis

Erynnis
sassacus

Hesperia
tessellata

Ancyloxypha numitor

Hylephila phylaeus

pocahontas

♀   ♂

Polites peckius

Poanes hobomok

♂

Catia otho egeremet

145

from *juvenalis* by not having two whitish spots on the underside of each hind wing just back of the front edge. *T. brizo* is about the size of *juvenalis;* it lacks the white dots, has two distinct rows of arrow-head, black marks on each front wing, and has more gray scales. Larva on oaks and probably legumes. *T. icelus* is like a small *brizo* with more gray on the outer third of the front wing. Larva on willow and poplar. *T. lucilius* is about the size of *icelus;* it has minute but distinct white dots on the front wings. Larva on columbine (*Aquilegia*).

Pholisora catullus is much like *T. lucilius* but is blacker, the white dots are more scattered, and it lacks the mottlings of *Thanaos*. Larva on lamb's quarters (*Chenopodium*) and Amarantaceæ.

PAMPHILINÆ

In this subfamily, however the sexes may differ above, they are much alike below. Except where stated, the light areas on the species mentioned here are yellowish. The larvæ of the following (Pl. 28) feed on grasses: *Ancyloxypha numitor; Erynnis* (or *Pamphila*) *sassacus; Catia otho egeremet* (the light areas, greenish yellow); *Hylephila phylæus; Polites mystic* (Much like *E. sassacus* but the "brand" on the male is more like that of *H. phylæus;* lower side of the hind wings is more distinctly banded or spotted than is *sassacus*. It is often caught with this species but is abundant later in the season); *Polites peckius;* and *Poanes hobomok* (the variety *pocahontas* is always female; the light markings are cream-color).

MEGATHYMINÆ

Our only genus, *Megathymus,* is Southern and Western. The adults are stout-bodied and have a wing expanse of about three inches. The antennal tip is neither pointed nor recurved but it is turned slightly to one side. Their larvæ bore in the pith of *Yucca*. This genus has been variously placed and at one time was considered to belong with the moths.

HETEROCERA

See p. 115 for some of the distinctive characteristics of Moths.

SPHINGIDÆ

These trim creatures are, for the most part, called Hawk Moths from their strong flight, but some are called Humming-bird Moths. Although strong of flight, the wings, especially the hind ones, are small in comparison with the body, which is usually stout and tapered at the hind end. None have ocelli. Adults feed and, with a few exceptions, are crepuscular. When at rest, their long tongues are tightly curled up under their head like a watch spring. The larvæ are hairless, except when very young, and usually have a horn (absolutely harmless) at the hind end of the body. In some species, especially when the larvæ are full-grown, this horn is reduced to a tubercle and in some it is entirely absent. The name of the family and its English equivalent, "Sphinx Moths," come from the more or less sphinx-like attitude of the larvæ when at rest with their front segments elevated and the head drawn in. Pupation takes place in or on the ground and some pupæ have a "handle" which is really a sheath for their long tongue. There are many species, but they are difficult to characterize in few words and I must regretfully refer the reader to more special books, such as Holland's *Moth Book,* for the identification of the majority.

Humming-bird Moths have the unmothlike habit of flying freely in the bright sunlight and, when hovering at flowers, they closely resemble humming-birds. Parts of the wings are transparent. It has been said that scales develop in the pupa but are rubbed off on emergence. Both *Hemaris* and *Hæmorrhagia* are used as the generic name. Pl. 86 shows the typical (summer) form of the Northern race of *thysbe.* The spring form, *cimbiciformis,* differs, among other ways, in having the outer margin of the transparent areas an even line. There are also two seasonal forms of the Southern race. *Hemaris diffinis* is smaller than *thysbe* and has the dark areas on the ab-

domen black instead of reddish. When flying it suggests a bumblebee. The thorax of *H. gracilis* is greener
in life than *thysbe* and has a pair of reddish, longitudinal
lines on the under side of its thorax. These are Eastern
species, *gracilis* being confined to the Atlantic States.
There are others in the West. Larvæ feed on relatives of
the honeysuckle, such as snowberry (*Symphoricarpos*)
and *Viburnum*. They usually pupate in fallen leaves and
generally make a poor sort of a cocoon. The pupæ do
not have free tongue-cases.

Amphion nessus flies in even broad daylight during
May and June. It has a wing-expanse of two inches or
more, but its body is only about an inch long; its general
color consists of various shades of brown; there is a narrow, yellowish-white band across the abdomen; the hind
wings have reddish centers and yellowish-white front
margins; the outer edge of each front wing has two
marked indentations. The larva feeds on grape, Virginia
creeper, and other plants. It has a short, rough tail-
horn, a brown body-color with black and yellow dottings,
and the third and fourth segments somewhat enlarged.
It pupates in fallen leaves, usually spinning a few threads.

Sphecodina abbotii has a wavy outer margin of the
front wings similar to that of *nessus* but, among other
differences, the basal half or two-thirds of the hind wings
is yellow. It flies, as a rule, just after sunset. The larva,
which feeds on grape and Virginia creeper, has two color-
forms, green and brown; it has an eye-like tubercle
instead of an anal horn. Even more than most of its relatives, it thrashes its tail about. Eliot and Soule say:
"We have seen orioles try to pick up an *abbotii* larva on
our woodbine, and dart away with a scream when it lifted
its snake-like anal end with the tubercle shining like an
eye. The caterpillars make a squeaking noise; how they
make it we do not know." Other Sphingid larvæ make
a similar noise. The tongue-case of the pupa is not free.

The adults of the common Striped Sphinx (*Deilephila
lineata,* Pl. 86) may be found flying at, apparently, any
hour of the day or night from July to November.
Celerio is probably a better generic name. "When full-
grown the caterpillars are three inches long and vary
greatly in coloring and markings. There seem to be two

styles of dress: one is yellowish green with a series of connected spots along each side of the back, each spot being colored crimson, yellow, and black; the other dress is black, with a yellow line down the middle of the back, and yellow spots of various sizes along the sides. These two styles may be varied in many ways" (Dickerson). There is a distinct anal horn. Although it is sometimes called the Purslane Sphinx, the larvæ feed on a great variety of plants including apple, grape, Virginia creeper, and currant. Sometimes the larva makes a loose, open cocoon at the surface of the ground, but usually it goes just below the surface and spins no threads. The tongue-case of the pupa is not free.

Deilephila intermedia is much like *lineata* except that it has only two pairs of dark marks on its abdomen and the veins of the front wings are not marked with whitish. It is not usually common but ranges from Canada to Mexico, and a nearly related species is found in the Eastern Hemisphere. The larva feeds on grape, *Epilobium,* and other plants.

Pholus pandorus (Pl. 86) may be but a form of *satellitia.* It flies at dusk, and later, from June to November. The larva, which feeds on grape and Virginia creeper, is green when young and has a long horn, which often curls over its back; but the full-grown larva is tailless and usually brown. It then has six oval, cream-colored spots on the sides and a black, polished, eye-like tail-spot. The pupa, with adhering tongue-case, is usually formed underground. It is a widely distributed species with several local races.

Pholus achemon has a brown general color, the basal three-fourths of the hind wings are pink, and the dark markings on the hind margin of each front wing are reduced to a rectangular spot near the middle and a smaller, triangular spot near the outer end. Larval and pupal habits like those of *pandorus.* The larva's light spots are more elongate and have an irregular outline.

For some reason, or none, *Ampelophagus myron* is called Hog Sphinx. Plate 86 shows a larva bearing on its back the cocoons of an Ichneumonid whose larvæ had been feeding on the tissues of the moth's larva. Such cocoons may be found on many kinds of caterpillars but this species is much afflicted by the parasites. The principal food plants of *myron* are grape and Virginia creeper. A cocoon is made among fallen leaves. *A. chœrilis* (or *pholus*) is much like *myron* but the front wings are brownish. Its larva feeds on *Viburnum* and *Azalea*. There are two annual broods.

A. versicolor differs from *myron* in having a white median-dorsal line and, on the thorax, a pair of white side-lines, white markings on the green front wings and a broad, whitish hind-margin of the hind wings. The larva feeds on *Hydrangea, Decodon,* and buttonball (*Cephalanthus*).

Phlegethontius (or *Protoparce*).—*P. sexta* (Pl. 29) was so named because of six orange-yellow spots on each side of the adult's abdomen. Similarly there is *P. quinquemaculata* with five such spots. These species are also called *carolina* and *celeus* respectively. The general color of the adult *sexta* is grayish brown; *5-maculata* is much lighter and, among other differences, the dark lines corresponding to the two outer ones on the hind wings of *sexta* are fused to form a band and the three inner lines are distinctly zigzagged. The mature larva of *5-maculata* may be distinguished from that of *sexta* by the fact that the lower ends of the light markings on the side of the abdomen curve backward below the spiracles (breathing holes). In the South the pupa is sometimes called "Hornblower" because the free tongue-case suggests a wind instrument. The green or brown larvæ are called Tobacco Worms or Tomato Worms, according to the crop on which they are found. They also eat the leaves of potato and other Solanaceæ.

The Modest Sphinx, *Pachysphinx modesta,* is not usually common but, when seen, always attracts attention. The shaded portions of the wings (Pl. 29) are brown, tinged on the hind wings with pink; the dark spot near the angle of each hind wing is purplish black. A Western form, *occidentalis,* has whitish front wings and largely pink hind wings. The larvæ feed on poplars and willows, pupating in the ground. Some authors place this species in the Oriental genus *Marumba*.

The Twin-spot Sphinx, *Smerinthus jamaicensis geminatus,* may have more or less than "twin" spots. The

PLATE 29

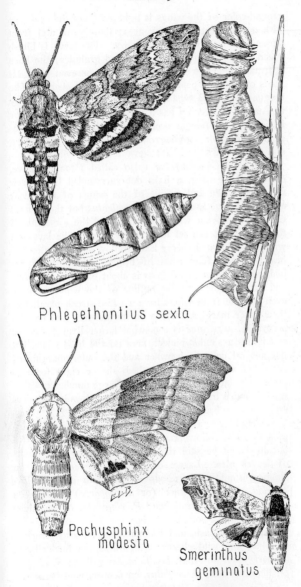

Phlegethontius sexta

Pachysphinx modesta

Smerinthus geminatus

ground-color of the wings is light gray but the eye-spots (Pl. 29) are set in a pink area; the thorax and front wings are marked with rich brown. The larva is bluish green with yellowish white lines and granules; the horn is usually blue but sometimes greenish or even pink. It feeds on willows, poplars, birches, and wild cherry. The tongue-case of the pupa is not free. Adults fly from May to August. *S. cerisyi* has a wing-expanse of about four inches and the single ocellus on each hind wing consists of a dark spot surrounded by first a light ring and then a dark one. Its larva feeds on willow.

Adults of *Calasymbolus* (also called *Paonias*) have, on each hind wing, a light dot surrounded by a dark ring. The size and outline of the wings of *C. myops* are almost exactly those of *S. geminatus* but the general color of the front wings is brown and the eye-spots of the hind wings are set in a yellow area. The larva on wild and cultivated cherry has a yellow side-stripe on the head; usually four rows of bright red spots on the body; horn green. *C. astylus* is about like *myops* in size and general color but the outline of the wings is more even and the front wings have a white streak parallel to their outer margins. Larva on huckleberry and dangle-berry. *C. excæcatus* is somewhat larger than *geminatus* and it has a similar pinkish area on the hind wings but the general color is browner and the outer margins of the front wings are saw-toothed, six or eight teeth to each. The larva on Rosaceæ and a large number of other trees is much like *myops* but has two yellow longitudinal stripes on the back and no red spots.

Sphingid larvæ are so easily recognized as being Sphingids that the following additional notes may be helpful but it should be said that larvæ often eat other sorts of leaves also. Larvæ of *Xylophanes tersa* feed on *Bouvardia* and buttonwood. *Dilophonota ello,* on *Euphorbia. Phlegethontius* (or *Protoparce*) *rustica* on *Chionanthus* and *Jasminium;* P. *cingulata,* on morning-glory and sweet-potato. *Sphinx* (or *Hyloicus*) *kalmiæ,* on laurel, lilac, ash, and *Chionanthus;* S. *drupiferarum,* on plum and wild cherry; S. *gordius,* on huckleberry, bayberry, and birch; S. *luscitiosa,* on willow; S. *chersis,* on lilac and ash; S. *eremitus,* on pepper, wild bergamot, and *Salvia*. *Dolba hylæus* larvæ are said to complete their growth in twenty days on black alder and sweet fern. *Chlænogramma jasminearum,* on ash. Larvæ of *Ceratomia amyntor* have four short thoracic horns in addition to the anal one and feed chiefly on elm; the black and yellow larvæ of *C. catalpæ* feed on *Catalpa. Lapara bombycoides* and *coniferarum,* on pines. *Cressonia juglandis,* on hickory, walnut, ironwood, and wild cherry.

SATURNIIDÆ

These Giant Silk-worm Moths are the amateur's delight because of their large size, beautiful colors, and often conspicuous cocoons. The antennæ of the males are feathered to their tips and are always larger than those of the female. The mouth-parts of the adults are poorly developed and apparently functionless; but the huge larvæ are certainly hearty feeders and, fortunately, have many enemies. Whoever tries to raise Saturniid adults from wild cocoons is almost sure to get more parasites than moths.

The Asiatic Ailanthus Silk-moth (Pl. 30, *Philosamia walkeri,* usually called *cynthia*) was brought to America about 1861, presumably in the hope that silk from its cocoon might be used commercially. That hope has not yet been realized and the larvæ occasionally occur in large enough numbers to be injurious to ailanthus trees—their original and favorite leaf, although they feed also upon wild cherry, linden, sycamore, lilac, and other plants. The full-grown larva is green with black dots; the tubercles are pale to quite blue except that those of the lowest (substigmatal) row are banded with black; the head, legs, props, and anal shield are yellow except for blue markings on the last two; spiracles (or "stigmata," the row of breathing holes along the sides) are black with a white dot at each end. The larvæ eat their cast skins. The cocoon is spun on a leaf which has first been fastened to the branch with silk, the pupa hibernating. Hanging cocoons like this are hard for birds to peck. The adults may be recognized by the white tufts on their abdomens. Distributed locally (especially near cities) along the Atlantic Coast.

PLATE 30

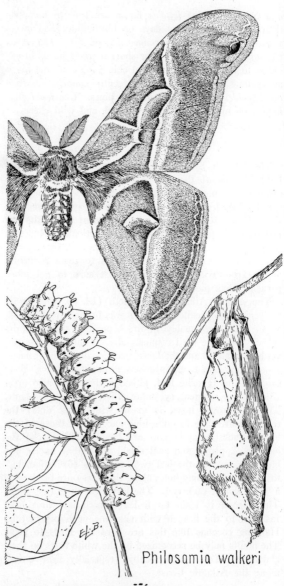

Philosamia walkeri

PLATE 31

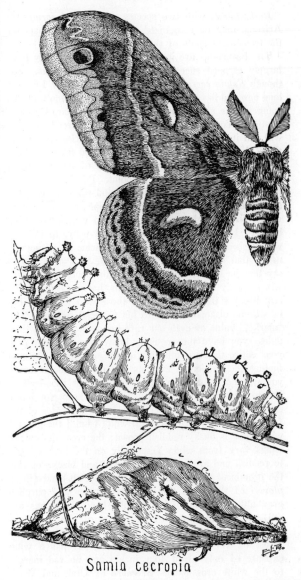

Samia cecropia

Rothschildia, with two species, *orizaba* and *jorulla,* in Arizona, may be recognized by the triangular shape of the translucent spots of the fore and hind wings.

The Saturniids are indeed fortunate moths; they have largely escaped successful "English" christenings. Although *Samia cecropia* (Pl. 31) was named by Linnæus long ago and has been a common and popular moth in this country ever since moths were at all popular, Cecropia is still its common name. I hope my children's children will call it Cecropia even though it was nicknamed something else by a lady who wrote very good fiction but did immeasurable harm to unalloyed love of nature by encouraging the commercial viewpoint. People forget that the Limberlost stories are fiction, and my mail was for some time filled with letters from people, ranging all the way from an eight-year-old boy, who wanted to sell a battered Luna so that he could get a pony, to invalids who wished to get money to buy medicine by selling the moths that came to their bedside lamps. Permit me to say that he who goes to Nature with money in his eyes will not only be blind to her truths, her glories, and the real benefits that she offers to those who love her, but he will be disappointed as to his financial returns. The "market" value of even our rare insects is so small that, unless you have the requisite knowledge and can give your entire time to collecting, classifying the spoils, and finding the particular markets for the particular sorts, you will not usually be paid for worn-out shoe-leather. But to return to more pleasant things: Except for interesting variations, Cecropia's head, body, and bases of the fore wings are a rich red with white bands; the general wing-color is dusky reddish brown; the crescents on the wings vary from white (especially on the hind wings) to reddish and are bordered with red and black; outside the prominent white band there is a reddish band (in *S. gloveri* of the West this band is broader and purplish gray although inside of the white band the wings are red); the outer border of both pairs of wings is light clay-brown. *S. columbia* occurs in northern United States (west of Wisconsin) and in Canada. It has a wing expanse of only about four inches and no red margin to the white cross-band. *S. rubra* of Utah and Wyo-

ming westward is about the size of *columbia* but the
general wing color is rather uniformly light red; it lacks,
as does also *gloveri,* the round dark areas near the hind
angles of the fore wings. The larva of *cecropia* is about
four inches long; green with bluish tints, especially along
the back, two rows of blue tubercles along each side,
two rows of yellow ones along the back, and two pairs
of red ones on the thorax. It feeds on a great variety
of trees and shrubs. The large cocoons, which when cut
open have distinctly the appearance of one cocoon inside
another, are fastened to a branch or other support but
not to leaves. Some cocoons are much larger and puffier
than others, probably because the larvæ that made them
were better fed. This species ranges from the Atlantic
to the Great Plains.

I am sorry that such an authority as Holland should
have called *Callosamia promethea* (Pl. 32) the Spice-
bush Silk-moth when "Promethea" was already in common usage. Furthermore, he says truly: "The insects
subsist in the larval stage upon a great variety of deciduous shrubs and trees, showing a special predilection for
Lauraceæ, Liriodendron, Liquidambar, and wild-cherry."
(Spice-bush and sassafras belong to the family Lauraceæ.) The mature larva is from two to three inches
long; head, yellowish-green; body, "frosted" bluish-green;
six rows of small black tubercles; two pairs of red
tubercles on the thorax; one yellow tubercle on the
eleventh segment; the legs and the anal shield yellow.
The cocoon is much like that of *walkeri* but tends to be
darker and slimmer. The general color of the male's
wings is such a dark maroon that it is sometimes practically black and all but the marginal markings are ob-
scured; the female is much lighter colored.

C. angulifera is a larger species than *promethea.* The
males have wood-brown wings. The females are like
promethea, but lack the contrasting marginal border, the
ground color shading into it. The V marks are usually
distinct in both sexes on all wings. Its larva feeds
chiefly on the tulip-tree (*Liriodendron*). The cocoon is
wrapped in leaves like Promethea's but with the difference that usually no "stem" fastening it to the twig
is made so that the cocoon falls to the ground when the

PLATE 32

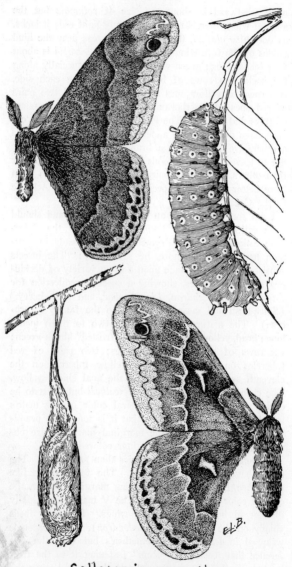

Callosamia promethea

PLATE 33

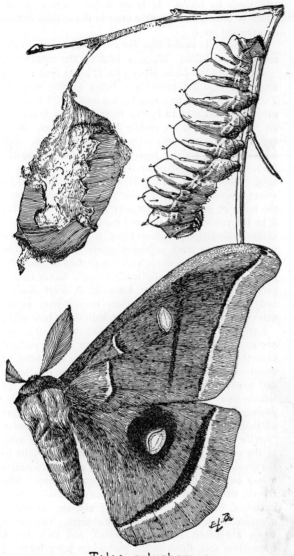

Telea polyphemus

tree sheds its leaves. It is an Atlantic Coast species which is usually not common even in the Middle States, its principal home.

The Saturniid moths thus far mentioned belong to the subfamily Attacinæ. We now take up the Saturniinæ.

Technically the Luna Moth (Pl. 87) has been known as *Actias luna* but probably a better generic name is *Tropæa*. However that may be, the moth itself is rather generally considered to be our most beautiful insect but its lovely green fades rapidly to a light gray. It is rather common and, once seen, is rarely forgotten. The larva feeds on walnut, hickory, sweet-gum (*Liquidambar*), persimmon, and other trees. When mature, it is about three inches long. It varies somewhat in its colors, especially those of the tubercles, and suggests the larva of *polyphemus* but may be distinguished from it by the yellow lateral line and the absence of the seven oblique side-stripes. When about to pupate, the back usually changes from yellowish green to pinkish. The cocoon is very thin and rattles when pressed or when the pupa moves. It is usually made between leaves on the ground. In some sections Luna is at least double-brooded. The early-spring adults usually have purple outer margins on the wings; later individuals lack these.

Larvæ of Polyphemus (*Telea polyphemus,* Pl. 33) are sent to the American Museum every season so that, even though they are the color of leaves, they must be frequently seen by the "laity." They feed on oak, birch, and a great variety of other trees, and somewhat resemble those of *luna*. More than their relatives, *polyphemus* larvæ have the habit of elevating the front part of their bodies and pulling in their heads to assume a "terrifying attitude"; clicking their jaws probably adds to the effect. Many books say that the cocoon falls to the ground in the autumn (There is but one annual generation) but this is by no means always the case. The cocoon, which is more solid than Luna's, contains a long, unbroken, easily unreeled thread of silk that would be commercially valuable if labor were cheaper. The adult's wings are ochre, sometimes pinkish, and each has a transparent spot, those on the hind wings being bordered inwardly by blue and set in a black ring.

The larvæ of the Io moth (*Automeris io,* Pl. 88) should be handled carefully since their spines are sharp and are connected with glands which secrete an irritating fluid. They feed on a great variety of plants, including corn, and when young "follow the leader," each spinning a silken path for the guidance of those which are behind. The thin, semitransparent, brown cocoon is spun among leaves on the ground. There are several other species which may be recognized as *Automeris* from their general resemblance to *io.* Another generic name is *Hyperchiria.*

CITHERONIIDÆ

Another name for the family is Ceratocampidæ. The adults have mouth-parts but probably do not feed. Pupation occurs in the ground, no cocoons being formed.

The black and yellow (or orange) larvæ of *Anisota senatoria* (Pl. 36) feed on oak, often in large colonies. The adult female has a yellow body and brownish-yellow wings, largely free from dark dots and with a tendency toward violet at the margins of the front wings. The male is reddish brown and the central halves of the front wings are slightly translucent. The larva of *A. virginiensis,* on oak, is dark greenish, with two purplish red stripes and three rows of black spines on each side. It is covered with white granules and has a pair of long, black "lashes" on the second segment. The adult female is much like the female *senatoria* but is more thinly scaled and with a definite violet band along the outer margin of each front wing. The male (Pl. 36) is like the male *senatoria* but darker and the central areas of the front wings are transparent, with definite boundaries. The larva of *A. stigma,* on oak, chestnut, and hazel, is brown, dotted with white. It has a very narrow, dusky, mid-dorsal line and a wider one on each side along the spiracles; body spines longer than in the other species. The adult female is much like the female *senatoria* but with about half an inch greater wing expanse, is more heavily scaled, and with a tendency to have at least the front wings thickly dotted with black. The male is much like its female, but smaller and with a tendency to

PLATE 34

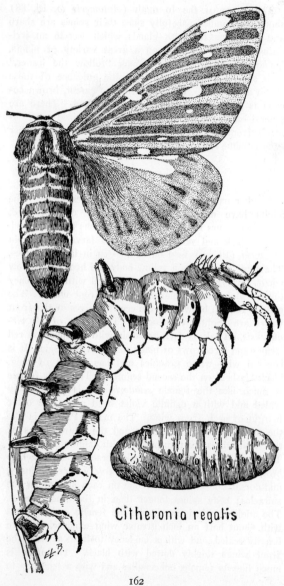

Citheronia regalis

PLATE 35

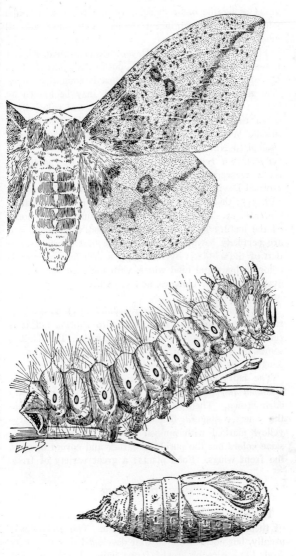

Eacles imperialis

violet along the outer margins of the front wings; the wings have no translucent areas. The pupæ are all much alike.

The Rosy Maple Moth (*Dryocampa rubicunda,* Pl. 88) is sometimes, probably correctly, put in the genus *Anisota.* Its larva feeds on maple. The pupa is somewhat shiny. The adult, though variable in color, may be known by being a fluffy combination of rose color and pale yellow, often tinged with pink. It is most abundant in the Middle West but it is occasionally injurious from Mississippi to New York.

Citheronia regalis.—Names applied to the adult and larva respectively, Royal Walnut Moth and Hickory Horned Devil, tell two of the food plants of this species (Pl. 34); there are a variety of others, including butternut, ash, persimmon, sweet gum, and sumac. The horns of the mature larva are reddish, tipped with black, and are perfectly harmless. Perhaps the best short description of the adults is by Kellogg: "a rich brown ground-color on body and hind wings, with the fore wings slaty gray with yellow blotches, and veins broadly marked out in red-brown."

The Pine-devil (*Citheronia sepulchralis*) is said to range along the coast from Maine to Florida but it is certainly rare in New Jersey, for example. The adult is somewhat smaller than *regalis* and has uniformly brown wings. The larva feeds on pine.

The hairy larvæ of the Imperial Moth (*Eacles* or *Basilona imperialis,* Pl. 35) vary from green to very dark brown. Their horns are proportionately larger in the younger stages. The adult female is rich canary-yellow marked with pinkish purple; the male has the same colors but the purple is darker and covers most of the front wings. Food plants: a great variety of trees.

EUCHROMIIDÆ

These largely Southern moths are day-flyers and some of them much resemble Hymenoptera. The proboscis is usually, but not always, so well developed that they may feed. The cocoons are of felted hair. The family has also been called Syntomidæ and Amatidæ.

PLATE 36

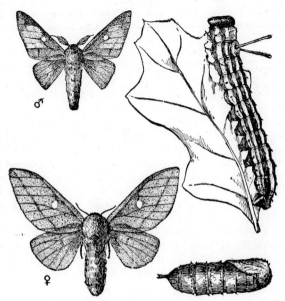

Anisota senatoria

A. virginiensis

Lycomorpha
pholus

Scepsis
fulvicollis

Hypoprepia
fucosa

Lycomorpha pholus (Pl. 36) may be recognized by the black and yellow markings. Its larva is said to feed on lichens. The adult is common on flowers and is found throughout the United States.

Scepsis fulvicollis (Pl. 36).—The wings are brown, except for the transparent central part of the hind wings; the abdomen is metallic blue-black; and there is a yellow color. The larva feeds on grasses. Adults frequent golden-rod flowers.

Ctenucha virginica.—The adult, which has brown wings, metallic bluish-black body, and orange head, is found at the flowers of blackberries, *Spiræa,* and other plants in the Appalachian region. The larva feeds on grasses.

LITHOSIIDÆ

The larvæ are hairy, somewhat after the fashion of the Arctiidæ, of which Lithosiidæ is sometimes considered to be a subfamily. Cocoons are made of silk and larval hairs by some species but others are said to have naked pupæ. The adults have thread-like antennæ and, usually, well-developed mouth-parts. They are popularly called Footman Moths.

Hypoprepia fucosa (Pl. 36) has three lead-colored stripes on the front wings, the ground color being yellow and red. *H. miniata* is very much like it but the dark markings are darker, and the light portions are bright scarlet. The larvæ of each feed on lichens.

ARCTIIDÆ

Topsell, in his *History of Serpents* (1608), said the larvæ of these moths were called Palmer-worms by reason of their wandering and roguish life, although by reason of their roughness and ruggedness some call them Beare-wormes (modern: Woolly Bears). Keats referred to the adults when he wrote:

> "All diamonded with panes of quaint device,
> Innumerable of stains, and splendid dyes,
> As are the Tiger Moth's deep damask wings."

There are more than 2000 species. The larvæ are hairy, usually very much so. The cocoons are made of silk and larval hairs. The adults of some genera have aborted mouth-parts; others have well-developed probosces.

The color and markings of the Beautiful Utetheisa (*Utetheisa ornatrix bella,* Pl. 89) vary greatly but there is nothing in its range (Quebec to Mexico and Antilles) which closely resembles it except the Southern, typical *U. ornatrix,* which has "washed-out" front wings. Although the adult is not common at lights, it is easily flushed in the daytime by walking through the meadows in which its food plants grow. The larva is recorded as feeding on cherry, elm, and other plants, but I have found it only on and in the green seed-pods of *Crotalaria* (Rattlebox) and doubt if it feeds on anything but Legumes.

Nature seems to make the Haploas and other Arctiids by guess; they are so variable. Pl. 89 shows one of the more constant species, *Haploa clymene.* Species of this genus tend to have a dark band, more or less complete, running from the hind margin of each front wing to near its apex; these wings are often also margined with dark color but in some forms they are immaculate. The larvæ are classed as "general feeders" but more careful study will doubtless discover decided preferences.

Plate 89 shows *Estigmene acraea.* It is the male that has yellow hind wings. The spotting varies greatly in both sexes, and there are a number of local races. The name Salt-marsh Caterpillar is misleading. As a matter of fact, the species is found throughout North America, the larva being a general feeder.

The unsightly nests made in late summer by the Fall Web-worm, *Hyphantria cunea,* are frequently confused with the spring tents of *Malacosoma americana.* The nest of *cunea* has a lighter texture and covers all the leaves upon which the colony of larvæ are feeding. It occurs on more than a hundred different kinds of trees, apple and ash being among the favorites. The figures on Pl. 37 indicate the great variability that exists in the markings of both larvæ and adults. The pupa, slightly protected by a loose cocoon, hibernates in crevices of bark, loose soil, etc. The eggs are laid in masses on the under side of leaves.

The larva of *Isia isabella* (Pl. 89) has caused much comment. Kellogg calls it "the woolliest woolly bear," and notes that "hedgehog" is a popular name; Holland connects the phrase "to caterpillar," in the sense of quickly yielding to unpleasant circumstances, with this species because, when disturbed, the larva curls up and lies motionless (a trick of the hedgehog, also); while Comstock recalls the "Hurrying along like a caterpillar in the fall" when speaking of the larva's apparent haste to find a snug place in which to curl up for the winter. When spring comes, it hustles for a little food, plantain being a favorite, and then pupates in a cocoon made of silk and larval hairs. The relative amount of black in the larva's "fur" varies greatly and is said to foretell weather but I forget what is what, although some experiments which I once made indicated that past, not future, moist conditions increase the amount of black. There are two annual broods.

Diacrisia (also called *Spilosoma*) *virginica* is the Yellow-bear of our gardens. The dense, long hair of some individuals is, however, white and of others reddish. The adults (Pl. 89) have up to four small black dots on each of their white wings. One of the several broods hibernates in the pupal stage.

Apantesis.—There are twenty or more species in the United States alone. It is rather characteristic of the genus that the front wings are checkered somewhat after the fashion of the species *nais*, shown in Pl. 89. The prevailing colors are red, brown, and white. The larvæ are general feeders, especially on low-growing things such as plantain.

Numbers of the gay Harlequin caterpillars (*Euchætias egle*, Pl. 89) are frequently seen on milkweed, feeding together in apparent disregard of birds. Most birds do not seem to care for hairy larvæ at any rate, but probably this species gets additional protection, advertised by its colors, from the acrid nature of its food. The cocoon is formed under loose stones and leaves. One brood of adults flies in June, another in late summer. It and the next species are given, by some authors, the generic name *Cycnia*.

PLATE 37

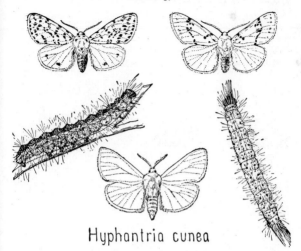

Hyphantria cunea

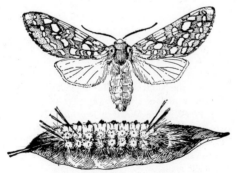

Halisidota caryae

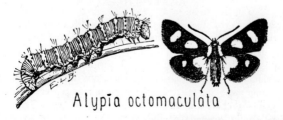

Alypia octomaculata

Pygarctia eglenensis also feeds on milkweed. The predominating color of the larval hairs is dark gray; its head is orange, while that of *egle* is black. The adult resembles *egle* but is somewhat smaller and has the front margin of the front wings, the head, and the collar orange. *Ammalo inopinatus* resembles *eglenensis* but the wings are almost white instead of gray.

"The Hickory Tiger" is one of the English names of *Halisidota caryæ* (Pl. 37) and, like the specific name, refers to the larva's fondness for hickory leaves but, as a matter of fact, it feeds on other trees also. It has also been called Tussock Moth, but that name should be reserved for a species of Liparidæ whose larvæ these resemble. The cocoon, which is made in some sheltered nook, is composed of larval hairs pushed through a very thin envelope of silk. The author of *Insect Lives; or Born in Prison* quaintly describes the color of the moths as being the same as that of hickory-nut meat.

Halisodota tessellaris is much like *caryæ* but the larva has no "black buttons down the back" and its body hairs are usually tinged with yellow or brownish. It is sometimes too common in our gardens and on shade trees. The adult *tessellaris* is much paler, being pale straw-color, and has bluish-green lines on the thorax. That description of the adult also fits the Southern *cinctipes*, which is larger and has the lower part of its legs gartered with black. The Western *argentata* has the white spots silvery and the ground-color of the front wings dark brown. The adult of the Northern *maculata* might be loosely described as like *caryæ* except that the white spots are dark spots.

AGARISTIDÆ

Members of the genus *Alypia* are called Foresters. Translating the specific name, *Alypia octomaculata* (Pl. 37) is called the Eight-spotted Forester. Its larva, which feeds on the leaves of grape and Virginia creeper, is a combination of orange, yellow, black, and white. It has a hump near its tail. Pupation occurs in a very thin cocoon of chips and silk at, or slightly below, the surface of the ground; or the larva may gnaw into wood to pupate. The velvety-black adult has yellow spots on the front wings, white on the hind. It frequently flies by day. Although the Eight-spot is confined to the northeastern quarter of the United States, other sections have similar species.

NOCTUIDÆ

We have about 2500 species of this family in the United States. "Quite two thousand too many," most farmers and gardeners would say, because Cut-worms are young Noctuids. But not all young Noctuids are cutworms. The adults, often called Owlet Moths, fly by night, and some have shiny eyes. They come abundantly to lights and some species crowd "sugar bait," sipping the sweets. Like the adults, the larvæ, as a rule, feed by night. Those which are cut-worms are naked and hide by day just under the surface of loose earth or beneath stones and other shelters. They may be distinguished from "White-grubs," larvæ of beetles that have somewhat similar habits, by the fact that they have fleshy prop-legs on their abdomen. Cut-worms curl up, head to tail, when at rest or when disturbed. Some clamber over plants, eating the leaves, but their common name is derived from the habit of gnawing through the stems of tender annuals. Many cut-worms hibernate in snug underground cells and, so, are ready to attack vigorously our seedlings in the spring. Many other Noctuidæ, especially those whose larvæ feed on trees, hibernate as pupæ. *Agrotis ypsilon* (Pl. 38) is a good example of an adult cut-worm of our gardens. Others shown on Pl. 38 are *Euxoa messoria, Mamestra picta, Rhynchagrotis anchoceloides, Noctua clandestina* and *N. c-nigrum.* The larva of *Xylina antennata* (Pl. 39) feeds on apple and other plants; the adult hibernates.

Acronycta is possibly correctly called *Apatela* in some books, and, commonly, Dagger Moths. More than forty species have been recorded from New Jersey alone. *A. americana* (Pl. 38) is one of our largest species. The hind wings are brownish. With sufficient imagination you can see near the hind, outer angle of the front wings of *americana* and some other species the "dagger" which is responsible for the common name of the genus. *Americana's* larva is one of the hairiest of Noctuidæ. With its dense, pale-yellow hairs it resembles an Arctiid but the hairs are scattered over the body instead of being grouped on tubercles as is the rule among the Arctiidæ. It feeds on maple (its favorite), elm, oak and other forest trees. Larvæ of this genus often rest near the base of a leaf with the front end of the body curved back so that they are somewhat fish-hook-shaped. When disturbed, *Acronycta* larvæ are given to curling up and dropping off of their food plant. They pupate in loose cocoons placed on rough bark or under ground-débris.

Acronycta hastulifera, according to its specific name, "bears a spear" instead of a dagger. Its larvæ are often abundant on alder and have been recorded on maple. They suggest those of *americana* but their color varies from pale to deep chocolate-brown. Eliot and Soule, whose *Caterpillars and their Moths* is not only a model of careful work but also shows what pleasure and profit ladies may get from a "crawlery," point out that these larvæ "are subject to fungoid diseases which kill many of them, and their stiff bodies may be found on branches of the alders, apparently unharmed, but they break at a touch and are filled with fungoid growth." As a matter of fact, fungi and bacteria vie with insect parasites as enemies of caterpillars in general.

The larva of *Acronycta hamamelis,* as its specific name signifies, feeds on witch-hazel but it is also found on various forest trees. This larva differs from its two relatives just mentioned in being almost hairless; it varies from light yellow to reddish brown and has a double row of white spots on its back. These, its food plants, and its fish-hook resting position will usually identify it.

The old, large genus *Hadena* is now split beyond hope of simplification. Two common, wide-spread, destructive cut-worms which were in it are *devastatrix* and *arctica* (Pl. 38). The larvæ attack garden and field crops. The adults have dark brown front and light hind wings. The larvæ of *turbulenta* are sometimes noticed on green briar (*Smilax*) because of their gregarious habits.

The Fall Army-worm (*Laphygma frugiperda,* Pl. 38) appears later than the true Army-worm (*Cirphis uni-*

PLATE 38

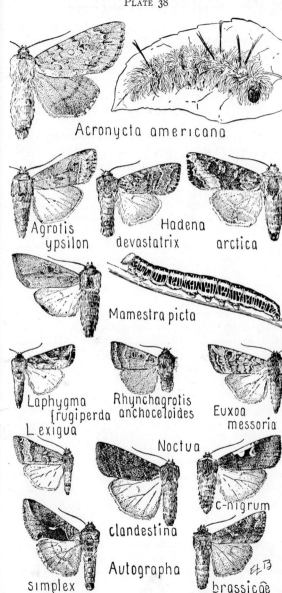

Acronycta americana

Agrotis ypsilon

Hadena devastatrix

arctica

Mamestra picta

Laphygma frugiperda
L. exigua

Rhynchagrotis anchoceloides

Euxoa messoria

Noctua

clandestina

c-nigrum

simplex

Autographa

brassicae

173

puncta) and the larvæ are not so choice about their food. They eat almost any crop, scattering more than do the Army-worms. The pitch-black stripe along each side and the four black spots on the back of each segment distinguish this "worm" from *Cirphis*. The naked pupæ hibernate about half an inch below ground. Adults emerge in the spring and the female covers her egg-clusters, placed on grass, with hairs from her own body. There are two or three generations a year but the larvæ that appear in late summer are the most destructive. The adult has a "general yellowish, ash-grey color, with the second pair of wings almost transparent, but with a purplish reflection." In the West there is a related species, *L. exigua* (Pl. 38), which is called the Beet Army-worm because of its ravages among the sugar-beets.

The Army-worm (*Cirphis unipuncta*, Pl. 39) is a conspicuous example of a species which occasionally gets ahead of its insect parasites and other ills, increasing its numbers to such an extent that its larvæ eat all the available food, chiefly grasses, in a given place and are forced to move *en masse*. However, Fate is not to be permanently outdone and soon there comes a time when the species is relatively rare. And then again the pendulum swings. Nature is "balanced" but not very steady. This dull-brown moth gets its specific name from the "one point" of white on each front wing. Other generic names are *Leucania* and *Heliophila*. Adults appear early in the season (June in the North), and yellowish eggs are laid in rows at the bases of grass leaves, each female depositing, all told, about seven hundred. The larvæ are nearly, or quite, two inches long when full-grown. They are grayish-black with three longitudinal yellow stripes on the back, the median one being the narrowest, and a wide greenish-yellow stripe on each side. They feed at night, hiding by day at the grass roots, and about midsummer pupate, without a cocoon, just under the surface of the ground. Adults emerge about two weeks later but their offspring are not usually numerous enough to be very destructive. The next brood of adults either hibernate or they lay eggs the same season and the larvæ hatching from these eggs hibernate. The number of an-

PLATE 39

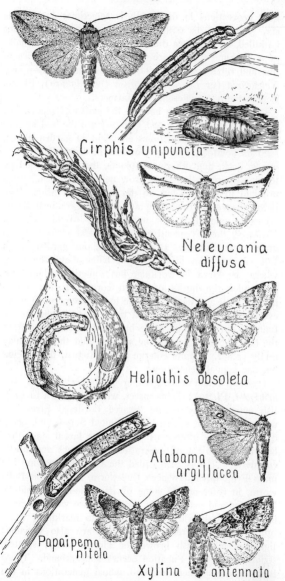

Cirphis unipuncta

Neleucania diffusa

Heliothis obsoleta

Alabama argillacea

Papaipema nitela

Xylina antennata

nual generations in the South is sometimes as high as six. Army-worms with white eggs on them should not be killed, as these are the eggs of some parasite, usually of a Tachinid fly. There are numerous other species in this and related genera. The Wheat-head Army-worm, *Neleucania* (or *Leucania*) *diffusa* (or *albilinea*), Pl. 39, is sometimes troublesome to farmers.

Larvæ of *Papaipema* bore in the stalks of plants. *P. nebris* and its variety *nitela* (Pl. 39) are the best-known, for the larvæ are sometimes abundant in garden plants, such as potatoes, tomatoes, and corn, especially if rag-weeds, dock, and other wild plants, the natural food of the species, are allowed to grow near the garden. Eggs are laid in the fall but do not hatch until May. The larvæ then start tunnelling and, if they confined themselves to one plant, not much injury would be done. However, they frequently leave the first plant and migrate some distance. It is then that our garden plants fall victims. An infested plant wilts above the place where the larva is working, but sometimes the larvæ get under the husks of green corn and remain unnoticed until an attempt is made to use the corn. (However, see *Heliothis*) Pupation takes place in the larva's tunnel. No cocoon is made but, just before it pupates, the larva bores a hole in the stalk so that the adult may easily escape. Adults emerge about August, there being but one annual generation.

Holland remarks concerning *Heliothis obsoleta* (or *armigera*, Pl. 39) : "This insect, which is known to English entomologists as the 'Scarce Bordered Straw,' is unfortunately not scarce in the United States, and, being of a singularly gluttonous habit in the larval stage, has become the object of execration to farmers and horticulturists." It has been called the Corn Ear-worm, Tomato Fruit-worm, Tobacco Bud-worm, and Cotton Boll-worm, in reference to some of its various food habits. The color and markings of the adults are variable, some being yellowish white, with nearly no markings, while others are dull green. The larvæ are also variable: light green, reddish brown, or almost black; spotted, striped, or plain. Pupation occurs underground. There is no cocoon. There are two annual generations in the

North but there may be five or six along the Gulf. In the North, winter is usually passed as a pupa. When feeding on young corn, the larvæ eat the leaves but later they feed on the tender ears and sometimes do as much as $50,000,000 damage a year in this way. When feeding on tobacco, they are called the False Bud-worm to distinguish them from the True Bud-worm (*Chloridea virescens*); as such they eat not only the flower-stalks and seed-pods but also the precious leaves. Not finally but for the sake of stopping somewhere, they do about $20,000,000 damage annually to cotton by boring into the bolls. In the North, winter plowing kills many of the pupæ, and, in the South, cotton may be protected by sowing trap-crops of corn, but everywhere the best plan with this, as with other insect pests, is to send an S.O.S. to your State Entomologist or the United States Department of Agriculture for special information and help. It is for this, among other things, that you pay your taxes.

Autographa (Pl. 38) is variously split into several genera. For example, the Celery Looper, *Autographa simplex* of Holland's book, will be found under *Plusia* in some books and the specific name may be *falcifera*. Except for this hint (and it applies with equal force in the case of other genera) to those who might be confused when more than one book is used, it need not concern us further since the only species we can mention in any detail was, no later than yesterday, still in the *Autographa* pigeon-hole. If you find a brown Noctuid-looking moth with a wing expanse of 1.0 to 1.5 inches and with one, or more, not strictly circular, silver spots near the middle of each front wing, it is a fairly safe bet that it is either *Autographa* or closely related to it. Some of the species fly by day. The larvæ are called Loopers or Semi-loopers because they walk somewhat like Measuring-worms (Geometridæ) on account of not having any prop-legs on the third and fourth abdominal segments. *Autographa brassicæ* is a close second to *Pieris rapæ* when it comes to injuring cabbage, cauliflower, and the like. The larva is colored much like the ordinary cabbage worm, but it has longitudinal white lines when young and it loops. The cocoon is a thin transparent affair attached to the leaf on which the larva was feeding.

There are two or more generations annually, winter probably being passed in the pupal state.

The genus *Catocala* shares the amateurs' "love" with the Saturniidæ and the Sphingidæ. Many of its species are pretty. They are also interesting because they have bright colors on the hind wings, which are covered when at rest by the "protectively colored" front wings and are usually displayed only at night when they cannot be seen —at least, by our eyes. Plate 90 shows an exhibit in the American Museum illustrating the fact that, however conspicuous when flying in daytime, Catocalinæ are concealed in plain sight when resting. I will not swear that I ever saw a live *relicta* so neatly placed on just the right spot of just the right tree, a birch, but it surely does require sharp eyes to see a resting *Catocala* or, for that matter, almost any moth when it is naturally resting. The adults of *Catocala* are sometimes called Under-wings because of the conspicuousness of these parts. He or she who "sugars" for moths will probably find varieties of those illustrated here, as well as totally different species, for they are fond of sweets and are sometimes numerous. The larvæ tend to be plump in the middle, tapering toward both ends. They pupate in flimsy cocoons, which are usually placed under débris on the ground. Winter is at least usually passed in the egg state.

Mrs. Stratton Porter, in lamenting her lack of knowledge concerning the life-history of these moths, took another whack at some of us: "Professional lepidopterists dismiss them with few words. One would-be authority disposes of the species with half a dozen lines. You can find at least a hundred Catocala reproduced from museum specimens and their habitat given, in the Holland *Moth Book,* but I fail to learn what I most desire to know; what these moths feed on; how late they live; how their eggs appear; where they are deposited; which is their caterpillar; what does it eat; and where and how does it pupate. . . . This will tend to bear out my contention that scientific works are not the help they should be to the Nature Lover." Lord bless us! If Dr. Holland had put in all that (He couldn't have done it) for each of the thousands of species his books help us to identify, he not only would have deprived us of the pleasure of finding out these things for ourselves but most of us would not have been able to own the resulting tomes. Perhaps it will be noticed that I am saying little about eggs. I have to draw a line somewhere, and people have not often asked me about eggs. I hope I have told in this little book something about all the sorts of insects' eggs that have excited the curiosity of my unspecialized visitors and correspondents. Of course, tomorrow some one may ask a question which I have not been asked before and very possibly I shall be unable to answer it. Incidentally, entomological oölogy is a nearly virgin field and may be very interesting.

Catocala ultronia (Pl. 90) is a variable species, several forms having been given distinctive names. The larva feeds on plum, apple, and wild cherry leaves. The pupa in its cocoon, which is formed in July under chips or dead leaves, is covered with a bluish, easily rubbed bloom. Adults fly from late July to October. Eggs are well hidden in crevices of the bark of their food-trees.

The *Catocala cara* (Pl. 90) larva on willow or poplar has a purplish head streaked and spotted with pale testaceous. Its body is light to dark clay or wood brown; on each side of the back is a smoky, longitudinal band and a wavy, broken one on each side along the spiracles; the dorsal warts are dull carmine or yellowish-brown; the underside is reddish, with a large black patch between each of the first three pairs of abdominal legs. Adults are to be found from July to September.

Catocala relicta (Pl. 90) larvæ feed on poplar and also, probably, willow and white birch. They are greenish-white, thickly spotted with yellowish-brown, the ninth and twelfth segments and the head being marked with black. The cocoon is rather thick and is usually made in fallen leaves drawn together by the larva. Adults, of which there are several forms, appear from July to September.

Catocala vidua (Pl. 90) larvæ eat walnut, butternut, hickory, and oak. They are pale lilac with stripes composed of black dots, giving a gray appearance; their heads are striped with dull lilac and white and have orange spots, above, with a black hair in the center of each. Pupation is said to occur in June. Most of our adult specimens were caught in August and September

Plate 40 shows *Catocala concumbens* (larva on willow and poplar), *C. grynea* (larva on apple and plum) and *C. amica* (oak).

Euparthenos nubilis (Pl. 40) larvæ feed on locust.

Alabama argillacea (Pl. 39) claims a paragraph because it gets into the New York subways and newspapers. It belongs 'way down South in the cotton fields where, until the invasion of the boll weevil, it was Cotton's most serious pest. Its breeding range is from Argentina to as far north as cotton grows. The larvæ are greenish, variously spotted or striped with black according to their age. They feed on the cotton leaves, buds, and even tender twigs, pupating in a thin cocoon made in a folded leaf. Sanderson says: "The moth is a dull olive-gray color which sometimes has a purple luster and which is marked with darker lines. Like most of the owlet moths it flies only after sunset, but unlike them it is not confined to the nectar of flowers for food, as its mouth is peculiarly adapted to piercing the skin of ripe fruit and feeding upon its juices." After stating that there are at least seven generations annually on the Gulf Coast and three at the northern limits of the species, he notes that "if none were killed, the progeny of a single moth after four generations would amount to over 300,000,000,000 individuals, or if placed end to end, the third generation would be enough to circle the earth at the equator over four times." That is a fairly good-sized "if," but make it much smaller and you still have a sufficient reason for a considerable migration away from a crowded home.

Erebus odora (Pl. 40) drifted into my Question Box because it was "big enough to be a Saturniid but isn't in the book"—one concerning the Saturniidæ, etc., of the vicinity of New York City. Size does not always count. This Noctuid does not belong in the North although, being a strong flier, it gets even into Canada. Holland records its having been found in a snow-storm at Leadville, Colorado. All the Northern captures I know about were females in September. Although I have seen it flying back and forth in its tropical home just at dusk, or even at mid-day if the place was shady, I have never recognized its larva, which is said to feed on Legumes.

PLATE 40

C. grynea

Catocala concumbens

C. amica

Euparthenos nubilis

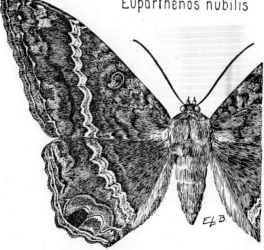

Erebus odora

The Hypeninæ have been classed as a separate family. They are commonly called Deltoids because the outline of their wings, when at rest, is frequently triangular like the Greek capital Delta; also Snout Moths because the palpi of many species are enlarged and so held as to resemble a beak. For the most part the adults are dull-colored, obscurely marked, and not likely to arouse comment by any but the collectors, and even they have not been enthusiastic although these moths come readily to light and sugar-bait. However, they have their interesting points. Secondary sexual modifications are common, the males frequently having wings, feet, antennæ, or palpi shaped differently from those of their mates. The larvæ of *Epizeuxis americalis* have been found in the nests of ants (*Formica rufa*). In July Mr. Grossbeck found a swarm of adult *Epizeuxis lubricalis* (Pl. 41) in a hollow tree. The larvæ feed on decaying wood and, probably, also on dead leaves and grasses; they are usually found under chips. *Hypena humuli* is frequently injurious to hops.

NOTODONTIDÆ

The adults superficially resemble the Noctuidæ. They come freely to light and often to sugar-bait. The larvæ have no claspers at the hind end of the body and so they more generally wave this portion in the air than do other caterpillars. Sometimes the anal segment has a pair of fleshy projections but these seem to correspond rather to humps on other segments than to prop-legs. The pupæ are usually naked.

The yellow-necked, yellow-striped caterpillar on apple and other trees that seems, when disturbed or when at rest, to be trying to touch its tail with its head is fairly certain to be *Datana ministra* (Pl. 41). It is somewhat fuzzy, especially when young, and is given to associating with its brothers and sisters, the whole family gathering in a mass and going through their gymnastics at the same time. The naked pupæ winter in the earth. Adults emerge in June and July. Their front wings are reddish-brown; their hind wings pale yellowish. The eggs are laid in flat masses of about a hundred on the leaves of

PLATE 41

Epizeuxis lubricalis

Schizura concinna

Datana ministra

♂ ♀

E·L·B·

Hemerocampa leucostigma

their food plants. The larvæ of *Datana integerrima* are darker than those of *ministra*. They lack the yellow neck-band and they seem to have more fine white hair. They feed chiefly on walnut and hickory. The adults are browner than (not so reddish as) *ministra* and the fine lines which enclose a dark area near the base of the front wings do not diverge from each other so much. You may find *Datana angusii,* and other species as well, but the larvæ of all, as far as I know, throw themselves into the posture shown for *ministra*.

The larva of *Schizura concinna* (Pl. 41) feeds on apple and other orchard trees as well as on rose, black-berry, and a great variety of plants. It is frequently noticed because of the prominent bright red hump on the first abdominal segment. The head is also red; the body is black, striped with yellow. Holland, quoting Sir George Hampson, says the pupæ of Notodontidæ are naked. Two paragraphs above I put in a "usually" be-cause I have it on good authority that the larvæ of this species become fully grown in late summer or early fall and then spin loose silken cocoons to which are attached bits of earth and rubbish, so that they closely resemble their surroundings as they lie on the ground beneath rub-bish, or just under the surface of the soil. After some time the larvæ transform to pupæ, in which stage the winter is passed. The adult's gray front wings have a curved cross-row of brown shades near the middle.

LIPARIDÆ

The best known and worst liked species of the family is *Hemerocampa leucostigma,* which is popularly called the Vaporer or White-marked Tussock Moth. The latter name refers to the larva (Pl. 41) with its four white tussocks. This larva is further adorned with three long pencils of black hair, a coral-red head and, in addition to yellow and black stripings on the body in general, two small red protuberances on the sixth and seventh ab-dominal segments. These red swellings are said to give off an odor disagreeable to the larva's enemies. All in all, it would be a pretty creature if it only would not eat the leaves of our shade trees, among which it seems to be no respecter of species. I am not sure how the name Vaporer arose but I remember that, when I got to swinging things about, my mother used to ask me not to "vapor" around her face. Well, this larva is much given to spinning a long thread, hanging by it from a tree and allowing itself to be swung by the breezes. Perhaps that is the reason for the name. The grayish cocoon is placed on tree trunks, fence corners, and similar places. It is composed of larval hairs held together by silk. The adult female is a stay-at-home, for she has no wings. She merely crawls to the outside of the cocoon, mates, lays her batch of four hundred or so eggs on the cocoon, protects them with a firm, frothy-looking covering, and dies. The general color of the male is ashy gray. There are from one to three generations a year, depending on the climate. The species over-winters in the egg-stage. Slingerland and Crosby note that the Tussock Moth is beset with many enemies. After mentioning birds and predacious insects they say "as many as 90 per cent of the caterpillars and pupæ sometimes fall a prey to more than twenty different kinds of hymenopterous and dipterous insect parasites. Unfortunately, however, there are fourteen hyper-parasites which work on the true parasites and thus materially lessen their effectiveness. There are also tertiary parasites which destroy these hyper-parasites, thus presenting a very complicated and interesting case of insect parasitism." If you once get a tree free from this species, it may be kept free by banding the trunk with sticky paper, or the like, unless the tree is so close to others that larvæ may be blown to it. The reason back of this protective method is that the females can not fly.

About 1868 an amateur entomologist in Massachusetts was breeding the Gypsy Moth (*Porthetria dispar*, Pl. 42), using specimens which he had obtained from Europe. His reason for doing this has been variously stated. An excuse that might now be made for him is that "he did not know it was loaded." At any rate, some of the specimens went off and started to colonize America. Millions of dollars have since been spent in an effort, so far unsuccessful, to free us from the invader. The U. S. Bureau of Entomology is now engaged in an attempt to establish here European parasites that hold it and the Brown-tail Moth in check there. The male Gypsy Moth is olive-brown; the whitish female rarely flies and then but feebly, although the wings are rather well developed. Adults appear from June to September but most abundantly in early July. The eggs, which are yellowish, nearly globular, and about a twentieth of an inch in diameter, are laid in masses of from less than 200 to more than 1000 and covered with buff-colored scales from the under side of the female's abdomen. These masses are placed anywhere that the female happens to be. As she does not crawl far from the pupal shell in which she dwelt and as the larvæ are much given to pupating under overhanging stones, on fences, buildings, wagons, railroad cars, and the like, as well as on vegetation, there is where the eggs are to be found. Though the larvæ may develop in a few weeks, they rarely hatch until the next April or May. More than 500 species of plants, including conifers, are in their dietary. The full-grown larva is about 2.25 inches long, brownish-yellow with long hairs and four rows of tubercles; there is one tubercle of each row on each segment, those on the anterior segments being blue, those (especially of the two middle rows) on the posterior segments being red. The larvæ are largely nocturnal and spend the day congregated in groups on a limb, trunk, or in some protected nook. They pupate about July, also often in groups. Each rather conical, dark-brown pupa, about an inch long, lies among a few threads securely attached to some of them by its terminal spine. If you should see something outside of New England which you think may be the Gypsy Moth or the Brown-tail Moth in any of their stages, send it at once to your State Entomologist or to the U. S. Bureau of Entomology at Washington.

We do not know how the Brown-tail Moth (*Euproctis chrysorrhœa,* Pl. 42) crossed the Atlantic from Europe, but it happened near Boston in the early nineties. Its American range is now from Rhode Island to Nova Scotia. Unlike those of the Gypsy Moth, these females fly freely, so that wind may be a factor in their spread. They are white, except for the yellowish-brown hairs at the tip of their abdomen that give them their name. The

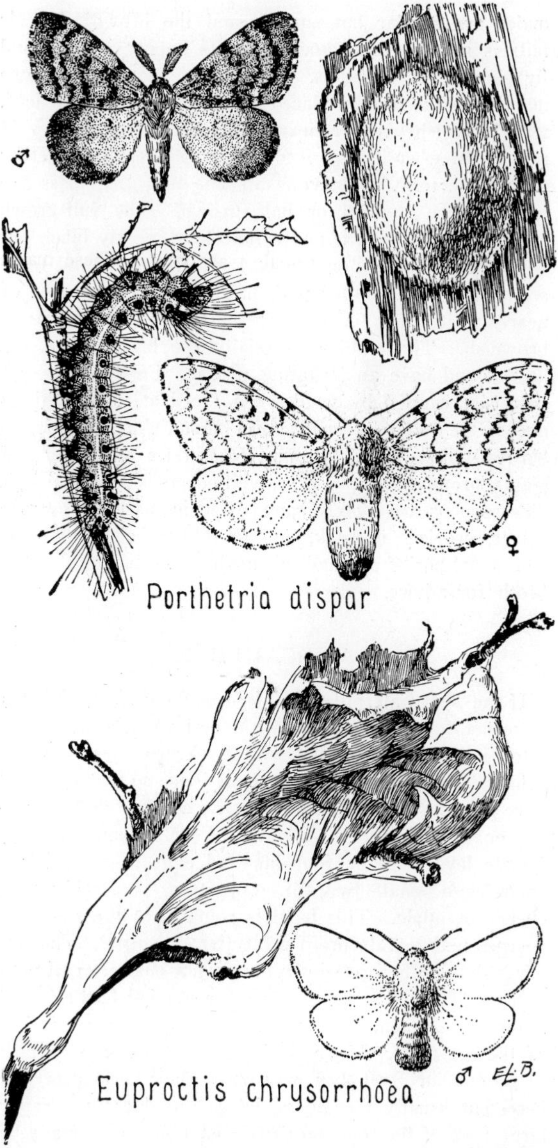

PLATE 42

Porthetria dispar

Euproctis chrysorrhœa

ELB.

males are similar but smaller and the brown of their
tails is not so conspicuous. Adults appear in July and
fly abundantly to lights. The female covers her egg-
mass, which is usually placed on the under side of a leaf,
with brownish hairs from her body. The larvæ hatch in
two or three weeks and feed in groups, webbing together
the tender terminal leaves. In this nest they pass the
winter when a third or half grown. The full-grown
larva is about an inch and a half long, nearly black but
with a red tubercle on the back of the ninth and tenth
segments. It is clothed with hair, there being a row of
nearly white tufts on each side of the body and the rest
brownish. These hairs, especially the brown ones, are
barbed and have an irritating poison. Furthermore, the
hairs are carried by wind when freed at molting times
and, if they gain entrance to the human skin, give rise to
"brown-tail rash." The larva feeds on a wide range of
plants, preferring apple, pear, wild cherry, oak, and maple.
The cocoons are loosely spun, often in masses, in curled
leaves, crevices in bark, and in other sheltered places.
The pupal period averages about three weeks. See Gypsy
Moth for advice.

LASIOCAMPIDÆ

If the Tent Caterpillar (*Malacosoma americana,* Pl. 43)
were not so common and such a pest we who are interested in nature would be willing to go miles to see a
colony. We might even bring eggs home so that we could
have it in our garden. The adults, which are dull yellowish or reddish brown, appear in early summer. The
female lays three or four hundred eggs in a band that
encircles a small twig of some tree, preferably wild
cherry or apple. This band is rounded at the ends and
covered with a waterproof protective "varnish." The em-
bryos develop before winter but do not emerge until next
spring. Their first act seems to be helping brothers and
sisters spin a temporary silken tent around what is left
of the egg-mass. If this is in a good place from which
to go out for food they may make their permanent tent
here, but usually they move in several days to a fairly
large fork of the tree and there construct the, to many of

PLATE 43

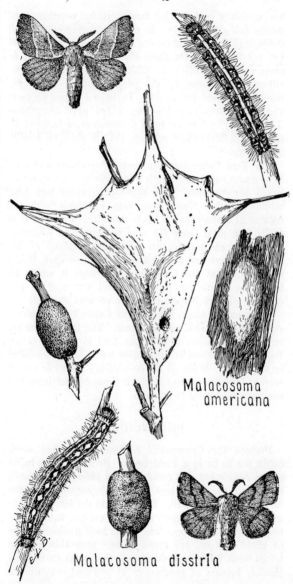

Malacosoma
americana

Malacosoma disstria

E.L.O.

us, unsightly web. The family sticks together until nearly full-grown, resting in the tent during storms and the heat of the day and coming out to feed when it is cool but not too cold. On these excursions they follow, to some extent, definite paths which may be recognized by silken threads spun by the passing larvæ. They get *wanderlust* when full-grown. Perhaps I object to them then more than ever for they crawl over everything. They are really hunting for a protected place in which to spin tough, oval, white cocoons, held in place by irregular threads.

The Tent Caterpillar is a native American; and long before man cared about such things Nature had so established her "balance" here that *Malacosoma* was kept within bounds. Now, when man interferes with the balance of Nature man is likely to suffer. I wonder if it really is a good thing for man to engage in wholesale destruction of *Malacosoma* egg-masses. Many of his friends, bacterial or other parasites in those eggs, would be destroyed at the same time. Perhaps it would be better for us to confine our control measures to our orchards and let Nature take care of wild cherries.

The common name, Forest Tent Caterpillar, of *Malacosoma disstria* (Pl. 43) is wrong. The larvæ make no tent although, when young, they feed in groups, eating the leaves of almost any deciduous tree. Maple is said to be a favorite. Many of the cocoons are placed in curled leaves. The egg-masses resemble those of *americana* but are more square-cut at the ends.

BOMBYCIDÆ

Perhaps the Commercial Silk-worm, *Bombyx mori,* ought not to be in a Field Book. Probably, even in its native Asiatic home, it could not now exist without man's help, since the larval legs have so degenerated that the larvæ cannot climb well. They will eat the leaves of several kinds of plants, such as Osage orange, but they do best on white mulberry. The adults have a wing-expanse of about 1.75 in., are creamy white and, although the wings seem fairly well developed, the moths do not fly, possibly because of generations of artificial confinement.

Each female lays about 300 eggs. There are many races that have been produced by man's selection. Some have one, others may have three or more, generations a year; also the color of larvæ and cocoons differ. If labor were cheap enough in America to make the rearing of silk-worms pay, some of our native Saturniidæ might be profitable.

GEOMETRIDÆ

Larvæ of this family are familiar to almost everyone, but only a small proportion of those larvæ that come within our range of vision are really seen, since most of them stiffen themselves and pass for a twig. Others, those that develop into the small, delicate, green moths you may have noticed about lights, cover themselves with bits of their food. When next you gather Black-eyed Susans and Field Daisies look carefully on the flowers for a collection of flower-bits fastened to the back of a Geometrid larva (Pl. 44). The name of this family means "earth measurers" and in English we call the larvæ Measuring-worms, Inch-worms, Span-worms, or Loopers. The saying that when they walk on our clothes they are planning a new suit for us is probably as logical as "earth measuring" and more interesting to us personally. Their peculiar locomotion is due to their lacking all but two or three pairs of abdominal legs. With legs only at each end of the body they must hump themselves to get along. The adults are slender-bodied. The wings are broad and the pattern on the front wings is, in many cases, continued on the hind wings. About 1,000 species have been described from this country alone.

Imagine a tiny gray flower-pot having a gray cover decorated with a dark central spot and a dark ring near the edge. That is like an egg of the Fall Canker-worm, *Alsophila pometaria* (Pl. 44). The female places several hundred of them in a flat mass, keeping the rows regular, on the bark of almost any deciduous tree. This is usually done in November but sometimes not until spring. The larvæ, especially at first, skeletonize the leaves instead of eating them entirely. They get to be about an inch long; black, with a stripe of yellow on each side below the spiracles and three narrower whitish stripes above them. These larvæ, like many of their relatives, often let themselves part-way down to the ground by means of silken threads. If it is not your tree, it is rather amusing to see them climb up these threads again, for all the world like sailors going up ropes. About the first of June they do not go back, but, instead, go to a depth of from one to four inches underground, where each spins a thin tough cocoon, pupates, and remains until late autumn or early spring. The adult males are brownish-gray and have good wings. The females have much the same color but are wingless. However, the females are not so sedentary as those of the Tussock Moth. They scramble out of the earth and make for a tree upon which to lay their eggs. This is when we can easily get the better of them, for we need only put a sticky barrier around the trunks of our trees to keep the females from climbing up. But there are two things to remember: first, one can never be quite sure when the females are going to come out, for they may choose a warm spell in midwinter, and, second, there is *Paleacrita vernata* (p. 194).

Calocalpe undulata (Pl. 44) has its wings zigzagged with yellow and brown. It gets a paragraph because of its nest. The female lays a cluster of eggs in early summer on a terminal leaf of wild cherry. I do not know just how they do it but the larvæ fasten together the leaves at the end of the twig and the whole family feeds on the walls of the nest. When these walls are nearly eaten, the larvæ bend other leaves and fasten them against the nest so that they may have fresh walls to eat. Finally, they all leave to pass the winter underground as pupæ. This species occurs also in Europe, but probably it is on both sides of the Atlantic naturally and not because of man's migrations.

Synchlora ærata (Pl. 44) is delicate pale green and the wings are crossed by two lighter lines. This description fits many species of the Geometrinæ but to make it more definite without becoming technical would be difficult. At any rate, it is the larva which is of interest here. It feeds on the fruit and also on the foliage of raspberry and blackberry. Like its relatives on the daisies, it covers itself with rubbish fastened to its back with silk.

PLATE 44

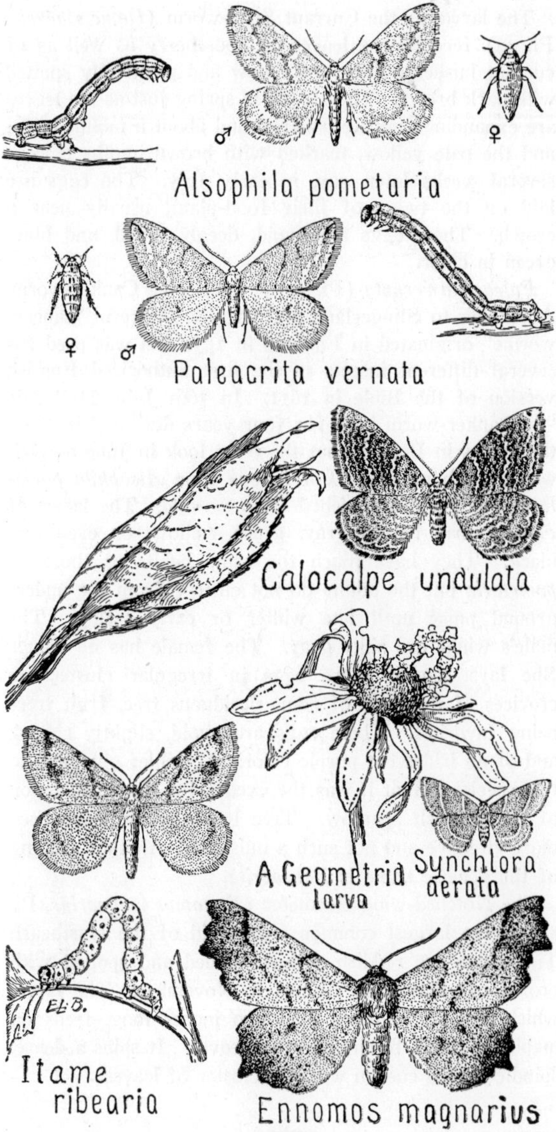
♂
♀
Alsophila pometaria
♀
♂
Paleacrita vernata
Calocalpe undulata
A Geometrid larva
Synchlora aerata
E.L.B.
Itame ribearia
Ennomos magnarius

The larvæ of the Currant Span-worm (*Itame ribearia,* Pl. 44) feed on the leaves of gooseberry as well as of currant bushes. They are yellow and plentifully spotted with dark brown. They hatch in spring just as the leaves are expanding; pupate underground about a month later; and the pale yellow, marked with brown, moths emerge several weeks later, say, in early July. The eggs are laid on the twigs of their food-plant, usually near a crotch. These eggs are ovoid, deeply pitted, and blue-green in color.

Paleacrita vernata (Pl. 44) is the Spring Canker-worm. According to Slingerland and Crosby, the term "canker-worme" originated in England in 1530 and was used for several different insects in the first authorized English version of the Bible in 1611. In 1661 John Hull said "the canker-worm hath for four years devoured most of the apples in Boston, that the trees look in June as if it was the 9th month." For a long time *Alsophila pometaria* was not distinguished from *vernata.* The larvæ of *vernata* may be ash-gray, green, yellow, or even dull black. They have much the same habits as those of *pometaria* but the adults do not emerge from the underground pupæ until late winter or early spring. The male's wings are silky gray. The female has no wings. She lays 400 or more eggs in irregular clusters in crevices of the bark of some deciduous tree, fruit trees being favorites. These eggs are ovoid, slightly ridged, and of an iridescent purple color. My chief objection to this species is that it was the excuse for the introduction of the English sparrow. Tree bands would have been more effective and not such a nuisance. Another spelling of the generic name is *Palæacrita.*

The Notched-wing Geometer (*Ennomos magnarius,* Pl. 44) is the largest common Geometrid of the Northeast. The wings are reddish yellow, shaded and spotted with brown. It flies from August to November. The larva, which gets to be more than two inches long, feeds on maple, chestnut, birch and other leaves. It spins a dense, spindle-shaped cocoon within a cluster of leaves.

In the preceding account of Macro-lepidoptera a number of families have been skipped. For the most part they are very poorly represented in our fauna. Among them are DIOPTIDÆ (*Phryganidia californica* in California), PERICOPIDÆ (bright contrasting colors), EUPTEROTIDÆ (*Apatelodes*), EPIPLEMIDÆ, THYATIRIDÆ, DREPANIDÆ (front wings of typical species sickle-shaped at apex), and LACOSOMIDÆ. The larvæ of the last make portable cases of leaves, chiefly oak, and silk (Compare Trichoptera and Psychidæ).

For years the order has been divided into MACRO-LEPIDOPTERA and MICROLEPIDOPTERA. The terms are misleading, for many Macrolepidoptera are smaller than some Microlepidoptera; but, although some Microlepidoptera are large, most of them are very small and, as a whole, they are more primitive than the Macrolepidoptera. Up to this point we have been discussing the former; the following are Microlepidoptera.

PSYCHIDÆ

Plate 91 shows a bag such as is frequently noticed on many sorts of trees. A larva of *Thyridopteryx ephemeræformis* made it of silk in which are fastened leaves or bits of twigs. If we examine such bags during the winter, we shall find many of them to be empty but others will be found full of soft yellow eggs. Riley, one of our pioneer economic entomologists, wrote as follows: "Those which do not contain eggs are the male bags and his empty chrysalis skin is generally to be found protruding from the lower end. About the middle of next May these eggs will hatch into active little worms, which from the first moment of their lives commence to form for themselves little bags. They crawl on to a tender leaf and, attached by their anterior feet with their tails hoisted in the air, they spin around themselves a ring of silk, to which they soon fasten bits of leaf. They continue adding to the lower edge of the ring, pushing it up as it increases in width, till it reaches the tail and forms a sort of a cone. As the worms grow, they continue to increase their bags from the bottom, until the latter become so large and heavy that the worms let them hang instead of holding them upright as they did while they were young. This full-grown condition is not attained, however, without critical periods. At four different times during their growth these worms close up the mouths of their bags and retire for two days to cast their skins or moult, as is the nature of their kind, and they push their old skins through a passage which is always left open at the extremity of the bag, and which also allows the passage of excrement. During their growth they are very slow travellers and seldom leave the tree on which they were born, but when full-grown they become quite restless, and it is this time that they do all their travelling, dropping on to persons by their silken threads and crossing the sidewalks in all directions. A wise instinct urges them to do this, for did they remain on one tree, they would soon multiply beyond the power of the tree to sustain them and would in consequence become extinct. When they have lost their migratory desires, they fasten their bags very securely by a strong band of silk to the twigs of the tree on which they happen to be. A strange instinct leads them to thus fasten their cocoons to the twigs only of the trees they inhabit, so that these cocoons will remain secure through the winter, and not to the leaf-stalk where they would be blown down with the leaf. After thus fastening their bags, they line them with a good thickness of the same material, and resting awhile from their labors, at last cast their skins and become chrysalids. Hitherto the worms had all been alike, but now the sexes are distinguishable, the male chrysalis being but half the size of the female chrysalis. Three weeks afterwards [late August or early September] a still greater change takes places, the sexes differentiating still more. The male chrysalis works himself down to the end of his bag and, hanging halfway out, the skin bursts and the moth with a black body and glassy wings escapes, and when his wings are dry, soars through the air to seek his mate." The wingless female does not leave her case but, after laying her eggs within its protection, stops the opening with what little remains of her body and dies.

Oiketicus abboti of the South places short pieces of twigs across the bag, making a sort of log cabin.

EUCLEIDÆ

The larvæ of this family are curious, slug-like creatures, with almost nothing resembling legs. They crawl on their flattened bellies. Be careful about handling them if they have spines, as these are easily broken off and are extremely irritating things to get in one's skin. Other names that have been used for the family are Cochlidiidæ and Limacodidæ.

The Saddle-back larva (*Sibine stimulea*, Pl. 91) is often noticed by reason of its curious shape and color. It feeds on apple, pear, cherry, and other things, including corn. Its spines sting like nettles but the pain may be allayed by ammonia or bicarbonate of soda. The larva is fully grown in late summer and the adult flies during June and July. The cocoon is a smooth ovoid with the larval hairs, retaining their stinging power, imbedded in it.

See Pl. 91 for the adult Green Slug Moth, *Euclea* (or, possibly better, *Parasa*) *chloris*. The larva on a variety of trees and shrubs is bright scarlet with four blue-black lines along the back and with yellow prickles. Sometimes, possibly when a molt is due, the ground-color of the larva is brownish-yellow. The cocoon is dark brown, egg-shaped, smooth, and very thin. The larva hibernates in this cocoon, not changing to a pupa until spring. Adults fly in June and July.

Phobetron pithecium is called Hag Moth because the dark brown larva has eight relatively long, fleshy, hairy appendages that cover the back, project from the sides and have a backward twist like locks of disheveled hair. They are, in fact, fleshy hooks covered with feathery, brown hairs among which are longer, black, stinging hairs. The cocoon is almost spherical and is defended by the hairy appendages that the larva in some way contrives to leave on the outside. These tufts give to the bullet-shaped cocoon a nondescript appearance and the stinging hairs afford a very perfect protection against birds and other vertebrates. "Unlike other species of

Limacodidæ, the Hag Moth larvæ do not seek to hide away their cocoons, but attach them to leaves and twigs fully exposed to view, with, however, such artful management as to surroundings and harmonizing colors that they are, of all the group, most difficult to discover. A device to which this insect frequently resorts exhibits the extreme of instinctive sagacity. If the caterpillar can not find at hand a suitable place in which to weave its cocoon it frequently makes for itself more satisfactory surroundings by killing the leaves upon which, after they have become dry or brown in color, it places its cocoon" (Hubbard). The larva is a rather general feeder and has been found on most orchard trees as well as on wild trees and shrubs in late summer. The adults fly in midsummer. The female is brownish marked with yellow; the male is much like that of *T. ephemeræformis* (Pl. 91) but smaller.

MEGALOPYGIDÆ

It is the cocoon of the Crinkled Flannel Moth, *Megalopyge crispata,* that gets this family into the Question Box, and *crispata* is the only Northeastern species that is at all common. The larva feeds on raspberry, blackberry, apple and other leaves. Like other larvæ of this family, it is extra well provided with legs, having the usual three pairs on its thorax and seven pairs on its abdomen. It is an oval, very hairy affair; the hairs are brown and form a ridge along the larva's back, sloping off on each side. The tough oval cocoon is fastened to the side of a twig very securely indeed and here the creature hibernates. But what arouses one's interest is that when the moth emerges, about July, it does so by lifting a flat circular lid at one end of the cocoon. The adult is a soft, fluffy, yellowish moth, with a wing expanse of about 1.25 in. or a little more. The front wings have irregular brownish markings near the front margin and rows of fine, curly, hair-like scales. The body is thick and woolly.

PYROMORPHIDÆ

These are small, blackish moths, often with brilliant markings, some of the species having a red collar.

If you have ever seen the larvæ of *Harrisina americana* on the leaves of grapes or Virginia creeper (Pl. 91) you will recall the sight, but there are other larvæ that feed on other plants in the same orderly fashion. The pupæ are in white, oval, flattened cocoons. Some of the adults emerge after a pupal life of only about two weeks but other pupæ hibernate. The yellow eggs are laid in loose clusters of about 100 on the under side of the food-plant's leaves.

COSSIDÆ

The adults' appearance suggests Sphingidæ but they have a very small head and almost no tongue. Furthermore, they, especially the females, are very feeble fliers. All the strength seems to be in the larvæ, which bore in the wood of trees. The adults are sometimes called Goat Moths, presumably because of their odor.

The Leopard Moth, *Zeuzera pyrina,* is an undesirable but interesting immigrant from Europe that is still largely confined to New York. The adult male (Pl. 45) is only about two-thirds as large as its mate; the semitransparent wings are white, spotted with black. The grub-like larva is pale yellowish, sometimes pinkish, except for numerous brownish-black spots. They bore in almost any tree and in many shrubs. If the young larva starts, as it usually does, in a twig that is too small for its continued existence, it crawls out and bores into a larger branch. Larval life takes nearly two years. Pupation occurs about May in the last larval burrow and adults emerge during June and July. Each female places well on to 1,000 eggs in soft, young wood and in crevices of old bark.

We have also native species of Cossidæ, the most common probably being *Prionoxystus robiniæ*. Its larvæ bore chiefly in oaks but also in chestnut, poplar, willow, maple, ash and, as its name indicates, locust. The larva is bad-smelling, reaches a length of 2.5 in. and after about three years of eating wood spins a loose cocoon in its burrow. The female's wings expand about 2.5 in.; they are gray, with irregular black lines and spots. The male is scarcely more than half as large. His front wings are darker than the female's and his hind wings are yellowish.

ÆGERIIDÆ

It is said that Sesiidæ, the commonly used name of this family, must, according to the rules of the game, give way to Ægeriidæ. Those of you who are just starting are fortunate in not having to unlearn so many names. The wings of the Ægeriidæ are usually more or less transparent and the adults depart from the usual habits of moths in that they fly by day (See also *Hemaris*). Please do not take "mimicry" too seriously but I quote Lugger to give the idea. "Many of the species of moths belonging here are very beautiful, and most of them are remarkable on account of the protective mimicry exhibited by them. This close resemblance to insects of different orders was observed long before the significance of protective mimicry was understood. The majority of the Sesiidæ mimic bees, wasps and flies. We all know from experience that bees and wasps can advance some very pointed arguments to be left alone, and any other insect that closely mimics such well armed warriors is very apt to be left unmolested. This mimicry is not simply a superficial one, since even their motions, if captured or disturbed, are like those of the insects imitated. Their attitude when resting, the sounds they produce, their hyaline wings, their ringed body, even the odor they give off, all are apt to warn us and to caution us. Yet though they pretend to sting they lack the necessary organ for that purpose." The larvæ are all borers and, like most concealed larvæ, rather uniformly yellowish-white except for their hardened parts such as the head. To illustrate the life histories I have selected some of those species that may be living in our yards. There are many more afield.

The larva of *Melittia satyriniformis* will be found in almost any kind of Cucurb but prefers squash or pumpkin. It lives in the stems, causing them to rot. Sanderson states that as many as forty larvæ have been taken from one vine. When fully grown (about 1 in. long) the larva leaves the plant and, going an inch or two below

PLATE 45

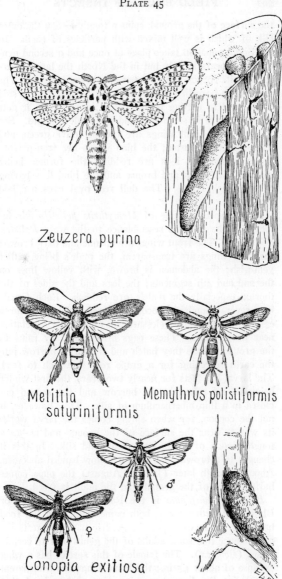

Zeuzera pyrina

Melittia
satyriniformis

Memythrus polistiformis

♂

♀

Conopia exitiosa

ELB

the surface of the ground, spins a tough cocoon the outer silk of which is well mixed with particles of earth. In the South pupation takes place at once and a second generation appears in July but in the North the larva hibernates in its cocoon and does not pupate until spring. The pupa has a horn-like process between its eyes that is said to be used in cutting the cocoon. At any rate, it gets to the surface in some way and the adult emerges. See Pl. 45. The front wings are opaque, olive green, and have a metallic luster; the hind wings are transparent; the abdomen and legs are reddish, the former being marked with black and bronze and the hind legs having a long black fringe. The dull red, oval eggs are laid singly.

As the specific name of *Memythrus polistiformis* indicates, it bears some resemblance to the wasp *Polistes*. See Pl. 45. The front wings are opaque and dark brown; the hind wings are transparent, the male's being rather yellowish; the abdomen is brown, with yellow lines on the 2nd and 4th segments; the legs and the sides of the thorax, especially the male's, are reddish. Each female lays several hundred chocolate-colored, finely sculptured eggs with apparent carelessness on almost any vegetation near grape vines. These eggs are washed by rains to the ground, where they hatch and the larvæ burrow into the earth searching for a grape root in which to feed. The larval life lasts for nearly two years, the first winter being passed naked in the burrow and the second enclosed in a thin hibernaculum of silk. This, however, is not the cocoon, for when spring comes the larva works its way to near the surface of the ground and makes a tough cocoon of earth, excrement, and silk. In this it changes to a brown pupa with a yellow-banded abdomen. About a month later (July or August) the pupa comes half-way out of the ground and the adult is freed.

Bembecia marginata is the Raspberry Root-borer or Blackberry Crown-borer, both names indicating the food habits of the larva, while the generic name suggests the resemblance that some adults of the genus bear to certain wasps (*Bembex*). The female of this species has a wing expanse of about 1.5 in.; the front wings are transparent except for the brown margins, tips, and a band that crosses each wing at about ⅔ of the distance from the base to the tips; the hind wings are altogether transparent, except, of course, for the veins and the outer fringe; the abdomen is banded with brownish-black and yellow, the former color predominating in front, the latter behind; the legs are largely yellow. The male is somewhat smaller than his mate and his abdomen has less yellow at the hind end. The adults emerge in, usually, late summer. Eggs are laid on the canes close to the ground. The larvæ, on hatching, crawl down the stem and hibernate under the bark just below the surface of the ground. In the spring they start to bore into the roots or the base of the plant, often girdling it. They spend the second winter in their burrows and the following spring work upward in the plant to a point above ground where, just inside the bark, they pupate. About a month later each pupa cuts the bark with its "horn," crawls partly out, and the adult emerges to mate and start the history anew.

The Peach-tree Borer (*Conopia exitiosa,* Pl. 45) once lived just outside my back door but I was not philosophical enough to enjoy its neighborliness. At that time its generally accepted generic name was *Sanninoidea.* I have seen an estimate of $6,000,000 for the annual damage done by this species—not all on my lot, of course. This moth ought to have stuck to wild cherries and plums, which are believed to have been its original food, although it feeds also on willow. The afflicted trees display distress signals by exuding large masses of gum where the larvæ are working, which is usually near the surface of the soil. The insect passes the winter as a half-grown larva. After attaining its full growth early the next season, the larva usually leaves its burrow and makes its unkempt cocoon of excrement, pieces of bark, gum, and silk on the trunk of the tree or on the ground. About a month later (which may be from June, or earlier in the South, to September) the adult appears. It has a wing expanse of an inch or more but the sexes differ markedly in appearance. The female is dark steel blue (sometimes with a reddish glint) except for the transparent hind wings and the orange band that covers the fourth and, in the North, the fifth abdominal segments. The male's wings are transparent, with blue edgings and blue cross-bands like those of *marginata;* the body is blue, banded with white or light yellow. Each female lays from 200 to 800 eggs about 0.02 in. long and much the color of the bark on which they are placed. I have never seen them but, according to the pictures, they are very pretty. I admit that the adults also are pretty. There is a generation every year. This species does damage wherever peaches are grown in this country, although it is an Eastern species. On the Pacific Coast it is joined in the work of destruction by *opalescens.*

We can blame *Conopia tipuliformis* on Europe but it is now well naturalized, having been here for about a hundred generations. It occurs also in Asia and Australia. We might expect from its name that it is very long-legged like Tipulidæ, but it is not. Both sexes have both pairs of wings transparent except for the golden markings, with purple reflections. The body is dark purple, with three yellow abdominal bands on the female and four on the male. The brown, spherical eggs are placed singly on currant stems and the larvæ work up or down the pith. The larvæ hibernate when nearly full-grown; pupate the following spring in a silk-lined cavity just under the bark; and adults emerge during June and July. There is one generation a year.

The work of *Conopia pictipes* in peach trees is often confused with that of *exitiosa,* but *pictipes* prefers old trees with rough bark and it works more often in the upper trunk and large branches than at the base of a tree. Its cocoon is similar to that of *exitiosa* but smaller. The adults of both sexes resemble the male *exitiosa* but are smaller. They fly during June and July. It is said that this species attacks June-berry and chestnut in addition to those "favored" by *exitiosa* but it rarely does much damage to any.

PYRALIDIDÆ

This is a large family of small moths and, although a number of the species are somewhat expensive to the farmer, he often does not know what is the matter.

The group does not seem to be a "popular" one. The following are samples of some of the subfamilies.

PYRAUSTINÆ

The wings are rather thinly scaled. Most of the species are yellow and white. The larvæ usually live in webs, sometimes gregariously.

The European Corn-borer, *Pyrausta nubilalis,* found its way to this country from Europe, probably in shipments of broom-corn about 1910, and has become a very serious pest. It was discovered in 1917 infesting corn near Boston. The mature larva is about an inch long, flesh-colored, often somewhat smoky or reddish dorsally; head dark brown; each abdominal segment has a cross-row of four dark spots, in each of which is a short, stout spine, and behind each row are two smaller spots. The insect has only one brood a year in some places; in others adults not only appear in May from larvæ that have overwintered in old stalks and pupated in the spring but there is another generation in midsummer. The larvæ bore almost anywhere in the corn plant: in the tassel-stalk, causing it to break; in the main stem, lowering the vitality of the plant; and in the ear, spoiling it for us. Unfortunately, because this fact makes the insect more difficult to control, it breeds in also a great variety of weeds.

The adult of the Grape Leaf-folder, *Desmia funeralis,* does not have the rather typical coloration of the sub-family. It is brownish-black, with two white spots on each front wing and one (sometimes divided on the female) on each hind wing. The larva feeds on the upper surface of a grape leaf, folding the leaf and fastening it by strands of silk. Pupation takes place in the fold. The pupæ of the second annual generation hibernate in their retreats, fallen to the ground.

Loxostege similalis is sometimes called Garden Web-worm but it is more at home on weeds than on garden plants. The markings of the yellowish and grayish-brown adult are difficult to describe. The thing that is apt to attract attention is the black-spotted, yellow larvæ in their fine web, which encloses skeletonized leaves. They pupate in silk-lined underground cells.

Larvæ of *Phlyctænia theseusalis* web tips of ferns.

NYMPHULINÆ

Small, for the most part brightly colored species, with narrow wings, the front pair being more or less angular. Many of the larvæ live on water plants and are semi-aquatic. Their life histories are probably interesting but have not been carefully studied. The young larvæ may have gills. The larvæ of *Nymphula obliteralis* live in cases on the leaves of greenhouse aquatics.

PYRALIDINÆ

This subfamily contains some rather troublesome species such as the Meal Snout-moth, *Pyralis farinalis*. The larva eats cereals, flour, and clover hay. It is whitish, a bit darkened at the ends, and has a reddish head. It lives in a long tube made by fastening food material together with silk. Pupation occurs in a cocoon outside of the tube. The adult has a wing expanse of about 0.75 in. It may be recognized by the front wings, which have chocolate-colored bases and tips, separated from the light-brown central area by curved white lines. It is rather generally distributed by commerce. There are from two to four generations a year, depending on temperature and other conditions.

The larva of *Hypsopygia costalis* is the Clover-hay Worm and is sometimes injurious.

CRAMBINÆ

The narrow front wings are sometimes drawn to a point and are usually whitish, ornamented with golden or silvery scales; the hind wings are broad and without markings; the palpi are very long. When at rest, the wings are wrapped so closely to the body that the moths look like small cylinders. The larvæ lie in silken tubes just above or below the surface of the ground.

The larvæ of *Prionapteryx nebulifera* in the Jersey pine barrens makes a tube of silk and sand leading from

PLATE 46

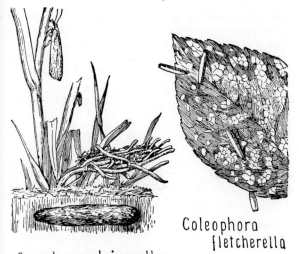

Crambus vulvivagellus

Coleophora
fletcherella

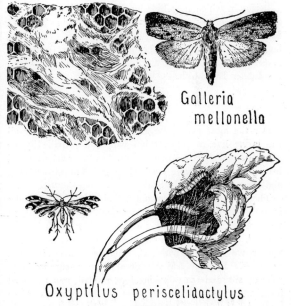

Galleria
mellonella

Oxyptilus periscelidactylus

an underground retreat to the leaves of sand-myrtle and huckleberry upon which it feeds. At night it carries pieces of leaves to its retreat for daytime meals.

Most of the larvæ of *Crambus* feed on grasses. That of *C. vulvivagellus* (The Vagabond, Pl. 46) is sometimes very destructive, feeding by night and retiring by day to a tube of cut grass and silk just below the surface of the ground. *C. caliginosellus* has similar habits, injuring young corn and, especially in the South, tobacco.

Larvæ of *Chilo plejadellus* bore in the stems of rice and allied plants.

GALLERIINÆ

The adult Bee Moth (*Galleria mellonella,* Pl. 46) has purplish-brown front wings and pale brown or yellowish hind ones. The female probably enters the bee-hives at night and lays her eggs while the bees are asleep for, when awake, they resent her presence. The larvæ feed by night on the wax of the combs. They make silken galleries in which they hide by day. The tough cocoons are usually placed against the side of the hive. The Bee Moth is found almost everywhere that honeybees are kept but its original home, probably Asia, is unknown. *Achroia grisella,* having much the same habits, is called the Lesser Bee Moth.

PHYCITINÆ

For the most part these are a silky gray. Nearly all the larvæ live in silken tubes which they make in the stems of plants, in seeds, in flower heads, or in crumpled leaves. *Lætilia coccidivora* feeds on the Tulip Soft Scale and the Cottony Maple Scale.

There are many leaf-crumplers but *Mineola indiginella* is apt to be noticed on home grounds. It has not been troublesome since spraying for the Codling Moth became general. The larvæ feed on apple, plum and cherry. In winter we can find withered, crumpled leaves fastened to twigs. If these leaves conceal a larva encased in a tube of silk and frass looking like a small, much-twisted horn, we probably have this species. In the spring, after

banquets on young leaves, the larva pupates in its case
and the adult, with silver-marked, pale brown, front
wings, emerges about July. *M. vaccinii* is the Cranberry
Fruit-worm.

Larvæ of *Acrobasis demotella* bore into the ends of
walnut twigs; *A. angusella,* into hickory leaf stems; *A.
caryæ,* into the twigs of hickory; of *A. rubrifasciella*
live in cases between leaves of hazel and alder; *A.
betulella,* in tubes between birch leaves; *A. comptoniella,*
in cases between the terminal leaves of *Comptonia* and
Myrica.

The Mediterranean Flour Moth, *Ephestia kuehniella,*
was first noticed in America about 1889. It is now rather
widely distributed in flour, "feed," and cereals. The
cylindrical larva is the color of pink flesh, with sparse,
long hairs and a reddish-brown head. Not only do the
larvæ destroy by eating, but they also spin threads as they
move about, so that the material in which they are becomes thoroughly mixed with webs. The larvæ are
sometimes so abundant in flour mills that the spouts and
machinery become clogged with silk. The thin cocoons
often have foreign material imbedded in the silk. The
wing expanse is somewhat less than an inch; the front
wings are dark gray crossed by wavy lines, the V-shaped
marks near the bases making a W when the wings are
closed; the hind wings are silvery gray; both wings are
fringed with hairs. Breeding continues throughout the
winter in warm places, giving as many as four or five
generations a year.

The common name, Indian-meal Moth, of *Plodia in-
terpunctella* is not inclusive enough, for the larva is fond
of all sorts of stored foods, including nuts and raisins.
It was called Indian-meal Moth by Fitch, who found it
in cornmeal in 1856. The larva can usually be distinguished from those of similar habits by a pale line that
divides the brown thoracic shield in halves. It is an active
creature that goes backward about as well as forward
and spins a web wherever it goes. The cocoon is usually
placed in a crack or corner. The wing expanse is a
little more than half an inch; the front wings are creamy
white at their bases and reddish brown, marked with
black, beyond; the hind wings are dingy gray, fringed

with long hairs. There are three or more generations a year, depending largely on temperature.

Larvæ of *Dioryctria zimmermanni* bore in pine; *Melitara prodenialis,* in "leaves" of prickly pear (*Opuntia*); *Zophodia grossulariæ,* in gooseberries; *Euzophera semifuneralis,* under bark of plum and cherry.

PTEROPHORIDÆ

If I should ever take up Lepidoptera as a hobby, I might be tempted to specialize on these delicate Plume Moths. The small, long-legged adults may be recognized by the fact that their wings, at least the hind ones, are so split as to form plumes. The larvæ suggest miniature Arctiids but, in addition to structural differences, they may be distinguished from Woolly-bears by their habit of living in tubes and loose webs. The pupæ are soft, hairy, and hang by their tails like butterfly chrysalids, although a few make an attempt at constructing cocoons. The family is not a large one. Less than twenty species have been recorded from New Jersey.

Oxyptilus periscelidactylus is shown on Pl. 46. Once again we quote from Riley: "The larva of the Grape-vine Plume invariably hatches soon after the leaves begin to expand; and though it is very generally called the Leaf-folder (from the fact that the larvæ live in a nest made by folding several leaves together), it must not be confounded with the true Leaf-folder [*Psychomorpha epimenis* of the Noctuidæ], which does its principal damage later in the season. At first the larva of our Plume is smooth and almost destitute of hairs, but after each moult the hairs become more perceptible, and when full grown the larva has hairs arising from a transverse row of warts, each joint having four above and six below the breathing pores. After feeding for about three weeks, our little worm fastens itself securely by the hind legs to the underside of some leaf or other object, and, casting its hairy skin, transforms to the pupa state. This pupa, with the lower part of the three or four terminal joints attached to a little silk previously spun by the worm, hangs at a slant of about

40°. It is of peculiar and characteristic form, being ridged and angular, with numerous projections, and having remnants of the larval warts; it is obliquely truncated at the head, but is chiefly distinguished by two compressed sharp-pointed horns; it measures, on the average, rather more than one-third inch, and varies in color from light green, with darker green shadings, to pale straw-color with light brown shadings. . . . The moth escapes from this pupa in about one week, and, like all the species belonging to this genus, it has a very active and impetuous flight, and rests with the wings closed and stretched at right angles from the body, so as to recall the letter T. It is of a tawny yellow color, the front wings marked with white and dark brown, the hind wings appearing like burnished copper, and the legs being alternately banded with white and tawny yellow."

We have, in the Northeast, a species of a related family, ORNEODIDÆ. It is called *Orneodes hexadactyla,* each wing being divided into "six fingers," making twenty-four in all.

TORTRICIDÆ

Like Pyralididæ, this is a large family of small moths. It gets its name from the habit that many of its members have of rolling leaves in order that they may have a sheltered place in which to feed. However, not all Tortricid larvæ roll leaves and not all leaf-rollers are Tortricids. The front wings are rather broad and usually square-cut at the outer end. When at rest, the wings are folded against the body. The following are examples of the principal subfamilies.

EUCOSMINÆ

The worm of many wormy grapes is the larva of *Polychrosis viteana.* If no accident, such as being eaten by humans, happens to this larva it leaves the grape berry and goes to a leaf. There it cuts a little flap, pulls the flap over and fastens it down to the main leaf with silk. The inside is then lined with silk and within this snug retreat the larva pupates. When this is done near the middle of the leaf two flaps are cut and drawn together to make the shelter. Finally, frost drops the leaf, and winter is passed on the ground. The first annual generation of adults emerges about June first. They are purplish-brown moths with a wing expanse of somewhat less than half an inch. The first-generation larvæ feed on grape blossoms and young grapes, making a slight web about them. They pupate and the second-generation adults emerge in midsummer. Occasionally there is a third generation.

Many of us have heard of the Codling Moth or Apple Worm (*Carpocapsa pomonella,* Pl. 47) and most of us have bitten into its larval galleries. Like the majority of our insect pests, it came from Europe; in its case, about 1750. In 1909 Quaintance estimated that it destroyed annually $12,000,000 worth of fruit and that $4,000,000 were expended annually in attempts to control it, not counting the salaries of professional entomologists and other small items! Mature larvæ pass the winter in cocoons placed, usually, on trunks of trees and rendered less conspicuous by having bits of bark mixed with the silk. The larvæ pupate in the spring, sometimes first leaving their hibernacula to spin new, thinner cocoons and at other times merely breaking open the hibernacula and closing them again with thin layers of silk through which the pupæ can push in order to free the adults. These adults fly just after apple-blossom time. They are well described by Slingerland and Crosby: "The front wings have the general appearance of watered silk, this effect being produced by alternating irregular lines of brown and bluish gray. Near the hind angle is a large, light brown area bounded on the inner side by an irregular chocolate brown band and crossed by two similar bands of metallic coppery or golden color in certain lights. The hind wings are coppery brown, darker towards the margin. The sexes are very similar, but the male may be distinguished by the presence of an elongate dark area on the underside of the fore wing and a pencil of black hairs on the upper surface of the hind wings." The scale-like eggs, about half the size of a pin-head, are usually laid on the leaves and then is the time for us to start spraying because the larvæ take a few mouthfuls of foliage before they bore into the young fruit. This generation usually goes in at the blossom end of the apple but later generations often go in at the side. In any case, it is not so much the amount of apple they eat that worries us as it is the difficulty in missing their excrement-filled burrows and themselves when we eat the fruit. Most of the larvæ leave their burrows before the apple falls and then they crawl down the limb to a suitable place for making a cocoon. There are from one to three, or, more, generations a year, depending on the climate. While this is distinctly an apple-worm, it feeds also on pears, quinces and even English walnuts. It is found nearly everywhere that apples are grown.

Mexican "jumping beans" are usually seeds of a species of Croton that contain wriggling larvæ of *Carpocapsa saltitans*. Kellogg says that another Tortricid larva, *Grapholitha sebastianiæ*, has similar habits.

Larvæ of the genus *Rhyacionia* feed in the shoots or bark of pines and hibernate in the shoots or in the masses of exuded resin.

The following mere samples of larval doings will give at least some idea of the multiple activities of one subfamily of moths. *Cymolomia exoleta* crumples gooseberry leaves; *C. inornatana* crumples wild cherry leaves. *Olethreutes dæckeana*, in stalks and leaves of pitcher plants (*Sarracenia*); *O. cyanana*, in rose shoots; *O. hebesana*, in seed pods of Tigridia, Iris, and other plants; *O. hemidesma* binds together leaves and makes galleries in flower spikes of *Spiræa; O. chionosema* twists apple leaves. *Pseudogalleria inimicella*, in stems of cat-briar (*Smilax*). *Eucosma cataclystiana*, in stems of rag-weed (*Ambrosia*); *E. strenuana*, makes spindle-shaped galls in *Ambrosia* stems; *E. otiosana*, in stems of beggar-ticks (*Bidens*); *E. suffusana* (an introduced European species), in flower buds and on young leaves of cultivated roses; *E. juncticiliana*, in goldenrod stems; *E. dorsisignatana*, in roots of the same; *E. nisella* in willow catkins; *E. scudderiana, desertana,* and possibly *obfuscana*, in galls on the stems of goldenrod but the galls themselves are probaby made by *Gnorimoschema gallæsolidaginis. Epiblema tripartitana,* in Cecidomyid galls on stems of Black-eyed Susan (*Rudbeckia*). *Epinotia signatana,* in tubes of silk and excrement under a web on underside of maple leaves; *E. timidella,* in similar tubes on underside of oak leaves. *Episimus argutanus* twists leaflets of sumac and leaves of other plants into a cone or spiral tube. *Proteoteras æsculanum,* in stems of horse-chestnut leaves. *Enarmonia piceafoliana* and *ratzeburgiana* mine spruce needles; *E. pyricolana,* in rosebuds. *Ancylis comptana* rolls strawberry (chiefly), blackberry and raspberry leaves; *A. platanana* makes tents between veins of underside of sycamore leaves. *Laspeyresia caryana,* on hulls of hickory and walnut; *L. prunivora,* in thorn apples (*Cratægus*); *L. nigricana,* in pods of cultivated peas. *Ecydytolopha insiticiana,* in gall-like swellings in twigs of locust. *Mellisopus latiferreana,* in fallen acorns. *Rhopobota vacciniana,* the Vine-worm or Blackhead, on cranberry. *Spilonota ocellana,* in buds of apple and other fruit trees. *Phthinolophus indentanus* webs leaves of huckleberry and bayberry.

TORTRICINÆ

Peronea minuta is the Fire-worm or Yellow-head of the cranberry. *Cenopis saracana* crumples leaves of sassafras; *C. testulana* fastens together wild cherry leaves. *Archips fervidana* makes nests on oak and cherry, sometimes "thousands" joining together and webbing up an entire bush or small tree. The larvæ of *A. rosana* (Pl. 47) feed on the leaves of currant and other small fruits, orchard and shade trees. Larvæ of *Eulia pinatubana* live in tubes made by fastening together the needles of white pine and then feed on the outer ends. And so on.

We now come to a series of families that contain "really rightly" *micro-lepidoptera,* but, as Smith said, "many of them are veritable gems of beauty, far ex-

PLATE 47

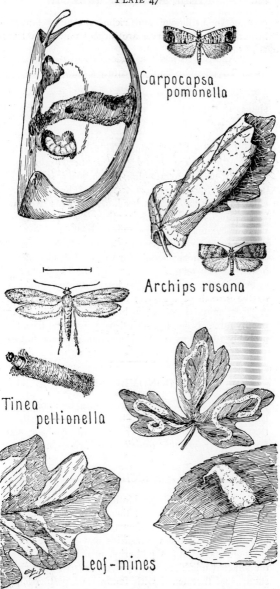

Carpocapsa
pomonella

Archips rosana

Tinea
pellionella

Leaf-mines

ceeding in brilliancy and richness their relatives of larger size." The larvæ are largely miners in leaves;

> "And there's never a blade nor leaf too mean
> To be some happy creature's palace."

Some larvæ of other orders also are leaf miners. The shape of the mine, as seen through the leaf, and the kind of leaf it is in are frequently quite characteristic of a given species. See Pl. 47. The long, narrow and more or less winding mines are called "linear mines." Some of these are very narrow at their beginning and gradually enlarge, resembling in outline a serpent; frequently the larger end is terminated by a blotch-like enlargement suggesting a head. Such mines are termed "serpentine mines." Other mines that start from a narrow beginning enlarge more rapidly and extend in a more or less regular curve; these are "trumpet mines." The mines of many species are mere disk-like blotches; hence, "blotch mines." In some of the blotch mines the epidermis of one side of the leaf is thrown into a fold by the growth of the leaf; these are "tentiform mines." A "tract mine" is merely a broad linear one. A "community mine" is one in which there are several larvæ; it is probably formed by several blotch mines running together.

YPONOMEUTIDÆ

Larvæ of *Plutella maculipennis* are common on cabbage and other crucifers. The pupæ can be easily seen through the delicate, lacy cocoons on cabbage stalks. Larvæ of *Argyresthia thuiella* mine arbor-vitæ leaves.

GELECHIIDÆ

The Angoumois Grain Moth, *Sitotroga cerealella*, is another pestiferous importation from Europe and "receives its name from the fact that in 1760 it was found to swarm in all the wheat-fields and granaries of Angoumois and of the neighboring provinces [of France], the afflicted inhabitants being deprived of their principal staple, and threatened with famine and pestilence from want of wholesome bread." It apparently landed in North Carolina about 1730. The larva feeds on seeds of cereals and the like. It hibernates as a larva wrapped in silk and pupates in the spring. The adult, which resembles the ordinary Clothes Moth, emerges in May or June and oviposits on young seed heads. There are two or three generations a year.

Larvæ of *Metzneria lapella* feed on seeds of burdock, hibernating in the burs. Those of *Telphusa belangerella* are rollers of alder leaves. Larvæ of various species of *Recurvaria* live in leaves of spruce, hemlock, juniper and arbor vitæ. Those of *Paralechia pinifoliella* mine pine needles. *Phthorimæa operculella* mines stored potatoes. *Gnorimoschema gallæsolidaginis* makes spindle-shaped, gall-like swellings in goldenrod (*Solidago*) stems; *G. busckiella* and *gallæasteriella* make galls in aster stems. *Anacampsis innocuella,* in curled leaves of poplar; *A. lupinella,* in folded-together leaves of *Lupinus perennis. Gelechia serotinella* fastens together the edges of a wild cherry leaf and lives within a tube of silk and frass placed in the fold.

XYLORICTIDÆ

Adults of *Stenoma,* when at rest, resemble gray and white bird-droppings.

ŒCOPHORIDÆ

Larvæ of *Eumeyrickia trimaculella* feed in decayed spruce stumps. Adults of *Agonopteryx* and *Depressaria* often hibernate in outhouses, piles of brush and the like. Larvæ of *A. pulvipennella,* in leaves, folded lengthwise, of *Solidago* and *Eupatorium;* of *A. robinella,* in similarly folded leaves of locust. Larvæ of *D. cinereocostella* fasten together leaves of water parsnip.

BLASTOBASIDÆ

Smith wrote: "These moths are usually small in size with a peculiar sheen to the prevailing gray shade of the forewings. The favorite time for flight is an hour before sundown, when sometimes hundreds can be taken.

The larvæ live in seeds, nuts, and buds, as well as Aphid
and Kermid galls." And in connection with *Valentinia
glandulella:* "Almost every acorn found on the ground
in midwinter contains one or more of the larvæ of this
species, often in company with a Tortricid and a Coleopterous larva."

COLEOPHORIDÆ

Coleophora.—Quoting Smith again (Most of the short
notes that I give concerning moths are culled from
his *Insects of New Jersey*): "As many of the species
in the adult stage are indistinguishable from each other,
the only reliable way to identify them is by breeding.
The larvæ are all case-makers, the cases distinctive for
each species. In shape they range from slender flattened
cylinders to one made of clusters of flowers. Almost
every plant supports one or more species, many are
confined to grasses, and others live in seed heads. In
general, the life histories are similar; eggs are laid in
summer, the larva makes a small case in which it hibernates in the next to the last stage. In the earliest days
of spring it resumes feeding for a few weeks, moths
issuing May to July." The cases may be found during
the winter attached to trunks and larger limbs. When
the trees leaf out, the larvæ move to the leaves. *C.
caryæfoliella:* cylindrical, dark brown cases on hickory.
C. corylifoliella: case flattened, with serrate edges, on
hazel. *C. fletcherella:* small, dark brown flattened case
on apple (Pl. 46). *C. laricella:* small, dark brown case
on larch. *C. limosipennella:* flat case, with serrate upper
edge, on elm. *C. malivorella:* black, pistol-shaped case
on apple. *C. pruniella:* large, black, pistol-shaped case
on wild cherry. *C. ostryæ:* reddish-brown, flat case on
ironwood. *C. querciella:* scimiter-case, front two-thirds
white, the rest black, on oak. *C. vagans:* grayish, cylindrical case on grass. *C. viburnella:* flat, brown case
with upper edge serrated, on *Viburnum.*

LAVERNIDÆ

Larvæ of *Batrachedra salicipomonella* live in Cecidomyid and Tenthredinid galls on willow leaves.

HELIOZELIDÆ

Antispila cornifoliella makes blotch mines in *Cornus* leaves; *A. viticordifoliella,* orange-colored blotch mines in wild grape leaves. The larvæ of *Coptodisca* are leaf-miners and some, at least, pupate in a case which they cut from the epidermis of a leaf and attach to a tree trunk. *C. lucifluella,* on hickory; *C. ostryæfoliella,* on ironwood; *C. saliciella,* on willow; *C. splendoriferella,* on *Cratægus,* apple, plum, and wild cherry.

TINEOIDEA

The family Tineidæ has now been split into a galaxy of families. Since the names of these are not likely to interest many of you, let us be content with notes on the superfamily as a whole. Most of the larvæ are leaf-miners, their life being passed in tunnels between the upper and under surfaces of a single leaf, which, however, they usually desert to pupate in a tough cocoon on a twig or on the ground.

Species of *Nepticula* are among the smallest of Lepidoptera, some having a wing expanse of not over 0.12 inch. *N. amelanchierella,* broad mines in leaves of June-berry (*Amelanchier*); *N. anguinella,* narrow, serpentine mines in oak leaves. *N. saginella,* moderately broad, serpentine mines in oak and chestnut leaves. *N. caryæfoliella,* very narrow, whitish mines in hickory leaves. *N. corylifoliella,* long, narrow, winding mines in hazel leaves; *N. juglandifoliella,* narrow, whitish mines in walnut leaves; *N. platanella,* large irregular, blotch mines on under side of sycamore leaves. *N. ostryæfoliella,* moderately wide, tract mines in ironwood leaves; *N. platea,* moderately wide, winding mines in oak leaves; *N. pomivorella,* in apple leaves; *N. prunifoliella,* narrow mines in wild cherry leaves; *N. rosæfoliella,* serpentine mines in rose leaves; *N. rubifoliella,* blotch mines, and *villosella,* narrow linear mines in blackberry leaves.

Bucculatrix larvæ are leaf-miners when young but later feed externally. They hibernate in slender cocoons which have longitudinal ridges and are usually fastened to the trunks or large limbs of trees.

The larvæ of *Lithocolletis* are leaf-miners and there are many species. The "samples" given here represent a very small part of merely the Northeastern fauna. Oak, especially, is largely omitted since it harbors so many species that make similar mines. OAK: *cincinnatiella*, large community mines on the under side of leaves; *conglomeratella*, leathery, brown blotch mines on upper side; *tubiferella*, long, sinuate, band-like mines, gradually increasing in width and frequently crossing, on the upper side of leaves. CHESTNUT: *macrocarpella*, upper side of leaves (also on oak?); *kearfottella*, narrow mines on under side, usually along a vein. MAPLE: *lucidicostella*, on under side; *saccharella*, irregular blotch mines on upper side; *aceriella*, broad tract mines on upper side of leaves. BIRCH: *betulivora*, small, nearly circular mine on upper side; *lentella*, community mines on upper side of leaves. LOCUST: *ostensackenella*, yellow blotch mines on both surfaces of leaves; there are other, more common ones but they are hard to differentiate. HICKORY: *caryæfoliella*, upper side of leaves. BASSWOOD: *lucetiella*, under side; *tiliacella*, nearly circular tent mines on upper side of leaves. ELM: *argentinotella*, under side; *ulmella*, irregular blotch mines on upper side of leaves. POPLAR: *salicifoliella*, under side of leaves (this species and others occur on willow); *populiella*, very small tent mine on under side of leaf. ALDER: *auronitens*, rounded, flattened mines on under side of leaves. HAZEL: *corylisella*, blotch mines on upper side of leaves. WITCH-HAZEL: *hamameliella*, whitish blotch mine on upper side of leaves. APPLE: *malimalifoliella*, small, much wrinkled, tent mine on the under side of leaves; there are others. HONEYSUCKLE (*Lonicera*): *fragilella*, under side of leaves. POISON IVY: *guttifinitella*, upper side of leaves. This very incomplete list might well give us many humble thoughts. What a world of creatures, each as important in its way as we in ours, and each doing its appointed task in the appointed way!

Larvæ of *Gracilaria* are all leaf-miners when young. Some leave the mines when half-grown and form cones by twisting and rolling the end of a leaf.

Larvæ of *Parectopa lespedezæfoliella* mine leaves of bush clover (*Lespedeza*).

The larvæ of *Ornix* or *Parornix* turn over the edge of a leaf, forming a flap, three or four often being present on one leaf. *O. guttea* (abundant) on apple; *kalmiella,* on sheep laurel (*Kalmia*); *preciosella,* on swamp huckleberry; *cratægifoliella,* on black thorn; *conspicuella,* on birch; *prunivorella,* on wild cherry; *quadripunctella,* on chokecherry. *Marmara salictella* mines long lines in the tender inner bark of young willows. *Proleucoptera smilaciella* makes blotch mines in leaves of cat-brier (*Smilax*); pupæ in hammock-like cocoons on under side of leaves. Species of *Phyllocnistis* make long, winding, thread-like mines in leaves: *ampelopsiella,* of Virginia creeper; *vitifoliella,* of grape; *liriodendrella,* of tulip tree. *Tischeria citrinipennella* makes trumpet-shaped mines in oak leaves; *quercitella,* dentate mines on upper side of oak leaves; *solidaginifoliella* mine goldenrod leaves; *malifoliella* make yellowish-brown blotch mines in apple leaves; *ænea,* funnel-shaped blotch mines in blackberry leaves.

The larvæ of *Setomorpha insectella,* an almost cosmopolitan species, feed on hair and other dry animal products, but, in America at least, do not often become injurious in houses.

Larvæ of *Xylesthia pruniramiella,* in woody excrescences on plum trees.

The larvæ of *Tinea* feed on rotten wood, fungi, dry animal products, and the like. There have been more than a dozen species recorded from New Jersey alone, although the adults have very secretive habits.

There are three species of Clothes Moths (See also Buffalo-bugs), each belonging to a different genus but all are Tineids and all are Old World species which have long been associated with man, "corrupting" his treasures.

Tinea pellionella (Pl. 47) has a case-making larva, the case being cylindrical, about as long as the larva. Herrick writes: "The young larva, of course, soon finds its case too small and, as it grows, it has to enlarge the case from time to time. This enlargement is done in a very interesting manner. Without emerging from its case, the larva cuts a slit halfway down one side, thus forming a triangular opening. Into this opening it inserts a triangular gore of the woolen material upon which it is feeding. This process is repeated on the opposite side of the case and without leaving its retreat it turns around and repeats the same thing on the other half of the case. Thus the case is enlarged in diameter, but it remains for the larva to lengthen its home. This is done by additions to each end of the case. On the outside the case appears to be composed of fibers of the material upon which the larva has been feeding, but inside the case is lined with a soft layer of fine silk. By transferring the larva to different colored materials a curiously parti-colored case may be obtained, for the insect will use the various materials for the enlargements. The larva completes its growth by fall and seeks a secluded place in which to secrete itself and spend the winter in a torpid condition. The larvæ have been observed to leave the carpets upon which they were feeding and drag their cases up a wall fifteen feet high and fasten them to the ceiling. In the spring, the larvæ transform to pupæ in the cases within which they have lived during the winter." About three weeks later the moths emerge. They have a wing expanse of about half an inch; the front wings are shining, yellowish brown, with indistinct dark spots; the hind wings are lighter and plain; both pairs are fringed with long hairs.

The second species, *Tineola biselliella,* has a webbing larva. It makes no case but feeds, naked, usually in a fold or crevice of the material it is eating and often under the web of silk that it spins wherever it goes. The cocoon is an irregular affair of silk and food material, somewhat resembling the case of *pellionella.* The adult is about the size of *pellionella;* the front wings are yellower and without spots; the hind wings are pale.

The third species, *Trichophaga tapetezella,* is, as yet, rather rare in America. Mr. Wm. T. Davis has bred it from larvæ in barn-owl pellets, but the larvæ are usually found in fur robes and woolens. The larvæ burrow into their food material, making silk-lined galleries, within which they eventually pupate. The adults have a wing expanse of about 0.75 in.; the bases of the front wings are black, the rest being white, clouded with gray; the hind wings are light gray; the head bears long white hairs.

Larvæ of *Prodoxus intermedius* bore in stalks of *Yucca* in great numbers.

Pronuba yuccasella.—"No discovery in recent years has been more interesting to students of insects and plant life than that which was made in 1872 by Professor Riley, of the intimate relationship which subsists between the beautiful plants, known as Yuccas, and the genus of moths to which the present species belongs. It has been ascertained that the fructification of the various species of Yucca is almost absolutely dependent upon the agency of the female moth; and, strangely enough, it has also been ascertained that the pollination of the flowers is not the result of mere accidental attrition of the wings and other organs of the insect when engaged in seeking for nectar in the flower and when engaged in laying her eggs, but that she deliberately collects the pollen with her mouth, which is peculiarly modified to enable her to do this, and then applies the pollen to the stigma with infinitely better care than it could be done by the most skillful horticulturist using the most delicate human appliances" (Holland). The moth's actions are not altogether altruistic for she lays her eggs in the seed capsules and her young feed on the tissue that would not develop if she did not pollinate. When full-grown, the larva crawls out and hibernates in a tough cocoon on or in the ground, pupating when spring comes. The generic name may, unfortunately, be changed to *Tegeticula*.

MICROPTERYGOIDEA

The HEPIALIDÆ (Ghost Moths) and MICROPTERYGIDÆ are rare moths closely related to Trichoptera (p. 112). The larvæ of some, at least, of the Hepialidæ bore in roots; those of Micropterygidæ are usually leaf-miners.

DIPTERA

See p. 39. Members of this order are Mosquitoes, Gnats, and Flies. The last name is applied, with modifying adjectives, to many other insects; but true flies never have more than one pair of wings. The pair of small, knobbed organs, called balancers or halteres, just back of these wings represents a second pair of wings. The scale-like affairs above the halteres and back of the roots of the wings are called squamæ or calypteres; there may be two pairs, one pair, or none. An alula is a small lobe sometimes present at the base of a wing. Eggs of Diptera are sometimes called nits; the larvæ are called maggots, wrigglers, or bots. Pupation often occurs inside the larval skin. About 10,000 species are already described from North America.

The venation of the wings and the arrangement of the thoracic bristles are important in classification; also the antennæ, which vary greatly from group to group. Unfortunately there are several systems of names for the veins and cells of the wings but the following (See Pl. 53) is in rather general use.

The vein that forms the front margin of, and runs for a variable distance around, the wing is the costa (or marginal). The next vein back of it is the auxiliary (subcosta). Then come the longitudinal veins (1st to 5th; called, for short, 1st to 5th veins). The last three of these are often branched. The 6th and 7th longitudinal veins when present are called anal veins. There may be a few or many cross-veins. The cell between the costal and auxiliary veins is the costal; that between the auxiliary and "first vein" is the subcostal; then, in order along the margin of the wing, are the marginal, first submarginal, second submarginal (between branches of the "third vein," if branched), and the more or less numerous posterior cells, numbered from front to back, the first posterior being the "apical cell." The discal cell is near the center of the wing; and at the base from front to back are the first and second basal, anal (not always present) and axillary cells. A cell is "complete" when it is entirely closed by veins. The adjectives anterior, posterior, anal, apical and so on are often used in a more general way merely indicating positions on the wing.

Some Diptera have either thread-like or feathery antennæ with numerous similar joints; others, such as the ordinary house flies, have stubby antennæ with only three joints, the third bearing an arista or style. An arista is a usually dorsal, bristle-like appendage; a style is much the same thing but stouter, usually tapering, and always placed at the tip of the antenna.

The space between the eyes and above the roots of the antennæ is called the front; between the antennæ and the mouth-opening is the "face." The "vertex" is the top of the head between the eyes. "Cheeks": the side of the head between the eyes and the mouth. An orbit is the part of the head around an eye, its anterior part is made up of the frontal and facial orbit. Parafacials: the sides of the face when different from the central part. Oral vibrissæ are bristles at the mouth-opening.

The various parts of the thorax and its bristles have been given special names. Pl. 53 shows the achrostical (*a*) and dorsocentral (*d.c.*) series of bristles divided by the transverse suture (*t.s.*). The letter *a* is placed on the scutellum. The postscutellum (metascutellum) is a convexity just below the back part of the scutellum. The sides of the thorax are the pleuræ. Sterno-pleura between the front and middle coxæ; hypopleura above a hind coxa.

As in other orders, recent work on the classification of flies has cast considerable doubt on the value of some of the older major groupings. At any rate, they are being changed and it seems that the best we can do here is to take a middle ground. The following key to adult flies includes practically all of the families, as now recognized, of Canada and the United States. It is based on that of Brues and Melander with modifications that have been at least "passed," whether approved or not, by Dr. C. H. Curran. For further details see his book *The Families and Genera of North American Diptera.*

Some authorities group as a suborder Orthorrhapha the Nematocera (2 in the following key. The name is sometimes given as Nemocera) and those Brachycera given in the key from 16 to 30 inclusive except the Phoridæ, Platypezidæ, Pipunculidæ and Syrphidæ. According to that system these four families make up the series Aschiza of the other suborder, Cyclorrhapha, and the remaining families make up its series Schizophora (29). The Schizophora are then divided (31) into the sections Myodaria and the Pupipara. Finally, the Myodaria are divided (32) into the subsections Acalyptratæ and Calyptratæ. The head of an adult in the Cyclorrhapha group has what is known as a "frontal suture." Such a fly in emerging from the puparium breaks off the end of the puparium by means of a sac ("ptilinum") that is pushed through this suture. Later the ptilinum is withdrawn into the head and the frontal suture closes to form the characteristic seam above the antennæ. Since the puparium usually breaks all around, the flies are called Cyclorrhapha ("circular seam"). The Orthorrhapha have no frontal suture and their pupal cases usually open in front by a dorsal, longitudinal "straight seam."

1.—Wings at least sufficiently developed to be useful in flight. ....2.

Wings either totally absent or usually so poor as to be useless in flight. (For the most part wingless species of otherwise winged families.)...........38.

2.—Antennæ usually longer than the thorax and usually containing at least 6 freely articulated joints (e.g., Fig. 6, p. 229). Palpi usually long, hanging downward, and having more than 2 joints. Body very rarely with bristles. No calypteres. Anal cell widely open, rarely narrowed at the wing-margin; discal cell usually absent. —Suborder NEMATOCERA ....3.

Antennæ shorter and usually having less than 6 freely articulated joints, the third of which may be subdivided and usually bears a style or arista (e.g., Fig. 7, p. 229). Palpi short, less than 3-jointed, projecting forward. Anal cell narrowed or closed, sometimes very short or even absent (Figs. 1 to 5, p. 229); discal cell usually present.—Suborder BRACHYCERA. ..16.

3.—Mesonotum with a usually distinct V-shaped suture beginning on each side in front of the wings, the pointed middle part close to the scutellum. Legs very long and slender, easily breaking at the trochanter joint. Female with a conical, usually protruding, hardened ovipositor. Costa going around the wing; 9 or more veins ending in the wing-margin.—Superfamily TIPULOIDEA, p. 238.

    Not so. ....**4.**

4.—Wing with a network of fine folds or creases. Legs long and slender.—BLEPHARICERATIDÆ. The flat, aquatic larvæ cling to stones in swift streams by means of ventral suckers, one on each of the six sections of the body, which are marked off by sharp constrictions. The even flatter, heavily chitinized, shining black or brown pupæ are fastened by three pairs of pads. The adult females feed on other insects.

    Wings without an extensive secondary venation. ..**5.**

5.—Antennæ long, with 10 to 36 cylindrical or bead-like joints. Wings with greatly reduced venation, less than 7 veins reaching the margin, but the costa continuing around the wing, though weakened behind. Ocelli usually absent.—CECIDOMYIIDÆ, p. 242.

    Not this combination of characters. ....**6.**

6.—Ocelli present. ....**7.**

    Ocelli absent. ....**11.**

7.—Discal cell present.—ANISOPODIDÆ (Antennæ 12 to 16-jointed. Pulvilli wanting but empodium pulvilliform. Eight veins reaching wing-margin. Fourth posterior cell widely open. See Tipuloidea) and RACHICERIDÆ (The genus, *Rachicerus,* formerly in Leptidæ but see **18.** Fourth posterior cell closed. Antennæ comb-like. Not common)

    No discal cell. ....**8.**

8.—At least the four posterior tibiæ without apical spurs but may have spur-like projections. Coxæ much less than half the length of the femora. Antennæ stout, 10- or 11-jointed, the middle joints shorter than broad. Strong anterior veins crowded close to the costa.— SCATOPSIDÆ. A few very small black flies. At least some larvæ live in excrement; others may live in ants' nests.

    Not so. ....**9.**

9.—Eyes more or less connected by projecting above the bases of the antennæ. Coxæ not more than half the length of the femora.—SCIARIDÆ. These have usually been classed in the family Mycetophilidæ. The principal genus is *Sciara,* whose larvæ are gregarious and sometimes travel in "armies" when looking for better food or when about to pupate.

    Not so. ....**10.**

10.—Antennæ placed below the eyes, usually near the margin of the mouth-opening; they are rarely longer than the head and thorax; the joints are short, broad, and compact. Legs stouter and shorter than is usual among Nematocera.—BIBIONIDÆ, p. 243.

Antennæ arising at most slightly below the level of the middle of the eyes.—MYCETOPHILIDÆ. This large and varied group of small Fungus Gnats has been variously divided into a number of subfamilies or families. The larvæ feed chiefly on fungus, including cultivated mushrooms, and on decaying vegetation, often living in the soil of potted plants. Some feed on foliage, covering themselves with their own excrement. They often spin webs and at least some pupate in a dense cocoon. Luminous larvæ have been described but their light may in some cases have been borrowed from luminous fungi that they had been eating.

11.—Costa ending at or near the apex of the wing. ..12.

Costa continued around the wing-margin, although often weaker along the hind margin. ....14.

12.—Wings very broad; the posterior veins poorly developed. First abdominal segment with a conspicuous fringed flap-like scale above.—SIMULIIDÆ, p. 244.

Wings narrow and relatively long, the posterior veins developed. ....13.

13.—Wings lying flat over the back when at rest. Femora sometimes swollen. Front legs not relatively lengthened. Metanotum short and without a longitudinal groove. Mouth-parts fitted for piercing.—CERATOPOGONIDÆ, p. 242.

Wings lying roof-like over the back when at rest. Legs, especially the front, long and slender. Metanotum long and with a median longitudinal groove. Mouthparts not fitted for piercing.—CHIRONOMIDÆ, p. 242.

14.—The short and broadly ovate or pointed wings held sloping roof-like against the body when at rest; no cross-veins except sometimes near the base. Tibiæ without apical spurs. Second antennal joint not enlarged. Densely hairy body, legs, and wings, some of the hairs being much like the scales of Lepidoptera.—PSYCHODIDÆ, p. 239.

Wings longer and narrow, not held sloping against the sides of the body; wing margin and veins usually scaly; veins straight or nearly so; radius 4-branched. Second antennal joint enlarged, antennæ of male usually "feathered" with long hairs. Legs usually long and moderately hairy or scaly. Slender species.—CULICIDÆ, p. 239.

Neither of these. Subcosta ending in costa at or beyond middle of wing. ....15.

15.—Apical veins strongly arched. Basal cells reaching distinctly beyond the middle of the wing. Joints of antennal flagellum indistinctly separated.—DIXIDÆ. We have a few species of *Dixa*. The aquatic larvæ are usually bent double and swim with the bent part foremost. The first two abdominal segments have "false

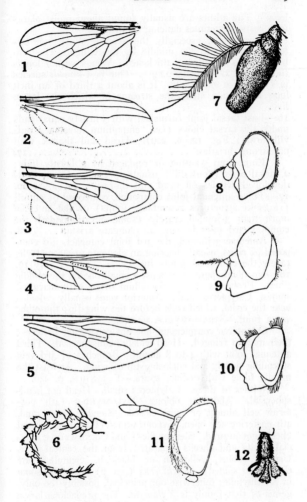

1, *Chrysopilus*. 2, *Dolichopus*. 3, *Eristalis*. 4, *Syrphus*. 5, *Syritta*. 6, *Limonia* antenna. 7, *Volucella* antenna; plumose arista. 8, Female and, 9, male *Brachyopa*. 10, *Syrphus*. 11, *Microdon*. 12, Tip of tarsus with pulvilliform empodium.

legs." The adults are usually found about moist places in forests, sometimes dancing in swarms.

Basal cells, especially the second, short, not extending nearly to the middle of the wings. The two basal joints of antennæ thickened. Wings with 7 longitudinal veins.—THAUMALEIDÆ. Our best-known species is *Thaumalea americana*. It is about a third of an inch long and found along the streams in which the larvæ live.

16.—Last tarsal joint furnished with 3 nearly equal pads under the tarsal claws (*i.e.*, "empodium developed pulvilliform"; Fig. 12, p. 229). Head and thorax with no strong bristles. ....**17.**

Empodium wanting or replaced by a bristly hair; 2 tarsal pads ("pulvilli") usually present. Often well-developed bristles on head and thorax. ....**20.**

17.—Third antennal joint compound, composed of annuli (ring-like structures resembling joints) or the antennæ more than 3-jointed, rarely (some Stratiomyidæ) the complex 3rd joint bearing an elongate arista. ......**18.**

Antennæ 3-jointed, the 3rd joint compact, not composed of rings, usually bearing an elongate arista or style, rarely the two basal joints fused. ....**19.**

18.—No tibial spurs or at most a small one on the middle tibiæ. Proboscis short. Scutellum often with marginal spines. Calypteres small. Anterior veins usually crowded near the costa, which ends before the wing-tip; the other veins faint.—STRATIOMYIDÆ, p. 246.

Calypteres conspicuous, but not concealing halteres; their margin fringed. Head widely hemispherical. Third antennal joint with 4 to 8 annuli. Branches of 3rd vein spreading widely and enclosing tip of wing. At least the middle tibiæ with distinct spurs.—TABANIDÆ, p. 246.

Neither of these. Calypteres small. Head not hemispherical. Abdomen oblong.—XYLOMYIIDÆ (4th posterior cell almost or quite closed. Slender flies); and, 4th posterior cell open, XYLOPHAGIDÆ (Facial orbits and cheeks not sutured. Slender flies) and CŒNOMYIIDÆ (Facial orbits and cheeks separated from the central part. Usually robust, yellowish or blackish. Scutellum of *Cœnomyia* spined). *Rachicerus* (See 7) is put by some in Xylomyiidæ; otherwise our principal, possibly the only, genus of that family is *Xylomyia*. The predacious larvæ of *X. pallipes* have been found under bark. The larvæ of Xylophagidæ, despite the name, and of Cœnomyiidæ are also apparently predacious. Possibly our only species of the latter is *Cœnomyia pallida*.

19.—Calypteres very large. Head very small, placed low down, composed almost entirely of eyes, the face and front very narrow or even lacking.—CYRTIDÆ, p. 249.

Not so.—RHAGIONIDÆ (Middle tibiæ with spurs. Venation not complex. See p. 248) and NEMESTRINIDÆ (Tibiæ without spurs. Venation intricate, many veins ending before the wing-tip). Little is known about the latter but the larva of one species is an internal parasite of beetle larvæ.

20.—Wings rounded apically; strong anterior veins and very weak oblique ones; no cross-veins and therefore no basal cells. Coxæ not widely separated by the sternum. Antennæ placed low; appearing to be 1-jointed because the small basal joints are set in a cavity of the 3rd joint; with a 3-jointed arista. Palpi projecting, not jointed. Hind legs long, the femora compressed. Small, humpbacked, quick-running flies.—PHORIDÆ, p. 253.

Not so. ....**21.**

21.—Wings pointed at the apex; no cross-veins; veins with small setæ above. Thorax with bristles but no hairs. Third antennal joint rounded, with a long, nearly terminal bristle.—LONCHOPTERIDÆ. We have a few species of *Lonchoptera*. They are small, brownish or yellowish. Males are rarely found. The larvæ live in decomposing vegetable matter in moist places.

Not so. ....**22.**

22.—Two or more submarginal cells; the 3rd vein branched. ....**23.**

Only one submarginal cell; the 3rd vein simple. **28.**

23.—Front concave between the eyes. ....**24.**

Front scarcely or not at all concave. ....**25.**

24.—At most one ocellus; and at most two veins reaching the wing margin behind the apex. Body without bristles. Antennæ with a clubbed style. Proboscis with a fleshy expanded tip. Palpi vestigial.—MYDAIDÆ. This is a small family of large flies that resemble thin-bodied Asilidæ but are not predacious. Our only Northeastern genus is *Mydas* (Pl. 51). The larvæ of at least some species live in rotten wood feeding on other larvæ.

Three ocelli. At least 4 veins reach the wing margin behind the apex or extend toward it. Body usually with bristles; face usually bearded. Proboscis fitted for piercing; not fleshy. Palpi usually prominent.—ASILIDÆ, p. 250.

25.—Costa usually continuing around the wing; 4th vein ending back of the wing-tip. ....**26.**

Costa not continued beyond the apex of the wing; 4th vein ending before the wing-tip. Proboscis hidden. Antennæ without a style. Body bare.—SCENOPINIDÆ, p. 249.

26.—Five posterior cells, the 4th often closed. Thorax with some bristles. Abdomen long and tapering.—APIOCERIDÆ (4th vein ending before the apex of the wing. At least the scutellum bristly. Antennæ with a very short style. Eyes separated. Palpi broadened at tip. Large flies) and THEREVIDÆ (4th vein ending back of wing-apex. Body usually furry rather than bristly, sometimes nearly bare. Palpi not broadened apically. See p. 250).

At most 4 posterior cells, the 4th not closed. Thorax usually without true bristles. Abdomen usually oval or oblong. ....**27.**

27.—Antennæ usually ending in a small style, style-like process, or circlet of bristly hairs. Tibiæ usually with spicules. Proboscis usually long, thin and not incurved. Body usually furry and stout but sometimes (Systropodinæ) slender and wasp-like. Anal vein reaching the margin; anal cell closed, if at all, near the wing-margin. Alula usually distinct.—BOMBYLIIDÆ, p. 250.

Antennal style longer than the 3rd joint. Tibiæ without spicules. Proboscis short, sharp, and incurved. Body slender, nearly bare. Anal vein not reaching the margin; anal cell closed far from the wing-margin.— EMPIDIDÆ, p. 253.

28.—Usually a "false vein" running obliquely between the 3rd and 4th longitudinal veins (Figs. 3 to 5, p. 229). Anal cell closed very near the wing margin. Head and body usually without bristles. Arista in a dorsal position, very rarely terminal. Ocelli present. Eyes of males usually meeting on top of head.—SYRPHIDÆ, p. 253.

Head relatively very large, hemispherical; front and face very narrow. Arista dorsal. Head and body rarely with true bristles. Wings much longer than abdomen. Anal angle of wings not developed; anal cell closed near the wing-margin. Ovipositor large, with swollen base and long, sword-like point, bent under the abdomen.— PIPUNCULIDÆ. There are not many species of these Big-eyed Flies. At least some larvæ are parasitic on Heteroptera.

Neither of these. ....**29.**

29.—No frontal lunule. Parafacials not marked off by a suture. ....**30.**

Frontal lunule present. Parafacials marked off by a suture that extends above the antennæ and is indistinct only in some Conopidæ.—(Series Schizophora). ....**31.**

30.—Anterior cross-vein situated at or before the basal fourth of the wing. Second basal and discal cell united (Fig. 2, p. 229). Calypteres rather large and fringed. Proboscis usually soft. Male genitalia more or less bent under the body. Color usually metallic green.—DOLICHOPIDÆ, p. 252.

Anterior cross-vein situated far beyond the basal fourth of the wing or the second basal cell complete. Anal cell pointed posteriorly (If not and especially if the proboscis is rigid, the specimen is probably one of the Empididæ, p. 253). Proboscis not so rigid that it can be used for piercing. Antennæ with terminal arista.

Face small and broad. Hind tibiæ and tarsi swollen, especially in males. Head and thorax with bristles. Females sometimes bright-colored.—PLATYPEZIDÆ. Since the hind tarsi are often very broad and flat these have been called Flatfooted Flies. They somewhat resemble the House Fly but are very much smaller. The larvæ live in mushrooms.

31.—Coxæ close together at the base; the legs attached ventrally.—(Myodaria). ....**32.**

Coxæ widely separated at the base, the legs attached near the sides of the thorax. Usually leathery flies that, as adults, live on mammals and birds (Braulidæ on bees).—PUPIPARA, p. 272.

32.—Second antennal joint with a longitudinal seam along the upper outer edge extending almost the whole length. Posterior calli definitely formed by a depression extending from behind the base of the wings to above the base of the scutellum.—Calyptratæ. ....**35.**

Second antennal joint rarely with a well-developed dorsal seam. Posterior calli not marked off, except in *Gasterophilus* and Cordyluridæ. Calypteres small.—Acalyptratæ. ....**33.**

33.—Mouth-parts vestigial and sunken in a very small oral pit. Antennæ sunken in the facial grooves which form a rounded pocket. Arista bare.—GASTEROPHILIDÆ, p. 261.

Not so.—A large number of, for the most part, small families whose classification has not yet been agreed upon. Since the differentiating characters are largely technical only the following list is given here. ......**34.**

34.—Posterior spiracle with several hairs, visible only with high magnification, on the border in addition to the pubescence.—Chiefly SEPSIDÆ (Head rather spherical. Scutellum usually convex, not elongate. Palpi very small. Arista bare or nearly so. Abdomen somewhat elongate and usually narrowed at base. Small flies) but *Krœberia* of ROPALOMERIDÆ (Head broad, flattened above. Scutellum and thorax flattened, the former elongate. Rather large flies) occurs in the South. The principal genus of Sepsidæ is *Sepsis*. They can usually be found at fresh droppings of horses and cattle vibrating their wings and "pirouetting in a unique and pretty dance."

CONOPIDÆ, p. 259. Proboscis distinctly longer than the head, slender, stiff, and often folding. Head wider than thorax; front broad in both sexes. Face with a grove or grooves under the antennæ. No body bristles. Abdomen club-like, the tip bent down.

CORDILURIDÆ, also called Scatophagidæ and now classed with Calyptratæ. See Muscoidea.

CLUSIIDÆ, also called Heteroneuridæ.—Rather rare with us. Second antennal joint usually with a triangular projection on the outer side; bristles usually present near apices of tibiæ. Larvæ have been found in decaying wood and under bark. They "skip" like those of *Piophila*.

HELOMYZIDÆ.—Area bearing the fronto-orbital bristles short. Usually a row of spines along the costa. Tibiæ with spurs and pre-apical bristles. Adults found in shady, damp places, including caves.

BORBORIDÆ.—Hind metatarsi short and thick in our species; subcostal vein wanting or indistinct. Usually found about excrement or near water.

CŒLOPIDÆ, also called Phycodromidæ.—Last tarsal joint flat and enlarged. Head, body, and legs coarsely bristly. Mesonotum and scutellum flattened. Several species occur on the Pacific shore.

TETANOCERATIDÆ, also called Sciomyzidæ.—Femora with bristles, a characteristic one usually present near the middle of the front face of the middle ones. First vein ending at middle of wing. Larvæ aquatic. The adults are somewhat sluggish, usually brown or yellow; many with receding chins and markings on the wings. See *Tetanocera*, Pl. 52.

LAUXANIIDÆ, also called Sapromyzidæ.—Second antennal joint with a dorsal bristle. Lower edge of front femora bearing bristles. Anal vein abruptly shortened. See *Sapromyza*, Pl. 52. Larvæ in decaying vegetation.

LONCHÆIDÆ.—Head hemispherical in profile. Eyes large and vertically semicircular. Cheeks and front narrow. Third antennal joint more or less cylindrical. Metallic black species. *Lonchæa polita* has been reared from both fungus and human excrement.

OTITIDÆ, p. 259.—Anal crossvein usually angulate so that the anal cell is acutely produced or at least the anal cell apically angled. Setæ usually on top of first vein. Ovipositor hardened and more or less projecting, usually flattened. Palpi developed. So defined, the family is now split up into several subfamilies or families, call them what you will. Of these, PYRGOTIDÆ lacks ocelli.

TRYPETIDÆ, p. 259.—Wings usually banded or spotted, the chief difference from Otitidæ in venation is that the subcosta, which is free from the first vein, ends steeply in the costal break much before the end of the first vein. Seventh segment of female abdomen long and hardened, usually flattened.

MICROPEZIDÆ.—Arista dorsal, located near the base of the 3rd antennal joint. Front legs shorter than hind pairs, from which they are widely separated; front coxæ short. Second antennal joint without a projection.

TANYPEZIDÆ.—Rare with us. Much like Micropezidæ but eyes large, the cheeks and hind orbits narrow.

PIOPHILIDÆ.—Costa not spiny; first vein not hairy; anal vein shortened. Eyes round, occiput convex. No ovipositor. The Cheese Skipper, which you have probably not seen unless you have lived long or quite near to Nature, belongs here. It is the larva of *Piophila casei* (Pl. 54). The "skip" is accomplished by holding the tail with the mouth, pulling hard, and letting go. Why it skips I do not know. It feeds on cheese, bacon and other fatty material.

PSILIDÆ (Also classed with the Calyptratæ. See 37).—Of our few species the larvæ of *Psila rosæ* burrow in the roots of carrots, parsnips, celery and parsley.

DIOPSIDÆ.—Each eye at the tip of a "horn" projecting from the side of the head, the horn also bearing an antenna. Front femora somewhat thickened. Scutellum bituberculate. Chiefly Old World. We have only *Sphyracephala brevicornis,* with relatively short eye-stalks; most often found on skunk-cabbage and associated plants.

CANACEIDÆ.—Upper part of face swollen, separating the antennæ. Cheeks and front wide. Third antennal joint spherical. *Canace snodgrassi* has been recorded from New Jersey.

EPHYDRIDÆ.—Anal cell absent and the front with bristles. Other distinguishing characters quite technical. They are small, bare dark-colored flies that live in wet places. Some larvæ live in fresh water but some in the strongly alkaline lakes of the West and in pools about salt works. In the West they are sometimes washed ashore in such quantities that the Indians dry them for food. The Californian *Psilopa petrolei* larvæ have the remarkable habit of living in pools of crude petroleum.

CHLOROPIDÆ, also called Oscinidæ.—Front with at most very weak bristles; anal vein with a slight curvature near the middle. Comstock says: "The larvæ of the different species differ in their habits; many species infest the stems of wheat, oats, rye, clover, and grasses; some live in burrows or cavities in plants made by other insects; a few feed upon the egg-shells or cast-off skins of insects; some live in excrement; and species of *Gaurax* develop in the egg-sacs of spiders."

ASTIIDÆ.—A small group sometimes united with either Chloropidæ or Drosophilidæ. The 1st and 2nd veins end very close together before the basal third of the wing; no anal cell.

DROSOPHILIDÆ.—See p. 260.

GEOMYZIDÆ.—Now divided by some authors between Trichoscelidæ and Opomyzidæ. In any case they are small flies and some of the larvæ mine leaves.

AGROMYZIDÆ.—When arista is present the basal joint is shorter than broad. Species of *Cryptochætum* (without arista) were introduced from Australia to California as parasites of the Cottony-cushion Scale. For the most part, the larvæ of our native species mine leaves; for example, *Phytomyza aquilegiæ* makes the snake-like mines in the leaves of columbine. *Agromyza æneiventris* makes swellings on poplar and cottonwood twigs.

MILICHIIDÆ and OCHTHIPHILIDÆ are small groups sometimes classed under Agrozymidæ. Some of the larvæ feed on plant-lice and scale-insects.

35.—Mouth-opening small, the mouth-parts vestigial or wanting. Front broad. Antennæ in the facial groove or grooves. Few bristles and no sternopleural ones. Lower calypter with the margin only slightly pubescent.— ŒSTRIDÆ, p. 261.

Not so. ....**36.**

36.—Hypopleura with a row of bristles. Fourth vein usually curving forward and narrowing or closing the first posterior cell.—TACHINOIDEA, p. 262.

Hypopleura with hair or bare; fourth vein usually straight, broadly curved forward. (The subfamily Egeniinæ of Muscidæ has one to three hypopleural bristles but the apical cell is not narrowed and there is no metascutellum. At present *Lutzomyia americana* is our only species.) ....**37.**

37.—Oral vibrissæ absent. Mesonotum without bristles except above the wings.—PSILIDÆ. Acalypterate flies of slender build and with long antennæ belonging to the genus *Loxocera*. See **34.**

Oral vibrissæ almost always present. Mesonotum with dorsal bristles. Calypters variable in size; the venation also variable.—MUSCOIDEA, p. 267.

38.—Coxæ widely separated by the sternum; the legs appearing to be attached near the sides of the thorax.— PUPIPARA, p. 272.

Not so. ....**39.**

39.—Antennæ consisting of at least 6 freely articulated joints. ....**40.**

Antennæ consisting of at most 3 freely articulated joints. ....**46.**

40.—Mesonotum with a complete V-shaped suture.— TIPULIDÆ, p. 238.

Not so. ....**41.**

41.—Eyes meeting over the antennæ. ....**42.**

Eyes widely separated above the antennæ. ....**44.**

42.—Abdomen enormously swollen, the apical four segments slender. Termite guests.—CECIDOMYIIDÆ, p. 242.

Not so. ....**43.**

43.—Scutellum and halteres present.—SCATOPSIDÆ, couplet **8.**

Scutellum and halteres absent.—SCIARIDÆ, couplet **9.**

44.—No ocelli. Associated with termites.—PSYCHODIDÆ, p. 239.

Not associated with termites. ....**45.**

45.—Halteres present.—CHIRONOMIDÆ, p. 242.

No halteres.—MYCETOPHILIDÆ, couplet **10.**

PLATE 48

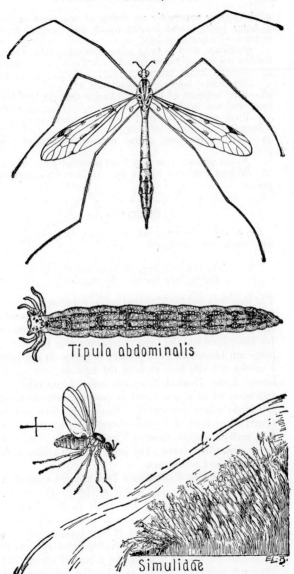

Tipula abdominalis

Simulidae

237

46.—Antennæ apparently consisting of one more or less globular joint. Hind femora robust and laterally compressed.—PHORIDÆ, p. 253.

Antennæ with 2 or 3 quite evident joints. Hind femora not laterally compressed. ....**47.**

47.—Frontal lunule present. ....**48.**

No frontal lunule.—EMPIDIDÆ, p. 253.

48.—First segment of hind tarsi longer than the 2nd segment and not swollen. ....**49.**

First segment of hind tarsi short and swollen.—BORBORIDÆ; see **34** of this key.

49.—Arista with long, sparse rays.—DROSOPHILIDÆ, p. 260.

Arista pubescent or bare; 3rd antennal joint orbicular. Wings mutilated by the fly.—HELOMYZIDÆ, couplet **34.**

TIPULOIDEA

See p. 227. These are the Crane Flies or Daddy Long-legs—those who complain

> "My six long legs, all here and there,
> Oppress my bosom with despair."

The long legs and the V-shaped suture between the wings usually distinguish typical members of this superfamily from other true flies. Tipuloids are sometimes mistaken for mosquitoes and the large ones—some over two inches long—are blamed on New Jersey; but they do not bite. I cannot tell you how to keep the legs on your specimens. Some Tipuloid larvæ are called Leather-jackets and many of them are found in decaying vegetation on dry land; others are aquatic; others under bark and in fungi; some feed, at least incidentally, on roots; and a few, such as *Cylindrotoma* of Tipulidæ, on the leaves of violets and other plants. The pupæ are slim affairs with relatively short wing-cases.

Of the primitive TANYDERIDÆ (2nd and 3rd veins each 2-branched) we have only a few species of *Protoplasa*. *Bittacomorpha clavipes* of the small family PTYCHOPTERIDÆ (2nd and 3rd veins with a total of only 3 branches reaching the margin) is very conspicuous with its white-banded black legs and swollen metatarsi. As it drifts through the air it looks like a rimless wheel. Its larvæ are aquatic. In these two families only one anal

vein reaches the margin but the many species of winged
TIPULIDÆ have two complete anal veins (Pl. 48). *Chionea*
is a genus of wingless Tipulidæ. Some, at least, of its
species are mature in winter and when walking on snow
are easily seen. TRICHOCERIDÆ have ocelli. Some species
of our genus *Trichocera* often gather in swarms, especially in early spring and late autumn, to "dance" a few
feet above the ground. Other species are found in cellars where potatoes in which their larvæ have fed are
stored. Of ANISOPIDÆ (also called Rhyphidæ) we have
chiefly *Anisopus*. They lack the V on the thorax and
most authors separate them from Tipuloidea. They resemble spotted-winged mosquitoes. Like many Tipulidæ,
their larvæ feed on decaying vegetable matter.

PSYCHODIDÆ

See p. 228. The Moth Flies are rarely more than a
sixth of an inch long. They fly but weakly in shady
places but are often found at lights and on windows.
Some larvæ live in decaying vegetation; others in water.
Fortunately we probably have but one species, *vexator,*
of the blood-sucking genus *Phlebotomus,* of which other
species carry such diseases as Peruvian verruga.

CULICIDÆ

See p. 228. Everyone knows a Mosquito, or thinks that
he does. The proboscis of the female is fitted for sucking but the male's mouthparts are so rudimentary that
he cannot "bite." His antennæ are very plumose. The
larvæ are aquatic. They are the "wrigglers" such as most
of us have seen in standing water. Owing to the medical
interest in mosquitoes they have been extensively studied.
The following, among other, subfamilies (or families)
have been recognized.

1.—Proboscis, even of females, short, not fitted for
piercing. Wings hairy, scaled only at margin. Mesosternum without ridge. Sternopleura divided by transverse suture.—Corethrinæ. The transparent, predacious
larvæ use their antennæ in capturing prey. They get
their oxygen by absorption from the water. The eyes
of these Phantom Larvæ are dark. The two other pairs

of dark spots are "air sacs." I do not know how the air, if it be real air, gets into them. The pupæ float upright and have respiratory trumpets on their heads.

Proboscis much longer than head; the female's fitted for piercing. Wings fully scaled. Mesosternum ridged.
....2.

2.—Palpi of female at least a third longer than the proboscis. Abdomen sometimes without scales. Scutellum crescent-shaped, with marginal bristles evenly distributed. —Anophelinæ.

Not so. ....3.

3.—Scutellum evenly rounded. Clypeus much broader than long. Calypteres not ciliated.—Day-flying, not-biting Megarhininæ.

Scutellum trilobed, with marginal bristles only on the lobes. ....4.

4.—Base of hind coxæ in line with upper margin of lateral metasternal sclerite, a small triangular piece between bases of middle and hind coxæ. Day-fliers.— Sabethinæ. The larvæ of *Wyeomyia smithii* live in the water in pitcher plant leaves.

Not so.—Chiefly Culicinæ (anal vein extending well beyond fork of cubitus) but also Uranotæniinæ.

The eggs of *Anopheles* (Pl. 49) are laid singly, each having a lateral "float." The larvæ are rarely found in foul or brackish water. Unlike Culicinæ, the breathing siphon on the end of the abdomen is very short and a resting larva floats horizontally. Adults usually have spotted wings. They are to be feared because they may be carrying malarial "germs" which they sucked in along with the blood of a former victim. If so and if the malarial organism had worked its way from the mosquito's stomach to its salivary glands, the mosquito biting us is likely to infect us with malaria.

The many species of Culicinæ have been divided into genera on technical characters. Most of what we called *Culex* are now *Aedes*. The Tropical *A. ægypti* (also called *Stegomyia fasciata*) carries yellow fever and dengue. Such Tropical diseases as dengue and filariasis are carried also by other Culicine females. The eggs of *Culex* (Pl. 49) are laid in a floating, raft-like mass; those of *Aedes* singly. The salt-marsh mosquitoes with banded legs are *Aedes*. The larva of *Tæniorhynchus* (= *Mansonia*) *perturbans* sticks its breathing siphon into the air-chambers of aquatic plants instead of coming to the surface to breathe.

PLATE 49

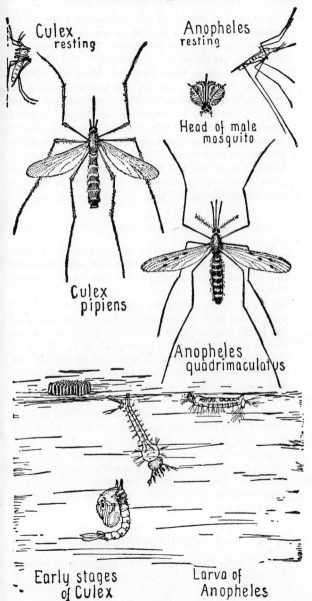

Culex resting

Anopheles resting

Head of male mosquito

Culex pipiens

Anopheles quadrimaculatus

Early stages of Culex

Larva of Anopheles

The pupæ of mosquitoes are humpbacked wrigglers or, rather, "flappers," that breathe by means of a pair of trumpet-shaped tubes on their backs. They can move but usually do not do so unless disturbed.

A film of oil on water kills such larvæ and pupæ as come to the surface for air. Of course, draining all breeding places would exterminate mosquitoes but I hope that this will never be completely done because it would exterminate many other things as well. Nature's balance, involving chiefly fish and dragonfly larvæ, does fairly well in most cases, particularly if man is not careless with tin cans, tubs and the like. To be sure, extreme cases require extreme measures, particularly in the case of a disease-bearing species.

CHIRONOMIDÆ AND CERATOPOGONIDÆ

See p. 228. These are the Midges, strictly speaking. "The larvæ are soft-skinned, worm-like, often blood-red in color and usually aquatic, as are also the active pupæ, though some live in decomposing vegetable matter, or in the earth. These midges are often seen, especially in the early spring or in the autumn, in immense swarms, dancing in the air, and have doubtless in many cases given rise to exaggerated stories of mosquitoes. . . . While at rest they usually raise their fore legs in the air and keep them constantly vibrating" (Williston). Most of the adults are harmless, but Sand Flies, Punkies, and No-see-ums, belonging to the genus *Culicoides,* often make our life miserable. They are the smallest blood-suckers, some of them being only 0.04 in. long. Some larvæ live under bark and fallen leaves, and in sap flowing from wounded trees. The pesky *Culicoides* are now out of the Chironomidæ and classed in a separate family, Ceratopogonidæ. This may please the more gentle midges. *Chironomus* has many inoffensive species; the larvæ are common in tubes in soft mud.

CECIDOMYIIDÆ

See p. 227. No attempt will be made here to indicate the subfamilies. The layman usually knows these only

by their works. Many of them are gall-makers (p. 443)
or live in galls made by other species; some breed in
decaying wood and bulbs, others under bark and in fungi,
while still others feed on plant lice and other insects.
Unlike most Diptera, many of these pupæ are enclosed
in a cocoon formed by an exudation from the larvæ.
The genus *Miastor* contains species whose larvæ sometimes develop eggs which hatch, without fertilization, inside their "mothers," the children then devouring their
parent.

Sanderson says of *Mayetiola destructor:* "Probably
no other insect does so wide-spread damage as the
Hessian Fly, attacking our chief staple, wheat, as well as
rye and barley. One-tenth of the whole crop, valued at
$50,000,000 to $70,000,000, is generally conceded to be
destroyed by this pest every year. In certain sections
the loss often amounts to from 30 to 50 per cent., and
in 1900 was estimated at fully $100,000,000." It (Pl. 50)
is a European insect that was first noticed on Long
Island shortly after the Hessian troops landed there.
The adults are dark-colored gnats, about 0.1 in. long.
The larvæ imbed themselves in the plant, especially where
the stem is covered by a leaf, absorb the sap, and weaken
the straw. The "flax-seed" is the puparium.

The Wheat Midge, *Diplosis tritici,* was introduced from
Europe a few years after the Hessian Fly. Its larvæ
feed on the developing wheat-heads and pupate in underground cocoons. The larvæ of *Dasyneura leguminicola*
feed on clover seed. The Pear Midge, *Contarinia py-
rivora,* is another immigrant from Europe; it causes a
lumpy growth in the fruit, the larvæ working chiefly at
the core.

BIBIONIDÆ

See p. 227. The name March Flies is misleading, as
adults rarely appear that early. Some are common about
fruit-tree blossoms. The larvæ feed on excrement, decaying roots, and logs. The white-winged, rather long-
legged, clumsy fly that frequently occurs in large numbers in meadows and is sometimes seen on windows is
Bibio albipennis (Pl. 50).

SIMULIIDÆ

See p. 228. Those who know the Black Flies of the
North woods, or the Buffalo Gnats and Turkey Gnats
of other sections, know some adult Simuliids: stout, humpbacked, short-legged, biting pests with very interesting
larvæ (Pl. 48). Groups of the black larvæ sit on their
tails on rocks, sticks and leaves in shallow, swift-flowing
water. They cling by means of "suckers" at the hind
end of the body; they also have a front pair of appendages that they use when crawling. Miall's *Aquatic
Insects* is a model of scientific accuracy and charming
diction. He says: "If seriously alarmed, the larva lets
go, and immediately disappears from sight. But by
watching the place attentively, we shall before long see
the larva working its way back, and in a minute or two
it will be found attached to the very same leaf from
which it started, or to some other leaf, equally convenient,
which it happens to fall in with. I found the difficulties
of observation in fast-flowing water crowded with leaves
very great, until at last it occurred to me to push a
white plate in among the leaves. Then the dark-colored
larvæ became perfectly evident on the white ground, and
I was able to see exactly how they managed. When
disturbed by the plate, some of them let go and drift a
few inches away. They are not very easily frightened,
and most of them remain holding on by their suckers.
Those which quit the leaf remain stationary in the tor-
rent or nearly so, and on close observation a thread, or
perhaps a number of threads, become visible on the white
ground. These threads are in general stuck all over with
small vegetable particles, like fine dust, which make them
much more apparent. The threads extend in all directions from leaf to leaf, and the larva has access to a
perfect labyrinth, along which it can travel to a fresh
place by help of the current and with the speed of
lightning. . . . Although the larva commonly slides along
a thread previously made, and easily seen to be an old
one by the small particles which cling to it, it can upon
a sudden emergency spin a new thread, like a spider or
a Geometer larva. . . . When the time for pupation
comes, special provision has to be made for the peculiar

circumstances in which the whole of the aquatic life of the Simulium is passed. An inactive and exposed pupa, like that of Chironomus, may fare well enough on the soft muddy bottom of a slow stream, but such a pupa would be swept away in a moment by the currents in which Simulium is most at home. Before pupation the Insect constructs for itself a kind of nest not unlike in shape to the nests of some Swallows. This nest is glued fast to the surface of a water-weed. The salivary glands, which furnished the mooring-threads, supply the material of which the nest is composed. Sheltered within this smooth and tapering cocoon, whose pointed tip is directed up-stream, while the open mouth is turned down-stream, the pupa rests securely during the time of its transformation. When the cocoon is first formed, it is completely closed, but, when the insect has cast the larval skin, one end of the cocoon is knocked off, and the pupa now thrusts the fore-part of its body into the current of water. The respiratory filaments, which project immediately behind the future head, just as in Chironomus, draw a sufficient supply of air from the well-aerated water around. The rings of the abdomen are furnished with a number of projecting hooks, and, as the interior of the cocooon is felted by silken threads, the pupa gets a firm grip of its cocoon. If it is forcibly dislodged a number of the silken threads are drawn out from the felted lining.

"A serious difficulty now appears. The fly is a delicate and minute Insect, with gauzy wings. How does it escape from the rushing water into the air above, where the remainder of its life has to be passed? . . . During the latter part of the pupal stage, which lasts about a fortnight in all, the pupal skin becomes inflated with air, which is extracted from the water, and passed apparently through the spiracles of the fly into the space immediately within the pupal skin. The pupal skin thus becomes distended with air, and assumes a more rounded shape in consequence. At length it splits along the back, in the way usual among Insects, and there emerges a small bubble of air, which rises quickly to the surface of the water and then bursts. When the bubble bursts, out comes the fly."

The larvæ have, on their heads, brushes that gather up food brought to them by the stream. I found them in large numbers where a much-used road crossed a small brook; the automobilists apparently wondered what I was looking for in that cold water but passed on in ignorance of things far more interesting than so-many miles an hour.

STRATIOMYIDÆ

See p. 230. Some of the Soldier Flies are gay with yellow or green and black cross-stripes on their flat, broad abdomens; the abdomen is so wide in some species that it extends on each side of the folded wings. There are numerous species, their larvæ having various habits. Aquatic larvæ (such as those of *Stratiomys,* Pl. 50, and *Odontomyia,* Pl. 92) have a circlet of bristles on their tails that opens out flat when the larva is at the surface taking atmospheric air into its tracheal system through its tail spiracles but folds together when the larva wishes to free itself from the surface film. Many, or most, of these aquatic larvæ pupate in the mud at the water's edge. Larvæ also occur in cow dung (*Chloromyia*), in privies (*Hermetia*), under stones, in tree sap (*Geosargus*), in decaying wood (*Pachygaster*), in moss, in catsup, and on vegetables, such as potato tubers and growing lettuce. Some are carnivorous; others are vegetarians. Pupation occurs in the larval skin.

TABANIDÆ

See p. 230. These (Plates 50 and 92) are surely of popular interest. They are the Horse Flies, Green-headed Monsters, Gad Flies, Breeze Flies, Ear Flies or Deer Flies. Only the females bite; the males content themselves with sipping sweets from flowers. The predacious larvæ live in water or in moist earth, apparently hibernating as mature larvæ and pupating, free from the larval skin, the following spring. The somewhat flattened larvæ have a circle of fleshy protuberances around each segment, aiding them in locomotion. There are many species; for example, about forty of *Tabanus* and

PLATE 50

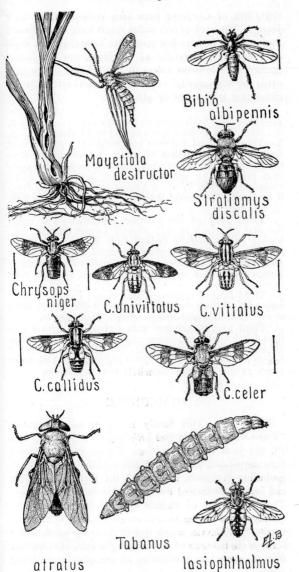

Mayetiola
destructor

Bibio
albipennis

Stratiomys
discalis

Chrysops
niger

C. univittatus

C. vittatus

C. callidus

C. celer

Tabanus

atratus

lasiophthalmus

thirty-five of *Chrysops* have been recorded from New Jersey. The eyes of the males touch each other above; those of the females are somewhat separated; but those of both sexes, especially of *Chrysops,* are beautifully marked with brilliant colors in life. These colors may often be temporarily restored in dried specimens by moistening with water or glycerine.

1.—Hind tibiæ with spurs at the tip. . . . . .2.
    Hind tibiæ without spurs at tip; ocelli absent. . . . . .3.
2.—Third joint of antennæ composed of 5 superficially separated rings, the first of which is much longer than the following ones; ocelli present.—*Chrysops* is the common genus. The wings very often have broad, black cross-bands. The Western *Silvius* is distinguished from it by having the second antennal joint only half as long as the first.

    Third joint of the antennæ composed of 8 rings, the first of which is only slightly longer than the following ones.—*Goniops* (wings dark in front, clear behind; eyes of female acutely angulated above) and *Buplex* (wings nearly clear or else uniformly darkened; female's eyes not so angulated; proboscis often very long).
3.—Third joint of antennæ with 4 rings; front of female very wide. Wings darkened and spotted with rings; when at rest, held in a roof-like position. —*Hæmatopota.*

    Third joint of antennæ with 5 rings and with a distinct basal angle or process above (The Southern *Diachlorus* differs in not having this process); front of female not unusually wide. Hind tibiæ without long hairs (such as the Western *Snowiella* has).—*Tabanus.*

RHAGIONIDÆ

See p. 231. This family has been called Leptidæ. "These trim-appearing flies [*Rhagio,* Pl. 51; *Chrysopilus,* Pl. 92] have rather long legs, a cone-shaped abdomen tapering towards the hind end, and sometimes a downward projecting proboscis, which with the form of the body and legs has suggested the name snipe-flies" (Comstock). They are usually of medium size for flies and are frequently found resting head-down on grass stems and tree trunks. The larvæ, which live in decaying wood, under bark, in the burrows of wood-boring insects, in moss, and even in water, are predacious, as are also most of the adults.

The subfamily Vermileoninæ (antennæ inserted above the middle of the eyes; each front tibia with a strong apical spur) includes the interesting *Vermileo,* larvæ of which live in sand, constructing pits like those of ant-lions and for the same purpose, catching prey.

Atherix is in the typical subfamily, Rhagioninæ (front tibiæ without spurs; hind ones with two each). The females "have the remarkable habit of clustering in large numbers on branches or rocks overhanging water, where they deposit their eggs in common and, dying as they do so, add their bodies to the common mass, which may contain thousands of individuals. . . . It is said that the larvæ feed upon the bodies of the dead mothers until the mass is loosened and falls into the water, where the larvæ complete their growth. Other writers state that the larvæ drop into the water when hatched" (Comstock). Indians used to gather these masses and eat them cooked. Quite probably these and the other subfamilies have equally interesting and still unknown habits.

CYRTIDÆ

See p. 230. Also called Acroceridæ. These rarely noticed, small-headed flies have curious habits. You may find *Opsebius pterodontinus* about the webs of the common grass-spider, *Agelena nœvia,* and can recognize it by the tooth-like projection on the front margins of the wings. Its larvæ live in the spiders and its relatives have similar habits. The tables are turned; in this case the fly eats the spider.

SCENOPINIDÆ

See p. 231. Also called Omphralidæ. We have only one Eastern genus, *Scenopinus,* of the Window Flies and, of this, only *fenestralis* (Pl. 51) is common. It is bluish, with reddish-yellow legs; the head is placed so low that the thorax seems quite convex. It is on our windows because its worm-like larvæ are under our carpets, eating "moths." Each of the larva's abdominal segments, except the last, is constricted, so that it appears to have nineteen segments.

ASILIDÆ

See p. 231. Plate 51 shows *Leptogaster, Bombomima* (or *Dasyllis*), *Erax,* and *Asilus* of the large family of Robber Flies, the two last-named being the more typical. They are frequently seen swooping upon insect victims in mid-air or snatching them off of leaves and carrying them away to a convenient spot where the sucking of vital fluids may be quietly completed. The hairier and stouter type is just as predacious and possibly their resemblance to peaceful bumblebees helps them to get close to their prey, although this mimicking may be a protection against enemies that fear the sting of bees; or, again, it may just "happen so." The eyes bulge out so that the head seems to be hollowed between them; the proboscis is stout, rather than long; the legs are strong and usually bristly. The larvæ, also, are predacious, feeding upon other larvæ in rotting wood, under bark, fallen leaves, or in loose soil. There are a number of subfamilies.

THEREVIDÆ

See p. 232. The Stiletto Flies are like delicate, long-legged Asilidæ but the front of the head is not hollowed out between the eyes; it may even be convex and the eyes of the males may join on top. Their habits are those of the Asilidæ. *Psilocephala* (Pl. 51) is a common genus.

BOMBYLIIDÆ

See p. 232. If you see a fuzzy fly hover in mid-air and suddenly dart a few feet away to hover again, you may feel certain that it is a Bee Fly. That name, and the "real" name for the family is just as bad, has always confused me, as it seemed to go with certain more bee-like Asilids, but it does not. Plate 92 shows samples of *Bombylius* (larvæ live in the nest of bees, such as *Andrena*) and *Villa,* there called *Anthrax.* The larvæ of some species of *Villa* are probably parasites of Lepidoptera but those of others, especially of those whose adults have wing-markings, are parasites of Lepidoptera's

PLATE 51

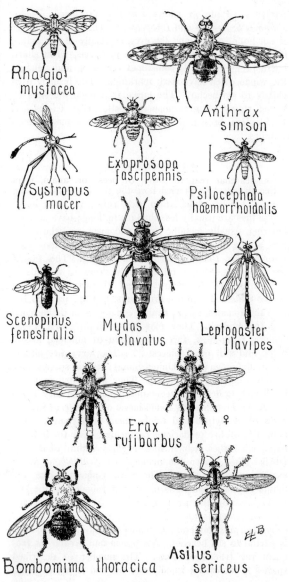

Rhagio
mystacea

Anthrax
simson

Systropus
macer

Exoprosopa
fascipennis

Psilocephala
haemorrhoidalis

Scenopinus
fenestralis

Mydas
clavatus

Leptogaster
flavipes

♂ Erax
rufibarbus ♀

Bombomima thoracica

Asilus
sericeus

ELB

parasites. Plate 51 shows *Anthrax* (formerly *Spogostylum*), *Systropus* and *Exoprosopa*. The Bombyliid face is not hollowed out and the eyes, especially of the males, almost or quite touch above; the proboscis, when short, has a broad tip but is sometimes very long and slender; the wings often have dark markings. The beak is used chiefly to sip nectar. The larvæ feed upon the eggs or young stages of grasshoppers, beetles (e.g. *Cicindela*), Lepidoptera, bees, and wasps. There are numerous sub-families.

DOLICHOPIDÆ

See p. 232. As spelled here the name refers to long eyes; "Dolichopodidæ," also used, refers to "long legs." These flies are usually less than 0.3 in. long; have slender, tapering, usually metallic green abdomens, and the tarsal part of the long legs are often relatively quite long (see *Psilopodinus*, Pl. 92). Prof. Aldrich said: "This family perhaps surpasses any other natural group of animals in the variety of secondary sexual characters possessed by the males. These are ornaments, and are paraded before the females, as are similar ornaments in the peacock and turkey-cock. They may occur in the tarsi, tibiæ, femora, wing-apex, face, third joint of antenna, arista, palpi, and still other places. . . . The larvæ are almost wholly unknown in the United States; several species have been worked out in Europe. They are found in moist earth rich in decaying vegetation, upon which they feed; Dr. A. D. Hopkins has found larvæ of *Medeterus* in burrows of Scolytidæ and thinks them predacious. . . . In adult life all are predacious, capturing chiefly the minuter soft-bodied flies, which they enclose within their soft labella [lips], after the manners of *Scatophaga,* while extracting the juices." The most common place for adults of some genera is on shaded foliage but the sun is favored by the great majority. Wet earth at the edge of water is also favored, while *Hydrophorus* and *Campsicnemus* stand on the surface of water. *Thinophilus* is partial to sea beaches. *Neurigona* and *Medeterus* frequent the trunks of trees. The number of described species is increasing rapidly and the end is not in sight.

EMPIDIDÆ

See p. 232. A question that one always expects, when out walking with non-entomologists, is "What are those little things dancing in the air?" The only way to answer truthfully is to catch some and find out, for they may be Homoptera, Coleoptera, Hymenoptera, Diptera, or even some other order. If Diptera, they may belong to any of a number of families; the Chironomids are great dancers (Williston told of such an immense flight that their wings produced a "noise like that of a distant waterfall, and audible for a considerable distance."), but the Empididæ are called the Dance Flies. At least some of the many species have a curious, "almost human" habit in connection with these wedding dances: the males bring gifts to the brides. The gifts are captured insects, sometimes enclosed in frothy bubbles, with other species done up in a web made from a secretion of glands in the front feet. The females keep their presents during the mating process.

The larvæ also are probably predacious. Some live in decaying vegetable matter; others are aquatic.

PHORIDÆ

See p. 231. These minute flies would probably not be noticed unless you were looking for them, although they are sometimes to be found on windows. The life histories are varied, but those of the dwellers in ant-nests are probably the most interesting. *Apocephalus* larvæ live inside the heads of adult ants; the larva of *Metopina pachycondylæ* curls around the neck of ant larvæ and shares the food which the ants bring to their larvæ. The larvæ of some species feed in mushrooms, including cultivated kinds. There is still much to be discovered concerning the unusual life-histories in this family.

SYRPHIDÆ

See p. 232. This family is rich in species. Because of the interesting habits of many, the economic importance of some, and the relative—though far from absolute—ease in identifying genera, it is given extra space here. The key, kindly furnished by Dr. Curran, includes practically all of the common American genera. The adults are so frequently seen feeding on nectar and pollen that they are called Flower Flies. Some are almost bare and resemble wasps; others are hairy and resemble bees, even in the buzzing noise they make; but all are quite harmless.

1.—Antennæ with terminal style.—Nearly bare species: *Cerioides* (wasp-like; 3rd antennal segment cylindrical) and *Pelecocera* (3rd antennal segment subtriangular). Body and eyes hairy: *Callicera*.
    Antennæ with dorsal or subapical arista..........2.
2.—Third vein deeply looped into the apical cell (Fig. 3, p. 229) ....24.
    Third vein at most moderately curved into the apical cell (Figs. 4 and 5, p. 229) ....3.
3.—Anterior crossvein situated distinctly before the middle of the discal cell and almost perpendicular. (Fig. 4, p. 229) ....4.
    Anterior crossvein ending at or beyond the middle of the discal cell and strongly oblique (e.g., Fig. 5, p. 229) ....17.
4.—A stripe along each eye separated from the rest of the face by a groove. Face usually black.—*Cheilosia* (eyes pilose) and *Cartosyrphus* (eyes bare).
    Face with only very short grooves below the eyes. ....5.
5.—Front or face (or both in females) with transverse wrinkles.—*Chrysogaster* (antennæ short; 3rd segment broad) and *Orthoneura* (antennæ long; 3rd segment narrow).
    Without such wrinkles....................................6.
6.—Face rather evenly convex; without tubercle or prominent oral margin (Fig. 11, p. 229).—*Mixogaster* (abdomen strongly constricted basally) and *Microdon* (abdomen broadest near the base; slug-like larvæ live in nests of ants and termites).
    Face with tubercle (Fig. 10, p. 229) or with projecting oral margin. ....7.
7.—Antennæ as long as face.—*Paragus* (antennæ and abdomen drooping) and *Chrysotoxum* (Not so. Wasp-like).
    Antennæ relatively shorter ....8.
8.—Arista plumose.—*Ornidia* (Metallic green. Face with strong swelling on each side) and *Volucella* (See p. 258) have arista loosely plumose (Fig. 7, p. 229) but *Copestylum* has them densely so and brush-like.
    Arista bare. ....9.

9.—Thorax with scale-like, appressed hairs.—*Eumyiolepta.*

Thoracic hair normal. ....10.

10.—Face black. ....11.

Face at least partly yellow or reddish. ....13.

11.—Abdomen narrow at base.—*Neoascia* (3rd antennal joint at least twice as long as broad) and *Sphegina* (that joint relatively shorter).*

Abdomen not narrowed basally. ....12.

12.—Eyes hairy.—*Pipiza* and allied genera. Larvæ of *Heryngia salax* (= *P. radicum*) feed on Root-lice; others on Woolly Aphids.

Eyes bare.—*Nausigaster* (3rd antennal joint very large; orbicular). 3rd joint not orbicular: *Pyrophæna* (wings longer than abdomen), *Platycheirus* (front tibiæ or tarsi of male broad; Pl. 52); *Melanostoma* (slender; usually with reddish marks); and *Myiolepta* (stout; face of female concave, of male tuberculate).

13.—Abdomen long and slender; usually narrow at base. —*Baccha* (face tuberculate) and *Sphegina* (face concave).

Abdomen not constricted basally but it may be slightly wider toward the tip. ....14.

14.—Face with a tubercle. ....15.

Face concave.—*Rhingia nasica* (mouth margin produced as a long snout) and *Brachyopa* (mouth not snout-like; Figs. 8 and 9, p. 229).

15.—Eyes and body with long pile.—*Leucozona americana.*

Not so. ....16.

16.—Pleura and sides of mesonotum with sharply defined yellow markings.—Face strongly produced in middle, receding below: *Mesogramma* (Pl. 52). Femora simple. Larvæ of *politum* said to feed on corn pollen) and *Toxomerus* (male hind femora strongly curved). Face not strongly produced: *Doros* (large; rather slender; wasp-like), *Sphærophoria* (male genitalia large) and (abdomen usually broad and flat) *Syrphus* and *Xanthogramma.*

Not so. *Didea* (abdomen very broad and unusually flat; markings usually greenish). Abdomen narrower: *Eupeodes* (male genitalia remarkably long), *Scæva* (Front of both sexes strongly swollen. Wings without minute hairs) and *Syrphus* (Front not strong swollen. Wings with minute hairs. See p. 258).

17.—Marginal cell closed and petiolate. Hind femora with a sharp, tooth-like projection near apex below.— *Milesia* (Pl. 92).

Marginal cell open. ....18.

18.—Apical cell longest in the middle.—*Citibæna* (= *Eumerus*). The larvæ live in bulbs but probably are secondary pests.

Apical cell longest in front. . . . .**19.**

19.—Hind femora with one sharp tooth near apex below. —*Spilomyia.*

Not so. . . . .**20.**

20.—Face carinate or concave.—*Syritta* (Small. Hind femora remarkably swollen), *Tropidia* (Larger. Hind femora with triangular process near apex below), *Heliophilus* (Also called *Xylota* and *Zelima*. Femora not like either *Syritta* or *Tropidia*), and *Pocota* (resembles bumblebees).

Face with more or less distinct tubercle; not carinate. . . . .**21.**

21.—Arista plumose.—*Sericomyia* (abdomen with transverse bands), *Condidea* (abdomen with yellow spots) and *Arctophila* (abdomen with long, erect pile).

Arista bare. . . . .**22.**

22.—Pale markings due to "dust" (very short, fragile hairs). Wasp-like.—*Sphecomyia* (face strongly extended below) and *Temnostoma* (not so; Pl. 52).

Pale markings, if any, not due entirely to "dust." . . . .**23.**

23.—Metallic, with black markings. Rather cylindrical. —*Chrysosomidia* (= *Calliprobola*).

Not metallic.—*Somula* resembles "yellow jacket" wasps and *Criorrhina* resembles bumblebees. Neither of these: *Crioprora* (face strongly extended below) and *Cynorhina* (not so).

24.—Marginal cell open. . . . .**25.**

Marginal cell closed and petiolate.—*Meromacrus* (thorax with tomentose yellow spots) and *Eristalis* (No such spots. See below).

25.—Hind femora with a strong triangular projection near apex.—*Merodon.* The larvæ are a serious pest in bulbs.

Not so. . . . .**26.**

26.—Pile of thorax yellow, rather long and dense.— *Mallota.*

Pile of thorax short and not so dense. . . . .**27.**

27.—Mesonotum with yellow, pollinose stripes (rarely almost absent).—*Elophilus* (or *Helophilus*) and allied genera. It has been reared from brackish water and carcasses.

Mesonotum not noticeably striped. . . . .**28.**

28.—Hind legs with tubercles and spurs.—*Polydontomyia.*

Not so. Mesonotum densely and evenly brownish-yellow pollinose.—*Pterallastes.*

PLATE 52

Platycheirus

Mesogramma
marginata

Sphærophoria
cylindrica

Temnostoma
alternans

Eristalis
tenax

Cuterebra
buccata

Trichopoda
pennipes

Physocephala
sagittaria

Belvosia
bifasciata

Epalpus
signiferus

Tetanocera
plumosa

Scatophaga
stercoraria

Sapromyza
philadelphica

E. B.

Volucella bombylans differs from our other members of the genus by being furry; Pl. 92 shows the subspecies *evecta*. *V. fasciata* is black with yellow markings on the thorax and three rather broad yellow bands on the abdomen; the wings have indistinct dark bands. Some say that the larvæ of *Volucella* feed on the larvæ of bumblebees and wasps but probably they are merely scavengers in the nests of these Hymenoptera. The brilliant green *Ornidia obesa* was formely put in *Volucella.*

About the middle of the 18th century Réaumer, known also for his thermometer, wrote voluminously and exceedingly well on the life histories of insects. It was he who called the larva of *Eristalis tenax* the Rat-tailed Maggot, a name which has stuck. This creature is extremely interesting but one must be interested in order to enjoy it, for it usually lives in foul water, such as privy vaults and the fluid in decaying carcasses. The yellow and black adults, Drone Flies, resemble honey bees, and it was this which led Ovid, Virgil, and other ancient writers to tell about bees originating from dead animals. Pl. 52 shows both adult and larva. The larva's tail lengthens and shortens like a telescope so that the tip may reach the surface of the water and the larva breathe atmospheric air through it while feeding on decaying matter under water. Pupation occurs out of the water in the larval skin. This was originally an Old World species but it is now almost cosmopolitan. Other species of the genus have similar habits.

Syrphus (Pl. 92) and other Aphid-eating genera such as *Mesogramma, Paragus, Melanostoma, Platy-cheirus, Baccha, Sphærophoria, Allograpta* (not included in the key), *Eupeodes* and *Scæva* should be classed among our friends. I have seen ants stop milking their Aphid cows to threaten a female *Syrphus,* and the ants even ran from the upper to the under side of the leaf and back again to keep her in sight but always she succeeded finally in depositing a minute egg in the midst of the herd. I do not believe the ants reasoned that here was an enemy of their friends; they were merely naturally pugnacious toward any intruder and, at any rate, they never noticed the eggs, which doubtless hatched in the course of time into flat, transversely wrinkled, green larvæ, pointed in front and eyeless, but able to search out the sedentary Aphids and to suck their juices.

Species of *Elophilus, Polydontomyia* and *Meromacrus* are scavengers. The larvæ of most of our genera not otherwise mentioned here live under bark or in decaying wood.

CONOPIDÆ

See p. 233. *Physocephala sagittaria* (Pl. 52) gives a fair idea of the family; some are even more wasp-like, some less; all are "thick-headed." They feed on nectar and pollen but the female from time to time leaves this sweet pastime to lay an egg on some bumblebee, wasp, or grasshopper. The larval and pupal periods are passed in the abdomen of the host.

OTITIDÆ

See p. 234. The name Ortalididæ for these must be dropped because it was used first for birds. These flies, like the Trypetidæ, have prettily marked wings. Numerous species are found in meadows. Some, such as *Tritoxa flexa,* Pl. 54, have been bred from onions but the life-histories of most are unknown. The same plate shows *Pyrgota undata,* now placed in the family PYRGOTIDÆ.

TRYPETIDÆ

See p. 234. Also called Trypaneidæ. One nickname is Peacock Flies because they spend much of the time strutting about with brown- or black-spotted wings elevated and waved back and forth. See *Euaresta,* Pl. 54. Several species make galls on goldenrod (Pl. 77); the larvæ of others mine leaves, live in roots, berries and various fruits. It is the latter habit that has fixed on them the nickname Fruit Flies.

Adults of the Apple Maggot, *Rhagoletis pomonella* (Pl. 54), are to be found from July to September. By means of her sharp ovipositor the female punctures the skin of the apple and lays her eggs directly in the pulp. The white larvæ, which taper somewhat toward the front, make winding burrows through the pulp and attain a length of 0.25 in. or more. They then bore out, usually after the apple has fallen, and go about an inch underground, where they spend the winter and spring in a brownish puparium. The larvæ of similar flies, *Rhagoletis cingulata* and *R. fausta,* are the Cherry-worms, known to us all. The currant and gooseberry worm is the larva of *Epochra canadensis.*

When people make laws to prevent the artificial spread of an insect from one part of the world to another it is said that they are "quarantining against" that insect. Probably no insect has been more widely and vigorously quarantined against than the Mediterranean Fruit Fly, *Ceratitis capitata.* It attacks many succulent fruits, including the citrus ones. It broke through our lines into Florida and its extermination there cost a fortune. Without doubt it will come again somewhere.

DROSOPHILIDÆ

See p. 235. The little Red-eyed Pomace-fly, *Drosophila melanogaster* (Pl. 93 has a very poor picture of one. See your fruit-basket during summer), also called Sour Fly and Vinegar Fly, has become famous in the study of heredity and sex. Its larvæ feed on ripe, or over-ripe, bananas and other fruit, also on vinegar, stale beer and the like. The average duration, at living-room temperatures, of the egg period is about 2 days; of the larval period, about 6 days; and of the pupal period, about 5 days. I have kept unmated adults alive, under the same conditions, for about three months. A bit of banana in a milk bottle is all the apparatus one needs to breed this creature and twenty generations a year are easily reared. These facts and its other virtues make it an ideal laboratory animal. Not only have simple cases of Mendelian inheritance been conveniently studied but more complex ones and also the relations between body-characteristics, including sex, and the chromosomes in the germ-cells have been analyzed by its aid. The adults are slaves to light (heliotropic).

Put a number of them in a bottle and they will all crowd to the part which is nearest the window, no matter how much you may turn the bottle about. The males are a trifle smaller than the females and have the hind part of the abdomen more largely pigmented. The males have relatively immense "sex combs" on their front legs. These may be for the sake of appearing more attractive to the females as the males go through their courtship dance, but, on numerous occasions, I cut them off without thereby noticeably decreasing the success of the combless males in the rivalry which I then staged with normal males. The "sex combs" may be to clean his antennæ, but how does she keep hers clean? These "combs" may just happen to be.

There are a number of closely related species.

GASTEROPHILIDÆ

See p. 233. The names of the family and of our only genus, *Gasterophilus,* have usually been spelled without the central *e,* and the species have been classed with Œstridæ. They are the Bot Flies of horses. We have three species: *intestinalis,* looking like a honey-bee with spotted wings; *nasalis,* smaller and wings unspotted; and *hæmorrhoidalis,* having its abdomen red-tipped. Eggs are laid on horses and swallowed by them when they lick themselves. The larvæ attach themselves to the walls of the digestive tract and live there until ready to pupate, at which time they pass out with the excrement.

ŒSTRIDÆ

See p. 236. The subfamilies (or families) of our Gad Flies, also called Bot Flies, Warble Flies and Breeze Flies, may be distinguished as follows.

1.—Postscutellum undeveloped. **Large,** robust species. The abdomen with very short app**ress**ed hairs. Rodent parasites.—Cuterebrinæ (Pseudogametinæ and Dermatobiinæ in the Tropics).

 Postscutellum strongly developed (as in Tachinidæ). More slender, generally hairy flies. ....**2.**

2.—Middle part of face narrow. Hypopleuræ with a fan of strong hairs.—Œstrinæ.

Middle part of face broad, forming a slightly convex plate. Hypopleuræ with a bundle of hairs.—Hypodermatinæ (possibly not to be separated from Œstrinæ).

Among Cuterebrinæ the larvæ of *Cuterebra* (*Bogeria*?) *buccata* (Pl. 52) and others live under the skin of rabbits. This subfamily seems to be related to Sarcophagidæ.

Œstrus ovis is the Sheep Bot. Its larvæ live in the head-cavities of sheep, causing the disease known as staggers or false gid.

Species of *Hypoderma* are the Warble Flies of cattle. Hadwen's work has changed our ideas concerning their life-histories. Eggs are laid on the hair, chiefly of the hind legs, but, instead of being taken into the mouth when the animal licks itself, they hatch there and the larvæ bore through the skin, migrate to the region of the animal's gullet, and later to the skin of its back. There, chiefly along the spine, they cause the swellings or "warbles." When full-grown they come out and pupate in the ground. The bad effect on the animal's health and the decreased value of "grubby" hides are often serious.

TACHINOIDEA

Tachinoidea is a rather easily recognized group but its subdivisions are very difficult to classify and the limits are not clear. Some authors place the Œstridæ here. The following treatment is suggested by Dr. Curran.

Postscutellum absent (no strong convexity beneath the scutellum, although there may be a slight swelling). Antennæ generally plumose but rarely so to the apex. Thorax usually black and gray striped or metallic.—Sarcophagidæ, including the Calliphoridæ.

Postscutellum strongly developed, rarely rather weak. Antennæ plumose (usually to the end), pubescent or bare. Thorax often striped, rarely metallic (if so the abdomen with strong, erect bristles).—Tachinidæ, including the Dexiidæ.

SARCOPHAGIDÆ

As treated here the family includes what have been also known as Metopiidæ and Calliphoridæ. The species of the former have been included in the Tachinidæ while the latter have been placed in the Muscidæ. The groups can be separated only upon fine, technical characters but those species with bare arista may be considered as belonging to the Metopiinæ (Miltogramminæ) and, with us, those with metallic coloring may be placed in the Calliphorinæ and all others in the Sarcophaginæ. This separation may appear crude but it will work in most cases.

The Sarcophaginæ are popularly called Flesh Flies, a translation of the scientific name. The principal genus is *Sarcophaga* (Pl. 93). Although the larvæ of most of the species justify the names by feeding on flesh, living or dead, those of others feed on dung and decaying vegetable matter. Some live under the skin of turtles; others in the stomachs of frogs; while still others devour living snails and insects. Nasal myiasis in man is due to the species of this genus. The eggs of some species hatch in the female's body, so that she lays living and rather large larvæ. It is claimed that 20,000 eggs have been found in the ovaries of a single female of others.

The term Blow Fly usually refers to the Calliphorinæ. Species of *Protocalliphora* have the disagreeable habit of breeding in nestling birds, causing their death, but this is now offset by the discovery that other kinds of Calliphorinæ, particularly *Phormia regina,* can save human lives. Their larvæ are used in surgery to cleanse deep wounds and diseased bone. Some of our species, particularly in the East, may be distinguished as follows.

1.—Thorax with a fairly distinct median dark stripe (When the stripe is very faint try 4). Abdomen metallic blue or green; not maculated. ....2.
　　Thorax with the median stripe light, or else no distinct stripes. ....3.
2.—Face light yellow. Thorax metallic with very distinct stripes.—*Cochliomyia* (formerly *Chrysomyia*, Pl. 93) *macellaria.* The mature larva is about 0.75 in. long.

Its pointed shape and a ring of bristles between each pair of segments have given it the name Screw Worm. It feeds on carrion but also on living animals, including man, the eggs being laid in open wounds or in the nose. In the latter case the larvæ work their way into the cavities of the head and sometimes cause death.

Face reddish-brown. Thorax non-metallic; stripes rather indistinct.—*Cynomyia cadaverina* (Pl. 53).

3.—Abdomen grayish, non-metallic. Thorax without distinct stripes and usually covered with a yellow "dust." The space between the eyes white. More than 2 pairs of acrostical bristles; 2 anterior and 3 posterior dorsocentrals.—*Pollenia rudis* (Pl. 53). On account of its habit of overlapping the wings when at rest, it often appears narrower than *Musca domestica*. The exact date of its introduction from Europe is unknown. It has been bred from manure, but probably only when the manure contained earthworms, as it has been bred from these common creatures. The adults are rather sluggish and have been called Cluster Flies from their habit of congregating in masses, especially about the ceilings of rooms. They are looking for a place to hibernate and may find it in closets, behind curtains, or in other nooks. When mashed, these flies are very greasy and have an odor which has been described by some as like honey and by others as "very disagreeable." It is even more susceptible to attack by a fungus (*Empusa*) than is *Musca domestica*.

Not so. ....**4.**

4.—Thorax not metallic. No spines on 3rd longitudinal vein except at its junction with the 2nd. ....**5.**

Thorax and abdomen bright metallic blue or green. Spines on the first section of the 3rd longitudinal vein. ....**7.**

5.—Distal third of arista naked. Bucca ("cheeks") red in front; black behind.—*Cynomyia cadaverina* (Pl. 53).

Distal third of arista bearing some hairs. Bucca unicolorous.—*Calliphora*. A female lays up to several hundred small eggs on meat or dead animals. They hatch in a few hours, sometimes even before they are laid. The pupal stage is reached in a week or ten days and lasts about two weeks. Pupation usually takes place under the food mass, often slightly below the surface of the ground. The following three species occur also in Europe. ....**6.**

6.—Bucca black. Beard red.—*C. vomitoria*.

Bucca brownish or reddish. Beard black.—*C. erythrocephala*.

Bucca black. Beard black.—*C. viridescens*.

7.—Two stout bristles on dorsal hind margin of the 2nd

PLATE 53

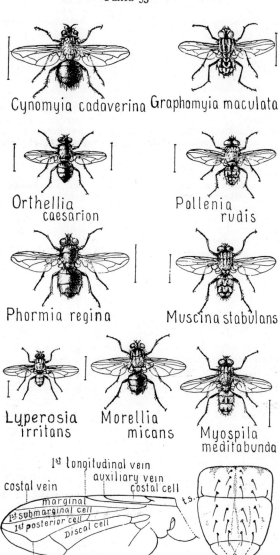

Cynomyia cadaverina Graphomyia maculata

Orthellia
caesarion

Pollenia
rudis

Phormia regina

Muscina stabulans

Lyperosia
irritans

Morellia
micans

Myospila
meditabunda

costal vein

1st longitudinal vein
auxiliary vein
costal cell

marginal
1st submarginal cell
1st posterior cell

Discal cell

t.s.

4th longitudinal vein

d. c.

abdominal segment.—*Lucilia sylvarum,* the bluest of our Bluebottles.

Not so. . . . .**8.**

8.—Acrostical bristles in front of the transverse suture wanting or feebly developed. . . . .**9.**

These bristles well developed. The front, between the eyes, usually distinctly margined with white. . . . . . .**10.**

9.—Squamæ brownish, especially the rim. Eyes of male separated by more than twice the width of the ocellar triangle. Acrostical bristles absent or scarcely stronger than the hairs.—*Phormia terrænovæ,* a Northern species.

Squamæ white or with a grayish tinge; the rim pale. Eyes of the male not more widely separated than the width of the ocellar triangle. Acrostical bristles coarse, though short.—*Phormia regina* (Pl. 53). The Surgical Fly (p. 263) occurs throughout our region.

10.—Both costal scales at base of wing black or brown. Normally two pairs of postsutural bristles. Metallic greenish or bluish.—*Lucilia lepida (cæsar,* Pl. 93). It has been reared from excrement and garbage, although carrion is the chief larval food of this genus.

Only the basal scale (epaulet) black; the other reddish. Normally three pairs of postsutural acrostical bristles. Metallic green; the abdomen usually, and sometimes the thorax, brassy or bronzed; very rarely bluish. —*Lucilia sericata.*

TACHINIDÆ

How large this family is nobody knows and few are qualified to identify the species, despite the fact that they are both interesting to the student and beneficial to all men. Many of them are common and easily recognized but so many are not that, as one Dipterist remarked, "they give a headache." As here treated, the Dexiidæ are included as well as several other family names proposed by various authors. Curran states that "there is no character or group of characters that does not lose its value in the diagnosis of groups (subfamilies, tribes, etc.) and it is therefore obvious that the so-called families are not tenable if we go beyond the fauna of a small or limited region." The Dexiidæ were separated because they had plumose arista while the Tachinidæ supposedly had bare or pubescent arista.

Amateur Lepidopterists often raise Tachinids instead of Lepidoptera when they work with caterpillars which were hatched afield. The other large orders of insects also furnish hosts for these guardians of the Balance of Nature. Pl. 52 shows *Belvosia bifasciata* and *Epalpus signiferus;* the former is parasitic on various Cerato-campidæ. *Trichopoda pennipes* on the same plate has been bred from the Squash Bug, *Anasa. Bombyliopsis* (*Bombyliomyia*) *abrupta* (Pl. 92) is often seen at the edge of woods and in clearings.

In the last edition of his excellent *Introduction to Entomology* Comstock wrote as follows—a volume could be written—about Tachinid life-histories: "The manner in which the larva finds its way into the body of its host differs greatly in different species of tachinids. Many observations on this have been made at the Gipsy Moth Laboratory and reported by Townsend. In many species the female fastens her eggs to the skin of the caterpillar; when the larvæ hatch they bore their way into their host and live there till they are full-grown. In some of the viviparous species the female punctures the skin of the caterpillar with the sheath of her ovipositor and deposits the larva within the body of the host. Some species deposit their eggs on the leaves of the food-plant of their host; these eggs are swallowed when the leaves are eaten. But most remarkable of all is the method practiced by *Eupeleteria magnicornis;* this is a viviparous species which infests the larva of the brown-tail moth. It attaches its larvæ to the surface of stems and leaves by a thin membranous case, which is cup-shaped and surrounds the anal end of the larva. Attached to the stem or leaf by this base, the maggot is able to reach out in all directions as far as its length will permit. As the maggot is deposited on the silken thread with which the caterpillar marks its trail as it leaves its nest, it is in a position where it can attach itself to the caterpillar when it is on its way back to the nest."

MUSCOIDEA

See p. 236. Some authors unite these with the Tachinoidea. Within the Muscoidea the groups are very difficult to separate since, so far as found, no diagnostic character holds throughout. For this reason there is a tendency to consider them as all one family, Muscidæ.

Being a bit conservative, I still keep the groups as families but, being a bit liberal, I have no objection to your changing "dæ" to "næ," making them subfamilies. In any case, we shall probably soon be out of date. The following is a modification of the Brues and Melander key.

1.—Fourth vein often bending forward, narrowing the apical cell at the margin. If the apical cell is not narrowed, then the eyes are not widely separated, or cruciate (crossing) bristles are present on the front, and the lower calypter is longer than the upper, and the abdomen proper contains only 5 segments; if the eyes are widely separated (females and some males), the oval, more or less bristly abdomen is somewhat distinctive. Scutellar suture complete. ....2.

Apical cell not narrowed at margin. No cruciate frontal bristles. Eyes broadly separated in both sexes. Lower calypter not longer than the upper. Scutellar suture interrupted in the middle. Abdomen more or less elongate.—Cordyluridæ.

2.—Fourth vein curving backward (if curving forward, the arista not feathered to the tip). Arista sometimes bare. Abdomen usually bristly. Neither the hypopleural nor pteropleural hairs or bristles present.—Anthomyiidæ.

Fourth vein bending or curving forward. Arista feathered to tip. Basal bristles of abdomen reduced. Either the hypopleural or pteropleural bristles or hairs present.—Muscidæ.

CORDYLURIDÆ

These have usually been classed with the Acalyptratæ and the family name has usually been Scatophagidæ. The species of *Scatophaga* (Pl. 52, possibly *Scopeuma* is a better name) are common about cow-dung, in which their larvæ live. They are moderately large, yellow-haired flies, with rather slim bodies and longish legs. These adults are predacious, catching even bees. Others of the numerous genera have other habits. The larvæ of some live in the stems of plants and some are said to be parasitic in caterpillars.

ANTHOMYIIDÆ

This is a large family of inconspicuously colored, small to moderately large flies. The squamæ are usually of considerable size. The larvæ have four rows of thread-like processes on the segments. The common Radish-worm is the larva of *Paregle radicum.* The larva of *Hylemya cilicrura* is a general feeder in roots of cabbage, radish, onion, seed corn, and the like. It is an importation from Europe, first noted in this country in 1856. The common Cabbage Maggot is the larva of *Hylemya brassicæ,* which also attacks cauliflower and radishes. Just as the plants are commencing to make a good growth, they suddenly wilt and die although not cut off as by a Noctuid larva. Old cabbage stumps should not be allowed to stay in the garden, as they harbor late-generation larvæ and overwintering pupæ. A troublesome pest in onion bulbs is the Imported Onion Maggot (*Hylemya antiqua*), although the native *Phorbia ceparum* does some damage (*Chætopsis ænea* of the Ortalidæ is another onion maggot). The larvæ of *Pegomya rubivora* girdle the inner bark of the tips of young raspberry and blackberry shoots. The larvæ of *Pegomya hyoscyami* make tortuous mines and large blotches in the leaves of beet and spinach. Pupation takes place in loose soil or under fallen leaves. Chittenden notes that "in many cases infestation can be traced directly to the insect having bred in lambs-quarters and similar weeds." *Ophyra leucostoma* breeds in excrement.

Especially in May and June, *Fannia canicularis,* an at first slight small edition of *Musca domestica,* is sometimes abundant in houses. Those who do not know that insects do not grow after getting functional wings believe them to be the young of the larger and more common insect. However, all the veins run without sharp bends to the margins of the wings. The early spring adults have probably been hibernating in the house. The larvæ of the Lesser Housefly live in waste vegetable matter, in the manure of different animals, and especially in human excrement. They have also been found in Yellow-jacket Wasp nests where they were probably cleaning up the debris.

MUSCIDÆ

The notorious Tsetse Flies of Africa are classed near here, usually as a separate family, Glossinidæ. Our more common Muscidæ may be separated as follows:

1.—Proboscis of both sexes elongate, rigid, fitted for piercing and sucking blood.—Stomoxydinæ. . . . . .2.
    Proboscis not stiff, the labella fleshy, fitted for lapping. . . . . .3.
2.—Palpi much shorter than the proboscis.—*Stomoxys calcitrans* (Pl. 93), the Biting Housefly. Specimens taken on the borders of woods often have brownish wings. Their superficial resemblance to *M. domestica* and their biting habits have given rise to the error that the latter species is adding to its many sins by sucking blood. Both sexes suck blood. On account of *calcitrans* being more troublesome during rains, it is sometimes called the Storm Fly. Another common name is Stable Fly. It has been, probably unjustly, accused of carrying infantile paralysis. The larvæ feed on a wide range of decaying matter, including fermenting grass cut from lawns, horse manure, and human excrement. It is worldwide in its distribution.
    Dark ash-gray, with a faint tinge of yellow. Thorax and abdomen with no distinct markings. Much smaller than *Musca domestica*. Palpi nearly as long as the proboscis.—*Lyperosia irritans* (Pl. 53). The name Texas Fly was based on the supposition that this species originated in the West. It came from Europe to the vicinity of Philadelphia about 1887 and is now found from Canada to the Gulf and at least as far west as Idaho. It was formerly abundant in the East but is now rather rare. The name Horn Fly comes from the habit which the adults have of clustering about the base of the horns of cattle to suck blood. The larvæ live in cow dung.
3.—Thorax with three blackish stripes. Abdomen nonmetallic in color, maculated. Squamæ slightly dusky. Some, at least, American specimens lack the yellowish color on the scutellum which has been recorded for European ones.—*Graphomyia maculata* (Pl. 53). The larvæ live in excrement.
    Thorax with the median stripe light or with no distinct stripes. . . . . .4.
4.—Abdomen opaque brown, a pair of triangular black spots on each of the 2nd and 3rd abdominal segments of the male (these spots faint or wanting in the female). Squamæ yellowish (See also **8**)—*Myospila meditabunda* (Pl. 53). The larvæ live in excrement. Only a few (several dozen) eggs are laid by each female. The eggs have a black stripe on each side and, as continuations of

these, a black curved appendage. This fly is common to
both Europe and America

 Not so. ....**5.**
5.—The 4th longitudinal vein slightly bent. ....**6.**
 The 4th vein sharply bent. ....**7.**
6.—First posterior cell narrowly constricted at the margin. Bluish-black, shining. Tip of scutellum not reddish.
Median light stripe on the thorax rather distinct. Tip of
abdomen brown with a hoary coating.—*Morellia micans*
(Pl. 53). Breeds in excrement, often abundant in human
fæces.

 First posterior cell scarcely constricted at the margin.
Black, not shining. Tip of scutellum sometimes reddish.
—*Muscina assimilis* (legs and palpi wholly black) and
M. stabulans (tibiæ and part of femora reddish; apex
of scutellum and the palpi reddish yellow; Pl. 53). The
larvæ feed on excrement and a variety of decaying substances, including fungi and vegetables. *M. stabulans* has
been reared from the pupæ of other insects but the pupæ
had probably died first, as it is not likely that the species
is parasitic. Both species are widely distributed in
Europe and America, *stabulans* usually being the com-
moner.

7.—Abdomen non-metallic. ....**8.**
 Abdomen metallic. Metallic between the eyes. A
prominent bristle on the inner surface of each middle
tibia.—*Orthellia cæsarion* (Pl. 53). The brilliant blue
larvæ are often abundant in cow dung.
8.—Thorax with distinct stripes only in front, if at all.
Not more than 2 pairs of acrostical bristles; 2 anterior
and 4 posterior dorsocentrals.—*Myiospila meditabunda*
(See **4**).

 Thorax with four stripes. Not more than 2 pairs of
acrostical bristles; 3 anterior and 4 posterior dorsocentrals.—*Musca domestica.*

As in many other flies, the males of *Musca domestica*
(Pl. 93), the House, or Disease, or Typhoid Fly, have
their eyes nearer together than the females. The sides
of the abdomen of the males are brownish yellow on
the basal half, or less, and grayish elsewhere. The
females usually have the sides of the abdomen reddish
toward the base, being otherwise grayish over all the
abdomen with a variable pattern of darker gray or
black. It takes the egg about twelve hours, on the average, to hatch. In about five days the larvæ are full-
grown and the pupal stage lasts from five days to a
month or longer. The puparium is the old larval skin,
hardened and brown. Each female usually lays from

one to two hundred eggs in the garbage or manure which is the food of the larvæ. Adults may hibernate, but so also do pupæ and larvæ. See *Fannia*.

Before the days of modern plumbing and the general fear of flies that breed in dirty places but do not wipe their feet, the "Swat the fly" campaigns were very necessary in keeping our food from being contaminated. Now, fortunately, conditions are better in all but backward communities.

PUPIPARA

See p. 233. Quite probably the BRAULIDÆ should be put elsewhere but their affinities are still uncertain. They are very tiny louse-like insects with short, thick legs, vestigial eyes, and neither wings nor halteres. Each last tarsal joint has a pair of comb-like appendages. Eggs of the single genus, *Braula,* are laid among the brood of bees, at least of *Apis*. The larvæ feed on the bees' food. Adults ride about on adult bees.

The other families live on warm-blooded vertebrates. The larvæ develop in their mother's body to such an extent that they are born as pupæ or as full-grown larvæ just ready to pupate. Hence the name of the group.

The NYCTERIBIIDÆ are wingless, long-legged parasites on bats. The small head can be folded back into a groove on the flat, broad mesonotum. The STREBLIDÆ also are parasites of bats. The palpi are leaf-like, projecting in front of the head but not sheathing the proboscis. Some are winged.

The HIPPOBOSCIDÆ have the head partly sunk into a hollow in the thorax. The head and body are often flattened. The palpi are not as described for Streblidæ. Eyes round or oval. Tarsal claws strong and often armed with a series of small teeth. Wings usually present but not, for example, in *Melophagus ovinus* (Pl. 54), the Sheep-Tick, which is, of course, not a tick but an insect. Young adults of *Lipoptena depressa,* a parasite on deer, have wings which they shed when they have found their deer. The yellowish-winged *Olfersia americana* (Pl. 54) is fairly common on hawks, owls and some other birds.

PLATE 54

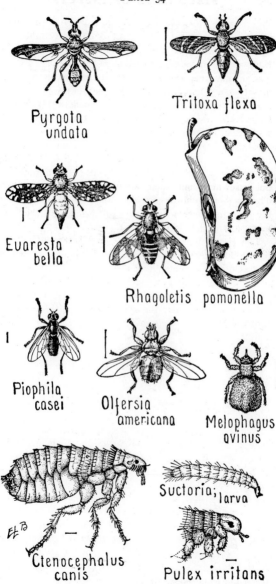

Pyrgota
undata

Tritoxa flexa

Euaresta
bella

Rhagoletis pomonella

Piophila
casei

Olfersia
americana

Melophagus
ovinus

Ctenocephalus
canis

Suctoria; larva

Pulex irritans

SIPHONAPTERA

See p. 39. This order, the Fleas, has been called Suctoria and Aphaniptera also. One suborder, FRAC-TICIPITA, has the head divided above the antennæ into two distinct parts by a suture; but we are more likely to be interested in the other suborder, INTEGRI-CIPITA. The following are of the latter. The family PULICIDÆ contains, among others, the common Dog Flea, *Ctenocephalus* (or *Ctenocephalides*) *canis,* the usually rare with us Human Flea, *Pulex irritans* (See Pl. 54 for both), and the Rat Fleas that transmit disease such as bubonic plague. The larvæ are worm-like. They live in rubbish and dust such as accumulates at the edges of carpets and in the folds of upholstery. The pupæ are enclosed in cocoons.

The Jigger Flea or Chigoe, *Tunga penetrans,* belongs to the TUNGIDÆ, also called Dermatophilidæ. (A mite that also burrows into human skin is often called Jigger or Chigger.) This flea infests birds and mammals, including man. The male feeds externally but the female works her way under the skin, causing a serious ulcer through which the eggs are released.

COLEOPTERA

See p. 39. Beetles may usually be recognized, when adult, by the fact that their front wings ("elytra") are usually hardened. The elytra do not overlap but in most species meet in a line (the "suture") along the middle of the back. However, in Staphylinidæ and some other groups or species within groups (sometimes as a secondary sexual characteristic) they do not completely cover the abdomen. The larvæ have no abdominal legs except (often) on the last joint. About 22,000 species are known from North America.

An old way of splitting this large order into smaller pieces is by grouping the families into a number of "series." These do not correspond to the more modern "superfamilies"; and technical studies, particularly of larvæ, cast doubt upon the scientific accuracy of the old groups and the order in which they were arranged. Nevertheless, the old has its good points. The following is given as a help both in identification and in translating from the old to the still somewhat chaotic newer.

What are here given as the superfamilies Brentoidea, Curculionoidea, and Scolytoidea of the present suborder Polyphaga were made the suborder Rhynchophora, distinct from "genuine Coleoptera." The head is usually more or less prolonged in front to form a beak; palpi usually rigid and not clearly evident; prosternal sutures wanting.

The "genuine Coleoptera" were as follows.

Series I.—ADEPHAGA. See p. 277, where it is ranked as a suborder. The first three ventral abdominal segments are united; the sides of the first separated from the very small median portion by the hind coxal cavities. There is a suture on each side of the prothorax marking off the top of it from the sides. Tarsi 5-jointed. Antennæ usually nearly or quite thread-like.

Series II.—CLAVICORNIA. The antennæ usually have the terminal joints more or less enlarged ("club-like"), rarely serrate ("saw-like"). First ventral abdominal segment visible for its entire breadth, except in Rhysodidæ. If there are 5 tarsal joints, the 5th is distinct, not fused with the 4th. This was and still is a troublesome series. They were divided into subseries as follows:

1.—Elytra usually short, leaving most of the abdomen exposed. Wings usually present and, when not in use, folded under the elytra. Skin of the dorsal part of abdomen "horny."—BRACHELYTRA. The Pselaphidæ and Staphylinidæ of the present Staphylinoidea (p. 293).

Elytra usually covering most of the abdomen; when not, the wings either absent or not folded under the elytra when at rest. Not all of the top of the abdomen horny. ....2.

2.—At least one pair of tarsi 5-jointed.—PENTAMERA. This large subseries included the present Hydrophiloidea (p. 290), most of the Silphoidea (p. 291), most of the Cucujoidea (p. 295), the Dermestidæ (p. 312), the Histeridæ (p. 295), Dryopidæ (p. 316), Rhysodidæ (p. 316), and some other, mostly small, families.

Tarsi 4-jointed, except the front ones of some male Mycetophagidæ.—TETRAMERA. A few Silphoidea such as Clambidæ; some Cucujoidea such as Erotylidæ and Colydiidæ; and several other small families, including Heteroceridæ and Georyssidæ.

Tarsi at least apparently 3-jointed.—TRIMERA. The Coccinellidæ (p. 297), Endomychidæ and Lathridiidæ of the Cucujoidea; also Monotomidæ.

Series III.—SERRICORNIA. Antennæ more or less "saw-toothed" from the third joint outward; rarely club-shaped. The Elateroidea (p. 301), Bostrichoidea (p. 326), Cupesidæ (p. 277), Cantharoidea (p. 308), Cleroidea (p. 310) and Lymexyloidea (p. 316).

Series II and III were sometimes united under the name POLYMORPHA.

Series IV.—LAMELLICORNIA, here the Scarabæoidea (p. 331). Antennæ with the outer 3 to 7 joints enlarged on one side to form a club, which is either a comb or a number of plates. Front tibiæ toothed or scalloped on the outer edges and usually enlarged. Tarsi usually 5-jointed, the front one sometimes reduced or absent.

Series V.—PHYTOPHAGA (p. 341). The families Cerambycidæ, Chrysomelidæ and Mylabridæ (or Bruchidæ), each of which is likely to be made into a superfamily and split into families. The tarsi usually with the 4th joint small and firmly united to the 5th so that the tarsi appear to be 4-jointed; the 3 basal joints usually pubescent beneath; the 3rd joint grooved or divided, the 4th joint attached near the base of the 3rd. Labrum visible.

Series VI.—HETEROMERA (p. 317). This roughly corresponds to Tenebrionoidea and Mordelloidea, including Meloidæ.

The order is here divided into three suborders: Archostemata, Adephaga, and Polyphaga (p. 290).

ARCHOSTEMATA

It is not clear that these are the most primitive beetles but they must be put somewhere and they do not fit well elsewhere. We have only two very small families.

CUPESIDÆ.—*Priacma* is in the extreme West. Otherwise, our only genus is *Cupes*. Its head and thorax are narrower than the combined elytra, which are beautifully sculptured in sunken rows separated by ridges. The principal species is the pale brownish or ashy gray *concolor* about 0.3 in. long. It occurs on dead wood and under bark. Some authors give this family a superfamily pigeon-hole of its own, Cupesoidea.

MICROMALTHIDÆ.—See also p. 317. *Micromalthus debilis* is about 0.1 in. long, narrow-bodied, shiny black with yellow antennæ and legs; elytra not completely covering the abdomen. It is said that "eggs are produced by larvæ as well as by the adult females; that there are seven or eight forms of larvæ; that the two sexes are developed through two distinct lines of larvæ; and that viviparous as well as oviparous pædogenesis [p. 83] occurs in the life-cycle. The larvæ are found in decaying oak, chestnut, and pine logs, where they make burrows in the decaying wood, on which they feed."

ADEPHAGA

These are almost completely predacious beetles. Their distinguishing characters are given on p. 275.

On the Pacific Coast there are several species of *Amphizoa,* family AMPHIZOIDÆ, that cling to objects in running water. They walk, not swim. Their head has no antennal grooves beneath. PSEUDOMORPHIDÆ is another small family. Its species have antennal grooves beneath between the eyes and the maxillary fissures. These two families are practically Carabidæ but the mentum and submentum are not separated by a distinct suture. Another troublesome little family is RHYSODIDÆ. It has recently been shifted from Polyphaga to Adephaga. Its few species occur under bark. The head and prothorax have deep longitudinal grooves. The families of Adephaga likely to be noticed are the following.

1.—Legs not fitted for swimming although the Haliplidæ are aquatic. ....2.

Aquatic. Legs fitted for swimming. ....3.

2.—Antennæ arising from the front of the head, above the base of the mandibles; 11-jointed, thread-like, with at least the 6 outer joints pubescent. Usually the head is vertical and wider than the thorax. Eyes usually prominent (bulging). Legs slender. All tarsi distinctly 5-jointed. Usually metallic green or bronze or, like *lepida* and *dorsalis* that live on white sand, grayish-white.—CICINDELIDÆ, Tiger Beetles. See p. 280 and *Cicindela*, Pls. 55 and 94.

Antennæ arising from the sides of the head between the base of the mandibles and the eyes; 11-jointed, usually distinctly thread-like (However, see *Scarites*, p. 283), with at least the 6 outer joints pubescent. Eyes usually moderate in size (However, see *Elaphrus*, p. 283). Head usually horizontal or slightly inclined, and usually narrower than the thorax. All of the tarsi distinctly 5-jointed. Usually black, blue, green, or brown, and a few are spotted.—CARABIDÆ. See p. 281 and Pls. 55 and 94, also the next two paragraphs.

Having the characters given above for Carabidæ but no scutellum; prosternum covering the mesosternum.—OMOPHRONIDÆ. *Omophron* includes a few circular, yellow beetles, checkered with dark green, that live by day in damp sand and come out at night to seek their prey.

Antennæ 10-jointed. Hind coxæ much enlarged, covering part of the hind femora and 3 to 6 abdominal segments. The beetles are small, oval, brown or yellow, more or less spotted with black. Back very rounded. Widest near the front of the elytra.—HALIPLIDÆ, p. 285.

3.—Antennæ 11-jointed, usually thread-like and not pubescent. Hind legs longest and adapted for swimming, being more or less flattened and fringed with long hairs (These hairs may be flattened against the legs and hard to see). Tarsi 5-jointed; the 4th joint of the anterior and middle tarsi obsolete in some of the smaller species.—DYTISCIDÆ, p. 286.

Antennæ short, thick, and stumpy; the third joint enlarged. Eyes divided by the sides of the head into an upper and underneath portion, giving the insects the appearance of having two eyes for looking up into the air and two for gazing down into the water. Middle

Plate 55

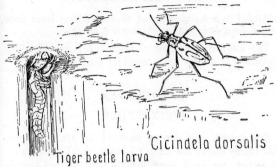

Cicindela dorsalis

Tiger beetle larva

Cychrus
elevatus

Carabus
vinctus

Harpalus
caliginosus

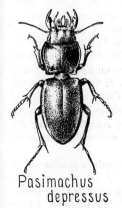

Pasimachus
depressus

Dicaelus
elongatus

Poecilus
lucublandus

and hind legs forming broad, short paddles; front ones rather long and slender.—GYRINIDÆ, p. 289.

The following grouping of families into superfamilies follows that of the Leng-Mutchler Catalogue.

CARABOIDEA

CICINDELIDÆ

See p. 278. So far as most of us are concerned, this family means the genus *Cicindela,* the Tiger Beetles. However, we have three genera with more Carabid-like habits.

1.—Hind coxæ touching each other. Eyes prominent..**2.**
    Hind coxæ separated. Eyes small. . . . .**3.**
2.—Third joint of maxillary palpi shorter than the fourth.— *Cicindela.*
    Third joint longer than the fourth. — *Tetracha.* Southern.
3.—Sides of elytra widely inflexed. Thorax scarcely margined.—*Amblycheila.* Western.
    Sides of elytra narrowly inflexed. Thorax distinctly margined.—*Omus.* Pacific Coast.

Adult *Cicindela* have much very fine recumbent hair, as well as erect bristles. "They are long-legged, rather slender, active beetles, predatory in habit, living usually in the open sandy places, and flying readily when disturbed. The larvæ are uncouth creatures, with large head and prominent jaws, that live in vertical burrows [usually] in sandy soil, watching at the mouth for such unwary creatures as may come their way" (Smith). The larvæ have a hump on the fifth abdominal segment. This hump is provided with forward-pointing hooks that help the larvæ to hold back if their prey should try to get away. See Pl. 55. The burrow, which is often a foot or more deep and within which the larva pupates, may be recognized by the smooth, circular depression, worn by the larva's feet, surrounding the opening.

The following are some of the common species in the Northeast.

C. dorsalis (Pl. 55) is white with variable black markings; along the seashore in July. Pl. 94 shows *gener-*

osa (a variety of *formosa*), which lives on sandy plains, and *sexguttata* (the number of white dots is variable) of sunny woodland paths. *C. repanda* of pond and river banks, is bronzy-brown above with three white marks on each elytron: one at the shoulder, one at the apex, and one which is somewhat like an eighth-note in music, in the middle. *C. hirticollis* is like it but hairier and the shoulder spots are upturned at their tips. *C. tranquebarica* is larger (about 0.6 in. long), the tips of the shoulder spots are down-turned; frequents sandy roads. *C. punctulata,* which is dark above (greenish-blue beneath) except for small white dots, is abundant on roads, garden paths, and even city streets, flying freely to light in midsummer; each elytron has a row of green punctures along the suture in addition to densely placed, uncolored ones. *C. modesta* is black and *C. rugifrons* is green. Each has three large white spots and is a variety of *scuttelaris*. They are found in pine barrens.

CARABIDÆ

See p. 278. Most of the many Ground Beetles are plain black or brown. Ornamental hairs are found only in *Brachynus* and *Chlænius* but erect setæ are present and are important in technical classification. Althougl some bright-colored Lebiini hunt by day on plants, mos of the family hide under stones or other cover. If dis turbed, they run rapidly but rarely fly except by night when some species swarm about lights. They are bene ficial because of their predacious habits. The larvæ are relatively long, and rather flat. They have sharp, projecting mandibles and a pair of posterior bristly ap pendages. They usually live in underground burrows, pupating iin small earthen cells.

Cychrus (now divided into several genera) is usually rather rare; and, since the violet or brownish-purple beetles are reasonably large, they are often sought by collectors. The pronotum is more or less turned up at the edges (Pl. 55). The long, narrow, straight head and mandibles may be thrust into snail-shells in order to draw out the owners. The palpi are shaped like a long-handled spoon. The genus is to be found only where snails are common: in moist woods and similar places.

Carabus may be separated from *Calosoma* by the fact that the former has the third antennal joint cyclindrical and that the latter has it compressed.

The species of *Carabus* are black or brownish-black and about an inch long. Here are some samples. *C. sylvosus:* margins (upturned) of pronotum and of elytra blue; striæ on elytra very fine; usually in sandy woods. *C. serratus:* margins (slightly upturned) of pronotum and of elytra violet; elytra with two or three slight notches in the margin near the base; usually in damp places. *C. limbatus:* bluish margins; pronotum a half wider than long; elytra deeply striate; usually in moist upland woods. *C. vinctus* (Pl. 55): bronzed, pronotum with a greenish tinge at borders; usually under bark in low, moist woods. All may be caught by sinking bottles or cans, baited with molasses, in the soil.

Species of *Calosoma* are usually found under cover in gardens, fields, and open woods; sometimes abundant at light. Their common name, Caterpillar Hunters, should recommend them, as it is well given. Pl. 94 gives sufficient help in identifying *calidum* and *scrutator*. *C. externum* is about 1.25 in. long; margins of pronotum and elytra blue; pronotum with the sides rounded, flattened, and turned up behind. Mr. Davis told of a "specimen which was found under an electric light and squirted its acrid fluid into my face at a distance of about a foot." They will do that sometimes. *C. will-coxi* is similar to *scrutator* but only about 0.75 in. long; the thorax is relatively narrower, and the margins of the elytra are sometimes green. *C. frigidum:* about 0.8 in. long; black above, greenish-black below; pronotum and elytra with narrow, green margins; spots on elytra, green. *C. sayi:* similar but found from N. Y. southward, while *frigidum* occurs from N. Y. northward. *C. sycophanta* was recently introduced near Boston from Europe to aid in fighting the Brown-tail Moth and is now to be found in the vicinity of New York City and elsewhere. It is the size of *scrutator;* the pronotum and underside are dark blue; and there is no reddish margin on the green elytra.

, Even after I was supposed to know something about entomology I tried to place *Elaphrus ruscarius* in *Cicindela*. All of the genus have the general form of Tiger Beetles, but they are smaller and lack the ornamental hairs. They inhabit sand-bars and mud-flats. *E. ruscarius* is about 0.25 in. long; dull brassy above, metallic green beneath; the numerous, circular impressions on the elytra are purplish; legs, reddish-brown. Adults have been taken even at Christmas time as far north as Indiana.

A black Carabid which is an inch or so long and whose pronotum seems too big for it (suggesting a collar that has come loose and moved up the neck) probably belongs to *Pasimachus*. They occur especially where the soil is sandy and are caterpillar hunters. *P. depressus* (Pl. 55) is blue-margined, but often faintly. *P. sublævis* occurs on the beach; the pronotum and elytra are margined (often faintly) with blue; pronotum squarish but pushed in at the front and somewhat bulged at the sides; tip of closed elytra rounded.

Species of *Scarites* are narrow; the pronotum is rounded behind and somewhat "too big"; the wide, flat front tibiæ are toothed. The common species of our gardens is *subterraneus*. It is usually less than 0.8 in. long. The Southern *substriatus* may be only a variety of it an inch or more in length. These species are shiny black. The head has two, deeply indented, parallel lines; the sides of the squarish pronotum are nearly straight and it is separated from the elytra by a neck; the elytra are distinctly striate. They are often found in gardens and feign death by holding the body rigid for a time, but soon run off to shelter.

Numerous small species of *Dyschirius* and *Clivina* live in damp soil, especially shady or muddy banks, and may be collected by throwing water on the banks, forcing the beetles out of the ground for air or to satisfy their curiosity as to the state of the weather. They are usually less than 0.4 in. long and have two bristle-bearing punctures above each eye and at each hind angle of the pronotum. *Pasimachus* and *Scarites* have only one at each of these places. The pronotum of *Dyschi-rius* is globular or oval and that of *Clivina* is squarish. Other, less common, genera may be distinguished from *Dyschirius* and *Clivina* by the fact that their front tarsi are dilated, while those of *D.* and *C.* are slender, and by the absence of a neck between the thorax and the elytra. *Bembidion* and *Tachys* are remarkable for the speed with which they move and are recognized by the short, sharp, needle-like last palpal joint. *Bembidion quadrimaculatum,* less than 0.15 in. long, with four conspicuous yellow spots, is common in gardens. *Tachyta nana,* all black, and *Tachymenis flavicauda,* brown with a yellow tip, both less than 0.12 in. long, are common under the bark of dead trees.

Species of *Pœcilus* are among the most common of the Carabidæ, but it is difficult to describe, without technicalities, even *lucublandus,* which lives in tilled fields. Pl. 55 shows its general form; its color is greenish or bluish. *Amara* and *Platynus* (Pl. 94) are related and also large genera. *Triæna angustata,* shining bronze, is common in gardens, running rapidly on paths in midsummer, especially when weeding operations disturb its shelter. *Dicælus elongatus,* a black, shiny beetle often found under stones, may be recognized from the illustration on Pl. 55.

A slender Carabid, 0.75 in. long, with blackish head and elytra, and a narrow, reddish-brown pronotum, is fairly certain to be *Galerita.* If the head is strongly rounded behind the eyes, it is probably *janus.* *G. bicolor* is similar but has the back of the head tapering, rather than rounded. They are often abundant about lights but their home is in fence rows or open woodlands. The larvæ are bluish and yellow.

Pl. 94 shows *Lebia grandis,* which is credited with feeding on the eggs and young larvæ of potato beetles. It is fairly typical, although one of the largest, of its genus, the members of which live under stones and leaves but often climb plants to feed on injurious insects. Their tarsi are comb-like, a feature which probably helps them in climbing, and the elytra are square-cut at apex.

The beetles mentioned from *Bembidion* (above) to

this point have two bristle-bearing punctures above each eye. The Carabidæ which follow have but one.

Species of *Brachinus* (Pl. 94) have the tip of the elytra square-cut; the head is tapering behind and both it and the thorax are very narrow, as compared with the abdomen. They occur on the ground under things, usually in damp places. Many Carabidæ, when disturbed, give off a defensive fluid from a gland at the end of the abdomen but species of *Brachinus* do it with a distinct "pop." For this reason, they are called the Bombardier Beetles. The discharged fluid is either volatile or it is shot out in a fine spray, so that it looks like smoke.

Chlænius is often found under stones and logs in damp places. They have a pronounced musky odor and usually bronzed or green backs, very finely clothed with short hair. *C. sericeus* is all green, 0.6 in. long, with yellow legs, while other species of the genus are smaller and variously colored.

Pl. 55 shows one of the largest and commonest species of *Harpalus, caliginosus.* It is black with reddish-brown antennæ and tarsi. *H. pennsylvanicus* is also common and is superficially much like *caliginosus* except that it is rarely more than 0.7 in. long. For that matter, in almost any region there are a dozen or more species of *Harpalus* for which our figure would do except as to size. It might also pass for related genera such as *Selenophorus, Stenolophus,* and *Anisodactylus.* Unlike their relatives, some species of *Harpalus* are said to feed, when adult, largely on seeds. *Harpalus viridiæneus,* with shining, greenish-bronze back, is common under boards in farmyards.

Agonoderus pallipes (Pl. 94) is a small relative of *Harpalus* that often enters houses at night, attracted by the lights.

HALIPLIDÆ

See p. 278. The numerous species crawl about aquatic plants, usually in shallow water, but do not swim well. The larvæ are slender and each of the body-segments has a fleshy lobe on the back, the hind one being long and tapering. They feed on filamentous algæ and are thus an exception among the largely carnivorous Adephaga.

DYTISCIDÆ

See p. 278 for the characteristics of these Predacious Diving Beetles. Their larvæ (Pl. 56) are called Watertigers. The adults are said to hibernate in underwater earth but they come out from time to time, especially in the early spring. During the summer they are frequently attracted to lights. The males of certain genera, e.g. *Dytiscus* have the three basal segments of the front (and, to a lesser extent, of the middle) tarsi modified to form cup-like suckers that may help them to cling to the females while mating. Some females have furrowed elytra. The adults have large spiracles near the hind end and smaller ones along the side. When at rest, they hang head-down with the tips of the elytra sticking out of the water. In this way the spiracles have access to the upper air. When the beetle dives, a supply of fresh air is carried along under the elytra. Adults discharge, from behind the head and also from the anal glands, fluids which differ somewhat from species to species but all of which are probably defensive against fish and other enemies. The mature beetles live for a long time, Harris having kept a *Dytiscus* "three years and a half in perfect health, in a glass vessel filled with water, and supported by morsels of raw meat." Eggs of *Dytiscus,* as far as known, are laid singly in slits made by the females in underwater plant stems. It is said that *Acilius* lets the eggs drop upon the mud while swimming about and *Colymbetes* arranges its eggs upon leaves. Miall remarks that many a raw naturalist has put these beetles into his collecting bottle or aquarium, to find after a few hours that they have destroyed or mutilated almost his whole live stock. When a larva swims about in a leisurely way, the legs are the chief means of propulsion, but it can also make a sudden spring by throwing its body into serpentine curves. It may also creep on submerged leaves and cling to them when resting or lying in ambush. The

PLATE 56

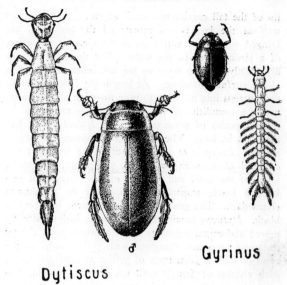

Dytiscus

♂

Gyrinus

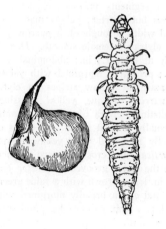

Hydrophilus

tip of the tail carries two small appendages. These, as well as the last two segments of the abdomen, are fringed with hairs which no doubt increase the effect of a stroke given to the water. But these appendages are chiefly used to buoy up the tail when the larva is at the surface breathing. At length the larva ceases to feed, creeps into moist earth near the edge of the water, makes a roundish cell there, and changes to a pupa.

The species of some genera, e. g. *Bidessus,* are less than 0.12 in. long. The following are among the largest species. *Colymbetes sculptilis:* about 0.7 in. long; top of head black, with two small, pale spots; pronotum, front of the head and margins of the elytra, dull yellow; a black, transverse, median bar on pronotum; elytra dark. The general color of *Dytiscus* is greenish-black. *Dytiscus fasciventris:* length, an inch or slightly more; abdominal segments reddish brown with darker margins; pronotum margined with yellow only on the sides or with a faint trace of yellow at base and apex; each elytron of female with ten grooves reaching beyond the middle. *D. hybridus:* a trifle more than an inch long; abdominal segments uniform black; pronotum like *fasciventris* but shorter; yellow margin of elytra of nearly equal width throughout, a narrow yellow bar near apices; elytra of female smooth. *D. verticalis:* length usually at least 1.4 in.; abdominal segments uniform black; pronotum margined with yellow only on the sides; marginal yellow stripes on elytra narrowing behind; narrow, oblique, yellow crossbars near apices often indistinct; elytra of females smooth. *D. harrisii:* length usually at least 1.5 in.; all edges of the pronotum distinctly margined with yellow; elytra marked much like *verticalis* but crossbar more distinct; females usually have the elytra grooved. *Cybister fimbriolatus* is about 1.3 in. long; brown with a faint greenish tinge; pronotum and elytra broadly margined with yellow; front of head, two front pairs of legs, and spots at sides of the third to sixth, inclusive, abdominal segments yellow; pronotum and elytra of female, except along the suture, with numerous, fine, short grooves.

GYRINOIDEA

GYRINIDÆ

All who observe have seen the steel-blue or black Whirligig Beetles (Pl. 56 and p. 280) gyrating in crowds on the surface of relatively still water or basking like turtles on logs and stones. When disturbed, Whirligig Beetles squeak by rubbing the tip of the abdomen against the elytra. They also give off a fluid that is sometimes ill-smelling but in other cases rather pleasantly suggests apples. Although they spend most of their active time on the surface of the water, they can fly well if they can climb out of the water so as to get a start, and they dive freely, carrying down a bubble of air at the tips of and under their elytra. The front legs are long and grasping. Adults are apparently not very predacious, but the larvæ seem to be. The female lays a number of elongate, oval eggs, end to end, upon the leaves of plants, usually beneath the surface of the water and sometimes at a considerable depth. The general appearance of the larva is that of a small centipede. The pupa of *Gyrinus* is so well hidden that few have seen it. Probably about the beginning of August the larva creeps out of the water by climbing up the water plants and then spins a grayish cocoon pointed at both ends, the adult emerging a few weeks later. Adults hibernate, coming out during mild weather for mid-winter dances.

The two principal genera are *Gyrinus* (length less than 0.35 in.; the scutellum distinct) and *Dineutes* (length 0.4 in., or more; scutellum hidden). *Dineutes vittatus:* 0.5 in. or longer; sides of pronotum and elytra with an indistinct, bronzed, submarginal stripe. *D. discolor:* about 0.5 in. long; above very dark, almost black, bronze, shining; below, yellowish. *D. emarginatus:* less than 0.5 in. long; above and below black, slightly bronzed, and not very shiny; middle and hind legs, narrow margin, and tip of the abdomen, paler. *D. americanus:* length a trifle under 0.5 in.; above black, strongly bronzed; beneath black, very shining; abdominal segments often tinged with brown; legs brownish-yellow; a common species with an apple odor.

POLYPHAGA

About as good a definition of this suborder as can be given is that it includes beetles that are not included either in Adephaga (p. 277) or, probably, in Archostemata (p. 277). We have about a hundred distinct families; but the distinctions are largely technical and not in every case generally accepted. Most of the specimens ordinarily collected can be placed in their proper family by using the list of "series" (p. 276) as a start. Also, general resemblance to one of the pictures may be a clue. If both of these fail, check your specimen with what is said about each family in turn until you find the right one—or don't.

HYDROPHILOIDEA

HYDROPHILIDÆ

Maxillary palpi usually longer than the antennæ and by the inexperienced student often mistaken for the moderately short antennæ, which are usually concealed beneath the head. Antennæ 6- to 9-jointed, the outer joints forming an abrupt club; all of the joints, excepting the basal ones, are pubescent. Metasternum usually large, often keeled, and often produced into a long spine behind. Tarsi on all legs 5-jointed, the first joint often very small and inconspicuous. The middle and hind tarsi are sometimes more or less compressed and fringed for swimming.

These are called the Water-scavenger Beetles. The adults do feed on decaying material, but they eat also water-plants and living animals; and, furthermore, not all are aquatic. The larvæ are largely predacious. The eggs of *Hydrophilus* are usually laid in a floating silken case with a handle-like mast (Pl. 56). The silk comes from glands at the hind end of the female's body. The larvæ are much like those of *Dytiscus* but clumsier and their tarsi never have more than a single claw, while those of the Dytiscidæ and the Gyrinidæ have two. Pupation occurs in moist earth near the water's edge, the pupa being kept from touching its cell's bottom by projecting hook-like spines. The adult's largest spiracles are well forward and air is taken in through the notch between the head and the thorax, the velvety hairs keeping out the water and the hairy club of the usually not noticed antennæ helping to break the surface film.

1.—Pronotum narrowed behind, not as wide as the two elytra.—Of those genera having not more than 10 rows of punctures on each elytron and the last joint of the maxillary palpi longer than the next to the last, *Helophorus* (antennæ 9-jointed) and *Hydrochus* (antennæ 7-jointed) are now made separate families, Helophoridæ and Hydrochidæ, by some authors.

Not so. ....2.

2.—First joint of each middle and hind tarsus elongated.
—Subfamily Sphæridiinæ, of which *Sphæridium scarabæoides* resembles Scarabæidæ in looks and habits. It is a European insect that was introduced in the latter part of the last century and is rapidly extending its range. It lives in dung. The adult is about 0.25 in. long; has a very convex back; shining black above except that the elytra have a reddish spot near the base and the apical fourth is yellowish.

Not so.—Possibly several subfamilies of which Hydrophilinæ (metasternum prolonged into a distinct spine; tarsi compressed) is the most important here.

Among the Hydrophilinæ the shiny black *Hydrophilus* (or *Hydrous*) *triangularis* is about 1.5 in. long. The under side of the abdomen is pubescent except for a broad, smooth streak down the middle of all but the first segment; the abdominal segments have more or less distinct triangular, yellow spots at the sides. It is sometimes attracted by lights. *Dibolocelus ovalis* is about 1.25 in. long; the abdomen, which is unmarked, is pubescent except for a narrow, smooth streak down the middle of the last three segments. *Hydrochara obtusata* is quite convex in cross-section, regularly oval in outline, and 0.6 in. long. It is common in brackish pools.

SILPHOIDEA

These are believed to be related to the Staphylinoidea. SILPHIDÆ is the important family. Our only species of PLATYPSYLLIDÆ is *Platypsyllus castoris*, a parasite of beavers. It is about 0.1 in. long and can sometimes be knocked or shaken out of dried beaver furs. Of the LEPTINIDÆ, *Leptinus testaceous*, a European species, is widely distributed in the nests of mice and bumblebees. Our native species are *Leptinillus aplodontiæ* in California and *validus* near Hudson Bay. Other relatively small families of very small Silphoidea are BRATHINIDÆ (in wet moss), CLAMBIDÆ (in decaying vegetation), SCYMÆNIDÆ (under bark, stones, and in ant's nests), and ORTHOPERIDÆ (= Corylophidæ. In decaying vegetable matter).

SILPHIDÆ

Hind coxæ more or less conical and prominent. Eyes sometimes absent. Antennæ with 11 (rarely 9 or 10) joints; gradually or suddenly thickened, usually forming a club at the apex, but sometimes nearly filiform. Abdomen with 5 or 6 visible ventral segments. Tibiæ sometimes fitted with spines for digging, sometimes slender and with large terminal spurs. Tarsi usually 5-jointed. The elytra are sometimes a little shorter than the abdomen.

Plate 95 is sufficient help in the identification of *Silpha* and *Necrophorus,* the only two genera of this family which ordinarily attract notice as Carrion Beetles, although there are not only numerous small species that feed on carrion but some on decaying fungi and a few are found only in ant's nests.

Species of *Necrophorus* are called Burying Beetles. It has been often said, either from hearsay or from observation, that they bury small carcasses and feed on them underground. Probably I have been unfortunate: I have furnished them with numerous carcasses but they ate them all on top of even loose sand. Perhaps the right species did not come to my feast. The sensory pits in the enlarged portion of the antennæ are doubtless olfactory and explain the adult's quickness in locating carrion. At least some larvæ feed on the fly larvæ there. The adults are black, usually marked with red or yellow. The following three have their hind (and, to a lesser extent, their middle) legs bowed. *N. americanus:* 1 in. or more long; pronotum rounded; orange-red on vertex of head, central part of pronotum, two irregular spots on each elytron, and club of antennæ. Usually found on reptiles. *N. sayi:* less than 1 in. long; pronotum rounded; orange-red in a cross-bar near base and a spot near apex of each elytron. Not usually common. *N. marginatus* Pl. 95; the elytral spots are sometimes connected along the margin, the basal spot sometimes divided. One of the commonest. The following three have straight legs. *N. orbicollis*: marked much like *sayi*. *N. pustulatus*: pronotum transversely oval, very little narrowed behind; orange-red on antennal club and two spots, the apical one sometimes double, on each elytron. Wholly black individuals have been recorded. *N. tomentosus*: not over 0.8 in. long; pronotum broader than long, very little narrowed behind; the disc clothed with yellow hairs; elytral markings resemble those of *marginatus* but are narrower.

Species of *Silpha* are extremely flattened. *S. surinamensis*: 0.6 to 1 in. long; rather elongate; eyes prominent; hind femora of males quite stout; black, usually with a narrower orange-red cross-bar (often broken into spots) near apex of each elytron. The following are oval in shape, the eyes are not prominent, and the hind femora are not enlarged. *S. inæqualis*: about 0.5 in. long; all black. *S. noveboracensis*: Pl. 95. *S. americana*: about 0.75 in. long; pronotum yellow with a black central spot; elytra brownish with the crinkly elevations slightly darker; pronotum nearly twice as wide as long; much narrowed in front. It occurs on toadstools and in dung as well as on carrion.

STAPHYLINOIDEA

The elytra are short, usually exposing much of the abdomen. The backs of abdominal segments are nearly, or quite, as horny as the thorax. The usually present wings are folded, when at rest, under the elytra. This description unfortunately includes also *Platypsyllus* (See Silphoidea) and several other troublesome but not common forms. If the body is greatly flattened see Hemipeplinæ of Cucujidæ. The Histeridæ, although not fitting the description, are placed here also.

Our principal family, STAPHYLINIDÆ, has a flexible, elongate abdomen, not enlarged apically. Each antennæ is at least 10-jointed (The rare MICROPEPLIDÆ have 9-jointed, club-tipped antennæ); each tarsus usually 5-

jointed. The small PSELAPHIDÆ (abdomen with 5 dorsal
segments) and CLAVIGERIDÆ (abdomen with 3 dorsal segments) have a solid, swollen abdomen and 3-jointed tarsi.
Others are PTILLIDÆ (= Trichopterygidæ. Most of them
are less than 0.04 in. long. Wings, if present, fringed
with long hairs. Usually found in decaying matter),
SCAPHIDIIDÆ (small fungus beetles with square-cut elytra and conical abdomens), SPHÆRITIDÆ (*Sphærites
glabratus* of the Pacific slope may be our only species),
and SPHÆRIIDÆ (small, convex species of *Sphærius* on
mud or under stones near water).

STAPHYLINIDÆ

About 3,000 kinds of Rove Beetles have already been
described from the United States and the number is
rapidly increasing. Probably fully 200 species can be
found in almost any region but their identification is
rather technical and no differentiation will be attempted
here. "They live in decaying animal and vegetable
matter, in excrement, fungi, or fermenting sap, and are
among the most universally distributed of all beetles.
Most of them are predatory, and some have been accused of feeding on living plants; but on the whole they
are of importance to the agriculturist only as scavengers" (Smith). *Creophilus villosus* (Pl. 95) is common
about carrion and excrement. When adults are disturbed,
they raise their tails as though they would sting, but all
the species are perfectly harmless. *Tachinus fimbriatus*
(Pl. 95) is often found in mushrooms.

PSELAPHIDÆ AND CLAVIGERIDÆ

These, particularly Clavigeridæ, have been called "Ant-
loving Beetles" because they are usually to be found with
ants. If the name be good the affection is mutual because the ants are fond of a substance excreted by the
beetles from special glands covered with small tufts of
hair. The beetles are said to be fed by the ants and
to ride about on their backs. The Pselaphidæ are apparently less myrmecophilus ("ant-loving").

HISTERIDÆ

First antennal joint long, more or less bent or curved; the 2nd joint attached a little to one side or the top of the 1st, the outer joints normally on an angle with the 1st, making the antennæ elbowed ("geniculate") ; the 8th and following joints forming a compact club. Elytra truncate, leaving the two end segments of the abdomen uncovered. All of the tarsi 5-jointed except in *Acritus* and *Æletes*, which have the hind ones 4-jointed. Compact beetles, with a very hard surface. (If the head is more or less prolonged into a beak, see also Heteromera, p. 317.)

It has been suggested that Linnæus, in naming the type genus of this family *Hister,* had in mind a filthy Mr. Hister of Juvenal's Satires. I have not looked up the original but, if the Roman was very bad, the name is not appropriate for all the Histeridæ, as some of them live in a fairly cleanly manner under bark and in ant's nests. Even those that take to carrion and excrement probably do not eat it but feed on the other more Hister-like insects.

CUCUJOIDEA

The limits of this superfamily are by no means clear and authorities greatly disagree.

OSTOMIDÆ (OR OSTOMATIDÆ)

This is the family formerly called Temnochilidæ and Trogositidæ. The tarsi are slender, the first joint very short. The elytra cover the abdomen. The 10- or 11-jointed antennæ are club-shaped. There are not many species and most of them live under bark. *Tenebrioides* belongs to part of the family in which the head is nearly or quite as wide as the front of the prothorax. *T. mauretanica* (the Cadelle) and *T. corticalis* are found in granaries throughout the world. The eighth antennal joint of *mauretanica* is about equal in width to the ninth; in our other species of the genus it is smaller. Pl. 57 is sufficient additional description of the blackish adult Cadelle. The dark areas shown in the illustration of the larva are reddish brown. It feeds on wheat, flour, and other foodstuffs. The fact that it has been found in milk has been used to help prove that milkmen enrich their goods with cornstarch. Webster recorded its feeding on even hellebore. It also feeds on other insects and it has been known to bore into the wood of grain bins.

NITIDULIDÆ

Some adults are much like the Histeridæ in form but the antennæ are straight; others suggest Staphylinidæ; and, in all, it is difficult to tell them "at a glance." The tarsi are more or less swollen and the first joint is not shortened. The elytra rarely reach the tip of the abdomen. In most species the pronotum has wide, thin sides. Some feed on fungi or carrion, others are found chiefly on flowers, but the majority feed on the sap of trees and the juices of fruits. Dury tells of trapping hundreds of specimens by laying chips on top of a freshly cut maple stump. They are also attracted to a mixture of vinegar and molasses. Some of the species are prettily marked with yellow or red. The genus *Glischrochilus* (= *Ips*) is often common under fallen, decaying fruit as well as about flowing sap. Its species are about 0.25 in. long and gaily marked with black and yellow or red. *Carpophilus hemipterus* is an introduced species that is found in grocery and bakery shops. It is about 0.17 in. long; black, except for the pale legs, a dull yellow shoulder-spot and an irregular area of the same color covering the distal half of each elytron. *Omosita* is often seen on greasy bones.

CUCUJIDÆ

Most of these narrow, elongate, somewhat flattened, brown beetles live under bark. The Cucujid head does not taper behind to form a neck; the scutellum is distinct; and the abdomen has five free ventral segments. *Cucujus clavipes* is all-red, 0.5 in. long, and flat as a piece of cardboard.

Some Cucujid larvæ are predacious but the following, among others, unfortunately is not. The enlarged figures of Pl. 59 are sufficiently descriptive of *Oryzæphilus* (no longer *Silvanus*) *surinamensis* except as to color. The adult is chestnut-brown and the larvæ are dirty white with darker areas. It is one of the most abundant of beetles in all kinds of stored grains, especially in the South, and it is sometimes destructive to dried fruits. It is not a weevil, but two of its nicknames are Grain-weevil and Sawtoothed-weevil, the latter referring to its thorax. "The larva when living in granular material, like meal, usually builds a thin case out of the particles and the whitish pupa may be found within. When the insect is living in substances like fine flour it does not build a case" (Herrick). It is cosmopolitan in its distribution. Several other Cucujids also feed on stored grain, fruits, and nuts, e.g. *Cathartus advena,* which is particularly fond of such as are stale. It is about the same size and color as *surinamensis* but the pronotum is straight-edged and nearly square.

CRYPTOPHAGIDÆ

They are usually less than 0.1 in. long and "often of a light yellowish-brown color, with a silken lustre produced by a very fine pubescence. Their habits are exceedingly variable, some living in fungi, others about wood and chip piles or in cellars, beneath dead leaves, in rotten logs, or on flowers." The last 3 of the 11 antennal joints are enlarged, loosely forming a club. Some of the males have only 4 joints, instead of 5, in each hind tarsus. The front and middle coxæ are very small and deeply imbedded.

COCCINELLIDÆ

All of the tarsi 3-jointed; second joint dilated and pad-like beneath. Antennæ 11-jointed, terminating in a more or less distinct 3-jointed club. Last joint of the maxillary palpi broad, hatchet-shaped. Head nearly concealed by the thorax.

Many of us have quoted: "Lady-bird, lady-bird! Fly away home. Your house is on fire. Your children do roam." Some of us add: "Except little Nan, who sits in a pan weaving gold laces as fast as she can." What is it all about? Many Lady-bird (Coccinellid) larva eat Aphids and this rhyme started in the Old Country, where they burn the hop-vines after the harvests. These vines are usually full of Aphids and Coccinellid "children." A Nan who can not roam but sits in a pan weaving gold laces is shown on Pl. 95. She is the yellow pupa. "Why 'Lady-bird' or 'Lady Beetles'?" That goes back still further to the Middle Ages when these beneficial insects were dedicated to the Virgin and were the "Beetles of Our Lady."

Plate 95 shows a number of common species, some of which are rather variable with respect to color and markings. Smith says that "in a very general way, and subject to many exceptions," those that are red or yellow, with black spots, feed on plant-lice (Aphids), and those that are wholly black, or black with red or yellow spots, feed on scale insects. The larvæ are often prettily marked with black, blue, or orange, and are even more greedy feeders on pests than are the adults. Some species have the curious habit of congregating, as adults, in great masses on mountain-tops to spend the winter. Horticulturists of California collect these masses "by the ton," put them into cold storage until wanted, and distribute them among the farmers at the proper season for controlling Aphids.

Although it is impossible to give here a key to the many genera and species, the family deserves at least the following steps in that direction.

The tribe Noviini includes the famous *Rodolia* (not, as often given, *Vedalia*) *cardinalis* that was introduced from Australia to California for controlling the Cottony-cushion Scale Insect. *Novius kœbelei* and *Lindorus lophantæ* were also introduced to help man fight his insect foes. The mandibles of Noviini are not toothed within; the body is pubescent; the eyes are finely, not coarsely, faceted and they are nearly covered by the pronotum.

Hippodamia (tarsal claws bifid, the two lobes unequal in length and acutely pointed; pronotum not margined at base), *Ceratomegilla* (claws with a large quadrate basal tooth; pronotum with a narrow but distinct margin along the base) and *Anisosticta* (claws simple) have the

middle coxæ close together; body elongate-oval, not
pubescent; femora extending beyond the sides of the
body; thorax not covering the eyes. See Pl. 95, where
Ceratomegilla is given the commonly used but technically
incorrect name *Megilla*. These are now included in the
tribe Coccinellini. It is *Hippodamia* that the Westerners
collect and put in cold storage until wanted.

Another group of the tribe Coccinellini has the middle
coxæ widely separated from each other; femora usually
not extending beyond the sides of the body; the thorax
somewhat covering the eyes, which are finely faceted;
body loosely jointed and usually rounded rather than
oval, its upper surface not pubescent. Some of the
genera including species more than 0.15 in. long may
be separated as follows.

Antennæ extending at least to the middle of the thorax.
—*Neomysia* (tarsal claws bifid) and *Anatis* (claws with
a large nearly quadrate tooth at base; elytra with numerous spots Pl. 95).

Antennæ only slightly longer than the head.—*Coccinella* (body usually rounded, strongly convex) and
Adalia (body oval, less convex). Species of each are
shown on Pl. 95. Adults of *A. bipunctata* often try to
hibernate in our houses. If any succeed and appear after
the days get somewhat warm, let them out of doors to
start the good work of eating plant-lice.

Epilachna belongs to a distinct subfamily, Epilach-
ninæ, in which the body is not pubescent and the mandibles are bifid at the tips and have several teeth within.
It should be disowned by its family. Except for *Epilachna* all our Coccinellids are distinctly beneficial because
of food habits, although the ignorant often accuse them
of being the authors of damage done by the Aphids and
Coccids upon which they are feeding. Some Coccinellidæ take a bit of pollen by way of a change, but
Epilachna is vegetarian. *E. borealis* (Pl. 95), larva and
adult, eats nothing but the leaves of pumpkin, squash,
and allied plants. The larva is yellow and armed with
six rows of forked, black spines. The adults hibernate.
E. corrupta, the Mexican Bean Beetle, eats the leaves and
green pods of beans and has now spread northward to
New England. It is somewhat smaller than *borealis* and
the elytral spots are relatively smaller.

ELATEROIDEA

The principal families are Elateridæ and Buprestidæ.

Of CEROPHYTIDÆ (middle and hind trochanters very long; antennæ of male comb-like, of female saw-like) we have only *Cerophytum* with *pulsator* in the East and *convexicolle* in the West.

CEBRIONIDÆ (six or more ventral abdominal segments; tibial spurs well developed; labrum fused with the clypeus) is a small Southern family including *Scaptolenus* (front tibiæ emarginate externally) and *Cebrio* (not so). PLASTOCERIDÆ differs in having the labrum free and tibial spurs very weak.

The tarsal claws of RHIPICERIDÆ have a large hairy pad between them. The few species occur usually on or near dead trees.

Adult MELASIDÆ (or Eucnemidæ) resemble Elateridæ but the labrum is concealed and the antennæ are somewhat farther from the eyes. The larvæ resemble Buprestidæ and live in wood that has started to decay.

THROSCIDÆ contains only a few small, oblong, black or brownish beetles which resemble Elaterids and Buprestids in form and in having the prosternum prolonged behind into a spine which fits into a cavity in the mesosternum. They differ from Elateridæ in having the pro- and meso-sterna firmly joined, and so without the power of leaping possessed by most click beetles. From Buprestidæ they are distinguished by having the ventral abdominal segments all free (Blatchley). They are usually found on dead wood or on flowers, and are inconspicuous as well as small.

ELATERIDÆ

Prothorax loosely joined behind (the basal part fitting loosely to the part bearing elytra); hind angles prolonged backwards into more or less elongated points. None of the 5 ventral segments of the abdomen more closely united than the others. Middle of the prosternum with a spine-like prolongation which projects into, but does not fill, the cavity at the middle of the mesosternum. Antennæ more or less saw-toothed, rarely fan-like or comb-like. Tarsal claws either simple, toothed, or comb-like.

PLATE 57

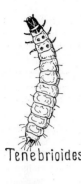

Tenebrioides mauretanica

Ludius
hieroglyphicus

An Elaterid larva

Elater
nigricollis

Melanotus
communis

Showing
the click apparatus

Alaus oculatus

These beetles have a unique method of getting on their feet if, by chance, they are on their back. The back can be bent between the pronotum and the elytra. When the beetle finds itself up-side-down it bends its body up and then suddenly a little more than straightens out. This bounces it into the air and it turns right side up as it goes. In the "little more than straightening out" the body is kept from bending too far by a spine on the hind edge of the prosternum (Pl. 57). This trick has won them various names such as Skip-Jacks, Click Beetles, Spring Beetles, and Snapping-bugs. Once, in Arizona, I had a guide who had never noticed them before. I made some of the species that came to the camp light perform. He immediately christened them Break-backs and began to count up how much he would win, after he got back to Tucson, by betting on "whether they would or wouldn't land right side up." I advised him to put his money on "would" and for nights thereafter he hung around my moth-tent, turning Elaterids on their backs to see whether they would or wouldn't. I do not know how he made out. Break-backs is really not a bad name.

Most of the species are brown or black and of medium or small size. The larvæ are commonly called Wireworms. They are long, narrow, cylindrical, hardshelled, brownish or yellowish-white creatures. Some live in the ground, feeding on the roots of grasses and other plants; some live in dead wood and under bark; and some, at least, are predacious.

Two species of *Alaus* occur in the Northeast (and elsewhere) but *oculatus* (Pl. 57) is the more common. The black-and-white adult flies throughout the season. It is called the Eyed Elater but those big spots on the thorax are, of course, not eyes. The larva, which lives in decayed trunks of apple and other trees, reaches a length of nearly 2.5 inches. Lugger concluded that this larva "largely subsists upon other insects" as all that he kept in decaying wood soon died if they were not provided with living insects, "which were soon discovered by these cannibals and devoured." If this be so, it is curious that *myops* is found only in pine, for we would expect that it would be predacious also and not so par-

ticular as to wood. The adult *myops* averages somewhat smaller than *oculatus* and the eye-like spots are not
only narrower and smaller but their gray margins are
indistinct.

In our South and the Tropics there are Elaterids that
have a pair of luminous spots on the pronotum. Several
years ago some enterprising person secured a large number of the Cuban *Pyrophorus noctilucus* and sold living
specimens at Coney Island.

The following United States species occur at least in
the Northeast and have relatively conspicuous characters that help in their identification but should not be
considered conclusive.

Adelocera discoidea is from 0.3 to 0.5 in. long; black
except for the yellow head and margins of the pronotum.
Hibernates under bark.

Elater nigricollis (Pl. 57): head and thorax black;
elytra all dull yellowish; occurs under bark and in
rotten wood, usually in damp woods (See *Ludius*). *E.
linteus,* similar, but usually smaller, and the elytra are
black along the suture and at the apex. Under bark,
usually in dry situations. In *E. sellatus* the black covers
all the elytra except for the yellow outer and basal margins. Under the bark of hickory, beech, and other trees.
E. verticinus (or *rubricollis*) is 0.5 to 0.7 in. long;
pronotum, except the apex and hind angles, red; otherwise black. Under bark and on flowers. *E. collaris* is
similar but is about 0.3 in. long and has no black on
pronotum. *E. sanguinipennis* is about 0.3 in. long;
pronotum black; elytra all red. *E. xanthomus* is about
the same size but only the bases of the elytra are red;
otherwise black.

Ludius (= *Corymbites*) *pyrrhos* is about 0.75 in. long;
dark reddish-brown; narrow; pronotum relatively long
and narrow. *L. tarsalis* is about the size and color of
Elater nigricollis. They belong to different groups of
genera, the Elaterini having the hind coxal plates suddenly dilated about the middle, the outer part much narrower than the inner, and the *Ludius* group having them
gradually, sometimes scarcely, dilated on the inner side.
It is such technical differences that make untechnical

catch-characters little more than hints. *L. hierglyphicus* (Pl. 57) is found northward, especially on pine.

Pityobius anguinus is an inch or so long but narrow; black; male's antennæ feathered. Usually on pine.

Melanactes piceus is 1 to 1.4 in. long and polished black. It occurs under stones and rubbish in dry situations.

Melanotus communis (Pl. 57) is found under the loose bark of fallen trees and is widely distributed. With a strong lens its claws are seen to be comb-like, a characteristic of the genus.

BUPRESTIDÆ

Prothorax fitting closely to the elytra; hind angles of prothorax usually not, or at most slightly, prolonged. Middle of the prosternum prolonged and fitting rather tightly into the mesosternum. First and second ventral segments of the abdomen more closely united than the others. The junction of these segments may be (1) very indistinct, making the first and second segment appear as one large segment; (2) with a more or less distinct line indicating the point of contact; or (3) the junction may be distinct but not so markedly so as that between the other segments. Elytra nearly or entirely covering the abdomen. Antennæ more or less saw-toothed. All of the tarsi distinctly 5-jointed. Body hard and not flexible. Many of them resemble the Elateridæ in general form, but the thorax and abdomen are more firmly united.

These are usually elongate, usually stout (but sometimes cylindrical) beetles, with broad thorax, and elytra tapering back from the shoulders. A large proportion of them are bronzed or metallic in color or reflection, and others are gaudily marked with red or yellow bands or spots. Many of them have the upper surface deeply grooved or pitted, and, altogether, they are very characteristic in appearance. Most of them are active and fly readily. One nickname is Square-heads referring to their broad, flat, square-cut front.

The larvæ are wood-borers, usually living under bark and making broad, rather shallow furrows, galleries, or chambers. In shape they are much elongated, somewhat flattened; the body segments well defined; head small; the anterior segments much enlarged so as, apparently, to form part of the head, giving rise to the common names

PLATE 58

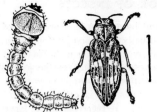

Chrysobothris
femorata

Dicerca
divaricata

Photuris
pennsylvanica

Photinus
scintillans

Calopteron
reticulatum

Phengodes

Chauliognathus
pennsylvanicus

Hammer-head or Flat-head borers. Adults are fond of basking in the sunshine, usually on their own food-plant, and may best be collected by holding an umbrella under branches and then jarring them. A key to the genera involves numerous technicalities.

Chrysobothris femorata (Pl. 58) is called the Flat-headed Apple-tree Borer, the name referring to the larva, which, however, attacks almost any deciduous tree. Adults appear about May, or later, and are given to sitting on tree trunks, where they are somewhat difficult to see on account of their dull metallic brown color and roughened elytra. When flying, the bright metallic greenish-blue abdomen is quite conspicuous. The young larvæ make shallow galleries in the sapwood, but as they get older they form somewhat dilated, irregular, flattened burrows in the heartwood, where they hibernate. In the spring they excavate a pupal cell near the surface, completing the life-cycle in one year.

The larva of *Dicerca divaricata* bores in peach, cherry, beech, maple, and other deciduous trees. The adult (Pl. 58) is coppery or brassy above; the size and the spreading tips of the elytra, whence the specific name, help to identify it. The males have a little tooth on the under side of each middle femur.

Agrilus ruficollis, the Red-necked Cane-borer, causes the swellings, usually with numerous slits, that have been called "gouty galls" on raspberry and blackberry. Adults emerge in May and June. They are not over 0.3 in. long; head short but wide, black; pronotum coppery-red; elytra bronzy-black. "The young larva enters the bark at the axil of a leaf-stem, and eats around the stem in a long spiral. By early August the galls commence to form where the bark has been girdled, though sometimes no gall results from the injury, and the larvæ mine into the pith. The larvæ probably become practically full grown in the fall and remain in their burrows over winter, in which they transform to pupæ in late April" (Sanderson).

Buprestidæ are very fond of Conifers. The following occur on pine. *Chalcophora virginiensis* is one of our largest Buprestids, attaining a length of 1 or 1.25 inches. (Much larger Buprestids occur in the Tropics, the family home, and many of them are brilliantly colored.) In this genus the hind tarsi have the first joint elongated and the males have a distinct sixth ventral abdominal segment. This species is dull black, feebly bronzed, the impressions of the thorax and elytra often brassy; head with a deep, median groove, which is broader and deeper in front; pronotum one-third wider than long, sides rounded on apical third, disk with a broad median impression and two others on each side, in the regions of the front and hind angles; elytra each with four to six elongate impressed spaces that are finely and rather densely punctuate. *Buprestis lineata* is 0.5 in. or more long. Each elytron has, typically, two longitudinal, yellowish stripes. The general color, above, is metallic black; beneath, dull bronze; head and prosternum, yellowish. *Buprestis salisburyensis* is about 0.5 in. long; brilliant green with the sutural and outer margins of the elytra coppery red. *Dicerca punctulata* is superficially much like *D. divaricata* but smaller (about 0.5 in.) and has a pair of prominent, shining, longitudinal ridges on the middle of the pronotum and parts of a second pair outside of these. *Melanophila acuminata* is often nearly 0.5 in. long and all black. It is found on various Conifers. *M. fulvoguttata* is about the same size, and has three yellow dots on each elytron; found on spruce and hemlock. *M. ænola* is rarely longer than 0.25 in.; pronotum bronzy; elytra metallic black. The males of *Chrysobothris floricola* have a single, acute tooth on each front tibia; the tibiæ of *dentipes* have no tooth but are dilated at the tip (those of *femorata* have numerous fine teeth on the inner edge).

The following are among the more easily recognized of those on deciduous forest trees. *Buprestis fasciata* about 0.6 in. long; brilliant metallic green, often with blue iridescence; a wavy yellow band across each elytron back of the middle, a yellow spot back of this and sometimes one in front. On maple and poplar, *Chrysobothris scitula* is usually a little more than 0.25 in. long. Its color varies from blue to greenish, coppery, and violet. Each elytron has the following brilliant blue or green markings, which appear to be depressed: a somewhat variable streak or combination of spots at the base, one circular spot near the middle, and one two-thirds of the way to the apex. On birch, sumac, and dogwood. The several species of *Brachys* are leaf-miners and abundant. The adult larva makes a curious noise within the mined leaf by switching his body rapidly.

Pachyschelus purpureus mines in the leaves of the bush clover (*Lespedeza*). The adult is usually less than 0.2 in. long and the shoulders are so broad that, from above, it looks hunched up. The head and pronotum are black; elytra, purple.

CANTHAROIDEA

Body and elytra softer than is usual for beetles (but see Melyridæ). Seven or eight segments of the abdomen showing on the ventral side. Often with light-giving apparatus, which is visible on the under side of one or more segments of the abdomen. Antennæ usually 11-jointed; usually saw-toothed, rarely comb-like, or with long flat processes folding like a fan. Elytra thin and flexible; sometimes short; never embracing the sides of the abdomen. Legs long, slender, and often compressed. Tarsi without appendages beneath; the fourth joint more or less bilobed. For the most part, these are plain black, or brownish, or brownish-yellow species; some are black and yellow.

In the Lycidæ the middle coxæ do not touch each other; the elytra usually have net-like ridges ("reticulate") and none of the species are luminous. They are usually flat, widened behind, and often marked with strongly contrasting colors. In Cantharidæ (head not all covered by the prothorax; male antennæ sometimes with fan-like projections) and Lampyridæ (head more or less completely covered by the prothorax) the middle coxæ touch each other; the elytra are not reticulate; and, in contrast with the rare Atractoceridæ and Telegeusidæ of the Lymexyloidea, the antennæ are not attached at the sides of the front before the eyes. There are certain species that give a great deal of trouble in classification and have been put in a separate family, Phengodidæ. The males are covered by the above description of Cantharidæ but the females are, as far as known, luminous and larviform (lacking elytra and wings). See *Phengodes*, Pl. 58.

LYCIDÆ

Both larvæ and adults are predacious, the adults being active by day. In *Calopteron* the elytra gradually widen from base to apex and each has six longitudinal ridges; antennæ saw-toothed. The light areas of *C. reticulatum,* Pl. 58, are yellow and variable. *C. terminale* is black except for a yellow basal part of the elytra and a very narrow margin of yellow on the sides of the pronotum. *Cæniella dimidiata* is apt to be confused with *terminale* but its antennæ are comb-like, not merely saw-toothed. *Lycostomus* (a prolongation on front of head; 3rd antennal joint scarcely longer than the 4th) *lateralis* is black; sides of pronotum and front half of elytral margin yellow. *Celetes basilis* has much less elytral yellow and the antennæ, especially male's, are decidedly comb-like. *Eros aurora* has scarlet elytra; under-side of body black.

CANTHARIDÆ

Of the typical genera *Chauliognathus* (mentum very long, wider in front) is most often seen, particularly *pennsylvanicus* (Pl. 58; thorax wider than long; head black) and *marginatus* (thorax longer than wide; head yellow with black spots). They are called Soldier Beetles. The modified mouthparts gather nectar and pollen from a variety of flowers. The larvæ, however, feed on other insect larvæ, including, it is said, the injurious Plum Curculio. *Podabrus modestus* has the pronotum all yellow; elytra narrowly margined with yellow; legs mostly black. In *Cantharis* (= *Telephorus*) *rotundicollis* the head, pronotum and legs are reddish; elytra dark, gray-brown.

LAMPYRIDÆ

Nearly all Americans have seen Fire-flies, or Lightning-bugs, and many have seen Glow-worms. These are usually Lampyridæ, nearly all of which are luminous. In some species not only adults of both sexes but all stages, including eggs, are luminous. The light is caused by the combining of oxygen with a substance called luciferin. This is brought about in a practically heatless way by the enzyme-like action of another substance, luciferase. It is a highly efficient method of producing rays visible to man. Its use to the beetles is debatable. One theory is that the light is a sexual attraction. But, then, why are the larvæ luminous? Another is that it warns nocturnal birds not to eat them; but the birds could not see unlighted beetles at night and, at any rate, thousands of other kinds of nocturnal insects get along without lights. Possibly it just is.

In *Photuris* the head is not completely covered by the pronotum and the second antennal joint is longer than wide. Of our two species, *pennsylvanica* (Pl. 58) is more northern than *frontalis*. The antennæ of the rare *Calyptocephalus bifaria* have comb-teeth on each side. Species of *Phausis* have a small, jointed, needle-shaped appendage on the last antennal joint. In *Lucidota* the eyes are small and the light organs are feeble but in *Pyractomena* (thorax slightly ridged; female's light organs on the sides of abdomen) and *Photinus* (thorax not ridged; female's light organs on the middle of the abdomen) the eyes are large, especially in males, and light organs are well developed. One of the common species is *scintillans* (Pl. 58). Its females have only partially developed wings and do not fly.

CLEROIDEA

Taxonomists have rather recently made up this superfamily from bits of several others. The following four of the included families interest us here.

MELYRIDÆ

These, formerly called Malachiidæ, have soft elytra suggesting Lampyridæ but the abdomen, with only 5 or 6 segments visible beneath, has no light organs. The antennæ of some males are curiously knotted and the fourth tarsal joint is not bilobed. Adults are found on flowers or herbage, some only in moist or low places, where they are said to feed on insect eggs, larvæ, and smaller insects generally. The larvæ, so far as known, are predacious. *Collops quadrimaculatus* (Pl. 61) is one of our largest and commonest species. The head and abdomen are black; pronotum and elytra reddish-yellow, each of the latter having two blue or bluish-black spots.

CLERIDÆ

Antennæ with 11 or rarely 10 joints; rather short; usually serrate; the outer joints larger and forming an open or less compact club. First and fourth tarsal joints often very small; all but the fifth furnished beneath with membranous appendages. The species are usually pubescent and more or less cylindrical in form. The fourth tarsal joint is about the size of the third; whereas in the rather similar Corynetidæ it is small, usually indistinct, embedded between the lobes of the third.

Checkered Beetles are, for the most part, small, graceful and pretty. The thorax is usually elongate and often much narrower than either the head or combined elytra. Some look like ants; others resemble Lampyrids. The usually pubescent adults occur chiefly on flowers, about flowing sap and on foliage. Both they and the larvæ are predacious, especially on wood-boring larvæ. *Trichodes* (front margin of eyes indented; antennal club triangular) *nutalli* (bluish, with reddish-yellow markings) and *Zenodosus* (eye margin not indented; the 3-jointed antennal club not triangular) *sanguineus* (brown, with red elytra) are shown on Pl. 61.

CORYNETIDÆ

See Cleridæ. We have three cosmopolitan species of *Necrobia* (the last 3 antennal joints forming a small, compact club, not very flat; only 5 abdominal segments visible). They are known as Bone Beetles because they are usually found on carrion after most of the flesh is gone, probably feeding on other insects there rather than on the carrion. *N. rufipes* (Pl. 61) is called the Red-legged Ham Beetle from its frequent appearance in that staple. Herrick says: "When the larva gets ready to transform it makes a curious and interesting cocoon in a rather novel way. The larva leaves the fatty portions and gnaws its way either to the harder, more fibrous parts of the ham or maybe into a near-by beam. Here it makes a glistening white cocoon that looks much like paper. The cocoon is not made like the cocoons of most insects, but is composed of small globules of spit out of the mouth of the larva. These globules adhere to each other and when dry form the paper-like cocoon." The three species may be separated as follows (none exceed 0.25 in. in length) :

1.—Pronotum and base of elytra red; rest of elytra blue or green; head and abdomen black.—*ruficollis.*
    No red on dorsal surface, but bluish. ....2.
2.—Legs and basal joints of antennæ red.—*rufipes.*
    Legs and antennæ dark.—*violacea.*

DERMESTIDÆ

Hind coxæ grooved for the reception of the femora in repose. Antennæ with 11 (sometimes 9 or 10) joints; the last 3 joints forming a large club. Elytra usually covering the abdomen. Legs short. Tibiæ with spurs. Tarsi 5-jointed; claws usually simple. These are usually oval, plump, dark beetles less than 0.4 in. long. They often have the surface partly covered with pale gray or brownish spots composed of minute hairs which are easily rubbed off.

The most troublesome of these feed on dried animal matter. *Byturus* (tarsi with second and third joints lobed beneath; front coxal cavities closed behind; each tarsal claw with a large basal tooth) *unicolor* is one that does not. In view of the fact that adults of most of the other species mentioned here regularly leave hides and hair for a sojourn among flowers, it may be retaining the ancestral activities. The adult is about 0.14 in. long, reddish-yellow or reddish-brown, and covered with a thick coat of pale, tawny hairs. It appears about the middle of May and feeds on the flower-buds and tender foliage of red raspberries. The larva is plump, white, with tawny cross-bands and numerous short white hairs. It feeds in the cup of the berries. Pupation and hibernation occur in an earthen cell just beneath the surface of the ground. Some put this genus in a separate family, Byturidæ.

In 1908 Mrs. Slosson, the author of such charming

PLATE 59

Oryzaephilus surinamensis

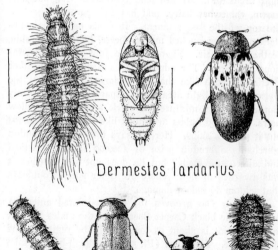

Dermestes lardarius

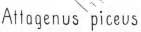

EL. B

Attagenus piceus

Anthrenus
scrophulariae

stories as "Fishing Jimmy," published a description of a strange beetle that was eating her collection of insects. She playfully called it *"Ignotus ænigmaticus."* This name was in proper form and by the rules of the game remained the scientific name of the beetle until the discovery was made that the beetle was an introduction from Transcaucasia and had a prior name. It is now *Thylodrias contractus.* It eats like a Dermestid but does not look like one. The female is wingless and the male has no hind wings.

The type genus of Dermestidæ, *Dermestes,* does not have the characteristics of *Byturus* and, unlike other common genera, it has no ocellus on the front of its head. The species are 0.25 in. or more long. *D. lardarius* is the common Larder or Bacon Beetle. The light areas (Pl. 59) are pale yellowish. The larva is brown, somewhat hairy, and has two curved spines on the top of the last segment. It feeds on animal substances such as smoked meats, cheese, hoofs, horn, skin, feather, and hair. There may be four or five generations a season. The adult of *D. vulpinus,* the Leather Beetle, is much like that of *lardarius* except that the elytra have no light areas, being sparsely and uniformly clothed with a mixture of black and grayish-yellow hairs. Its food habits are much like those of *lardarius* but it prefers skins. Herrick says that certain London merchants offered a prize of £20,000 for a "practical and effectual remedy" but he does not say whether it was awarded or not. There are other species outdoors that seldom do indoor damage.

Attagenus (no grooves for the 11-jointed antennæ) *piceus* is the black Carpet Beetle. In the males the last antennal joint is about as long as all the remainder of the antennæ. The larva (Pl. 59) is reddish-brown. Like most of the Dermestids, the adult does but little damage to our goods. It much prefers pollen as food. The larva goes in for almost anything of animal origin, especially woolens, feathers, and the dried specimens of entomological collections.

In *Anthrenus* the body is covered with small scales, not hairy; antennal club received in a deep pit at the apical thoracic angles. The larvæ of its species are

the Buffalo-moths or -bugs and some are the worst
enemies of entomological collections. *A. museorum*
has only 8 joints in each antenna, including the two-
jointed club; and the outline of the eyes is not indented.
It is found on flowers but is not a frequent visitor in
houses. The following species have 11 joints in each
antenna, including a three-jointed club, and, except for
verbasci, the outline of the eyes is indented. The
pronotum of *A. verbasci* is black, the central part
sparsely clothed with yellow scales, the sides more
densely with white ones; elytra black, with a large
basal ring and two transverse, zigzag bands of white
scales bordered by yellow ones; under surface of abdomen clothed with fine, long, grayish-yellow scales.
It is the common museum pest. *A. scrophulariæ* is the
Buffalo-moth. The elytra have brick-red, or dull yellow,
markings as shown in Pl. 59. I do not know why this
genus is connected, by name, with the buffalo, unless
the larvæ have a fancied resemblance to that animal.
Possibly it got its nick-name by being destructive of
buffalo robes in the days when such things were common.

This is as good a place as any to mention a number
of families that are not so apt to be noticed by any
but the specialist and that even specialists classify now
here and now there.

Among those that probably belong to the Cucujoidea
we have the following. RHIZOPHAGIDÆ has the single
genus *Rhizophagus.* They occur under bark. The
body is slender. The antennae are 10-jointed, including
a 2-jointed club. MONOTOMIDÆ are small, flattened
beetles usually under bark but sometimes in ant nests.
EROTYLIDÆ have 5-jointed tarsi, the 4th joint usually
very small; antennæ distinctly clubbed. Many are red
and black. Found chiefly on fungi. The larva of the
slender *Languria mozardi* (which with a few of the
other slender species are considered by some as belonging in a separate family, Languriidæ) bores in
clover stems. DERODONTIDÆ, a very few small fungus-
beetles. MYCETOPHAGIDÆ, another small family of
fungus-beetles. The upper surface is hairy, densely
punctured and with brown and yellow markings. The
tarsi are thread-like and 4-jointed except that the front
ones of males are 3-jointed. At least some COLYDIIDÆ

feed on small wood-boring insects. They have been put in Cucujidæ as a subfamily. MURMIDIIDÆ, MONŒDIDÆ and MYCETÆIDÆ are exceedingly small families. LATHRIDIIDÆ are rarely over 0.1 in. long; tarsi 3-jointed. For the most part they live under bark, stones or decaying leaves but some are on plants and *Corticaria ferruginea* has been found on dried drugs. ENDOMYCHIDÆ resemble Coccinellidæ but the tarsal claws appear to be 3-jointed as the very small third joint is concealed in the base of the terminal joint. They live in decaying wood and on fungi. Adult PHALACRIDÆ are usually shiny black and very convex. The larvæ live in flowers, especially Compositæ, and sometimes under bark.

Two families that may be Mordelloidea are PEDILIDÆ and EUGLENIDÆ.

DRYOPOIDEA includes some small but interesting aquatic insects. The small adult DRYOPIDÆ (formerly Parnidæ) cling with their long claws to sticks and stones in often swift streams. The last tarsal joint is longer than the other four combined. The abdomen has only 5 ventral segments. The flat aquatic larvæ are narrower than those of Psephenidæ. Adult PSEPHENIDÆ have more than 5 ventral segments. Their small flat, circular aquatic larvæ have been called Water-pennies. They cling tightly to stones usually in rapid streams but come out of the water to pupate under the last larval skin. HELMIDÆ larvæ are slender. They live in water or damp earth. HETEROCERIDÆ have enlarged tibiæ, armed with rows of spines, useful in digging in damp sand and mud. Splashing water into their galleries drives them out but the collector must act quickly, as they fly. GEORYSSIDÆ live in much the same way but, as they cover themselves with mud, it is difficult to see them unless they move.

In the DASCILLOIDEA we have DASCILLIDÆ, EUCINETIDÆ, and HELODIDÆ, small families of small beetles, some living in water, others on plants and in dead wood.

Some authors include Dermestidæ in the BYRRHOIDEA. Otherwise we have the following. BYRRHIDÆ have 5-jointed tarsi. The hind femora, when at rest, fit into grooves in the coxæ. They are found most commonly about the roots of coarse grasses in sandy places. *Chelonarium lecontei* of Florida may be our only species of CHELONARIIDÆ and *Nosodendron* our only genus of NOSODENDRIDÆ.

RHYSODIDÆ is a very small family of uncertain relationship. They are narrow, somewhat flattened; the thorax deeply wrinkled; head narrowed into a "neck." They live under bark.

The superfamily LYMEXYLOIDEA will be dropped if, as some urge, the type family, LYMEXYLIDÆ, is moved to the Cucujoidea. *Melittomma sericeum* (formerly put in *Lymexylon;* about 0.5 in. long; very narrow; brown with silky pubescence) lives under bark, especially that of oak logs. The very slender larvæ make small, irregular galleries. TELEGEUSIDÆ includes three or four Western species. For Micromalthidæ, formerly put here, see p. 277.

Tenebrionoidea has been considered to include Alleculidæ, Tenebrionidæ, Lagriidæ and Melandryidæ of our "Heteromera"; also MONOMMIDÆ. Of the latter we have less than a dozen species.

"HETEROMERA"

See p. 276. The name Heteromera has been used to cover a large number (a "series") of families in which the front and middle tarsi are 5-jointed and the hind ones are 4-jointed. Although this grouping is now for technical reasons being dropped, it is a convenient way to state distinguishing characteristics of some of the families, particularly as authorities are far from agreed as to superfamily groupings.

1.—Front coxal cavities closed behind. ....2.
   These open behind. ....4.
2.—Tarsal claws simple. ....3.
   Claws comb-like.—ALLECULIDÆ, formerly Cistelidæ. Looking much like Tenebrionidæ, they have more slender antennæ. They are usually brown, with a smooth, pubescent surface, and often taper toward the hind end. The larvæ, so far as known, live in rotten wood and resemble wireworms.
3.—Tarsi with the next to the last joint spongy beneath. Front coxæ prominent. Last antennal joint at least as long as the 3 preceeding ones combined.—LAGRIIDÆ. Species of *Arthromacra* are about 0.5 in. and of *Statira* usually less than 0.3 in. long. They are black or bronzed, with rather thin, flexible elytra.
   Next to the last tarsal joint not spongy beneath.—TENEBRIONIDÆ, p. 324.
4.—Head not strongly and suddenly constricted behind the eyes. ....5.
   Head thus constricted. ....7.
5.—Middle coxæ very prominent. Pronotum narrower at base than combined elytra, its sides rounded and without a sharp edge. Next to last tarsal joint broad, slightly bilobed. Body-covering rather flimsy in texture.—ŒDEMERIDÆ. One of the species, *Nacerda*

melanura (Pl. 62), is a cosmopolitan beetle that is rather common in city cellars, old boxes and lumber yards. It is dull yellow above, the elytra tipped with dark purple; each front tibiæ with one spur; tarsi with next to the last joint broadly dilated.

Middle coxæ not very prominent. ....6.

6.—Pronotum margined at sides, broad at base; its middle portion (disk) with impressions near base. Maxillary palpi usually long and drooping; its joint enlarged—MELANDRYIDÆ. These usually elongate, "loose-jointed" beetles feed on fungi and dead wood. *Penthe obliquata,* about 0.5 in. long, velvety black with reddish yellow on the scutellum (scutellum of *P. pimelia* black), is common under bark. See also below.

Pronotum not margined, narrower behind, disk not impressed at base. Head sometimes prolonged into a beak.—PYTHIDÆ. Our score or so of species are most apt to be found under bark, especially pine, or stones. They may be predacious.

7.—Pronotum with a sharp edge at each side; its base as wide as combined elytra. ....8.

Sides of pronotum more or less rounded and without a sharp edge. ....10.

8.—Antennæ thread-like. ....9.

Antennæ with long, flat processes folding like a fan (male) or somewhat saw-toothed (female).—Some (e.g. *Pelecotoma flavipes*) Rhipiphoridæ. See below.

9.—Hind coxæ with plates. Head with vertex lobed or ridged behind so that, when extended, it rests on the front edge of the pronotum. Abdomen usually ending in a pointed process.—MORDELLIDÆ, p. 319.

Hind coxæ without plates. Length less than 0.25 in.—Some Melandryidæ. See above.

10.—Pronotum narrower at base than the combined elytra. ....11.

Pronotum as wide at base as combined elytra. Elytra narrowed behind and usually shorter than the abdomen. Abdomen not ending in a spinous process. Antennæ comb-like in males, often saw-toothed in females.—RHIPIPHORIDÆ. A small family resembling the Mordellidæ in general appearance. "Adults occur on flowers and are much less common than the Mordellids. The larvæ that are known are parasitic, some in the nests of wasps and others on cockroaches" (Blatchley). See *Rhipiphorus flavipennis,* Pl. 60.

11.—Hind coxæ not prominent. Tarsal claws simple. Antennæ thread-like and simple. Head with an abrupt, narrow neck. Length less than 0.5 in., usually less than 0.2 in.—ANTHICIDÆ. These probably predacious beetles are found on flowers, in rotten wood, and in burrows in sandy places near water. Some of them resemble ants and others have a prominent horn on the pronotum.

Of the latter sort, *Notoxus* has the hind tarsi not longer than the tibiæ; they are much longer in *Mecynotarsus*.

Hind coxæ large, prominent. ....12.

12.—Tarsal claws simple. Head horizontal. Antennæ usually branched in male, saw-toothed in female. Tarsi with next to last joints very broad.—PYROCHROIDÆ. We have only about a dozen species and they are not common. Reddish pronotum and black or blue elytra is the usual color scheme. The larvæ, with broad heads, stout legs, and two spines on the tips of the abdomens, occur under bark. Adult *Dendroides* have very large eyes nearly touching each other.

Tarsal claws cleft or toothed; front of head vertical; length at least 0.25 in.—MELOIDÆ, p. 320.

MORDELLIDÆ

See above. "This family includes a large number of small, wedge-shaped beetles having the body arched, the head bent downward and the abdomen usually prolonged into a style or pointed process. The hind legs are, in most species, very long and stout, fitted for leaping; the antennæ long and slender and the thorax is as wide at the base as the elytra. The body is densely covered with fine silky hairs, usually black, but often very prettily spotted or banded with yellow or silver hues. The adults occur on flowers or on dead trees and are very active, flying and running with great rapidity and in the net or beating umbrella jumping and tumbling about in grotesque manner in their efforts to escape. The larvæ live in old wood or in the pith of plants, and those of some species are said to be carnivorous in habit, feeding upon the young of Lepidoptera and Diptera which they find in the plant stems" (Blatchley). *Mordellistena* has the most species in our region. They are usually not over 0.25 in. long. Their hind tibiæ have a distinct ridge near the apex and usually one or more oblique ones. Their eyes are coarsely granulated. The two following genera agree with it in having the last abdominal segment prolonged into a conical "style" and their tarsal claws comb-like, but their hind tibiæ have but a small ridge near the apex and their eyes are only finely granulated. In *Tomoxia* the style is short, obtuse, and the scutellum is usually indented behind; in *Mordella* (Plate 62) the anal style is long, slender, and the scutellum is triangular. *Anthobates* and *Anaspis* (4th joint of the front and middle tarsi smaller than the 3rd) are not especially rare but they have few and small species. Their abdomen is not prolonged at the tip and the tarsal claws are not cleft. They may be removed to another family.

MELOIDÆ

See p. 319. The family was nicknamed Blister Beetles because certain species such as the "Spanish-fly," *Lytta* (The old name *Cantharis* was "preoccupied") *vesicatoria* of southern Europe, were formerly ground up to make a blistering ointment. The active substance, cantharidin, is chiefly in the elytra.

Meloë (Pl. 60), unlike most beetles, has one elytron slightly overlapping the other. There are no hind wings (other wingless genera in the West). Among the Eastern species we have:

1.—Pronotum longer than wide.—*M. angusticollis.*
  Pronotum not longer than wide. ....**2.**
2.—Dull black. Pronotum with an impression on basal half of median line.—*M. impressus.*
  Blue or bluish-black. Thorax not impressed. ....**3.**
3.—Pronotum densely punctate. Elytra roughly sculptured.—*M. americanus.*
  Pronotum rather densely punctate. Elytra not roughly sculptured.—*M. niger.*

These species are called Oil Beetles because, when disturbed, they give off a disagreeable oily fluid. A female may lay several thousand eggs. The life-history is much like that of *Epicauta* described below except that the newly hatched larvæ clamber around flowers trying to get onto bees so that they may be carried to the bees' nests and find an easy living there. If they mistake, as many do, flies for bees the outcome is starvation.

Some of our other genera and a few of their species may be recognized as follows:

1.—Front not prolonged beyond the base of the antennæ. Labrum (upper lip) small, scarcely visible.—Tribe Horiini, of which *Tricrania sanguinipennis* should be looked for in sandy places. It is about 0.3 in. long; black, with brick-red elytra.

PLATE 60

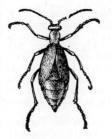

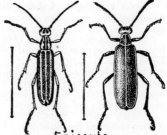

Meloë
angusticollis

Epicauta
vitatta   marginata

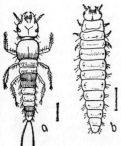

Hypermetamorphosis of Epicauta vittata

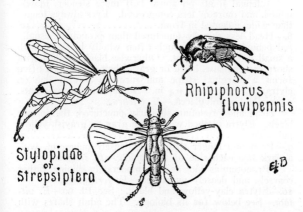

Stylopidæ
or
Strepsiptera

Rhipiphorus
flavipennis

E.B

Front prolonged. Labrum distinct. ....**2.**
2.—Mandibles prolonged beyond the labrum, acute at tip. ....**3.**

Mandibles not prolonged, obtuse. Elytra entire. Antennæ straight, not thickened toward the apex.—Tribe Lyttini. ....**4.**
3.—Elytra rudimentary. No wings. Tarsal claws not cleft.—Tribe Sitarini, to which *Hornia minutipennis* belongs. It is reddish-brown; length about 0.7 in.; in nests of solitary bees (*Anthophora*).

Elytra entire. Tarsal claws cleft.—Tribe Zonitini. *Nemognatha* has the outer lobe of the maxillæ (accessory jaws below or behind the mandibles) prolonged; it is not so in *Zonitis*.
4.—Second antennal joint at least half as long as the third.—*Macrobasis*. *M. unicolor*: 0.3 to 0.5 in. long; black, rather densely clothed with grayish hairs, which give it an ashy color; second joint of male's antennæ slightly longer than the next two and nearly twice as wide. The adults occur on various plants including potatoes and ironweed.

Second antennal joint much less than half the length of the third. ....**5.**
5.—Next to the last joint of tarsi bilobed.—*Tetraonyx*.

Next to last joint of tarsi cylindrical. ....**6.**
6.—Front femora with a silken, hairy spot on the under side. Second antennal joint very short. Mandibles short. Larvæ, as far as known, feed on eggs of grasshoppers.— *Epicauta*. ....**7.**

Front femora without a silken, hairy spot. ....**13.**
7.—Antennal joints of equal thickness throughout, cylindrical, and closely united. Eyes nearly as wide as long, feebly or not at all indented in front. ....**8.**

Antennal joints on apical half more slender, loosely united, and more or less compressed. Eyes always longer than wide, indented in front. ....**10.**
8.—Head less densely punctured than pronotum, usually red behind the eyes, though often wholly black or with a small red spot in front. Otherwise black, clothed with short, rather dense, black or gray pubescence, which often forms a marginal stripe and rarely a sutural line on elytra. Length about 0.4 in. Adults on various plants, especially Convolvulaceæ.—*E. trichrus*.

Head and pronotum similarly punctured, the former black. Elytra clothed with dense gray or grayish-yellow pubescence. ....**9.**
9.—Pronotum longer than wide, densely pubescent, with a dark line each side of the middle.—*E. strigosa*.

Pronotum as wide as long, moderately shining, rather coarsely and densely punctured.—*E. ferruginea*.
10.—Elytra clay-yellow and black. See Pl. 60.—*E. vittata*. See below for its biology. The adult shares with

Lema trilineata the name of Old-fashioned Potato Beetle but feeds also on tomatoes and various weeds.

Elytra without stripes on their middle. . . . . .11.

11.—Body, beneath, clothed with gray pubescence; elytra in part or wholly pubescent. . . . . .12.

Body, above and beneath, wholly black. Outer spur of hind tibiæ broader than the inner. Length, 0.3 to 0.5 in. During autumn on goldenrod especially, sometimes injures garden asters.—*E. pennsylvanica.*

12.—Elytra wholly clothed with uniform, gray pubescence; length 0.4 to 0.75 in. Adults on potatoes and other plants.—*E. cinerea.*

Elytra black, with gray margins and suture. Pl. 60. —*E. marginata;* may be only a variety of *cinerea.*

13.—Antennæ thread-like, the outer joints cylindrical.—*Pyrota.*

Antennæ thicker toward the apex, the outer joints oval or rounded.—*Pomphopœa,* with a deeply indented labrum; and *Lytta,* with labrum only slightly indented.

As an example of the curious life-histories to be found in this family we may quote from Riley's old account of *Epicauta vittata.* The victims are short-horned grasshoppers or "locusts" of the genus *Melanoplus.* "The locust lays its eggs underground in masses surrounded by an irregular capsule, and the *Epicauta* deposits its eggs in spots frequented by the locusts, but not in special proximity to the eggs thereof. In a few days the eggs of the blister-beetle hatch, giving rise to a little larvæ [*a,* Pl. 60] of the kind called triungulin, because each leg is terminated by three tarsal spines or claws. In warm, sunny weather these triungulins become very active; they run about on the surface of the ground exploring all its cracks, penetrating various spots and burrowing, till an egg-pod of the locust is met with; into this the triungulin at once eats its way, and commences to devour an egg. Should two or more triungulins enter the same egg-pod, battles occur until one is left. After a few days passed in devouring a couple of eggs, the triungulin sheds it skin and appears as a different larva [*b*], with soft skin, short legs, small eyes, and different form and proportions; a second moult takes place after about a week, but it is not accompanied by any very great change in form, though the larva is now curved, less active, and in form like a larva of Scarabæidæ; when another moult occurs the fourth instar appears as a still more helpless form of larva, which increases rapidly in size, and when full grown leaves the remains of the egg-pod it has been living on, and forms a small cavity near by; here it lies on one side motionless, but gradually contracting, till the skin separates and is pushed down to the end of the body, disclosing a completely helpless creature [c] that has been variously called a semi-pupa, pseudo-pupa, or coarctate larva; in this state the winter is passed. In the spring the skin of the coarctate larva bursts, and there crawls out of it a sixth instar [d] which resembles the fourth, except in the somewhat reduced size and greater whiteness. It is worthy of remark that the skin it has deserted retains its original form almost intact. In this sixth instar the larva is rather active and burrows about, but does not take food, and in the course of a few days again moults and discloses the true pupa. As usual in Coleoptera, this instar lasts but a short time, and in five or six days the perfect beetle appears. It is extremely difficult to frame any explanation of this complex development; there are, it will be noticed, no less than five stages interposed between the first larval instar and the pupal instar, and the creature assumes in the penultimate one a quasi-pupal state, to again quit it for a return to a previous state. It is possible to look on the triungulin and the pupal instar as special adaptations to external conditions; but it is not possible to account for the intermediate instars in this way, and we must look on them as necessitated by the physiological processes going on internally. Nothing, however, is known as to these."

Fabre and others have described the European species of *Sitaris* living in much the same way at the expense of the bees of the genus *Anthophora*.

TENEBRIONIDÆ

See p. 317. These are the Darkling Beetles. Quite probably future authors will subdivide this family. There are many species in the Southwest, where they occur like Carabidæ, but they are by no means lacking in the East. New Jersey, for example, has more than sixty species. The Eastern species are not usually found under stones, as are those in arid regions, but in dead wood, fungi, and dry vegetable products. The Western Pinacates (*Eleodes*), "the bugs that stand on their heads," are members of this family.

The larvæ of *Tenebrio obscurus* (Pl. 62) and *molitor* are the large Meal-worms which have the distinction of being the only insects injurious to man's goods that are purposely bred on a large scale for commercial purposes. They destroy large quantities of flour, meal, cereals and the like, but are bred and sold for soft-billed birds to eat. The larvæ are hard, cylindrical, and strongly resembles wire-worms (Elateridæ). That of *obscurus* is about an inch long when full-grown; yellow but shading off into yellowish-brown at each end and where the segments join. That of *molitor* is somewhat lighter. The pupæ are whitish and about 0.6 in. long; most of the abdominal segments have fringed side-expansions and the last one ends in two spines. The adults of both species are black or dark reddish-brown and about 0.6 in. long; *molitor* is shiny and *obscurus* is not. They are frequently attracted to lights. There seems to be, normally, but one generation a year, but in heated buildings this is not very definite. Related species occur under bark.

Alobates pennsylvanica is a black beetle, nearly an inch long, that is often common under the loose bark of dead trees. The genus differs from *Tenebrio* by the tarsal pubescence being fine and silky. The antennæ do not reach to the hind margin of the pronotum, which is not narrowed at the base.

We have two species of *Tribolium* that occur in meal, grain, and other vegetable products. To give them a common name different from that applied to *Tenebrio,* they have been called Flour Beetles, but neither name is very distinctive. *Tribolium ferrugineum* is red-brown; its head is not expanded beyond the eyes at the sides; its antennal club is distinctly three-jointed; and its length is less than 0.2 in. Its "cousin," *confusum* (Pl. 62), is darker; its head is expanded on each side in front of the eye; antennal joints gradually broader at tip. It has been recorded as breeding in pepper as well as in a variety of milder, starchy foods and it also eats the eggs and larvæ of other meal-feeding insects. The larvæ and pupæ are much like *Tenebrio* in miniature. Under favorable circumstances, a generation may be completed in five or six weeks and there may be several generations a year.

Bolitotherus cornutus occurs, often in numbers, in woody, "bracket" fungi such as grow on the sides of trees and stumps. The adults are black or brownish-black. What attracts attention are the horned males (Pl. 62). A related genus, *Bolitophagus,* is found with it, but more often under bark. In it each eye is completely divided and the antennæ are 11-jointed. There are two species, each not over 0.3 in. long and black; in *corticola* the pronotum has numerous tubercles, its margin is scalloped and, in front of the hind angles, deeply notched; in *depressus* the pronotum is merely coarsely punctured and its sides are evenly rounded.

Diaperis maculata is also common in hard fungi and under bark. It is about 0.25 in. long, oval and convex. The head and most of the elytra are reddish, otherwise black.

BOSTRICHOIDEA

In addition to the families mentioned below we have the *Cisidæ* (or Cioidæ) and SPHINDIDÆ. They are very small, cylindrical beetles that usually live under bark or in dry fungi. Some, however, make small holes in wood and even in books.

PTINIDÆ

As now restricted, this is a small family. The antennæ arise from the front of the head rather close together and the thorax has no side-margin. As in Anobiidæ and related families, the prothorax tends to over-grow the head. The tarsi are 5-jointed. *Ptinus* is our largest genus. In it the elytra have rows of small pits and are pubescent.

There is no such thing as *the* Book-worm among insects. A Ptinid has a record of having "penetrated directly through twenty-seven large quarto volumes in so straight a line that a string could be passed through the opening and the whole series of volumes suspended." This was *Ptinus fur* (Pl. 61), the small reddish-brown

PLATE 61

Collops
4-maculatus

Trichodes
nuttalli

Zenodosus
sanguineus

Necrobia rufipes

Sitodrepa
panicea

Ptinus
fur

Lasioderma
serricorne

Lyctus
striatus

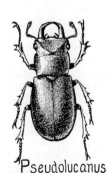

Pseudolucanus

Passalus
cornutus

Nicagus
obscurus

Spider Beetle whose female has two white patches on each elytron. However, almost any insect which feeds on dry, starchy material may eat books. *Gibbium psylloides* is 0.1 in. long, spider-like in shape, with a mahogany back and eyes near the front. It infests old buildings and occasionally appears in restaurant sugar bowls. *Mezium americanum* is somewhat similar but has its eyes on the sides of the head; head and thorax covered with yellow scales.

ANOBIIDÆ

The antennæ arise from the sides of the head in front of the eyes. The thorax is usually margined at the sides.

I had not been at the American Museum of Natural History very long before a mystified lady brought in some red pepper which had been kept in a tight tin box and which, nevertheless, had in it reddish-brown beetles about 0.1 in. long. A lens showed the characteristic form (Pl. 61) and bristling yellow pubescence of *Sitodrepa panicea,* the Drug-store Beetle. I assured her that even red pepper is not too strong for it. At least forty-five different drugs, including aconite, belladonna, squill, orris root, and ergot, are in its menu. It has been known to bore through tin-foil and sheet-lead. Printed books are not too dry for it; and it eats all sorts of seeds and dry groceries. There still remained in the visitor's mind curiosity concerning the sufficiency of air and water in the "tight tin box." I took her pepper and beetles, put them in a glass vial, corked it, sealed it with paraffin, and put it in an exhibition case, suggesting that she come back occasionally to see how her captives were getting along. I do not know that she did but at the end of two years and a half there had been numerous generations of offspring which, by that time, had reduced the pepper and part of the cork to such unnutritious powder that even *Sitodrepa* had to give up. Under favorable conditions there is a generation every two months.

The small burrows in cigars and cigarettes are usually the work of *Lasioderma serricorne* (Pl. 61), the Cigar and Cigarette Beetle. Although very fond of tobacco, its dietary is much the same as that of *Sitodrepa*. It

PLATE 62

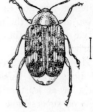

Mylabris obtectus

Mylabris pisorum

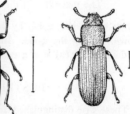

Tenebrio obscurus

Tribolium confusum

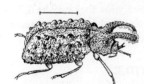

Bolitotherus cornutus

Nacerda melanura

Mordella 8-punctata

E.L.B.

averages less than 0.2 in. long, and the last 3 joints of the
antennæ are not enlarged like those of *Sitodrepa;* the
front angles of the pronotum are more acute. The white
larvæ resemble those of the Drug-store Beetle but are
hairier.

Anobium and several related species bore in the wood
of houses and furniture. In the role of Death-watch
they, or at least some of them, sometimes play a grim
joke on superstitious humans who believe that the ticking
sound which the beetle makes portends the death of some
one in the house. Swift had the right idea:

> "A kettle of scalding hot water ejected
> Infallibly cures the timber affected;
> The omen is broken, the danger is over,
> The maggot will die and the sick will recover."

They make the noise by bobbing their heads up and
down, tapping the wood. Instead of foretelling death, it
is doubtless a call for a mate and new lives.

BOSTRICHIDÆ

These are distinguished from the Ptinidæ by, among
other characters, their cylindrical form and by having the
first joint of the tarsi very short and imperfectly separated from the second. The eyes are small, rounded, and
somewhat prominent. From Scolytidæ they may be differentiated also by the loose-jointed club of the antennæ.
They are chiefly borers in twigs.

LYCTIDÆ

Lyctus striatus (Pl. 61) and related species bore into
dry wood of furniture, trimmings, and construction timber, often doing a great deal of harm that is difficult to
prevent. They are sometimes called Powder-post Beetles
and "all live in dry wood, either in cylindrical burrows
or beneath the bark, and sometimes in such numbers that
the timber is wholly destroyed by them." Frequently the
interior of the wood is largely reduced to powder before
the small exit holes of the beetle are noticed. The

common species are reddish-brown, cylindrical, and about
0.2 in. long.

SCARABÆOIDEA

See p. 276. This superfamily is the old "series" Lamell-
licornia. Not so long ago we were satisfied with only
two families, Lucanidæ and Scarabæidæ. I do not know
how many groups of genera will be raised to family rank
by the time you see this but I hope that the following
will suffice for now. The antennæ of Lucanidæ and related families are usually elbowed; the joints are not
flattened but form a comb-like club, the joints of which
cannot be brought closely together. The elytra cover
the abdomen, which has only five ventral segments visible
at the sides. The antennæ of Scarabæidæ and its relatives
are not elbowed; the end joints are plate-like and, when
brought together, form a compact club. The elytra usually
do not cover the last segment of the abdomen, which
usually has more than five ventral segments visible at the
sides.

LUCANIDÆ AND RELATIVES

These are the Stag Beetles and Pinching-bugs. Some
of the adults come freely to lights. The larvæ are flat,
white grubs, usually living in decaying wood. The "relatives" are a new family, SINODENDRIDÆ, of which *Sino-
dendron rugosum,* having antennæ not elbowed, maxillæ
not covered by the mentum, and the male having a "horn,"
is on the Pacific Coast; and PASSALIDÆ, of which *Passalus cornutus* may be our only species. *P. cornutus* (Pl.
61) can make a creaking or hissing noise by rubbing the
abdomen against the wings. The larvæ make faint sounds
by rubbing the middle coxæ with their very short hind
legs. Larvæ and parents live together, the former eating
wood that the latter chew for them. Some of the genera
still in Lucanidæ may be known as follows:

1.—Antennæ elbowed, the first segment nearly or quite as
long as the others together. Front coxæ near each
other. ....**2.**
     Antennæ not elbowed.—Æsalinæ, including *Nicagus*
(Pl. 61) and several other genera.
2.—Elytra smooth or nearly so. Front tibiæ with large
teeth on outer edges.—Lucaninæ, including *Lucanus* (man-

dibles of male as long as the abdomen) and *Pseudolucanus* (mandibles shorter). Of *Lucanus* we have only
elaphus. It occurs from New Jersey to Illinois southward. The female may be known by her black legs and
chestnut-brown elytra. *P. capreolus* (Pl. 61) used to be
called *dama*.

Elytra grooved and punctate.—Dorcinæ, including
Dorcus (margin of eyes indented) and *Platycerus* (eye-
margin not indented).

SCARABÆIDÆ AND RELATIVES

This large family (over 20,000 species and "increasing
by the discovery of about 300 new species every year")
contains such forms as the May Beetles (June-bugs), the
"shard-borne beetle with his drowsy hum" of Shake-
speare, and the Sacred Scarab of Egypt. The larvæ are
usually yellowish-white, with a brown, chitinized head
bearing prominent mandibles. They are wrinkled, fat
(especially at the hind end) "grubs" that live in excrement, in decaying wood, or in the ground, and normally
lie on their side with the hind end almost, or quite, touching the legs. What are given here as subfamilies will
probably be generally accepted as families. The reader
can then change "-næ" to "-dæ." Even some of the
tribes (names ending in "ni") have already been made
families by some authors.

SCARABÆINÆ

The name Coprinæ has also been used for these. They
feed on either excrement or decaying fungi. The enlarged clypeus covers the mandibles and each tibia usually
has but one terminal spur.

Canthon may be recognized by the slender, somewhat
curved, middle and hind tibiæ being but little enlarged
at the tip. The males never have horns. Other genera
have the middle and hind tibiæ much expanded at the tip
and the males usually have horns on the head or pronotum. Of these, *Chœridium* and *Onthophagus* rarely exceed 0.3 in. in length.

Species of *Canthon* are the black or bronzed Tumble-
bugs that make balls of dung and industriously roll them
about (Pl. 63) just as does their near relative, *Scarabæus*

sacer, considered sacred by the ancient Egyptians. It seems that this creature, in its form and actions, was believed by them to be emblematical of such abstruse things as the planetary movements and future life, not to mention minor matters. As a matter of fact, we have a great deal to learn about the whys and hows of ball-rolling. Comstock wrote that "this is one of the instances, rare among insects, where the male realizes he has some responsibility as a father, and assists the female in providing for the young." On the other hand, Fabre, observing *S. sacer,* tells of females helping each other to the extent of stealing the ball.

Some of these beetles do not roll their food to some distant hole for burial but dig a hole in the ground under or near the source of supply, usually cow dung. This hole is then provisioned and a single egg laid in it. Our three common species having this habit are plain black. *Pinotus carolina* (Pl. 63) is rarely less than 0.9 in. long and each elytron has but seven longitudinal striæ. *Copris minutus* is less than 0.5 in. long, while the size of *C. anaglypticus* is intermediate. Each has eight striæ on each elytron.

Phanæus includes brilliantly colored beetles. The males of our species have quite a horn on their heads and lack tarsi on their front legs. The first joint of the antennal club is hollowed out to receive the others. The male of *carnifex* is shown in Pl. 96. The female has a short, blunt tubercle in place of the male's horn.

Aphodiinæ

Each hind tibiæ has two spines; antennæ 9-jointed; abdomen covered by elytra. *Aphodius* is the largest genus, both as regards the number of species and by having the largest species. They are dung-feeders that frequently fly in great numbers during the warm autumn afternoons and, like their relatives, come freely to light.

Geotrupinæ

Antennæ 11-jointed, mandibles prominent and visible from above. The principal genus in the Northeast is

Geotrupes (Pl. 63). The antennal clubs are not very large and the plates are of equal thickness. Individuals of our common species range from 0.5 to 0.75 in. in length and vary from black to purple and dark metallic green. Some provision holes, as does *Copris,* with dung; others live in decaying "toadstools," especially in the underground stem. Some, possibly all, of the species can make a faint sound by rubbing the hind coxæ against the abdomen. As for other genera, their antennal clubs are large, round, and convex on both sides. The eyes of *Bolboceras* are partially divided by a process from the side of the head, and those of *Bolbocerosoma* (black and brown beetles in which the process between the middle coxæ has an erect tooth-like elevation) and of *Odontæus* (brown beetles without this "tooth") are entirely divided.

ACANTHOCERINÆ

Although even larger subfamilies are being skipped here, this one is included to mention *Clœotus* because its species are a bit exceptional. They live under bark and in rotten wood. They can roll up their bodies, less than 0.25 in. long, into a somewhat hemispherical mass.

TROGINÆ

Except for the Western *Glaresis* (9-jointed antennæ; each compound eye half-divided) this is the genus *Trox* (10-jointed antennæ; eyes not divided). Its species are oblong, convex, dirty-looking, brown beetles, that occur under or about carrion or old hides. The surface is usually roughly sculptured (Pl. 63) and covered with a crust of earth that is difficult to remove. Adults stridulate by rubbing the abdomen against the elytra, special areas being roughened "for this purpose." What they gain by making this noise is another question.

MELOLONTHINÆ

Here belong the June-bugs or Cockchafers. The adults, often very abundant about lights, feed chiefly on leaves and flowers. The abdominal spiracles are

PLATE 63

Canthon laevis

Geotrupes
blackburnii

Trox suberosus

Pinotus carolina

Pelidnota punctata

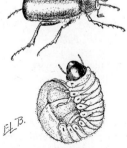

Phyllophaga

Macrodactylus
subspinosus

ELB.

placed almost in a line but not more than the front three spiracles are on the membrane connecting the dorsal and ventral parts of the abdomen. The larvæ live in the ground and feed chiefly on roots. Our principal genera may be separated as follows:

1.—Middle and hind tibiæ each with only one spur and this sometimes obsolete; hind tarsi with a single claw.—*Hoplia.*

Middle and hind tibiæ each with two spurs; all tarsi with two equal claws. ....2.

2.—Form elongate, slender; metallic green or bronzed or dull yellow. ....3.

Form robust, heavy; brownish, sometimes iridescent. ....4.

3.—Elytra pubescent, not densely scaly. Claws capable of being folded along the last joint of tarsi.—*Dichelonyx.*

Elytra densely covered with elongate, yellowish scales. Tarsal claws not as above.—*Macrodactylus.*

4.—Five ventral, abdominal segments. Elytra either uniformly and rather finely punctured or with punctured striæ.—*Diplotaxis.*

Six ventral, abdominal segments. ....5.

5.—Less than 0.5 in. long. Elytra with indistinct but regular grooves.—*Serica* (hind femora and especially the hind tibiæ slender) and *Autoserica* (these joints flat).

Usually more than 0.5 in. long. Most of the elytra usually without striæ or grooves.—*Phyllophaga.*

Adults of *Hoplia* are usually found on flowers during the day. The two sexes often differ in size and color. Adults of *Dichelonyx* are usually found on leaves of trees and shrubs. The eyes are rather large and prominent. The antennal club of males is nearly as long as the rest of the antennæ.

The name *Macrodactylus* (Pl. 63) means "long fingered" and all who grow roses will agree that it fits in both a literal and a figurative sense. There is little you can do to combat this pest unless you wish either to keep your roses, flowers and all, sprayed with poison when the beetles are around or plow deeply your lawn and the lawns of all your neighbors every winter in order to turn the young of the Rose Beetles out into the cold. It is of some help to go out several times a day and knock the adults that have made their appearance into a cup of kerosene. It is said that chickens die from eating them. The Rose Beetle feeds also on grape blossoms. Its specific name is *subspinosus.* A much less common species, *angustatus,* also occurs. The latter is more Southern in its distribution and confines its attention chiefly to oak and other wild plants. The specific distinctions are slight and technical.

Autoserica castanea is bronzy-brown in color; variations of this color are found but not commonly. This Asiatic species was first reported in the U. S. in a nursery near Rutherford, New Jersey. Its spread has been quite slow, but now extends in isolated places from Massachusetts to Virginia.

Species of *Phyllophaga* (Pl. 63) are the beetles that buzz and bang about the room in the early summer evenings, often going under the name of *Lachnosterna.* There are numerous species but distinguishing them is a matter of considerable difficulty. The female is said to deposit her eggs, enclosed in a ball of earth, among the roots of grass. The larvæ are "white grubs"; they get to be about as thick as a man's little finger and are frequently very injurious to the roots of various plants. Cases have been reported in which they were so numerous in lawns that they had completely cut the roots; the turf could be rolled up like a carpet. The larval stage of some species, at least, lasts for two or three years. Pupation occurs in an underground cell.

The remainder of the subfamilies have the abdominal spiracles placed in two lines on each side, the front three on the connecting membrane and the others on the ventral segments.

RUTELINÆ

Claws on each tarsus unequal in size, the inner one much more slender than the outer. Of the four native genera to be mentioned here, *Anomala* and *Strigoderma* have 9-jointed antennæ and the mandibles, when closed, are covered by the clypeus; *Pelidnota* and *Cotalpa* have 10-jointed antennæ and the mandibles are usually visible beyond the clypeus. The elytra of *Anomala* are convex, not notched at the base, shallowly striate, and with small holes (punctate); the thorax is not hairy. The elytra of *Strigoderma* are flattened, notched at the base, deeply striate but not punctate; the thorax is hairy and has impressed lines.

Anomala orientalis, first reported in this country in 1920 in a nursery near New Haven, Connecticut, is commonly straw-colored with black markings but variable to the extent that some specimens may be entirely black.

Cotalpa lanigera, the Goldsmith Beetle (Pl. 96), is found on willow and poplar, occasionally on oak, and at light. Its specific name refers to the whitish "wool" on the under side.

Pelidnota punctata is, by day, common on grape, drawing the leaves together for shelter, and by night at lights. It is dull reddish-brown or brownish-yellow above, with spots as shown in Pl. 63. The larvæ live in decaying stumps, especially of oak and hickory.

An introduced pest that has become very important recently is the Green Japanese Beetle, *Popillia japonica.* It is about half an inch long, and may be recognized by its being almost entirely green except for the brown elytra, which do not reach to the tip of the abdomen. When Messrs. Weiss and Dickerson, then inspectors for the New Jersey State Department of Agriculture, discovered it in 1916 in Burlington County, N. J., they could find only a dozen beetles. By 1919 it had increased to such an extent that 20,000 beetles could "be collected by hand by one person in a single day." By 1934 it had broken through "quarantine" lines and become firmly established in this country. The first beetles probably came in with the earth surrounding the roots of some ornamental plant such as iris or azalea. The adults skeletonize the leaves of almost all kinds of plants. They also eat such fruits as peaches. The larvæ feed on the roots of grasses, chiefly.

DYNASTINÆ

Claws on each tarsus equal in size; front coxæ transverse, not very prominent; body usually convex above. Of our more common genera, *Spilosota* and *Dyscinetus* have the head and pronotum plain; the others have at least a ridge or tubercle on one or the other or both. Our species of *Spilosota* are about 0.5 in. long; brownish-yellow; the mandibles are narrow and scarcely curved. *Dyscinetus trachypygus* is practically black; the mandibles are broad, rounded on the outer side, and curved. It is nearly 0.75 in. long and is found under rubbish along the shores of the sea, lakes and larger streams, as well as at lights.

Dynastes tityus is over 1.5 in. long. It is usually greenish-gray with brown or blackish spots scattered irregularly over the elytra. The common name, Unicorn Beetle, is scarcely correct, for the males have three horns on the pronotum, the ones on the sides slender, curved and very short, the median stout, with yellowish hair beneath, notched at the tip, and projecting forward to meet a long, curved horn arising from the head. The females have only a slight tubercle on the middle of the head. It is a Southern insect, rarely seen even in southern New Jersey, for example. I have found larvæ, pupæ, and adults abundant in rotten wood in southern Mississippi.

Strategus antæus, the Ox Beetle, is an inch or more long; shiny, dark reddish-brown, the male's pronotum almost black. The male has one stout horn on each side of the pronotum, and one on the front of the same segment; the female has merely a much reduced front horn.

Xyloryctes satyrus is also an inch or more long and rather stouter than the preceding species. Its color also is much like that of the preceding but the male, instead of horns on the thorax, has a long, stout one on the head. It is called the Rhinoceros Beetle, but this is confusing as that name is applied more aptly to certain Tropical species.

CETONIINÆ

These have the claws on each tarsus equal; coxæ conical, rather prominent; body rather flattened above; the antennæ 10-jointed. In flying, they usually "do not raise the elytra as most beetles do, but the inner wings pass out from the side under the elytra, which are a little narrower at the tips than the base and do not at all embrace the sides of the body. The members of this subfamily differ from the other 'leaf-chafers' in being for the most part flower beetles, the mouth organs being furnished with a brush of hairs with which they collect pollen. They are therefore mostly diurnal, flying about from flower to flower during the heat of the day. At night and in cloudy or rainy weather they are to be found beneath bark or other cover."

In the South *Cotinis* (or *Allorhina*) *nitida* (Pl. 96) is called the Fig-eater. When flying, it is easily mistaken for a loudly buzzing bumblebee. The head is deeply excavated, the front with a horizontal spine extending forward nearly to the upturned spine of the clypeus. Larvæ feed upon the roots of grass and other plants, sometimes becoming decidedly injurious.

The pronotum of *Euphoria* is triangular; scutellum not covered; side pieces of the mesothorax visible from above; elytra more or less wavy on the sides. Comstock calls *inda* the Bumble Flower Beetle—a name that covers the habits of humming when flying and of feeding in flowers. However, the name might well be applied to its relatives also. The adults often feed on fruit and green corn. The elevation between the middle coxæ is transverse; head and pronotum dark, feebly bronzed, the latter often with yellowish spots; elytra brownish-yellow, mottled with black spots that often tend to form cross-bands; pronotum woolly; length somewhat over 0.5 in. *E. limbalis* is similar in size and form but brilliant polished green.

Cremastocheilus differs from *Euphoria* in having the pronotum quadrate, with prominent angles. The species are uniformly blackish and, while not especially rare, are not often seen because they live in ants' nests. There are pubescent areas near the angles of the pronotum that are glandular and furnish agreeable food for the ants. Sometimes the ants even gnaw off the angles. The beetles are sluggish and "seem to be held in captivity by the ants, which pull them back into the vicinity of the nests whenever they attempt to escape." However, it is probable that the advantages are not entirely one-sided.

The name *Osmoderma* refers to the "odor of leather." The species are largely nocturnal and come to lights. *O. eremicola* is an inch or more long; shiny dark brown; head deeply excavated between the eyes in both sexes, the edge with a tubercle above the bases of the antennæ; elytra sparsely punctate. *O. scabra* is not more than an inch long; purplish-black, bronzed; head of male as in *eremicola,* of female nearly flat; elytra roughly sculptured. The larva of each lives in the hollows of beech, cherry, apple, and other trees, feeding upon rotten wood. In the autumn it makes an oval cell of fragments of wood strongly cemented with saliva. It pupates in this cell, the adult emerging next summer.

The pronotum of *Valgus* has a deep median groove, and the body is more or less covered with whitish scales instead of hairs. Adults hibernate in groups on the ground under some shelter such as a log. *V. canaliculatus* is 0.25 in., or less, long; reddish-brown, feebly shining; sides of pronotum, and base, middle, and apex of elytra sparsely clothed with yellowish scales; front tibiæ with three or more slender, widely separated teeth on the outer side. *V. squamiger* is slightly larger and darker; front tibiæ with 5 or 6 closely placed, stout, rounded teeth.

The hind coxæ of *Trichiotinus* touch each other; the pronotum is rounded at base and has no median groove; elytra not longer than wide; body pubescent. Three of our more common species may be partially separated as follows, all being a trifle less than 0.5 in. long. Elytra reddish-brown, tinged with green; head, thorax, body beneath, and legs, bright metallic green: *bibens*. Reddish-brown elytra with two short, oblique, whitish bars; head and thorax greenish-black: *piger*. *T. affinis* is much like *piger* but more shining and separated on technical characters.

"PHYTOPHAGA"

See p. 276. The name is not very distinctive because, of course, many other beetles eat plants. For the present, at least, a division into three families, Cerambycidæ, Chrysomelidæ, and Mylabridæ, will be enough.

CERAMBYCIDÆ

Antennæ usually very long (rarely short) ; their points
of insertion usually much embraced by the eyes and
usually upon frontal prominences. Sometimes the second antennal joint is so short as to be easily overlooked.
Eyes usually transverse, with deeply indented margin
or sometimes entirely divided. (Species with eyes
slightly or not indented may be hard to separate from
some Chrysomelidæ and, in that case, other characters
should be carefully compared.) Elytra usually covering
the abdomen, but in a few species very short (Those
species which are long and narrow and have short elytra
may be mistaken for Staphylinidæ.) Tibiæ with more
or less distinct spurs. Upper surface usually hairy, but
sometimes glabrous and shining.

Many of the numerous species are pretty and certain
to attract attention. That is one reason for giving them
extra space here. Do not expect the following keys to
fit every species you get, even in the Northeast. Good
authorities give each of the following subfamilies full
family rank. They also arrange the minor groupings
differently.

1.—Sides of pronotum somewhat flattened ("margined")
and usually toothed. Body usually broad and flattened.
Labrum fused with clypeus.—Prioninæ.
    Not so. ....2.
2.—Front tibiæ not grooved. Last joint of maxillary
palpi not sharp at tip, often more or less triangular.—
Cerambycinæ, p. 344.
    Front tibiæ usually with a more or less distinct
oblique groove on the inner side. Last joint of maxillary
palpi cylindrical, pointed at tip.—Lamiinæ, p. 353.

PRIONINÆ

The few species of *Parandra,* the Aberrant Long-
horns, are on good grounds often considered to be a
distinct family, PARANDRIDÆ (called Spondylidæ by
some). Their antennæ are not long and are fastened
at the sides of the head near the mandibles. The fourth
joint of the 5-jointed tarsi is small but distinct. The
tarsal joints are neither much dilated nor pubescent
beneath. The larvæ live under the bark of decaying
trees.

PLATE 64

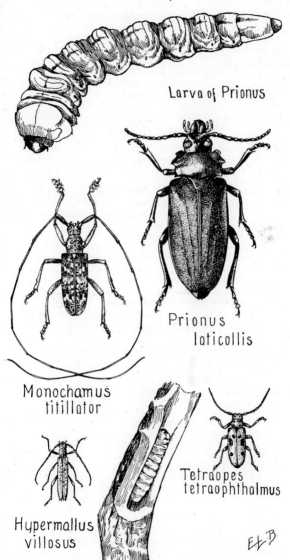

Larva of Prionus

Prionus
laticollis

Monochamus
titillator

Hypermallus
villosus

Tetraopes
tetraophthalmus

E⅃B

The true Prioninæ are more common. Some Tropical species are six inches or more long.

1.—Form elongate. Antennæ 11-jointed, the joints not overlapping. Width of pronotum more than twice its length, 3 sharp teeth on each side. Length, from 1 to 1.7 in. Light chestnut-brown, shining. Larvæ in stumps and logs.—*Derobrachus brunneus.*

Form, stout, broad. Antennæ (in our species) 12- to 20-jointed, the joints, especially in the males, more or less overlapping each other. Length from 0.9 to 2 in.; shining reddish-brown or black.—*Prionus.* ......2.

2.—Antennæ with 16 to 18 joints in the female and 18 to 20 in the male. Pronotum very short and broad; its teeth, especially the hind ones, not very distinct.—*P. imbricornis.*

Antennæ with only 12 joints. ....3.

3.—Elytra, combined, at base not wider than the pronotum. All joints of the hind tarsi densely pubescent beneath. Antennæ of male longer than the body, of female about half the length.—*P. laticollis* (Pl. 64). The larvæ live in the roots of many trees and shrubs, including orchard trees and small fruits such as blackberry. They are three years in reaching maturity.

Elytra, combined, at base wider than the pronotum. Basal joint of each hind tarsus nearly smooth. Middle and Southern States.—*P. pocularis.*

CERAMBYCINÆ

Larval characters indicate that the subfamily should be divided into four, Disteniinæ, Aseminæ, Lepturinæ, and typical Cerambycinæ; but, because of the diversity of opinion, I have here omitted tribal names.

1.—Base of antennæ not enveloped by the eyes. ......2.

Base of antennæ partly enveloped by the eyes. Head inserted in the thorax. ....8.

2.—Front coxæ transverse, not prominent. Second antennal joint a third or more the length of the 3rd. Head inserted in the thorax. ....3.

Front coxæ conical (globose in *Distenia*), prominent. Second antennal joint small. Usually a rather distinct "neck," this appearance being caused by the head being narrowed behind the eyes and thorax narrowed in front. Elytra usually tapering behind the middle. ....4.

3.—Second antennal joint more than a third as long as the 3rd. Antennæ densely punctured and pubescent. Scutellum rounded behind. Fifth ventral abdominal segment of the males transverse and the 6th visible; 5th segment of females prolonged and the 6th invisible. ..15.

Second antennal joint not more than a third as long
as the 3rd. Eyes finely granulate (i.e., the lines between
the facets are feebly impressed) and deeply emarginate
(i.e., margin indented). Pronotum and elytra not
spined. Antennæ of males thicker at the base than
those of females and usually longer than the body. ..18.
4.—Front coxæ globose. Mandibles chisel-shaped, not
fringed on the inner margin. Pronotum spined on the
sides, and elytra spined at tips. Body elongate; head
large. Eyes large, feebly emarginate. Antennæ long,
tapering; 1st joint as long as the head.—*Distenia undata*
varies from 0.7 to 1 in. long; dark brown, densely
clothed with short, gray pubescence; elytra marked with
three serrate cross-bands of darker pubescence. It
occurs beneath the bark of hickory, oak, and chestnut
trees.

Frontal coxæ conical. ....5.
5.—Joints 3 to 5 of antennæ much thickened at tips.
Mandibles simple, not fringed. Eyes nearly rounded,
suddenly and deeply emarginate.—Pl. 96 shows *Desmocerus palliatus*. Its larvæ bore in the stems of elder
(*Sambucus*).

Joints 3 to 5 of antennæ normal, usually slender.
Mandibles acute, fringed on the inner margin. Elytra
not colored as above. ....6.
6.—Elytra short, not covering the wings.—The abdomen,
front and middle legs, and basal joint of antennæ of
Necydalis mellita are dull-yellow; elytra reddish-brown
or yellow; otherwise black; 0.5 to 0.9 in. long.

Elytra of normal length. ....7.
7.—Front of the face nearly vertical. Neck, very short.
First joint of hind tarsi much longer than the other
joints combined.—In *Encyclops* the 1st hind tarsal joint
is cylindrical. *E. cærulea* is about 0.3 in. long; almost
linear; shiny blue or green.

Front of face oblique or horizontal. Elytra usually
tapering to the apex. Often on flowers. ....51.
8.—Second antennal joint small, not over a fourth the
length of the 3rd. Front coxæ not conical though sometimes prominent. ....9.

Second antennal joint about a third the length of
the 3rd. Front coxæ globose, widely separated. Rare
with us.—*Atimia confusa* is about 0.3 in. long; dull
black, clothed with rather long, yellowish pubescence,
with irregular, smooth, hairless spots; hind tarsi with
the 1st joint equal to the 2nd and 3rd combined. On
conifers.

9.—Eyes coarsely granulated (i.e., the lines between the
facets deeply impressed). ....10.

Eyes finely granulated. ....11.
10.—Front coxal cavities open behind. Abdomen normal in both sexes. Second antennal joint small.

Scutellum rounded behind, except in *Chion.* Eyes not divided, though always deeply emarginate. ....21.

Front coxal cavities angulated, closed behind. First segment of abdomen very long.—The species of *Obrium* are less than 0.3 in. long.

11.—Elytra either only about as long as the pronotum or elongated and awl-shaped. ....28.

Elytra normal. ....12.

12.—Scutellum either rounded behind or broadly triangular. ....13.

Scutellum acutely triangular. Front coxal cavities open behind. Eyes finely granulated. Many in the South and Southwest. The following are more Northern. ....29.

13.—Tibial spurs large. Pronotum without tubercles or spines. ....14.

Tibial spurs small; legs long and slender; femora very slender at base, strongly and suddenly club-shaped at apex.—*Rhopalophora longipes* is about 0.3 in. long; bluish black; pronotum red, with a small obtuse tubercle on each side.

14.—Tibiæ strongly ridged. Form slender; puncturation (pittings) sparse and coarse.—*Stenosphenus notatus,* breeding in hickory, is black; pronotum reddish with a central black spot; under side of head and thorax reddish; about 0.4 in. long.

Tibiæ not ridged. Form rather stout; puncturation fine. Our species usually have the elytra banded with yellow, or white, and black pubescence; eyes finely granulated and deeply emarginate, the lower lobe always large. ....32.

15.—Black or dark-brown. Cylindrical, scarcely depressed ....16.

Pale yellowish. Form, depressed. Length, about 0.3 in. Eyes coarsely granulated and very deeply emarginate. —*Smodicum cucujiforme.* Occurs under loosened bark of dead poplar, oak, and other trees.

16.—Eyes not wholly divided, often deeply emarginate. **17.**

Eyes divided, apparently four in number, rather finely granulated. Length, about 0.5 in. Dull, sooty, brown. Northern.—*Tetropium cinnamopterum.*

17.—Eyes moderate in size, finely granulated and hairy. Antennæ finely pubescent. Length, 0.5 in. or more. Black. Northern.—*Asemum mœstum.*

Eyes large, coarsely granulated, not hairy. About 1 in. long.—*Criocephalus.*

18.—Elytra bluish-black, with narrow, raised, longitudinal white lines on the middle. Pronotum with a very deep median groove. Femora distinctly club-shaped. General color, black; 0.5 to 0.7 in. long.—*Physocnemum brevilineum.* Larvæ bore in elm.

Elytra without distinct, raised, white lines. ......**19.**

19.—Pronotum very short, strongly rounded on the sides, red. Upper surface not shining; black. About 0.75 in. long.—*Rhopalopus sanguinicollis.*

Pronotum not very short, the width not much exceeding the length. Upper surface more or less shining. ..**20.**

20.—Front coxæ at least moderately separated.—*Merium* (pronotum with a broad, smooth, shining median space on the basal half) and *Hylotrupes* (pronotum with a narrow median elevation and moderate or small ones on the sides). *H. bajalus* is about 0.75 in. long; brown to black, with grayish-white pubescence that may form two irregular bands on the elytra. Breeds in pine and spruce. *H.* (or *Anacomis*) *ligneus* is usually not over 0.5 in. long; elytra yellow except for the apical third and a circular spot on each, which portions are, together with the head and pronotum, bluish-black. Breeds in cedar.

Front coxæ touching.—*Phymatodes* and *Callidium.* *P. varius* is black to (especially thorax and basal part of elytra) reddish-brown; 2 slightly curved cross-bars on elytra; about 0.3 in. long. The larvæ mine the inner bark of diseased oaks. *P. variabilis* (about 0.5 in. long; elytra blue, or yellow, or blue with yellow margins. Larvæ in oak bark. Probably a variety of *testaceous*) and *P. amœnus* (about 0.25 in. long; elytra bluish. Larvæ in dead grape stems) have the pronotum reddish-yellow. *P. dimidiatus* has an almost black pronotum; elytra reddish-brown, lighter at the base. The larvæ are "bark-slippers" of cord-wood. *C. antennatum* (over 0.5 in. long; surface rough) and *violaceum* (about 0.5 in. long; surface shining) are dark blue. They breed in conifers.

21.—With 6 cross-bands of yellow pubescence, 2 on pronotum and 4 on elytra. West of the Alleghanies.—*Dryobius sexfasciatus* Larvæ bore in dead beech and maple.

With not more than one yellow cross-band. ......**22.**

22.—Scutellum acute, triangular. Pronotum with a short spine on each side. Antennæ of female about the length of the body, of the male longer. Brownish, with sparse fine, gray pubescence; each elytron with 2 short spines at apex and usually with an oblique, yellow blotch in front of the middle. Length varies from 0.6 to 1.3 in.—*Chion cinctus.* Larvæ in hickory, oak, and plum.

Scutellum rounded behind. ....**23.**

23.—Each elytron with 2 pairs of elliptical, elevated, ivory-like spots on each; pale brownish-yellow.—*Eburia quadrigeminata.* Larvæ bore in hickory, ash, and honey-locust.

Elytra without pairs of ivory-like spots. ....**24.**

24.—Femora not distinctly club-shaped. Antennal joints and elytra with spines. ....**25.**

Femora distinctly club-shaped. Elytra without spines at tip.—*Tylonotus bimaculatus* (Antennæ grooved on the outer side; 2 rounded, yellow spots on each elytron; 0.5 in. long; larvæ in ash) and *Heterachthes* (antennæ not grooved or hairy; less than 0.5 in. long). *H. quadrimaculatus* is brownish-yellow with pale spots (sometimes tip also pale) on each elytron. Larvæ in hickory. *H. ebenus* is dull black.

25.—Not less than 0.75 in. long. ....**26.**

　　　Usually less than 0.75 in. long. ....**27.**

26.—Dark brown, with irregular spots of short, grayish pubescence. Pronotum without spines on sides.—*Romaleum atomarium.* Occurs beneath the bark of walnut, hickory, and hackberry.

　　　Reddish-brown with uniform pubescence of the same color. Pronotum with a small tubercle on each side of the median line.—*Romaleum rufulum.* Larvæ bore in oak and probably other trees.

27.—Antennæ and elytra with long spines; femora spinose at tips. Dull reddish-brown, irregularly clothed with grayish-yellow pubescence. Length, nearly, or quite, 0.75 in.—*Elaphidion mucronotum.* On various deciduous trees, also grape.

　　　Antennal spines small; femora not spinose at tips.— *Hypermallus incertus:* dark reddish-brown, mottled with small patches of grayish-brown pubescence; prothorax almost globose, wider than long, sides rounded; small elevations, sometimes connected, on each side of polished median line of pronotum; each elytron with two short spines at tip. *H. villosus:* Pl. 64; dark brown, clothed with grayish-yellow, somewhat mottled pubescence; pronotum rather rough and with coarse, deep punctures; the outer of the 2 spines on the tip of each elytron the longer. The larva of *villosus* is the Pruner. It breeds in a large variety of deciduous trees, developing in the heart of a small shoot and, when full-grown, girdling the shoot from within so that it may fall in the first high wind. Pupation and hibernation occur in this twig.

28.—Dull black, with sparse, long, grayish hairs. Elytra scarcely longer than the pronotum, a large, dull, yellow spot often nearly covering each elytron. Antennæ and legs reddish-brown. Less than 0.3 in. long.—*Molorchus bimaculatus.* Breeds in dead hickory, maple, ash, dogwood, red-bud, and walnut.

　　　Dull black; pronotum of male red, with narrow, black, apical and basal margins; elytra brownish, elongate awl-shaped. Femora swollen; hind legs yellow, the tips of the joints black.—*Callimoxys fuscipennis.*

29.—Pronotum not shining; its sides with a spine or large tubercle. Length not less than 0.5 in. ....**30.**

　　　Pronotum shining; its sides unarmed. Usually not longer than 0.3 in.; dark red; antennæ, legs, and often the suture of the elytra varying from dusky red to black. —*Batyleoma suturale.* Adults often abundant on flowers.

30.—Body pubescent; black; each elytron with a large rounded orange spot near the base.—*Tragidion coquus.*

Body not pubescent. ....31.

31.—Black; each elytron with a large triangular, scarlet humeral area.—*Purpuricenus humeralis.* Larvæ probably in oak and hickory.

Black; front half of elytra orange-yellow.—*Purpuricenus axillaris.*

32.—Head small, face short. Process of first ventral abdominal segment between the hind coxæ rounded. ..33.

Head large; face long. Process between the hind coxæ acute. ....38.

33.—Pronotum with 3 yellow cross-bands; excavated transversely at the sides near the base. ....34.

Pronotum without yellow cross-bands, but sometimes with yellow, oblique bars on each side; not excavated at the sides. ....36.

34.—Second joint of hind tarsi without hairs at the middle. Antennæ of male longer than the body. Velvety black; head, pronotum, and elytra with narrow, yellow crossbands, the third one from the base of the elytra W-shaped, the 3 behind it sinuous. Length 0.5 to 0.8 in. —*Cyllene caryæ.* Larvæ bore in hickory and elm. Adults in spring and early summer.

Second joint of hind tarsi densely pubescent. Antennæ not longer than the body. ....35.

35.—Pl. 96. Closely resembles *C. caryæ.*—*Cyllene robiniæ.* Larvæ bore in black locust (*Robinia*). Adults in late summer and fall.

Basal third of elytra orange-yellow, remainder black except for a yellow band behind the middle, and yellow tip; pronotum yellow, with 3 short, black cross-bars. A Southern and Western species.—*Cyllene chara.*

36.—Antennæ compressed, somewhat serrate. Black, dense yellow pubescence covering the greater part of the head and forming 2 short oblique bands on each side of the pronotum and 5 on each elytron, the first 2 of which are decidedly oblique and the last (apical) one broad and including a dark spot. Length, about 1 in. Northern.—*Glycobius speciosus.* Larvæ bore in maples and are often injurious.

Antennæ thread-like. ....37.

37.—Brownish-black, densely clothed with velvety pubescence; each elytron usually with a rounded, yellow spot at the base, a small one near it and the margin, a larger one before the middle, and 2 narrow, transverse, sinuous bands on apical half. Antennæ half the length of the body, which is 0.8 in. or more.—*Calloides nobilis.*

Not more than 0.75 in. long. Black; head and pronotum covered with grayish pubescence, the latter with a large, black spot in the center and a small, round one on each side; elytra marked with obscure, zigzag bands of grayish pubescence.—*Arhopalus fulminans.* Breeds in chestnut, oak, and butternut.

38.—Elytra flat on basal third. Not less than 0.3 in. long. ....**39.**

Elytra swollen on basal third. Ant-like species, not over 0.4 in. long. ....**49.**

39.—Front of head with one or more ridges. ....**40.**

Front of head without ridges. ....**44.**

40.—Ridges on the front of the head reduced to an elongate space. Length usually not much more, if any, than 0.5 in. ....**41.**

Ridges on face V- or Y-shaped. Length usually not much less, if any, than 0.5 in. ....**42.**

41.—Ridge on face divided or impressed longitudinally. Black; thorax with four spots of yellow pubescence; elytra with the sutural line and 3 oblique extensions from it dull yellow.—*Xylotrechus quadrimaculatus.* Usually on black alder.

Ridge on face scarcely divided. Shining black, with yellow margins.—*Xylotrechus nitidus.*

42.—A spine on the outer angle of the obliquely-cut apex of each elytron. Brownish, with white pubescence.—*Xylotrechus sagittatus.* Usually on dead pine.

No distinct spine on the outer angle of the obliquely-cut apex. ....**43.**

43.—Black or brown; yellowish or whitish pubescence arranged to form variable markings; usually 4 such markings on the pronotum, and 3 bands (the front one narrow and curved) and an apical spot on the elytra.—*Xylotrechus colonus.*

Black or dark brown; pronotum with light pubescence on front and back markings; each elytron with a narrow stripe of yellow pubescence running from the scutellum to about the middle and then curving to the outer margin, a short line of yellow in front of this and 2 behind it.—*Xylotrechus undulatus.* Breeds in spruce and hemlock.

44.—Pronotum with short, transverse lines or ridges. **45.**

Pronotum without transverse ridges. ....**48.**

45.—Middle and hind femora spined at apex. ....**46.**

Middle and hind femora not spined at apex. Black; whitish pubescence on thorax; pronotum with narrow, light, front margin; each elytron with a white or yellow marking which nearly forms a circle near the base, a jagged one just behind the middle, and an oblique one near the apex.—*Neoclytus caprea.* Breeds in ash, elm, and hickory.

46.—Pronotum with a longitudinal, elevated ridge. Antennæ thread-like. ....**47.**

Pronotum with a few distinct, transverse ridges arranged in a median row. Antennæ thickened towards the apex. Reddish-brown; elytra dark behind the first band

and with 4 nearly straight, narrow cross-bars of bright yellow pubescence, the one at the base the least distinct.— *Neoclytus acuminatus.* Breeds in a variety of trees.

47.—Blackish; 2 vertical yellow banads on the front of the head and 3 transverse ones on the pronotum; elytra with the base reddish-brown, the scutellum and 3 narrow bands yellow.—*Neoclytus scutellaris.* Said to breed in hickory, elm, and grape.

Very similar but the median yellow band is lacking from the pronotum and there is often a red spot (not of hairs, but in the "skin") on each side.—*Neoclytus mucronatus.* In hickory.

48.—Black with the following yellow markings: a marginal line on the pronotum, interrupted at the base; scutellum; an oval, oblique spot on basal third of each elytron; a strongly angulated band back of this; and an oblique bar back of the middle.—*Anthoboscus ruricola.* On hickory, elm, and oak.

Blackish-brown, except reddish basal half of elytra. Each elytron with the following markings of whitish pubescence: a narrow, oblique line on basal half; a long, narrow, curved band behind the middle; and a spot on the apex. Has been taken on hickory, grape, and oak.— *Clytoleptus albofasciatus.*

49.—Shining black or dark reddish-brown; each elytron with an oblique, wavy band. Looks like an ant.— *Euderces picipes.* Breeds in hickory and chestnut branches, possibly in other trees.

No such band. ....**50.**

50.—Eyes emarginate. Second antennal joint distinctly shorter than the 4th; 3rd joint with a spine. Black; femora and basal three-fifths of elytra reddish-brown, the latter marked with 3 narrow, oblique lines of whitish pubescence and separated from the black portion by a similar transverse line.—*Cyrtophorus verrucosus.* Bores in peach, linden, chestnut, and other trees.

Eyes not emarginate. Head and pronotum black; elytra with markings of silvery hairs.—*Tilloclytus geminatus.* Has been bred from sumac and hickory. Rare.

51.—Spurs of hind tibiæ not terminal but at the base of a deep excavation. Pronotum tuberculate at the sides.— *Stenocorus. S. vittiger* has 2 long, longitudinal, whitish stripes on each elytron. *S. cylindricollis* is also black (or reddish) but without whitish markings.

Spurs of hind tibiæ terminal. ....**52.**

52.—First joint of hind tarsi with the usual brush of hair beneath. Pronotum, with rare exceptions, distinctly tuberculate or spined at the sides. Head obliquely narrowed behind the eyes. ....**53.**

First joint of hind tarsi without the brush-like sole. Pronotum usually broadest at the base; its sides above base never spined or tuberculate. Head constricted behind the eyes. ....**58.**

53.—Antennæ scarcely reaching the base of the elytra. Pronotum with a sharp spine on each side. Elytra with longitudinal raised ridges. Black, mottled with brown and gray pubescence; reddish-brown spots on elytra. Length, 0.5 to 0.75 in.—*Rhagium lineatum.* Larvæ under pine bark, making a nest of chips.

Antennæ longer. Elytra not strongly ridged. ....**54.**

54.—Eyes globose and large or moderate in diameter. Pronotum with a short, acute tubercle on each side. ..**55.**

Eyes small. Pronotum angulated or rounded on the sides. Length, about 0.3 in. ....**56.**

55.—Elytra uniform reddish-brown, somewhat square-cut at tips.—*Centrodera decolorata.* In butternut and beech.

Elytra clay-yellow with irregular brown markings; tips rounded. Length, 0.5 in.—*Centrodera picta.* In hickory.

56.—Head, pronotum, and under surface black; elytra shining bluish-green; antennæ and legs pale brownish-yellow.—*Gaurotes cyanipennis.* Breeds in butternut and probably other trees.

Not so.—*Acmæops.* For two species see. ......**57.**

57.—Stout; usually dull brownish-yellow; pronotum with 2 black spots and each elytron with 2 longitudinal black stripes. Western.—*A. bivittata.*

Slender; head, pronotum, elytra, and under surface, yellow except for the black suture, a median stripe, and side margin on each elytron.—*A. directa.*

58.—Form slender, strongly tapering behind. Last ventral, abdominal segment of male deeply excavated. ....**59.**

Form less slender and less tapering behind. Last ventral segment not excavated. ....**62.**

59.—Longer than 0.75 in. Elytra strongly sinuate on the sides. Chestnut-brown to black, the elytra with paler areas.—*Bellamira scalaris.* Breeds in ash.

Smaller.—*Ophistomis.* ....**60.**

60.—Head and pronotum wholly black; elytra dull yellow, with margin and suture blackish.—*O. acuminata.*

Head and pronotum not wholly black. ....**61.**

61.—Elytra yellowish, usually marked with black.—*O. famelica* (antennæ black) and *O. luteicornis* (these yellow).

Elytra wholly black; head and pronotum reddish-yellow.—*O. bicolor.*

62.—Antennæ with impressed, pore-bearing spaces on the sixth or seventh and the following joints.—*Typocerus.* *T. lugubris* is all black. The elytra of *velutinus* are reddish-brown with four yellowish spots (which may be enlarged to form partial bands) on each; of *zebra* with one or two basal spots and 3 bands, all yellowish, on each.

Antennæ without such spaces. ....**63.**

63.—Pronotum rather triangular or bell-shaped, widest at base. ....**64.**

Pronotum more squarish or rounded, usually constricted in front and behind; hind angles not prolonged.—*Anoplodera.* ....**65.**

64.—Over 1 in. long. Antennæ serrate. Pronotum black, with yellow pubescence; elytra red, with black tips.—*Leptura emarginata.*

65.—Antennæ ringed with yellow; elytra reddish; pronotum black; abdomen of male red, of female black.—*A. rubrica.*

Antennæ not ringed with yellow...............**66.**

66.—Pronotum black with yellow margins; elytra black with four yellow cross-bands.—*A. nitens.*

Pronotum black; elytra sometimes dull yellow or with the tip alone dark.—*A. proxima.*

LAMIINÆ

Adults of this subfamily (p. 342) are, as a rule, not as brightly colored as those of the preceding one, nor are they as active by day as some of their relatives. The larvæ differ from the remainder of the Cerambycidæ in that they have no legs. Those species with elytra about half the length of the abdomen, and front tibiæ not grooved, belong to the tribe Methini, which some authors place in the Cerambycinæ.

1.—Elytra about as long as the abdomen and with a spine or protuberance near the scutellum. Rarely over 0.25 in. long. ....**2.**

Elytra about as long as the abdomen but without such a spine or protuberance. Usually at least 0.25 in. long. **3.**

2.—Frontal coxal cavities rounded.—*Cyrtinus pygmæus* is dark brown; antennæ ringed with yellow; elytra with a transverse blotch of white pubescence before the middle. On oak, hickory, locust, and box elder.

Frontal cavities angulated.—*Psenocerus supernotatus* is reddish-brown or blackish; scutellum, a narrow oblique band about the middle of the elytra, and a wider curved band, not reaching the suture, on apical third, white. Larvæ in stems of currant, gooseberry, grape, and sometimes in apple twigs.

3.—First antennal joint with a scar-like structure near the tip (except in *Dorcaschema*). Body elongate, nearly cylindrical. Antennæ as long as (in males much longer than) the body. Mostly large species. ....**9.**

First antennal joint without the scar-like structure. ....**4.**

4.—Tarsal claws (at least those on the front legs) arising at opposite sides of the joints and separating widely. **5.**
  Not so. ....**8.**
5.—Front coxal cavities rounded; middle coxal cavities closed or nearly so. Body usually broad. Antennæ usually very long in males. ....**21.**
  Front coxal cavities angulate; middle cavities open. **6.**
6.—Tarsal claws simple (except the outer one of the front and middle tarsi in some males of *Saperda*). ..**7.**
  Tarsal claws cleft or with appendages. ....**35.**
7.—Small, flattened species. Pronotum with a spine or tubercle on the sides. Usually long, erect hairs in addition to the ordinary pubescence. Antennæ about as long as the body, the joints progressively shorter toward the tip. ....**29.**
  Rather large, cylindrical species. Pronotum without spines or tubercles. ....**34.**
8.—Front of the face large and flat. Front coxæ angulated.—*Oncideres cingulatus* is about 0.6 in. long; antennæ of male longer than the body, of female about as long; smoky or reddish-brown to clay-yellow, almost always lighter in a broad band across the elytra; usually 3 small black dots in a cross-row on the pronotum. The female lays her eggs in twigs of hickory and other trees; then chews a girdle around the twig below the eggs. The twig dies and, broken off by the wind, falls to the ground where the larvæ mature. Adults are somewhat abundant in August and September.
  Front of the face bent in. Form very slender and elongate.—*Hippopsis lemniscata* is about 0.5 in. long; dark reddish-brown; pronotum with 2 whitish lines on each side; each elytron with 3 whitish lines; antennæ pale brown, darker at bases, more than twice as long as the body, fringed with hairs beneath. Breeds in stems of ragweed (*Ambrosia*) and in other herbaceous plants.
9.—Legs, especially the front ones of males, relatively long. ....**10.**
  Legs not especially long and all about equal. Pronotum with a spine on each side. ....**16.**
10.—Pronotum with spines on the sides.—*Monochamus.*
  ....**11.**
  Pronotum without spines......................**13.**
11.—The sutural angle of elytra acute or projecting as a short spine. Brownish, the elytra mottled with gray. Antennæ of male sometimes 4.5 times as long as the body.—*M. titillator* (Pl. 64). The variety *carolinensis* is paler and not much over half as long. Breeds in pine.
  The sutural angle not prolonged. ....**12.**
12.—Black, distinctly bronzed; the elytra with very small

or no patches of white and brown pubescence. Length
0.6 to 1.1 in.—*M. scutellatus.* Breeds in pine.

Brown; elytra sparsely mottled with small patches
of gray and brown pubescence. Length about 1.2 in.—
M. notatus. Larvæ in the inner bark and sapwood of
dead and dying spruces and balsams.

13.—Elytra rounded at the tip; black or grayish-
brown. ....**14.**

Elytra pointed at the tip; black, densely clothed
with uniform ash-gray pubescence. Length 0.3 to 0.5
in.—*Hetœmis cinerea.* Breeds in walnut, mulberry,
osage-orange, and hickory.

14.—Thorax cylindrical, longer than wide Brown with
grayish pubescence. ....**15.**

Prothorax slightly narrowed behind the middle,
nearly as wide as long. Uniform dull black. Length
0.3 to 0.4 in.—*Dorcaschema nigrum.* Breeds in hickory.

15.—Pronotum transversely wrinkled, indistinctly punctured; length, 0.3 to 0.5 in. Breeds in mulberry and
osage-orange.—*Dorcaschema wildi.*

Pronotum not wrinkled, distinctly punctured; length,
0.3 to 0.5 in. Breeds in mulberry and osage-orange.—
Dorcaschema alternatum.

16.—Brownish. Antennæ of male not more than a
fourth longer than the body. ....**17.**

Shining black, pubescence whitish. Elytra coarsely
punctured and each with a small, black spot behind the
middle. Antennæ of male about twice as long as the
body, which is about 0.4 in.—*Microgoes oculatus.* Breeds
in oak and hickory.

17.—Elytra with a conspicuous non-pubescent space on
the apical half. ....**18.**

Elytra without a conspicuous bare space on the
apical half. Nearly 1 in. long. ....**20.**

18.—Length about an inch. ....**19.**

Length about 0.5 in. Brown; head, pronotum and
last third of elytra with reddish-yellow pubescence; basal
part of elytra mottled with grayish pubescence.—*Goes
debilis.* Breeds in oak, probably also in chestnut and
hickory.

19.—Pubescence white.—*Goes tigrinus.* Breeds in hickory, oak, and possibly other trees.

Pubescence dark brown; silvery and reddish-yellow.
A broad, transverse, lighter band across the elytra and
the tips of these have golden pubescence.—*Goes pulcher.*
Breeds in hickory.

20.—General pubescence brownish; elytra with small
spots of yellowish hairs arranged in irregular rows.—
Hammoderus tesselatus. Breeds in oak.

General pubescence grayish or whitish; elytra indistinctly cross-barred at base and again behind the
middle with pale-brown pubescence; scutellum some-

times clay-yellow.—*Goes pulverulentus.* Apparently breeds in elm, ironwood, beech, and oak.

21.—Basal joint of antennæ club-shaped. Pronotum with dorsal tubercles and a large, acute spine near the middle of each side. About 0.5 in. long. ....**22.**

Basal joint of each antennæ cylindrical. Spines on sides of pronotum, if present, behind the middle. ....**23.**

22.—Dark brown, with yellowish-brown pubescence; each elytron with a large, wavy, white cross-bar near the middle and a row of small alternate brown and white spots along the suture.—*Psapharochrus quadrigibbus.* Larvæ live in oak, hickory, beech, and hackberry.

Dark brown, with yellowish and gray pubescence in about equal proportions, the gray on the elytra in 3 obscure, oblique, nearly parallel bands; an indistinct, M-shaped, black mark behind the middle of each elytron.—*Ægomorphus decipiens.* On poplar and hickory.

23.—Females with an elongated ovipositor. This is a very unsatisfactory sort of character in a key, but I know of no better.—*Graphisurus obsoletus* is dull yellowish with small blotches and 3 undulated cross-bars on elytra. Length 0.4 to 0.6 in. *Urographis fasciata* occurs under bark of deciduous trees. It is grayish, sprinkled with black spots and usually having 2 larger blotches back of the middle of each elytron. Length 0.3 to 0.6 in.

Females without elongated ovipositor. Except as noted, usually not over 0.3 in. long. ....**24.**

24.—Pronotum distinctly angulate or more frequently with acute tubercles or short spines behind the middle. ....**25.**

Pronotum only feebly tuberculate or angulate at the sides a little behind the middle.—*Leptostylus* and allied genera including *Astylopsis* and *Astylidius.*

25.—Antennæ without fringed hairs beneath. First joint of hind tarsi as long as the next two. ....**26.**

Antennæ distinctly fringed beneath with hairs. First joint of hind tarsi as long as the next three. ...**28.**

26.—Form cylindrical. Elytra with erect hairs, which may be seen when viewed from the side; prostrate ash-gray hairs cover the black color. An acute spine on each side of pronotum near the base. Length 0.3 to 0.4 in.—*Dectes spinosus.* Breeds in ragweed (*Ambrosia*), the larvæ hibernating in the stems.

Form somewhat flattened. Elytra without erect hairs. ....**27.**

27.—Purplish-brown, mottled with black; elytra with numerous, small, irregular, black spots and a dark blotch, bordered behind by gray, back of the middle. Length 0.3 to 0.5 in.—*Leiopus variegatus.* Breeds under the bark of honey-locust and box elder.

Usually dull reddish-brown with sparse, grayish pubescence; elytra usually with 4 rows of small, black dots and with an acute-angular, black band behind the middle; pronotum with 3, small blackish spots.—*Leiopus alpha.* In sumac, apple, hickory, and locust.

Much like *alpha* but the oblique band on each elytron (making the acute angle when the elytra are closed) is replaced by an obscure band of gray.—*Leiopus punctatus.* Breeds in dogwood (*Cornus*) and plum.

28.—Each elytron with a distinct ridge on the outer side.—*Hyperplatys,* of which *aspera* is our common species. It is reddish-brown, with grayish pubescence; pronotum with 4 black dots in a transverse row; each elytron with 3 irregular rows of similar dots and usually a large, black blotch behind the middle.

Elytra without a ridge on the outer side.—*Lepturges,* of which we have several rather variable species, none of which are more than 0.5 in. long. The spines on the sides of the pronotum of *symmetricus* are rather broad and very close to the base. In the others they are more slender and acute, not so close to the base and the tips are recurved. The cross-bar on the elytra of *signatus* is interrupted at the suture; in *querci* (apex of elytra not black, cross-bar angular) and in *facetus* (apex black, bar transverse) it is broad and complete.

29.—Femora club-shaped. Vertex of head concave. Antennal tubercles prominent. ....**32.**

Femora not club-shaped. Vertex flat or convex. Antennal tubercles not prominent. Eyes coarsely granulated, lower lobe as wide as long.—*Eupogonius.* ......**30.**

30.—Spine on side of thorax acute, well marked. ....**31.**

Spine on side of thorax obtuse, small. Black, with broad line of yellowish pubescence on each side of pronotum.—*E. subarmatus.* On elm and linden.

31.—Elytral punctation feeble, almost obsolete near apex; pubescence ash-gray or yellowish, forming more or less transverse nettings.—*E. tomentosus.* Has been bred from apple twigs but is said to occur also on pine.

The punctation coarse, gradually finer, but distinct, at tip; pale yellow pubescence arranged in irregular, small patches.—*E. vestitus.* Breeds in dogwood, hickory, walnut, pine and perhaps other trees.

32.—Lower lobe of eyes elongate. Spines on sides of pronotum large, median. Pubescence mottled, gray, and black, mixed with short, scattered hairs on elytra.—*Hoplosia nubila.* Breeds in dry twigs of beech and linden.

Lower lobe of eyes as wide as long, squarish or somewhat triangular. ....**33.**

33.—Pronotum with spines on sides. Black; elytra variegated with dull brownish-yellow and with a broad, oblique band of white pubescence.—*Pogonocherus mixtus*. Beneath bark of dead pine, also on pear and willow.

Pronotum with feebly rounded sides. Pale grayish-brown; elytra with a narrow, curved, black band on basal third.—*Ecyrus dasycerus*. Breeds in red-bud, hickory, and probably other trees.

34.—*Saperda*. For *S. candida* see Pl. 96. The larva is known as the Round-headed Apple-borer but it also lives in quince, *Cratægus,* and *Amelanchier*. The larvæ usually work in the base of the trunk and in the large roots, more rarely in the large limbs. Their presence may often be detected by piles of "saw-dust" pushed out of the burrow through an opening in the bark. From egg to adult takes 3 years. Pupation occurs in the burrow. The adult, in emerging, makes a hole in the bark as big around as a lead pencil. Adults emerge throughout the season, starting in April. Two more of our species have complete, longitudinal stripes on the elytra: *puncticollis* (2 pairs of black dots on top of the yellow pronotum and 1 dot on each side) and *lateralis* (pronotum dark, with yellowish side stripes). The latter breeds in hickory and some specimens (variety *connecta*) lack the narrow, yellow sutural line but have developed oblique cross-bars. Virginia creeper is the food plant of *puncticollis*. The male *S. discoidea* has unmarked dark elytra; light grayish lines on the pronotum and the underside silvery; legs reddish. The female is yellow on the head, pronotum, scutellum, a crescentic bar in the middle of each elytron, and a spot in front and behind each of these. It breeds in hickory and butternut. *S. vestita,* the Linden-borer, is olive-yellow but each elytron has three small, black dots. Large specimens are an inch long. Our largest species is *calcarata* the Poplar- and Cottonwood-borer. It is usually at least 1 in. long; dense, gray pubescence, with front of the head, stripes on the pronotum, the scutellum, and numerous lines and blotches on the elytra, orange-yellow. *S. obliqua* (reddish, with lighter, oblique markings on the elytra, which are spined at the tips; 0.6 to 0.8 in. long) and *mutica* (black, with light markings; elytra not spined; 0.4 to 0.6 in. long) have distinct color-rings on their antennæ. The former breeds in alder; the latter, more Western, in willow. *S. cretata* is a fairly common apple-borer, especially in the Middle West. It is brown with two large, white spots on each elytron and white stripes on the sides of the pronotum; length, 0.5 to 0.8 in. *S. fayi* is rarely 0.5 in. long; darker and more slender than *cretata;* the elytral spots narrow, and near the suture, and an additional small spot at the base. Both make gall-like swellings in stems of *Cratægus. S. tridentata,* the Elm-

borer, is grayish-black; there is an orange stripe on
each side of the pronotum; each elytron has a narrow
orange stripe near the margin and 3 bands, of which
the last 2 are quite oblique and usually meet the corresponding one in the opposite side; the front of the
head is very flat; 0.4 to 0.6 in. long. *S. imitans* resembles it but the elytra are rounded at their apices,
instead of being somewhat truncate; the elytral markings are narrower, yellower, and the hind band is not
distinctly oblique.

35.—Each eye not divided but the outline deeply indented. Thorax cylindrical. ....**36.**

Each eye completely divided so that there appear
to be four eyes. Thorax dilated or tuberculate on the
sides. ....**43.**

36.—Antennæ without hairy pile. ....**37.**

Antennæ with thick, long hairs. Black, feebly shining; top of head, a stripe on each side of the pronotum
and often the margins of the elytra, yellowish. Length
0.3 in.—*Amphionycha flammata.*

37.—Nearly uniform gray above. Tarsal claws feebly
toothed or cleft.—*Mecas,* usually *inornata.* Breed in
stems of herbs.

Not uniform gray above. Tarsal claws broadly
toothed. Length 0.6 to 0.7 in. *Oberea.* ....**38.**

38.—Pronotum with small, rounded, black elevations or
callosities. ....**39.**

Pronotum without callosities. ....**42.**

39.—Pronotum with 4 callosities. Usually pale, dull
yellow; elytra, antennæ, and tarsi often nearly black.—
O. schaumii. Breeds in living twigs of cottonwood.

Pronotum with 2 callosities, and often a third spot,
black. There are several named color-varieties of each
of the following species. ....**40.**

40.—Tips of elytra rounded. Body, below, and femora
entirely red; head and thorax usually red, rarely more
or less black; 2 rounded, black spots on middle of
pronotum; elytra black.—*O. ocellata.* Probably breeds
in hackberry stems.

Tips of elytra rather square-cut. ....**41.**

41.—Shining black except the pronotum, which is yellow
with 2 or 3 black spots.—*O. bimaculata.* Breeds in raspberry and blackberry.

Typically the body, beneath, is largely yellow but it
is sometimes wholly black; pronotum yellow with 3
black spots; each elytron with a wide, dull yellow stripe
bordered with blackish.—*O. tripunctata.* Breeds in cottonwood and blackberry.

42.—Thorax pale reddish-yellow; antennæ, elytra, tibiæ,
and tarsi, nearly black; pronotum without black spots;
elytra rather densely clothed with gray pubescence.—

O. ruficollis. On sumac and sassafras, making double girdles.

Pale, dull yellow with a dark brown elytral stripe on each side.—*O. gracilis.*

43.—Elytra black; head and pronotum red, the latter with a black spot. On alder.—*Tetrops monostigma* (elytra with black hairs; Western) and *T. canescens* (elytra with grayish hairs; Eastern).

Elytra red with black spots; head and pronotum red.—*Tetraopes,* of which the following are the more common species. *T. canteriator:* pronotum with 4 round, black spots; black areas on elytra form, when elytra are closed, a heart-shaped space back of the middle; apex of elytra also black; 0.3 to 0.5 in. long. *T. tetraophthalmus:* pronotum with 4 black spots near the middle and sometimes a blotch in front and behind; see Pl. 64. *T. femoratus:* a Western species; resembles *tetraophthalmus,* but the apex and base of each antennal joint are narrowly ringed with gray; 0.5 in. or more long. They are usually found late in summer on milkweed in the stems and roots of which they breed. They stridulate loudly. The extent of the black markings varies somewhat.

CHRYSOMELIDÆ

Antennæ either moderately long or short and either thread-like, saw-toothed, or clubbed; their point of insertion rarely, or not at all, surrounded by the eyes and not upon frontal prominences. Margins of the eyes not, or scarcely, indented. Elytra usually covering the abdomen, sometimes leaving the last dorsal segment exposed and rarely not nearly covering the enlarged abdomen of gravid females. Legs usually short; hind femora frequently enlarged; tibiæ never serrate and often shining.

The Chrysomelidæ of the United States are never more than moderately long, as beetles go, and their bodies are often chunky. Nearly a thousand species are known from North America, about a twentieth of the number known from the rest of the world. One way of looking at the food habits of beetles is that adopted by the celebrated Coleopterists, LeConte and Horn: "As the function of the Cerambycidæ is to hold the vegetable world in check by destroying woody fiber, the Bruchidæ effect a similar result by attacking the seeds and the Chrysomelidæ by destroying the leaves." The potato-grower would have to be a philosopher in order to look at the Chrysomelid *Leptinotarsa* in that way. Moreover, as will be pointed out in the course of the discussion, not all Chrysomelidæ are leaf-eaters. No attempt will be made to enable the reader to identify a large proportion of the species he may find. This is partly because of technical difficulties, including the large number of species, and partly because many of the species are small and not usually noticed. Probably some, at least, of the following subfamilies will soon be generally accepted as families. All of them are diurnal.

1.—The front of the head enlarged so that the small mouth is far on the under side of the head. ....13.

    Not so. ....2.

2.—Antennæ widely separated at the base. Elytra hard. ....3.

    Bases of antennæ usually close together. Elytra more or less soft. ....12.

3.—The under sides of the central abdominal segments narrowed in the middle. The pygidium sloping and usually not covered by the elytra. ....8.

    Not so. ....4.

4.—Prothorax rounded on the sides, without distinct lateral margins. Prosternum very narrow. Head and eyes prominent. ....5.

    Prothorax usually with distinct lateral margins. Prosternum broad. Head and eyes not prominent. ..10.

5.—Antennæ separated by the entire front of the head. ....7.

    Not so. ....6.

6.—Prosternum very narrow, not distinct. Body clothed with dense silvery pubescence. First ventral abdominal segment about as long as all of the others combined. Elongate; more or less metallic. Semiaquatic.—Donaciinæ, p. 362.

    Not so.—Megascelinæ, of which *Megascelis texana* may be our only species.

7.—Hind femora greatly thickened. Hind tibiæ curved. —Sagrinæ, of which *Aulacoscelis* in the Southwest may be our only genus.

    Not so.—Criocerinæ, including Orsodacninæ, p. 363.

8.—Antennæ long and usually thread-like, sometimes thicker at the end, not "saw-toothed." Small, compact, cylindrical beetles with a flat, perpendicular head invisible from above.—Cryptocephalinæ. One of the variable and common species is *Cryptocephalus venustus*. It is nearly 0.25 in. long and, in the typical form, the head and pronotum is reddish brown, the latter having a narrow edging and two oblique spots yellow; the elytra are yellow, each with two broad, oblique, black or brown

stripes. It is found on potato and other garden, as well
as wild, plants.

Antennæ short, the joints "saw-toothed." ....**9.**
9.—Each side of prothorax with a groove into which an
antennæ fits. Elytra rough.—Chlamydinæ, p. 364.

Not so.—Clytrinæ. A small, chiefly Western group.
Larvæ of the Eastern *Coscinoptera dominicana* are said
to feed on vegetable debris in ants' nests.
10.—Third joint of tarsi deeply bilobed. Front coxæ
usually rounded. ....**11.**

Not so. Body oval, convex. Antennæ somewhat
thickened toward the apex.—Chrysomelinæ, p. 365.
11.—Prothorax as wide as combined elytra at base.
Legs flattened sideways. Femora with grooves into
which the tibiæ can be placed. Short, very convex
beetles.—Lamprosominæ. *Lamprosoma floridana* in the
Southwest and *L. opulenta* in California.

Prothorax usually narrower than the elytra. Legs
not compressed.—Eumolpinæ, p. 364.
12.—Hind femora slender. Tibiæ usually nearly cylindrical. Tarsi slender, not retractile.—Galerucinæ, p. 367.

Hind femora greatly thickened. Tibiæ often
grooved on the outside. Tarsi retractile.—Halticinæ
(or Alticinæ), p. 369.
13.—Head not concealed by the prothorax. Body usually spiny, narrowed in front, broad and truncate behind.
—Hispinæ, p. 371.

Head concealed under the prothorax, which and
the elytra are widely margined. Body oval or nearly
circular in outline.—Cassidinæ, p. 372.

DONACIINÆ

These look very much like certain Cerambycidæ.
Their larvæ live on the outside of the submerged roots
of water-lilies, skunk-cabbage, pickerel-weed, sedges,
and other aquatic or semi-aquatic plants. They pupate
in cocoons, a number of which are often fastened in a
row to the stems or roots of their food plants. The
adults of *Donacia* are commonly seen on the leaves of
water lilies and other aquatic plants in early summer
and fly from leaf to leaf when disturbed. The color is
usually more or less metallic greenish, bronze, or purple.
They are coated beneath with a satiny pile of fine hair.
Donacia has numerous species, all of which have the
tips of the elytra simple and the tarsi dilated, spongy
beneath. With the exception of this genus, we have
only *Hæmonia nigricornis,* which has narrow tarsi and

a distinct spine at the outer angle of each elytron. Adults of *Donacia* rarely enter the water, except to lay eggs, but those of *Hæmonia* are more aquatic.

CRIOCERINÆ

Three genera that have been grouped separately as Orsodacninæ are *Orsodacne, Zeugophora* (outline of eyes indented) and *Syneta* (outline of eyes not indented). The latter two have prominent front coxæ and on each side of the thorax a tubercle or angle. *Orsodacne* does not. Like Sagrinæ and unlike other Criocerinæ, they have a distinct, not very narrow prosternum and well-developed ligula. Our only species of *Orsodacne, atra,* is exceedingly variable and many of these variations have been named. It may be black, or there may be reddish or yellowish markings. It is about 0.25 in. long and is often abundant on willow and other very early blossoms.

In true Criocerinæ we have two genera: *Lema* (pronotum constricted near the middle) and *Crioceris* (not so).

The most frequently noticed species of *Lema* is *trilineata*. It is sometimes called the Old-fashioned Potato Beetle because it was at work eating potato leaves before the Colorado Potato Beetle came north and east. It usually lays its eggs along the midrib of a leaf, not in a cluster but at random. Its larvæ have a curious, but not unique, habit of piling their excrement on their backs. Pupation takes place underground. The adult is shown in Pl. 97. In *brunnicollits* the elytra are wholly dark blue; head and pronotum red. In *collaris* the elytra are dark greenish-blue; head, black; pronotum, red.

Of *Crioceris* we have two species. Both are from Europe and largely confined, as yet, to the East. Both attack asparagus. *C. asparagi* (Pl. 97) was introduced about 1862 near New York. The three yellow spots are sometimes joined. Adults hibernate under rubbish. The dark-brown eggs are usually laid in rows. There are several generations a year. *Crioceris 12-punctata* is a trifle larger; red with six black spots on each elytron.

It was introduced about 1881 near Baltimore. Adults emerging from hibernation eat the young shoots, but the larvæ prefer the ripening berries to "leaves." Both species pupate underground.

CHLAMYDINÆ

"The legs are closely contractile and when disturbed the beetles draw them and the antennæ in and feign death. They then resemble the excrement of certain caterpillars so closely as to render their detection difficult, unless the collector is in especial search for them, and it is said that birds will not pick them up for the same reason." The larvæ are case-making leaf-feeders and pupate in their cases, which they first attach to twigs. We have two genera: *Chlamys* (antennæ serrate from the fourth or fifth joint) and *Exema* (antennal serrations beginning at the sixth joint).

EUMOLPINÆ

These are usually of a uniform metallic color, although some are dull yellow or spotted. Their head is visible from above although the pronotum comes about to the eyes. The outline of the eyes is more or less indented. The claws are toothed or cleft. A few of the species are:

1.—Front ventral margin of thorax curved, forming lobes behind or below the eyes. (Only those beetles, belonging here, whose elytra are not pubescent or scaly are considered further.) ....2.
   Front ventral margin of thorax straight. ....3.
2.—Elytral punctures in distinct, regular rows. Middle and hind tibiæ indented on outer edge near apex. —*Paria canella* is quite common on a variety of plants and sometimes injurious to strawberries, raspberries, etc. It is exceedingly variable in color and markings, reddish-yellow and black being the usual elements. About all that can be said here is that it is neither 0.2 in. long nor bright blue (as is *Typophorus viridicyaneus*), nor has it a saddle-shaped, black space on the elytra (as has *Paria sellata*).
   Elytral punctures irregular. Tibiæ not indented.—*Chrysochus auratus* (Pl. 96). Usually common on dogbane.

3.—Side-margins of pronotum not distinctly flattened. **4.**

Side-margins of pronotum distinctly flattened. ....**6.**

4.—Not metallic above. Head without a groove above the eyes. ....**5.**

Metallic green or bronzed above. Head with a narrow groove above the eyes.—*Graphops.* The larvæ of *G. nebulosus* live in the roots of strawberries.

5.—Front femora with a small tooth. Third antennal joint not longer than the second.—*Xanthonia.* On oak and other trees.

Femora not toothed. Third antennal joint longer than the second.—*Fidia.* On grape and Virginia Creeper.

6.—Head with distinct grooves above the eyes. Middle and hind tibiæ indented near apex.—*Metachroma.* On oak and other trees.

Head without grooves above the eyes. ....**7.**

7.—Pronotum about a half wider than long; the sides rather broadly curved, angles prominent. Dull brownish- or reddish-yellow. Length usually not over 0.25 in.—*Colaspis brunnea.* Adults on various garden plants; larvæ on roots of grape.

Sides of pronotum not so.—*Nodonota* (third antennal joint distinctly longer than the second, the last 5 joints not abruptly wider) and *Chrysodina.*

CHRYSOMELINÆ

These are usually of moderate size and variegated in color. The antennæ are of moderate length; the outer joints somewhat enlarged. The eyes not prominent and their outline feebly indented. The pronotum has well-defined side-margins. The elytra cover the abdomen.

Phyllodecta is distinguished by the tarsal claws being toothed or bifid, and the tibiæ neither dilated nor toothed.

The genera mentioned in this paragraph have the third tarsal joint indented or bilobed. Species of *Prasocuris* are usually not over 0.25 in. long; upper surface brassy-green, or bronzed-black, with yellow stripes; pronotum without a thin margin at the base. *Plagiodera* (punctures of elytra in regular rows; tibiæ not grooved on the outer side) and *Gastroidea* (punctures confused; tibiæ grooved) have the sides of the pronotum thickened and unicolorous elytra. *G. cyanea* is uniform, brilliant, green or blue, and feeds on dock (*Rumex*). *G. polygoni* is like it but the pronotum, legs, base of antennæ, and tip of abdomen are reddish, and it feeds on knot-grass. Each is about 0.2 in. long. The pronotum of *Lina* (or *Melasoma*) is thickened at the sides, and the elytra are usually spotted; length, 0.25 to 0.4 in. The pronotum is dark metallic green, with yellow sides, in *scripta* and *lapponica*. The elytra are usually reddish (fading to yellow) with rounded black spots which are sometimes merged into transverse bands (*lapponica*) or are longitudinally elongate (*scripta*). Each feeds on willow and *Populus,* and each sometimes has the elytra wholly dark-colored. *L. tremulæ* is an introduced European species with a green pronotum and unspotted, dull yellow elytra; also on willow and poplar. The pronotum of *L. obsoleta* has reddish margins enclosing a rounded, black spot, or is reddish with 3 or 4 black spots at the center; elytra purplish-black with the margins, tips, and often two short, indistinct lines on basal half, reddish-yellow.

The third tarsal joint of the following genera of this subfamily is not, or scarcely, indented; the pronotum has a thin margin at the base; the insects are usually more than 0.25 in. long, robust, and convex.

Labidomera clivicollis feeds on milkweed. It is dark blackish-blue; elytra orange-yellow with variable, broad, curved, black markings; mesosternum prominent, forming a blunt tubercle between the middle coxæ; front femora of male strongly toothed.

Leptinotarsa has simple femora and the mesosternum is not raised above the level of the prosternum. *L. decimlineata,* the Colorado Potato Beetle (Pl. 97), has the elytral punctures confluent and in double rows. Until about 1855 it was confined to the southern Rocky Mountain region, where it fed on the wild relatives of the potato. Then man introduced potatoes to it, and it did the rest, spreading over the entire East. Adults hibernate underground. Each female lays about 500 eggs and there are two generations a year. In the South there is another species, *juncta,* which is somewhat similar but the third and fourth black bands on each elytron are usually united at the base and apex; the elytral punctures are regular and in single rows.

In *Zygogramma* the tarsal claws are parallel and united at the bases; claw-joint toothed beneath. The adults of *suturalis,* which occur on ragweed in the spring and on goldenrod in the fall, are brown, feebly bronzed; elytra striped with yellow and dark brown.

The elytra of our *Chrysomela* are without spots and the sides of the pronotum are thickened. Like *Calligrapha,* the last palpal joint is not shorter than the next to last.

The elytra of *Calligrapha* have dark markings and the sides of the pronotum are not thickened. To mention a few of the many variable species, first taking those with yellow and brown stripes on the elytra: *lunata* (chiefly on roses; median brown stripe of each elytron more or less divided by yellow) and *similis* (chiefly on ragweed; that stripe merely notched on the outer side) have the pronotum wholly brown; it is partly yellowish in *præcelsis* (the median brown spot on pronotum reaching the base) and in *elegans* (this spot not reaching the base of the pronotum; chiefly on *Bidens* and *Ambrosia*). Of those with irregular spots on the elytra: the pronotum is wholly dark in *philadelphica* (elytral suture pale but with, among other markings, a line each side of it; chiefly on dogwood), in *scalaris* (sutural stripe branched; a large crescentic shoulder-spot enclosing two spots; chiefly on hazel) and in *rhoda* (sutural stripe branched; each shoulder-crescent usually enclosing two spots; chiefly on hazel); the pronotum is yellow with reddish-brown spots in *multipunctata* (chiefly on *Cratægus*) and olive-green or brown, with pale apical and side margins, in *bigsbyana* (on maple, willow, and alder).

GALERUCINÆ

These are usually more oblong and have softer elytra than those previously considered. The head is exposed; the third antennal joint usually smaller than the fourth; hind tibiæ usually without terminal spurs. The following are the genera most likely to be noticed.

One of the "usuallies," above, was put there on account of *Galerucella:* the third antennal joint is longer than the fourth. The antennæ are at least half as long as the body; pronotum has a median and two lateral impressions; front coxal cavities open behind; tibiæ ridged on the outer sides and without terminal spurs;

first joint of hind tarsi not longer than the next two; tarsal claws bifid in both sexes. There are about a dozen species in New Jersey, for example, and different species, for the most part, live on different plants; but the one which attracts attention is the Elm-leaf Beetle, *G. xanthomalæna* (given a formerly used, shorter name, *luteola,* on Pl. 96). Yes. It is another foreigner. Most injurious species are immigrants; the principal reason for their becoming injurious is that their special enemies, which held them in check at home, did not come with them. *G. xanthomalæna* came in at Baltimore about 1834. The adult hibernates beneath bark, in cracks of buildings, and in other shelter. It may go into hibernation quite yellow and come out very dark green. The orange-yellow eggs are laid in clusters on the lower side of a leaf and the larvæ feed on the lower side also, gradually skeletonizing the leaf. When two or three weeks old, they enter the ground and pupate, emerging as adults in about a week. Usually it is the adults of the second annual brood that hibernate. Hints as to some of the other species may be gained from their food-plants. The following have stripes (often narrow and indistinct, especially in *americana*) on their elytra: *americana* on goldenrod; *notulata* on ragweed (*Ambrosia*); and *notata* on *Eupatorium*. The following have no elongate, dark markings on the elytra: *cavicollis* on peach, plum, and cherry; *rufosanguinea* on *Azalea; nymphææ* on water-lilies; *tuberculata* and *decora* on willow.

Among others, *Trirhabda* may be distinguished from *Galerucella* by having the third antennal joint shorter than the fourth; and the antennæ of *Monoxia* do not reach the middle of the body, tarsal claws bifid only in males.

Two species of *Diabrotica* (Pl. 97) are familiar to gardeners. *D. 12-punctata* is called the Southern Corn Root-worm because its larvæ live in the roots of corn (and other grasses) and are sometimes quite injurious in the South. It is called the Twelve-spotted Cucumber Beetle because the adults eat cucumber leaves, but they feed also on melons of various kinds. The hibernating adults are among the first insects to appear in the spring and the last to take shelter in the fall. The Striped Cucumber Beetle, which feeds also on all the melon family, is *D. vittata*. The larvæ live in the roots and in the base of the vine of cucumbers, melon, etc. Adults hibernate in the ground. *D. atripennis* (elytra black) and *D. longicornis* (elytra green or yellow, without black margins) have the outer edge of their tibiæ ridged. The latter species is called the Western Corn Root-worm.

Cerotoma trifurcata has the head, scutellum, and under side of the body black; pronotum and elytra dull yellow, rarely reddish; each elytron usually, but not always, with black basal and side margins, the latter extending nearly to the apex, and with three black spots close to the suture, the hind one the smallest; antennæ and the legs yellow; the tibiæ and often the femora in part, black; length about 0.17 in. Common on peas, beans and other legumes.

HALTICINÆ

This is the large group of Flea Beetles or Jumping Beetles. These names are applied especially to the small black species of *Haltica* and *Epitrix,* which are very injurious to vegetation in the mature or adult stage. Taxonomic rules may compel us to drop the *H,* leaving *Altica* and *Alticinæ.*

Œdionychis has the last joint of hind tarsi globosely swollen. Frontal coxæ open behind: *Haltica* (a feeble transverse impression on basal half of pronotum; each hind tibiæ with a short, terminal spur), *Disonycha* (first joint of hind tarsus short, as compared with the tibiæ, and rather broad; beetles distinctly more than 0.17 in. long), and *Phyllotreta.*

Of *Disonycha* the following are garden species. *D. triangularis:* black (with a faint bluish tinge on elytra) except for the pronotum, which is yellow with a pair of round, black spots and a small, linear one; length, about 0.25 in.; on a variety of plants, sometimes injurious to beets and spinach. *D. xanthomelæna:* resembles the preceding but, among other things, is usually smaller, has the pronotum entirely yellow, the elytra with a greenish tinge, and the abdomen yellow; it feeds upon a number of wild plants but is known as the Spinach Flea Beetle.

The hind tibiæ of *Phyllotreta* are not grooved on the outer edge, but slightly excavated near the tip and with a spur at the middle beneath. *P. vittata* (Pl. 97) is common all summer on cabbage and other Cruciferæ. The fifth antennal joint is longer than either the fourth or the sixth; the male has the fifth antennal joint thickened.

The two common, garden species of *Haltica* are distinguished from the others by having no longitudinal fold along the sides of the elytra; by the antennæ and legs being black; and by a deep groove that extends completely across the pronotum in front of the base. *H. chalybea* is the Grape Flea Beetle. It is usually not less than 0.17 in. long; metallic blue, rarely greenish; pronotum distinctly narrowed in front. *H. ignita* is usually not more than 0.17 in. long; color varies from a coppery-golden lustre through greenish to dark blue; pronotum only slightly narrowed in front. In addition to feeding on a variety of wild plants, it attacks strawberries and roses.

The following have the front coxal cavities closed behind and the last joint of the hind tarsi is not inflated, usually slender, although sometimes thickened in a side view. The antennæ of *Blepharida* are 12-jointed, instead of 11; tarsal claws bifid. *Chætocnema* has the hind tibiæ sinuate near the apex and with a distinct tooth on the outer margin. *Epitrix* (elytra with rows of stiff hairs) and *Crepidodera* (elytra without hairs; antennæ shorter than the body) have a distinct transverse impression in front of the base of the pronotum. The following lack such an impression: *Dibolia* (hind tibial spur broad, emarginate, or bifid at apex), *Mantura* (pronotum with a short, deep longitudinal impression on each side near the base), and *Systena* (pronotum without any impression).

Chætocnema confinis feeds on sweet potato, morning-glory and other Convolvulaceæ. It is less than 0.07 in. long; black, slightly bronzed; antennæ and legs, except hind femora, reddish-yellow; pronotum obliquely cut off at the front angles and with an angulation in front of the middle. *C. pulicaria* is locally common and sometimes injurious to corn and millet. It is about the same size; black, with faint greenish or bluish-bronzed lustre; the base of antennæ and tibiæ and tarsi yellowish; side of pronotum regularly curved and the front angles not cut off; head without punctures, but a row along the basal margin of the pronotum.

Of *Crepidodera* only *rufipes* (or *erythropus*) need be mentioned here. It is about 0.1 in. long; head, pronotum, and legs dull reddish-yellow, elytra dark blue; there are no punctures on the pronotum. On locust (*Robinia*), and sometimes injurious to grape, peach, apple, and other fruit trees.

In *Epitrix* we again have two garden species. *E. cucumeris* is not over 0.08 in. long; shining black, with reddish-yellow antennæ and legs, except the hind femora. The pronotum is not densely punctate and the impression in front of the base is well marked. It is the Cucumber Flea Beetle but it is not at all choice in its food, eating also leaves of potato and other plants. In *E. parvula* the pronotum is rather closely punctate and the impression is scarcely visible. It is about the same size and dull reddish-yellow. The adults feed on the leaves of potato, tomato, and egg-plant, but do their greatest damage by eating holes in tobacco leaves. The larvæ feed on the roots of common weeds, such as the nightshade and Jamestown weed.

And, finally, we note this pair of *Systena*. *S. hudsonias:* length, 0.17 in.; shining black except for the yellow third to fifth antennal joints. Common on many plants. *S. tæniata:* length, about the same; color variable, usually reddish- or brownish-yellow, shining; each elytron with a paler, median stripe; narrow side-margins of pronotum and under side of body usually black. Adults occur on various plants including cultivated ones.

HISPINÆ

Most of the larvæ live *in* leaves, feeding on the tissue between the two surfaces. See in this connection the Micro-lepidoptera and *Brachys*. The first three segments back of the head of a Hispine larva are wider than the rest of the body.

Microrhopala (antennæ either thread-like or the last 4 joints united into an oblong mass; elytra not, or only feebly, ridged) and *Octotoma* (the last 2 antennal joints enlarged; elytra with short, oblique folds) have 8 or 9 antennal joints. The others have 11, and some of them may be separated as follows:

1.—Elytra ridged ....**2.**
 Elytra not ridged. Body elongate.—*Stenispa. S. me-tallica* is uniform, shining black, slightly bronzed; length 0.2 in. The pronotum of *collaris* is red; length slightly over 0.25 in.
2.—Middle tibiæ strongly curved.—*Anisostena.*
 Middle tibiæ straight. The following species are about 0.25 in. long, except as noted. ....**3.**
3.—Each elytron with 10 rows of punctures; ridged. ...**4.**
 Each elytron with 8 rows of punctures; color varies from nearly uniform rose-red to nearly black, with a few indistinct reddish or yellowish spots; legs pale; length about 0.17 in.—*Anoplitis inæqualis (nervosa).* On locust.
4.—Each elytron with only 3 ridges.—*Chalepus* ....**5.**
 Each elytron with 3 ridges, and a fourth (at base and apex) between the second and third.—*Baliosus* (called *Chalepus* on Pl. 97) *rubra.* On locust (*Robinia*), bass-wood, and other trees.
5.—Elytra wholly black; pronotum wholly red.—*C. bi-color.*
 Elytra black, with red shoulders; pronotum red, with a dark center.—*C. scapularis.*
 Elytra and pronotum scarlet, fading to yellowish, with a black, sutural line becoming gradually broader as it reaches the apex.—*C. dorsalis.* The larva makes a blotch mine on locust.

CASSIDINÆ

On account of their form, these are often called Tortoise Beetles. Many of them are beautifully colored in life, but the golden hues rapidly fade after death. The oval, flattened, prickly larvæ feed upon the surface of leaves. "The larvæ are almost as disagreeable as the adult beetles are attractive, but are nevertheless very interesting creatures. Each of them is provided with a tail-like fork at the end of the body which is almost as long as the body, . . . Upon this fork are heaped the excrement and cast skins of the larva, and when covered by this 'umbrella' it is with great difficulty that the larva is distinguished from a bit of mud or a bird-dropping. The manner in which this fork increases with the size of the larva is rather interesting. At each moult, the fæci-fork of the last stage is held upon the new fæci-fork, and in this way those of the different stages are telescoped, the one inside the other, and the stage of growth of the larva may be readily determined by the number of cast skins held on the fork. From the likeness of this burden to a pack, the larvæ are known as 'peddlers.' In order to more firmly bind the excrement and cast skins to the fork, the larvæ fasten them together by a fine network of silken threads, which are attached to the spines at the sides of the body. When fully grown the larva fastens itself to a leaf, its skin splits open along the back, and from it comes the pupa, which is held to the leaf by its caudal fork, which is securely incased in the fæci-fork of the larval skin" (Sanderson). The adult hibernates.

Unless otherwise stated, the following feed chiefly on sweet-potatoes and other Convolvulaceæ.

Chelymorpha cassidea was called *argus*. The front of the pronotum is incurved, partially exposing the head; upper surface red or yellow, with four or six black dots on pronotum, and six on each elytron in addition to a sutural one near the base; under surface black; length, about 0.4 in. The eggs are laid in bunches, each egg being supported by a long stalk or pedicle. When fullgrown, the larva is about 0.5 in. long with the fæci-fork half as long again, slightly convex; dirty yellowish, with numerous dark-brown tubercles and prominent lateral spines. The yellowish to black back-color of the pupa is almost concealed by a bluish bloom or waxy secretion resembling mold. On milkweeds, Convolvulus, and, sometimes, raspberries.

In the following, the pronotum is rounded in front, covering the head; its side-margins are flattened (not thickened as in *Physonota*). The antennæ of *Cassida* and genera split from it do not reach beyond the base of the pronotum; those of *Chirida* and *Metriona* (formerly part of *Coptocycla*) extend beyond it.

Cassida (Jonthonota) nigripes is dull red or yellow after death; each elytron with three obscure black dots near the middle; base of antennæ, part of tibiæ, and tarsi, reddish; rest of legs and antennæ black. The eggs are laid in rows of three or more, so that several of the bright, straw-yellow larvæ, having two crescentic, black marks just back of the head and prominent, black-tipped spines, will be found together. The mass of excrement is usually much branched. The pronotum of C. (probably *Metriona* is the right genus) *bivittata* is yellowish, with a large, triangular, brownish-red space at the base; elytra dull yellow, with the suture and two stripes on each black or dark brown; under surface and legs black. Eggs are usually laid singly. The cream-colored, with a longitudinal band along the back, larva (Pl. 97) does not carry excrement but merely cast skins. It holds them at an angle from the body, instead of close over the back. *Metriona purpurata* is usually not common in the North. It is less than 0.25 in. long, with unspotted, brownish-red elytra.

Coptocycla (or *Metriona*) *bicolor* (Pl. 97) is common on bindweed. It is one of several "Gold-bugs." Harris said: "When living it has the power of changing its hues, at one time appearing only of a dull yellow color, and at other times shining with the splendor of polished brass or gold, tinged sometimes also with variable tints of pearl. The wing-covers, the parts which exhibit a change of color, are lined beneath with an orange colored paint, which seems to be filled with little vessels; and these are probably the source of the changeable brilliancy of the insect." Freshly emerged adults are dull orange and have three black dots on each elytron but, as the golden color is assumed, these spots disappear. After death, the elytra become dull reddish-yellow. Thanks to Mr. Leng, who sifted several hibernating adults from the fallen leaves in his garden just as the publishers were calling for "copy" for the first edition, I was able to give a figure colored from life. The under surface and last four joints of the antennæ are black; the flat margins of the pronotum and elytra are very thin and translucent. The egg has three spiny prongs; the larva's "pack" is trilobed in outline; the pupa is hidden by the larval pack and has three dark stripes on the pronotum, with similar markings over the abdomen.

The following two have dark markings on the elytra. In *Deloyala clavata* the disk of the elytra is quite rough from the numerous tubercles or elevations; base of pro-

notum and elytra, except for the apices and the middle
of the side margins, brown; under surface pale yellow;
length, 0.3 in. The disk of the elytra of *Chirida guttata*
is smooth; dull yellow; base of pronotum usually with
a large, black spot, enclosing two pale ones; disk of
elytra and shoulders black with irregular, yellow spots;
not over 0.25 in. long. "The larva is a pale straw-yellow
color during the first four stages when it carries excrement of the fæci-fork in a peculiar branched shape
much like that of the black-legged tortoise-beetle larva,
but after the last moult the color changes to a pea-green,
and all the excrement is removed from the fæci-fork,
which makes the larva very difficult to recognize on a
green leaf. Inasmuch as the larva does not feed and
remains entirely motionless during this last stage, this
change of color is very evidently of protective value.
The pupa is also a bright green, marked only by a ring
around each of the first pair of abdominal spiracles"
(Sanderson). The discal space on the elytra of *C. pennsylvanica,* a variety of *guttata,* is shiny black, without
spots.

MYLABRIDÆ

Front of head prolonged into a broad quadrate beak.
Antennæ short, serrate, inserted in front of the eyes.
Margin of the eyes more or less indented in front.
Elytra short, leaving the last dorsal segment exposed.
Front and middle legs of moderate length, their femora
not dilated; hind femora dilated and often toothed beneath. First tarsal joint elongate; this and the two following joints clothed beneath with a spongy pubescence;
third joint deeply bilobed; claws usually broadly toothed
at the base. All but one species are less than 0.25 in.
in length. Certain "Rhynchophora," such as Anthribidæ,
are difficult to separate from other beetles and the student
may have them, also, at this point.

These are the old "Bruchidæ." Species are, relatively,
not numerous. They differ from most of the Chrysomelidæ by having short, saw-toothed antennæ, and the
tip of the abdomen exposed. It has been suggested that
they and Chrysomelidæ should form a superfamily Chry-
someloidea. The larvæ live in seeds, especially of Legumes, and are often called "weevils"—a term that is

confusing because of its application to the Rhynchophora. We have, all of us, eaten the larvæ with our peas and beans, but—what's the difference? The eggs are usually laid upon the pod when the peas, for example, are quite small, and the young larvæ bore inside.

Spermophagus has two slender, jointed spurs on each hind tibia. The only Northeastern species, *robiniæ,* breeds in the seeds of the locust trees (*Robinia* and *Gleditschia*). The adult is about 0.3 in. long; dull reddish-brown, clothed with grayish-yellow pubescence; elytra with small, black spots arranged in five irregular, transverse rows.

Mylabris ("*Bruchus*") is the large and common genus. The hind tibiæ are without jointed spurs and the prominent, front coxæ touch each other. Only two species (Pl. 62) will be mentioned, but several others may be obtained either in ordinary collecting or, better because it gives the food habits, by breeding from seeds of wild plants. *M. pisorum,* the Pea-weevil, has a notch on the middle of each side of the pronotum and a tooth on the outer side of each hind femur. It is black, densely clothed with reddish-brown and whitish hairs, pronotum with a triangular, whitish space in front of scutellum; elytra with yellowish, grayish, and whitish hairs. There is but one generation a year and this species does not breed in dry peas. The adult hibernates. The newly-hatched larva has legs but it loses these when it becomes a fat, sedentary grub. Pupation occurs within the seed. *M. obtectus,* the Bean-weevil, has no notch on the sides of the pronotum and each hind femur has two fine teeth in addition to a larger one near the tip. It is black, clothed with grayish-yellow pubescence; abdomen dull reddish-brown; antennæ black, the apical half and four basal joints reddish; legs reddish-brown, underside of hind femora black. In the field the eggs are laid upon or are inserted in the bean-pod, but the eggs are also placed loosely among shelled beans. The larvæ and pupæ are much like those of *pisorum* but, unlike that species, more than one (28 have been recorded) may be in a single seed. The life-cycle takes from three to twelve, or more, weeks depending on conditions. Breeding is continuous throughout the year if it is warm enough.

"RHYNCHOPHORA"

This group of superfamilies has never been very popular. Furthermore, the taxonomy is difficult, possibly one of the main reasons for the unpopularity. These two facts are sufficient excuse for giving short treatment here. Measurements of length are from the front margin of the eye or head (not the tip of the beak) to the tip of the abdomen. In giving the key to families, which is presented here in a slightly modified form, Blatchley and Leng say: "In using this key the student must remember that while the beak in many Curculionidæ is so long, slender, and curved downwards as to permit of immediately placing them in their family position, there are other species, especially in the Otiorynchinæ, whose broader beaks would suggest their belonging to the Scolytidæ or Anthribidæ. In such cases, if the antennæ are elbowed, he must find the serrate tibiæ that characterize the Anthribidæ; otherwise the specimen does not belong to those families."

1.—Beak rarely absent, usually longer than broad. Tibiæ never with a series of teeth externally. ....**2**.

Beak absent or extremely short and broad. Tibiæ with a series of teeth externally or, if these are wanting, with a prominent curved spine at apex. Antennæ short, but little longer than the head, always elbowed and with a compact club. Palpi rigid. Body short, more or less cylindrical, rarely oval.—SCOLYTIDÆ. See p. 387.

2.—Antennæ straight, without a distinct club, though the outer joints often more or less thickened. Beak present, at least in the female, and pointing directly forward. Form usually very slender and elongate.—BRENTIDÆ. See p. 378.

Antennæ straight or elbowed, always with a distinct club. ....**3**.

3.—Beak always short and broad; labrum (upper lip) present; palpi flexible. Antennal club rarely compact. Pronotum with a transverse, raised line near the base.—ANTHRIBIDÆ, p. 378.

Beak variable in length, often long and curved downwards; labrum absent except in the subfamily Rhinomacerinæ; palpi rigid. Antennal club usually compact.—CURCULIONIDÆ, p. 380.

BRENTIDÆ

This small family is our only representative of BRENTOIDEA. The only Northern species seems to be *Eupsalis minuta* (Pl. 65). It varies in length from about 0.25 to nearly 0.75 in. The color varies from reddish-brown to black; elytra with narrow, longitudinal, yellowish spots, often united to form two or three cross-bars. The length of the elytra is more than twice their combined width, and the pronotum is longer than broad. The mandibles of the male are curved, flattened, pointed, toothed on the inner edge; those of the female are small and pincer-shaped, at the end of a slender beak. The female uses this beak to bore deep holes in the wood beneath the bark of dead trees and she frequently takes the better part of a day at each hole, afterwards laying one egg in it. It is said that a male stands guard during the operation "occasionally assisting the female in extracting her beak; this he does by stationing himself at a right angle with her body, and by pressing his heavy prosternum against the tip of her abdomen; her stout forelegs serving as a fulcrum and her long body as a lever. When the beak is extracted, the female uses her antennæ for freeing the pincer or jaws of bits of wood or dust, the antennæ being furnished with stiff hairs and forming an excellent brush. Should a strange male approach, a heavy contest at once ensues, and continues until one or the other is thrown from the tree. The successful party then takes his station as guard" (Howard). The larvæ make extensive galleries in the solid wood of oak, also of other deciduous trees.

ANTHRIBIDÆ

This much-named family has been called Platystomidæ, Platyrrhinidæ, Choragidæ, Bruchelidæ, and, by error, Polystomidæ. They are usually found on dead wood or on those fungi which grow on trees. Little is known of their life-histories. *Eurymycter fasciatus* is about 0.3 in. long and has a conspicuous patch of white pubescence on the beak as well as a broad, white band across the

PLATE 65

Conotrachelus
nenuphar

Curculio

Calendra
larva

Calendra
oryzæ

Eupsalis
minuta

Scolytus rugulosus

Attelabus
rhois

379

elytra. *Brachytarsus sticticus* is not over 0.15 in. long, and breeds in the smut of corn and wheat. *Euparius marmoreus*, sooty brown mottled with gray, is very common on tough fungus on fallen logs, its color matching well with its surroundings. *Aræocerus fasciculatus*, less than 0.2 in. long, blackish mottled with yellowish and dark brown, is a pest in stored coffee and similar material.

CURCULIONIDÆ

This is a very large family, more than 20,000 species having been described to date. The maggot-like larvæ have no more than bristly elevations for legs; the front part of the body is usually the thickest and, when at rest, the larvæ are usually curled like a C. Pupation usually occurs where the larvæ live but some species pupate in the ground. The following subfamilies are recognized:

1.—Antennæ straight; the beak not grooved to receive them. ....**2.**
   Antennæ more or less completely elbowed; the beak grooved to receive them when at rest; antennal club compact. ....**9.**
2.—Antennal club with completely separated joints. ....**3.**
   Club composed of compactly united joints. ....**6.**
3.—Thorax without a side margin. ....**4.**
   Thorax acutely margined and excavated beneath. Three abdominal segments show beyond the tip of elytra. —Pterocolinæ, of which only *Pterocolus ovatus* is known from Eastern U. S. It is blue, less than 0.17 in. long.
4.—Labrum present; palpi well developed, flexible. Form elongate-oval.—Rhinomacerinæ. Feed on the staminate flowers of Conifers.
   Labrum absent; palpi short, rigid. ....**5.**
5.—Mandibles flat, toothed on inner and outer sides. Tibiæ with short terminal spurs at tip; claws free, bifid or acutely toothed. Form usually elongate-oval, somewhat depressed.—Rhynchitinæ. *Rhynchites bicolor* (elytra, pronotum and head, back of eyes, red, otherwise black; length 0.25 in.) breeds in rose "hips."
   Mandibles stout, pincer-shaped. Tibiæ armed at tip with two strong hooks; claws united at base. Form short-oval, robust.—Attelabinæ, p. 381.
6.—Tip of abdomen covered by elytra. Trochanters large, femora attached to their apex. Form pear-shaped; not over 0.2 in. long.—Apioninæ. There are many species of *Apion*, one of which is abundant in late summer on Wild Indigo. *Podapion gallicola* makes rather spherical galls on pine twigs and is rare.

Tip of abdomen exposed. Trochanters small. .....**7.**
7.—First antennal joint longer than the second. ....**8.**

First antennal joint no longer than the second. Beak short, broad. Hind coxæ very widely separated; legs elongate, clasping. Length less than 0.13 in.—Tachygoninæ, the only genus being *Tachygonus.*

8.—Hind femora very broad, their outer margin strongly curved, wrinkled. Beak very slender, cylindrical. Length about 0.14 in.—Allocoryninæ, *Allocorynus slossoni* from Florida being our only known species.

Hind femora normal. Beak short and broad. Length 0.5 in. or more.—Ithycerinæ, the large *Ithycerus noveboracensis* being our only species. Some authors place this subfamily in a separate family (Belidæ).

9.—Antennal club usually ringed, not shining. Tarsi usually dilated, third joint bilobed, brush-like beneath, though narrow and setose in some more or less aquatic species. Abdomen of male with an extra anal segment. ....**10.**

Antennal club with its basal joint usually enlarged or shining or both, feebly or not at all ringed. Tarsi frequently narrow; not brush-like beneath. ....**12.**

10.—Prosternum simple, or grooved to receive the beak; not forming a triangular plate in front of the coxæ. ..**11.**

Prosternum forming a triangular plate in front of the coxæ. Beak received in the breast in repose. Tarsi narrow, not dilated.—Thecesterninæ. *Thecesternus* is our only genus.

11.—Beak never long and slender; mandibles with a deciduous cusp, leaving a scar that is, however, often hard to see.—Otiorhynchinæ, p. 382.

Beak usually elongate; mandibles without scar.—Curculioninæ, p. 383.

12.—Tip of abdomen covered by elytra.—Cossoninæ.

Tip of abdomen not covered by elytra.—Calendrinæ, p. 386.

ATTELABINÆ

The larvæ of our only genus, *Attelabus,* feed on the inside of "houses" prepared for them by their mothers. Pupation is said to take place underground. I quote concerning *rhois* (Pl. 65) from the Fifth Report of the U. S. Entomological Commission, a most excellent classic by A. S. Packard: "The singular thimble-like rolls of this weevil may be found in June and July on the alder, and also occur on the hazel, according to LeConte [I have found them in large numbers on hazel]. When about to lay her eggs, the female begins to eat a slit near the base of the leaf on each side of the midrib, and at right angles to it, so that the leaf may be folded together. Before beginning to roll up the leaf she gnaws the stem nearly off, so that after the roll is made, and has dried for perhaps a day, it is easily detached by the wind and falls to the ground. When folding the leaf, she tightly rolls it up, neatly tucking in the ends, until a compact, cylindrical solid mass of vegetation is formed. Before the leaf is entirely rolled she deposits a single egg, rarely two, in the middle next to the midrib, where it lies loosely in a little cavity. While all this is going on her consort stands near by and she occasionally runs to him to receive his caresses, to again resume her work." As the habits are so interesting, a modification of Blatchley and Leng's key to our Eastern species is given.

1.—Surface shining; color, above, either mainly bright red or black. ....**2.**

    Surface pubescent; dull red (rarely blackish in the melanic Northern form). Length about 0.2 in.—*rhois.*

2.—Elytra bright red (except see *analis*). ....**3.**

    Black, faintly bluish, with a reddish spot on each shoulder. Length usually not 0.17 in. Front femora with a small, acute tooth. On oak.—*bipustulatus.*

3.—Front femora slender; not toothed in male. Elytra, pronotum, base of head, prosternum, and abdomen bright red (variety *similis* is darker); rest of body, including appendages, blue-black. Length rarely less than 0.2 in. It rolls the leaves of oak, possibly also of sumac, hickory and walnut.—*analis.*

    Front femora stout; 2-toothed in males. Color like *analis* except that all of the under surface of the body is usually dull red. Length usually less than 0.2 in. Sumac is probably its only food-plant although adults occur on oak and other trees.—*nigripes.*

OTIORHYNCHINÆ

Some authors give these insects the rank of a family. The deciduous cusps of the mandibles, mentioned in the key to subfamilies, are teeth which are probably useful to the beetle in getting out of the pupal case. They are soon lost but they leave a "scar," often difficult to make out, on the front of each mandible. Of the numerous species, the following deserve special mention.

Epicærus imbricatus is a little less than 0.5 in. long; greenish-brown; when fresh, there is a median, longitudinal stripe of pale scales on the pronotum, two irregular, white cross-bands on the elytra; the under surface and legs are nearly white. The adult feeds on a variety of plants, sometimes defoliating strawberries.

Species of *Brachyrhinus* (*Otiorhynchus*) have two short, fixed spurs on each hind tibia; the tarsi are dilated, spongy-pubescent beneath, the third joint deeply bilobed; the eyes are rounded or slightly oval; the beak is as long as the head, more or less dilated, and notched at the tip. *B. sulcatus* and *ovatus* have the hind femora distinctly toothed. *B. sulcatus* is brownish-black; about 0.3 in. long; the femoral tooth is small and acute; the prothorax is rather cylindrical; elytra with small, remote patches of short, yellowish hair; the tip of the beak has a forked ridge. The larva eats the roots of strawberry and, in greenhouses, other plants. It is usually not so troublesome in this way as *ovatus,* which is shiny black with reddish-brown legs and antennæ; length a trifle less than 0.25 in.; the femoral tooth large; tip of beak not ridged; prothorax rather globose; short, yellowish hairs on the prothorax and also on the elytra. Neither species has wings and both occur also in Europe. The adults have a troublesome habit, shared by other weevils, of nibbling at tender shoots, causing serious damage at times to ornamental shrubs.

CURCULIONINÆ

This subfamily contains the great majority of the species, only a few of which can be mentioned here.

Hypera punctata is the Clover-leaf Beetle. The larvæ hibernate in the stems and among the old leaves of clover. Many species of *Listronotus* and *Hyperodes* feed on aquatic plants.

The genus *Curculio* (or *Balaninus*) contains the Nut and Acorn Weevils. The species have a bulky body and a long, slender beak, which is longer than the body in the females of some species. It is used for drilling holes in nuts or acorns in order that eggs may be placed in the kernel. The mouth-parts at the end of the beak work vertically, instead of horizontally. Squirrels are fond of eating the larvæ, slightly opening many acorns, only to discard them if no larvæ are present. *C. proboscideus*

(Pl. 65) is 0.3 in., or more, long; dark brown, densely but irregularly clothed with yellowish, scale-like hairs; the second antennal joint longer than the third; the beak of the female often nearly twice as long as the body. The female lays its eggs in chestnuts by drilling a hole through the burr. When the nuts fall, the larvæ leave to hibernate underground, pupating the next July. The Lesser Chestnut Weevil, *C. auriger,* is rarely 0.3 in. long; black, with brownish scales; pronotum with a paler line near each side; elytra with numerous, pale, yellow spots, which sometimes form bands; second antennal joint shorter than the third; beak of female nearly twice as long as the body. It usually lays its eggs in the chestnuts after the burrs are opened and the larvæ remain there all winter, unless eaten. By reason of a fungus killing the chestnut trees, these beetles have been having a hard time. *C. caryæ* is the Hickory-nut and Pecan Weevil. The adult is about 0.3 in. long; brownish with sparse, yellowish hairs. *C. obtusus* is the Hazel-nut Weevil. The infested nuts fall early. Most of our other species feed on acorns. *C. rectus* has a beak which, in the female, is nearly twice the length of the body but in the other acorn-eating species the beak is relatively shorter. *C. rectus* has "the habit, not known in the other species, of sealing the egg-hole with excrement, thus forming a whitish spot."

Tachypterellus quadrigibbus, the Apple Curculio, is dark red; about 0.17 in. long; pronotum with three lines of white pubescence; each elytron with two prominent tubercles toward the back. The larvæ feed for about three weeks in the flesh of green apples and pupate there. Even more damage is done by the adults feeding on tender shoots or puncturing the ripening fruit in order to feed, causing it to become "dimpled and gnarled." Adults hibernate.

Anthonomus signatus, the Strawberry Weevil, is not over 0.13 in. long. The injury is done by the females, which lay their eggs in the strawberry buds and then cut the stems so that the buds fall to the ground. *Anthonomus grandis,* the Cotton-boll Weevil, is a Mexican insect that spread northward throughout practically the whole of the cotton belt, due to the shortsightedness of legislatures in neither appropriating sufficient money nor passing stringent enough laws to control it at the start.

Ampeloglypter sesostris is pale reddish-brown, about 0.12 in. long. It lays its eggs in grape canes, causing galls about twice the diameter of the cane and an inch or so long, with a deep scar on one side. There are usually a number of these galls in a row. *A. ater* is much like it, but black. It also lays its eggs in grape-vines but, instead of putting them in a longitudinal line, it deposits them in a circle around the cane, girdling the vine so that it breaks off.

Trichobaris trinotata is about 0.14 in. long; black, with white, scale-like hairs, except on the scutellum and two spots on the pronotum. Its larva is the Potato-stalk Borer but it lives also in nettle.

Craponius inequalis, the Grape Curculio, is not over 0.13 in. long; dark brown, with scattered patches of whitish hairs. The hibernated adults feed on grape leaves until the berries are about a fourth grown, when the female lays her eggs in them, the larvæ feeding on the seeds, and dropping to the ground to pupate under stones and the like, or just below the surface.

Ceutorhyncus rapæ larvæ live in the seed stalks of cabbage but more often in wild Crucifers.

Conotrachelus nenuphar (Pl. 65) is the Plum Curculio but it breeds also in peach, cherry, and apple, causing an annual loss in the United States of more than $8,000,000. It is about 0.25 in. long; dark brown, varied with black; pubescence brownish-yellow, forming a curved, forked line on each side of the pronotum; an elytral band of yellow and white hairs back of the middle. "The adults hibernate, and issue from their winter quarters about the time the trees are in bloom, feeding on the tender foliage, buds, and blossoms. Later they attack the newly set fruit, cutting small circular holes through the skin in feeding, while the females, in the operation of egg-laying, make the small, crescent-shaped punctures so commonly found on plums and other stone fruits. The egg, deposited under the skin of the fruit, soon hatches into a very small whitish grub, which makes its way into the flesh of the fruit. Here it feeds greedily and grows rapidly, becoming, in the course of a fortnight, the fat, dirty white 'worm' so well known to fruit growers. When the larva obtains full growth, which requires some twelve to eighteen days, it bores its way out of the fruit and enters the soil, where it forms an earthen cell in which to pupate."

Strawberry plants are often dwarfed or killed by the larvæ of *Tyloderma fragrariæ,* which mine out the interior of the crown.

CALENDRINÆ

This rather small group, also called Rhynchophoridæ, of usually large (relative to other Curculionidæ) beetles are the Bill-bugs and Grain Weevils. The larvæ of the larger species bore into the stems of plants; those of the smaller ones feed on seeds and grain. *Rhynchophorus cruentatus* is usually more than 0.75 in. long, shiny black or partly red, and lives in the cabbage palmetto of the Southern States. It is the largest of our species. The antennal club is wedge-shaped in *Rhodobænus* (third tarsal joint broad, spongy beneath, the brush narrowly divided) and *Sphenophorus* (this joint smooth, at least in the middle) ; the species of each are 0.2 in., or more, long. The antennal club of *Calendra* is oval, and the species are smaller. *Rhodobænus 13-punctatus* is black beneath; above, red with five black spots on the pronotum and a number of more or less confluent ones on the elytra. It breeds in the stems of a variety of weeds. An allied species attacks sugar cane in the West Indies.

"The corn bill-bugs (or 'elephant bugs'), as the species of *Sphenophorus* [*Calendra*] are commonly called, pass the winter in the imago [adult] stage among dead leaves and rubbish, and lay eggs early in the following summer, beginning probably in May. The larvæ hatch in June, feed on the bulbous roots of grasses and grass-like plants, including corn, pass into the pupal stage late in July, and begin to emerge as imagoes late in July, continuing into August and possibly for some time thereafter" (Blatchley and Leng).

The cosmopolitan *Calendra* (or *Sitophilus*) *granaria* or one of its relatives may have been the first beetle to attract man's notice as they were already feeding on cereals in the Old World when man started to do so. It is about 0.13 in. long; chestnut-brown to black; moderately shining; the pronotum with coarse, oval punctures; the elytra with small punctures in the longitudinal grooves. It is wingless and is found about granaries or wherever grain goes. The larvæ live inside the kernels, a single grain of wheat being food enough for one. This does not sound very destructive, but the females are very prolific and there are from three to probably more than six generations a year. *C. oryzæ* (Pl. 65) is called the Rice Weevil and is probably a native of India but now infests all sorts of stored grain in this country. It is less than 0.13 in. long; reddish-brown to black, not shining; each elytron with two reddish spots. It is more apt to be found in crackers and packages of cereals than is *granaria*.

SCOLYTIDÆ

The U. S. Department of Agriculture once stated that if the timber destroyed by Scolytidæ in the United States during the past fifty years were alive, its stumpage value would be more than $1,000,000,000. For the most part, these beetles live between the bark and the wood, making galleries which are often quite characteristic of the particular species that fashioned them and which cause the insects to be called Engraver Beetles. The insects are small and their taxonomy is difficult. The eyes are usually oblong (See Bostrychidæ). The following subfamilies have been recognized:

1.—Anterior tarsi with the first joint longer than the next three combined.—Platypodinæ or a separate family, Platypodidæ. Our only common genus is *Platypus*. They frequently come to light in the Southern States.
    Anterior tarsi with first joint shorter than the next three combined. ....2.
2.—Anterior tibiæ with a prominent process on the outer apical angle.—Scolytinæ.
    Anterior tibiæ without such a process.—Ipinæ.

Scolytus rugulosus (Pl. 65), the Fruit-tree Bark Beetle, is typical of the Scolytinæ. The numerous small "wormholes," which make the outside of the bark look as if it had received a load of shot, are formed by the adults in boring out. Each female then burrows in at a new place and eats a vertical tunnel partly in the bark and partly in the sap-wood. Along the sides of this tunnel she makes small pockets and puts an egg in each. The young larvæ tunnel at right angles to the "broad burrow" and each pupates at the end of its own burrow. When the adults emerge from these pupæ, they bore straight out and so give the tree the "shot" appearance. If the insects are very numerous, their galleries girdle the tree and it dies, although it happens that this particular species usually works in trees that are dying from some other cause. *S. 4-spinosus* terribly damages the hickory trees near New York and its "bird-shot" emergence holes are a common sight. *S. multistriatus,* introduced from Europe, is considered an important carrier of the Dutch Elm Disease. It is 0.1 to 0.12 in. long; thorax shiny black; elytra pitchy red; the small antennæ and legs light brown.

The subfamily Ipinæ contains most of our species. Their food-habits are various but they usually live in trees, some in the solid wood instead of just beneath the bark. It should be said that many, especially those living in diseased wood, seem to feed more on the fungus ("ambrosia") that grows in their galleries than they do on the wood. Probably emerging females carry, but not intentionally, the spores of these fungi when they leave their childhood homes to start a new establishment.

STREPSIPTERA

These curious creatures are sometimes classed as a family, Stylopidæ, of beetles. They are parasitic upon other insects. The always wingless female never leaves her host; Pl. 60 shows one sticking out of a wasp's abdomen. The same plate shows a typical winged male greatly enlarged. Female Hymenoptera that are "stylopized" tend to resemble males; and, to a lesser extent, stylopized males acquire feminine characters. Homoptera of several families are also favorite hosts. See p. 39.

HYMENOPTERA

See p. 39. These are the Sawflies, Ants, Bees and
Wasps. "Wasps" refers chiefly to certain Vespoidea and
Sphecoidea; but many Cynipoidea are "Gall Wasps"
and there are many "Parasitic Wasps." Ants and some
wasps and bees are "social." In a "colony" of a social
insect usually one female ("queen") does most, or all,
of the egg-laying and unmated females ("workers") do
most of the other work in connection with the family
nest. Among "solitary" species the mother does all of
the work and usually she does not live to see her children become adult.

Ideas concerning classification all the way from suborders to species are still very confused and many of
the characters used are necessarily technical. This is
unfortunate because the order should be one of the most
interesting to amateurs. Furthermore, when all of the
species are known it may turn out to be the largest.

Hymenoptera have the true first segment of the abdomen immovably attached to the thorax, appearing to
be a part of it and being called the propodeum or
epinotum. In general usage the segment following the
propodeum is considered to be the first abdominal one,
although it is really the second. That usage is followed
here. For wing venation see p. 442.

1.—First abdominal segment not definitely narrowed;
rather broadly (usually over its entire width) joined to
the thorax. Hind wings with 3 basal cells. Trochanters 2-jointed.—Suborder CHALASTOGASTRA (also
called Symphyta). ....2.
    First abdominal segment narrowed at least at its
juncture with the thorax so that the main part of the
abdomen is separated from the thorax by a deep constriction; in many so much of the first segment is
narrowed that it forms a "petiole." Hind wing with
less than 3 basal cells. Larvæ legless.—Suborder CLIS-
TOGASTRA (also called Apocrita). ....3.
2.—Antennæ arising between the eyes above the base of
the clypeus. Ovipositor stout, not coiled. Larvæ with
usually distinct thoracic and abdominal legs.—TEN-
THREDINOIDEA, p. 391.
    Antennæ arising below the eyes immediately above
the mandibles and under a transverse ridge. Each front

tibia with a single apical spur.—The family ORYSSIDÆ, sometimes made a distinct suborder, IDIOGASTRA (in which case the name Chalastogastra is limited to Tenthredinoidea. See also Siricoidea). So far as known, the legless larvæ of our single genus, *Oryssus,* are parasitic on the larvæ of wood-boring beetles.

3.—Trochanters 2-jointed except in some of the forms which have no stigma (a thickened spot on the front border of each front wing). Last sternite (ventral plate) of abdomen divided longitudinally, the ovipositor issuing some distance before the tip of the abdomen and provided with a pair of narrow sheaths as long as it is. —A group of superfamilies that has been called Terebrantia. .... **4.**

Trochanters 2-jointed except in Pelecinidæ (See *Pelecinus,* p. 399). The pronotum extends back to the tegulæ (scale-like structures, one in front of the base of each wing). Ovipositor issues from the tip of the abdomen and its outer sheaths form a more or less cylindrical tube. Antennæ straight or, if elbowed, without ring-like segments. The wingless forms with distinct ocelli.—SERPHOIDEA (also called Proctotrypoidea), p. 399.

Trochanters usually 1-jointed (Rarely there is a second which, then, is usually—but see Trigonalidæ— not distinctly separated from the femur). Last abdominal sternite not divided longitudinally; the ovipositor, if present, issuing from the tip of the abdomen as a sting without a pair of external sheaths.—A group of superfamilies called Aculeata. .... **5.**

4.—Usually less than 0.1 in. long and often metallic in appearance. Antennæ at least somewhat elbowed and with one or more ring-like segments between the shaft and lash; basal joint usually long, terminal ones often thick. Wings, if any, with but few veins and no stigma. Pronotum not extending back to tegulæ. Wingless forms with indistinct or no ocelli.—CHALCIDOIDEA, p. 397.

Antennæ straight, with not more than 16 joints. Front wings, if any, with no stigma and few veins but usually at least one closed cell. Pronotum extending back to the tegulæ. Body somewhat "flea-like."— CYNIPOIDEA, p. 398.

Antennæ straight, usually with more than 16 joints. Front wings, if any, with a stigma and closed cells. Pronotum extending back to tegulæ. Ventral segments of abdomen usually soft, membranous, and with a fold. —ICHNEUMONOIDEA, p. 394.

5.—First abdominal segment, sometimes also the second, shaped like a scale or knot, quite different from the rest of the abdomen ("gaster"). Pronotum extending back to the tegulæ. Not densely hairy. Social insects in

which there is usually a wingless "worker caste." True
Ants.—FORMICOIDEA, p. 399.

First abdominal segment may be narrow but not
scale-like; if nodiform and separated from the gaster
by a constriction, the second segment forms a part of
the gaster and is not separated from it both above and
below. ....**6.**

6.—Abdomen with 6 or less (often only 3) exposed abdominal segments. The abdomen is flat or concave below. Often metallic in appearance. Ovipositor an
extensile jointed tube. Trochanters 1-jointed.—CHRY-
SIDOIDEA, p. 407.

Not so. ....**7.**

7.—Pronotum extending back so that its hind angles or
tubercles touch or reach above the tegulæ. Wingless
forms densely hairy. Some of the winged forms fold
the front wings longitudinally when at rest. Trochanters rarely 2-jointed.—VESPOIDEA, p. 408.

Pronotum shortened, more or less collar-like, not
extending to the tegulæ although each hind angle is produced to form a lobe; rarely extended in front as a
neck. Trochanters always 1-jointed. ....**8.**

8.—Hind tarsi slender, the first joint not broadened or
thickened. First abdominal segment often narrowed
like a petiole. Hairs unbranched.—SPHECOIDEA, p.
416.

Hind tarsi usually with the first joint thickened or
flattened. Often very hairy. At least some of the
hairs branched or otherwise modified. First abdominal
segment not petiolate.—APOIDEA, p. 423.

TENTHREDINOIDEA

See p. 389. Sawfly larvæ have only one ocellus on
each side of the head, whereas "caterpillars" have several. Unlike larvæ of Lepidoptera, their abdominal legs
("prolegs"), if any, do not have circles of hooklets.
When Sawfly larvæ have prolegs there is a pair on the
fifth segment. The adults are called Sawflies because
the ovipositor is often somewhat saw-like and used for
making cuts in plant tissue.

In XYELIIDÆ the third antennal joint is long, usually
longer than all of the many following joints combined.
Larvæ feed chiefly on tree leaves and at least some have
10 pairs of prolegs.

PAMPHILIIDÆ.—The adult body is stout; the hind
margin of the pronotum nearly or quite straight; the
many-jointed antennæ slender, especially toward the tip.

Larvæ have 7-jointed antennæ; thoracic but no abdominal legs. Some larvæ are gregarious; some fasten leaves together with silk; some roll individual leaves; others feed openly. *Neurotoma fasciata* (Pl. 66) is a common species, chiefly on wild cherry.

Some students group the families having not more than a single apical spur on each front tibia as a super-family, Siricoidea, taking in Oryssidæ (p. 390) and the next three of the following families. In that case the name Tenthredinoidea is limited to the remaining families, all of which have two apical tibial spurs.

The pronotum of CEPHIDÆ is at most weakly indented behind and its front surface is not vertical; abdomen rather compressed. Larvæ bore in plant-stems, *Cephus pygmæus* in wheat, *Adirus trimaculatus* in blackberry and so on. The female *Janus integer,* after laying an egg in a currant stem, moves up a short distance and girdles the stem with her ovipositor.

The following families have the hind margin of the pronotum indented, often greatly so, and the front pronotal surface is more or less vertical; abdomen rather cylindrical.

Adult SIRICIDÆ have a triangular plate at the apex of the abdomen. They are called Horntails because of the strong ovipositor, used for drilling in the wood in which the larvæ are to feed. They pupate in their burrows and adults sometimes emerge in our houses from firewood or furniture. A common species is *Tremex columba* (Pl. 66). Even its larva, which bores in the trunks of diseased trees, has a "horn-tail." On emerging, the adult leaves a hole about the diameter of a pencil.

XIPHYDRIIDÆ have no triangular plate at the abdominal apex. The larvæ bore in dead wood.

The antennæ of CIMBICIDÆ are club-shaped. *Cimbex americana* (Pl. 66) is the largest of our common Sawflies. Its larvæ feed on leaves of trees, especially willow, and, when disturbed, spurt fluid from just above the spiracles (breathing holes). They pupate in brownish cocoons underground. (We may have to use the name *Crabro* in place of *Cimbex* and change the family name accordingly. This would be most unfortunate be-

PLATE 66

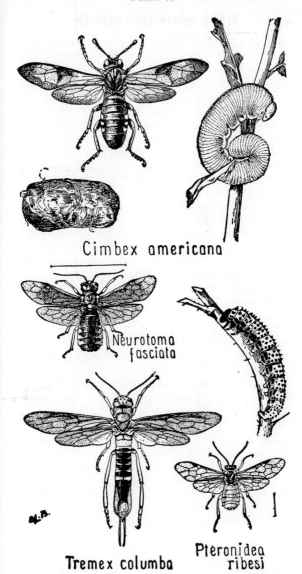

Cimbex americana

Neurotoma
fasciata

Tremex columba

Pteronidea
ribesi

cause we have been using *Crabro* as the name of a wasp.)

ARGIDÆ (antennæ with only 3 joints; the third very long, sometimes split in the male) and DIPRIONIDÆ (antennæ usually more than 6-jointed, often saw-like or comb-like) are small families.

TENTHREDINIDÆ includes most of the Chalastogastra. Most of the larvæ have prolegs, as well as thoracic legs, and feed on leaves. The imported *Pteronidea ribesi* (Pl. 66) often strips our currant bushes, the larvæ pupating underground. The Pear-slug (*Eriocampoides limacina*) and the Rose-slug (*Caliroa æthiops*) are also too common. Some larvæ of this family bore inside of leaves ("leaf miners"). *Caulocampa acericaulis* bores in the petioles of maple leaves. Some fold the edges of leaves. Some are gall-makers, as are *Pontania* and *Euura* on willow. Since these galls start before the larvæ hatch and continue if the larvæ be killed, it seems that the galls are caused by something the females inject when they lay their eggs.

ICHNEUMONOIDEA

See p. 390. As far as known, all of these species and practically all of the Chalcidoidea, the two largest superfamilies of Hymenoptera, are "parasitic" on other insects. Technically, either "parasitoid" or "predacious" might be a better term because these insects eventually kill their victims. Many millions of these Ichneumon "wasps" are working every year, with the assistance of other parasitic insects, in keeping down insect pests and insects that might be pests. To be sure, others, as "secondary parasites," also called "hyperparasites," prey upon the foes of our foes. It is one of the problems of professional economic entomologists to know one from the other; but in this group so much depends on the general looks of a species, its "habitus," that experience and named collections are almost necessary to correct identification. Numbers, as well as technical difficulties, prevent an even moderately satisfactory simplification of classification in these two superfamilies.

EVANIIDÆ have the abdomen joined in a somewhat

PLATE 67

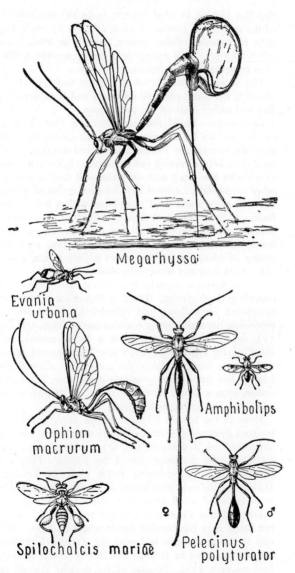

Megarhyssa

Evania
urbana

Ophion
macrurum

Amphibolips

Spilochalcis mariae

Pelecinus
polyturator

♀   ♂

flag-like fashion to what appears to be the top, instead of the end, of the thorax. *Evania* (Pl. 67) breeds in the eggs of roaches. Other genera, usually at least, have other "hosts." This family is sometimes made a distinct superfamily, Evanioidea.

The slender abdomens of AULACIDÆ and GASTERUPTIONIDÆ, the latter parasitic on wasps and bees, are also fastened rather high on the propodeum.

BRACONIDÆ.—Pl. 86 shows the cocoons (not "eggs") of one species on a caterpillar. That caterpillar will soon die because the Braconid larvæ had eaten most of its insides before coming out to pupate. Similar masses of cocoons are often seen on plants—all that is left of other caterpillars. Almost any out-door group of plant-lice will show some dead plant-louse with a hole in its back. A Braconid (probably *Aphidius*) or some other parasitic insect came out of that hole, having pupated inside of the host's skin. Before pupating, such an enemy of plant-lice usually makes a hole in the under side of its host and fastens the skin to the leaf.

ICHNEUMONIDÆ include the largest and most frequently noticed species. The first abdominal segment is broadened or bulbous, not cylindrical. Frequently a promising Saturnid cocoon contains one of these, *Ophion* (Pl. 67, possibly *Eremotylus* is a better name), instead of its rightful owner. The Ichneumonid larva which was feeding inside the caterpillar allowed its host to live until the cocoon was made, then killed the maker, spun a dense, brownish cocoon of its own as an additional protection, and pupated.

Most of the female Ichneumonoidea carry their ovipositors protruding from the tip of their body, but the ovipositors of *Megarhyssa* (Pl. 67) are long, even when compared with the large size of the insects. They are parasitic upon wood-boring larvæ such as *Tremex*. Delicate as the ovipositor seems to be, the female is able to pierce solid wood in order to deposit an egg in the burrow of the *Tremex* within the tree's trunk. I do not know how the females decide where to bore. The egg is not necessarily laid near the *Tremex* larva but the burrow must be reached and this is rarely, if ever, half an inch wide. Because of the popular interest in the subject, I assure you that the creature neither stings humans nor harms trees. We have several species. The wings of some have dark patches.

STEPHANIDÆ are a small family having slender antennæ of 30 or more joints. The hind femora are usually swollen and spined beneath. Ovipositor long. At least some of the species attack wood-boring larvæ.

TRIGONALIDÆ (see p. 409) are another small family. Some are found in the nests of social wasps. A species of *Lycogaster* is believed to attack *Eremotylus* parasites of Saturniidæ.

CHALCIDOIDEA

See p. 390. Here belong thousands of very small species. Without doubt one of the most interesting chapters in all biology could be written about these if we only knew enough.

Plate 67 shows *Spilochalcis mariæ* of the CHALCIDIDÆ. It is a parasite of caterpillars such as *cecropia*.

MYMARIDÆ, which may belong in Serphoidea, are egg-parasites, some of the adults being less than 0.01 in. long but still insects, complete in all their parts, powers, and psychology. Some hunt out *Notonecta* eggs under water, swimming rapidly with their wings.

TRICHOGRAMMATIDÆ.—Egg parasites. Twenty *Trichogramma* individuals have been reared from a single *Papilio* egg. Literally millions of *Trichogramma minutum,* an egg parasite, are now being reared in laboratories for the control of injurious insects. *Lathromeris cicadæ,* an egg-parasite of Cicadidæ, is said to have several generations during the two-month egg-period of the host.

EULOPHIDÆ.—Some are important controls of scale-insects. The several larvæ of *Tetrastichus asparagi* in a single egg of the Asparagus Beetle do not prevent it from hatching. They stay in the beetle larva until it makes a pupal cell. Then they pupate and later emerge as adults. *Euplectrus comstockii,* an external parasite of caterpillars, becomes adult from egg in a week.

Both PTEROMALIDÆ and ENCYRTIDÆ have a wide range of hosts, including scale insects. A number of species of Encyrtidæ practise "polyembryony": one egg, in developing, splits up and eventually produces many adults.

PERILAMPIDÆ.—A small but interesting family. For example, the larva of *Perilampus hyalinus,* a hyperparasite, waits inside of *Hyphantria* caterpillars until some other insect—a primary parasite—develops there. Then the *Perilampus* larva enters the other larva. The end result is a dead caterpillar, a dead parasite of the caterpillar, and a live adult of *Perilampus.*

Not all Chalcidoidea are enemies of other insects. *Harmolita* of EURYTOMIDÆ makes destructive galls in the stems of cereals. Another gall-making species is now in America to make it possible for us to grow Smyrna figs. It is *Blastophaga psenes* of the AGAONTIDÆ. The Smyrna fig has only female flowers which will not set fruit until they receive pollen. Pollen is present in the more perfect flowers of other varieties, "caprifigs." *Blastophaga* larvæ make galls in the ovaries of caprifigs. The male wasps are wingless but the females are winged. The newly emerged female leaves her home-flower dusted with its pollen. When she enters a Smyrna fig flower, as she may, to oviposit there, some of the pollen gets brushed off and fertilizes that flower so that it can set fruit. The female, however, is not repaid: the Smyrna flower is of such a shape that she cannot lay her eggs in its ovaries. She must go elsewhere and we get the figs.

CYNIPOIDEA

See p. 390. Several small families contain only parasitic species but the Cynipidæ are chiefly "gall-makers" on plants. Really, it is the plants that make the galls, the insects furnishing the stimulus. Suggestions as to what that stimulus is have ranged from mechanical injuries and injected chemicals ("enzymes") to bacterial infection. Whatever it is, the galls are so definite that they (see p. 443 and *Amphibolips,* Pl. 67) are more easily identified by the amateur than are the insects. Certain Cynipidæ, although breeding in galls, do not have any part in making them but merely feed on the plant tissue which grew because of the activities of another insect. A few of these "guests" eat their insect benefactors.

Some of the gall-makers have an interesting alternation of generations. Generation A produces a certain kind of gall from which hatches generation B. Adults of B differ from those of A and the galls produced by B differ from those produced by A; but B's children are A, starting the cycle over again. In these cases one of the alternate generations usually lacks males. Some Cynipids have no males at all.

SERPHOIDEA

See p. 390. The female *Pelecinus polyturator,* family PELECINIDÆ, has a very distinctive form. She uses her long abdomen to lay eggs on the underground larvæ of May Beetles. Unfortunately, Pl. 67 shows the femora, instead of the tibiæ, enlarged. Species of other families are, for the most part, small in size. SCELIONIDÆ live largely in the eggs of other insects and of spiders. Females of *Rielia manticida* settle on adult Mantids and, shedding their wings, stay there until the Mantid, if it be a female, lays its eggs. Then the *Rielia* which has picked a host of the right sex lays her eggs in its eggs. Some GALLICERATIDÆ (or Ceraphronidæ) live in *Aphidius,* itself a parasite of plant-lice. BETHYLIDÆ parasitize wood-boring larvæ. The wood may be in our houses and then the emerging wasps are unjustly accused. And so on. Serphoidea are considered by some to be closely related to Chalcidoidea; by others to Vespoidea. See p. 408, where a key is given to some of the families. Serphidæ have been called Proctotrypidæ.

FORMICOIDEA

See p. 391. Students still keep to one family, FORMICIDÆ, of ants but the "subfamilies" might well be called "families." In addition to males and sexual females, nearly every species has modified females, which rarely reproduce. These are the workers. There may be more than one size of worker, and some may be differentiated as "soldiers." It is the workers which we ordinarily see and, as they never have wings, many people think that all ants are wingless. However, the sexual forms, which are usually produced but once a year, usually are fully winged and indulge in a nuptial flight. After it the males die but the females lose their wings and settle down to the stay-at-home task of producing offspring. The rearing of all except the first of these offspring is attended to by the old-maid daughters unless the species has learned the trick of keeping servants ("slaves"). Many species eagerly gather the sweetish excretions of plant-lice and other insects—"Ants' cows." The "ants' eggs" sold for feeding birds and fish are really pupæ.

Ants may be kept alive as pets. To do this, be sure that you secure a queen. Many workers to take care of things are not required and, in fact, an unattended queen will often rear attendants, especially if she be young and fertile. Things go more smoothly if the workers have eggs, larvæ, and pupæ to start with. The simplest formicarium is a goblet set in a pan of water or covered with wire gauze. In this case considerable earth is necessary and one can not well see what is going on. Janet used a plaster box much like the one described on p. 13 except that he had several communicating chambers. Each chamber should have a glass cover and, except for the feeding chamber, be provided with a removable opaque cover to keep it dark when observations are not being made. The Fielde nest is made from two pieces of glass, one for top and one for bottom; the walls are made from strips of glass (laid flat) or of heavy toweling, the feeding door being a plug of cotton; there should be an opaque cover for top and bottom of all but the feeding chamber; moisture is supplied by wetting a slice of sponge in the feeding chamber. A little soil (or rotten wood) may be put in the Janet nest and should be in the Fielde nest. Feed sugar, bits of meat, fruit, or something of the sort. Workers have been kept for seven years and queens for about twice as long.

The narrowed, often otherwise modified, front part (the "waist") of an ant's abdomen is the petiole or pedicel. The thick part of the abdomen is the gaster. The long, first antennal joint is the scape; the rest of an antenna is the funiculus.

The following key, based on one kindly prepared by Dr. Wm. S. Creighton, is to the more common genera

PLATE 68

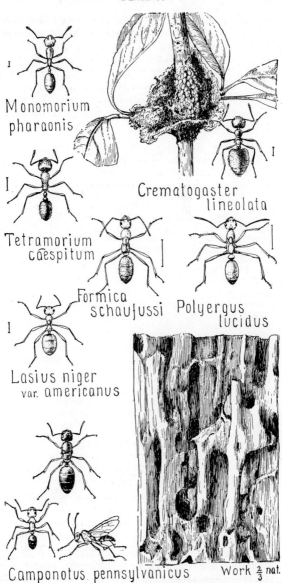

I Monomorium pharaonis

Crematogaster lineolata I

I Tetramorium caespitum

Formica schaufussi

Polyergus lucidus

I Lasius niger var. americanus

Camponotus pennsylvanicus

Work ⅔ nat.

and subgenera of our ants. It refers entirely to workers, and the characters used frequently hold only within our area. When a genus has been broken into subgenera only the latter names are given; some of them are likely to be full-fledged genera when subfamilies become families. Subfamily names have been put in merely to show where the genera go; the characters given are not always diagnostic of the subfamilies but merely of the genera given here.

1.—Anus circular; bordered by a fringe of close-set hairs. (Formicinæ, or Camponotinæ). ....30.

Anus slit-shaped; hairs, if any, not forming a close-set fringe. ....2.

2.—Gaster with a distinct constriction between its 1st and 2nd segments. (Ponerinæ).....................3.

Not so. ....7.

3.—Mandibles linear; a double row of teeth along the inner border.—*Stigmatomma* (chiefly, or only, *pallipes*).

Mandibles triangular; teeth of masticatory border in a single row. ....4.

4.—Tip of gaster directed forward and downward....5.

Tip directed rearward. ....6.

5.—Second gastric segment dilated behind to form the curved posterior border of the abdomen; terminal segments projecting forward and downward from the anterior edge of the 2nd. Clypeus with a projecting triangular lobe in the middle.—*Sysphincta.*

Terminal segments projecting forward and downward from the posterior edge of the 2nd gastric segment. Clypeus not as above.—*Proceratium.*

6.—Mandibular teeth fine, pointed, largely confined to outer half of masticatory margin; inner half toothless or with tiny denticles. Prothorax not margined.—*Ponera.*

Teeth coarser, rather blunt, extending over entire masticatory margin. Prothorax feebly margined.—*Euponera.*

7.—Petiole consisting of one segment. ....8.

Petiole including 2 segments. ....9.

8.—Mandibles linear; inserted at the middle of the anterior border of the head. Sting well developed.—*Odontomachus* (Ponerinæ). Fla. to Texas.

Mandibles triangular; inserted at the corners of the head. No sting. Have anal glands that give off a sometimes strong odor. (Dolichoderinæ). ....26.

9.—Antennal carinæ near each other; not covering the antennal insertion. ....10.

Antennal carinæ more or less covering the antennal insertions and separated by a triangular frontal area. (Myrmicinæ). ....11.

10.—Eyes large, oval, more than half as long as the sides of the head. Integument smooth and somewhat shining. —*Pseudomyrma* (Pseudomyrminæ).

Eyes consisting of only a few poorly developed facets. Integument coarsely sculptured, opaque.—*Acamatus* (Dorylinæ).

11.—Antennæ 6-jointed.—*Strumigenys.*

Antennæ with more than 6 joints. ....**12.**

12.—All 3 thoracic segments with dorsal spines or tubercles. (The species cultivate fungi on bits of vegetation that they carry into the nest). ....**13.**

Thoracic spines, when present, confined to the epinotum (See p. 389). ....**14.**

13.—Thorax with 3 pairs of spines or tubercles. Occipital lobes rounded. Workers polymorphic.—*Atta.*

Thorax with 4 pairs of spines. Occipital lobes angular. Workers monomorphic.—*Trachymyrmex.* Usually made a subgenus of *Atta. T. septentrionalis* occurs as far north as Long Island, N. Y.

14.—Antennæ 10-jointed with a club of 2 joints.— *Solenopsis.* The minute, yellow workers of *molesta* are common in open, grassy places, where they may have nests of their own under stones or they may tunnel the walls of nests of larger ants, stealing their food. The sting of the Southern *geminata* has won it the name Fire Ant.

Antennæ with 11 or 12 joints, thread-like or with a club of more than 2 joints. ....**15.**

15.—Postpetiole attached to the dorsal surface of a subtriangular gaster.—*Crematogaster. C. lineolata* (Pl. 68), in several varieties, is very common under stones, boards, etc. It often makes paper-like partitions in its nest or over Aphids and Coccids on plants—"cow sheds." The workers, which have a disagreeable odor, move in loose files and often carry the gaster over the thorax with the tip turned forward.

Not so. ....**16.**

16.—Except for *kingi* of Texas, workers dimorphic. The large workers with a disproportionately large head with parallel sides, prominent occipital lobes, and mandibles adapted for crushing seeds.—*Pheidole.* Called Harvesting Ants because they, like some others, gather seeds.

Workers monomorphic or polymorphic. ....**17.**

17.—Head with well-developed antennal scrobes extending almost to the occiput.—*Harpegoxenus. H. americanus,* our only (?) species, lives in colonies of *Leptothorax.*

Not so. ....**18.**

18.—The angle between the dorsal ("basal") and declivious (posterior) faces of the epinotum armed with spines or teeth; if not, the epinotum sharply angular and the dorsum flat, bordered by parallel lateral ridges. ....**20.**

That angle not armed, often much rounded with the basal face convex and not bordered by lateral ridges. ....**19.**

19.—More than 0.2 in. long. Antennæ 12-jointed.—*Mannica*. Western.

Not more than 0.1 in. long. Antennæ 11-jointed.—*Monomorium*. The red or yellow *M. pharaonis* (Pl. 68), often abundant in our houses, is one of the several introduced species. The black *minimum*, a native, makes small crater nests in sandy places. We have still others.

20.—Antennæ with 3-jointed club. ....**21.**

Not so. ....**23.**

21.—Petiole's 1st segment subrectangular in profile; no distinction between the anterior peduncle and the node.—*Myrmecina, graminicola* our only (?) species.

Not so. The node well developed and anterior peduncle distinct, though sometimes short. ....**22.**

22.—Antennal fossæ bordered in front by a ridge.—*Tetramorium*. *T. cæspitum* (Pl. 68), a common Lawn Ant, and several others are introductions from Europe.

Not so.—*Leptothorax*. Numerous species. *L. emersoni* obtains food by licking *Myrmica* workers and nests in little cells that communicate by means of slender galleries with *Myrmica* nests. *L. curvispinosus* nests in hollow twigs, empty galls, etc.; it is yellow, with 2 dark spots on the 1st gastric segment.

23.—Thoracic dorsum without sutures or impressions.—*Pogonomyrmex*. Southern and Western.

Not so. ....**24.**

24.—Postpetiole and petiole's node covered with coarse reticulorugose sculpture.—*Myrmica*.

These parts smooth or finely granulose, with occasional feeble striæ at the base. ....**25.**

25.—Clypeus with 2 carinæ.—*Stenamma*.

Clypeus smooth or striate but not carinate.—*Aphænogaster*.

26.—Dorsal face of epinotum with a conical dorsal projection—*Dorymyrmex*. The Southern and Western *pyramicus* our only (?) species.

Not so. ....**27.**

27.—Dorsal face of epinotum forming a posterior shelf or lamina that projects above the very strongly concave declivious face.—*Dolichoderus*. *D. mariæ*, with a bright red head and thorax, has large colonies in sandy places but another common species, *plagiatus* (large yellowish-red spots on gaster), has small ones.

Not so. ....**28.**

28.—Scale of petiole absent or vestigial; when present, so strongly inclined forward that there is virtually no anterior face to the node.—*Tapinoma*. Our Northern species is *sessile*. It nests under things, usually in sunny places, and has salmon-colored larvæ and pupæ.

The scale well developed; erect or, if inclined forward, there is a distinct anterior face. ....**29.**

29.—Head strongly cordate. Thoracic dorsum not impressed at the mesoepinotal suture. Size of workers variable.—*Liometopum.* Western.

Not so.—*Iridomyrmex.* Southern or introduced species. *I. humilis* is the "Argentine Ant," so troublesome about New Orleans and elsewhere.

30.—Antennæ 9-jointed.—*Brachymyrmex.* The very small *heeri depilis* is our only (?) Northeastern form. It nests under stones in shady woods and attends Coccids on roots.

More than 9 antennal joints. ....**31.**

31.—Mandibles narrow, falcate and pointed.—*Polyergus.* See below.

Not so. ....**32.**

32.—Thorax as seen from above "strangulate" (compressed in the middle); both pronotum and epinotum wider than the mesonotum. ....**33.**

Thorax not so but tapering gradually from pronotum to epinotum.—*Camponotus.* Carpenter Ants. The common big, black *herculeanus pennsylvanicus* (Pl. 68) sometimes migrates from its nests in logs or stumps to houses, becoming a pest, both by riddling woodwork with its large galleries and by hunting for sweets.

33.—Maxillary palpi 3-jointed.—*Acanthomyops.* Usually made a subgenus of *Lasius.*

These with more than 3 joints. ....**34.**

34.—Scale of petiole sharply inclined forward; the hind face notably longer than the front one. ....**35.**

Not so. ....**36.**

35.—Thorax as seen from above very strongly strangulate; mesopleuræ deeply impressed.—*Prenolepis.* Our only (?) species of the typical subgenus is *imparis.* The workers visit trees to "milk" Aphids or get the secretions of extrafloral nectaries. They may feed so well that the gaster becomes much distended and they have trouble in walking. In this "replete" condition they may be said to represent a temporary stage of the more extraordinary state of affairs in *Myrmecocystus.*

Thoracic strangulation confined to the dorsal portion; mesopleuræ only slightly impressed.—*Nylanderia.* Usually made a subgenus of *Prenolepis.*

36.—Epinotum short and high, the basal face not more than a third as long as the declivious.—*Lasius.* Much given to cultivating Root Aphids in nest-chambers. *L. niger* (Pl. 68) is said to be the most abundant of our ants and, hence, of all our insects. However that may be, it is certainly common throughout most of our area.

Not so. ....**37.**

37.—Maxillary palpi with 2nd and 3rd joints each at least 3 times as long as the terminal ones.—*Myrmecocystus.* Texas to Colorado and westward. "Replete" workers of Honey Ants are so gorged with food that they can not walk but hang up in the nest. Since they disgorge to their less-fed sisters they are really living food-jars.

Not so.—*Formica.* See below.

We have several species or subspecies of *Polyergus.* In the Northeast it is *lucidus,* the Shining Amazon or Slave-maker (Pl. 68). Its slaves are bred from pupæ of *Formica schaufussi* that are taken from their maternal nests by the warlike *lucidus* workers. The latter are unable to feed themselves, excavate their nests, or care for their own brood, and must depend for these important activities on the *schaufussi* workers. Hence the ants of this species are quite unable to live an independent life and may be regarded as permanently parasitic on fragments of *schaufussi* colonies which they bring together with great skill.

The following key to a few *Formica* applies chiefly to our Northeastern species.

1.—Clypeus with a notch in middle of anterior border. —*F. sanguinea;* subspecies *subintegra* is light red, with brown gaster, and *rubicunda,* among others, is deep red, with black gaster. They usually nest under stones in grassy places along the edges of woods and obtain slaves, or auxiliary workers, by kidnapping the larvæ and pupæ of *fusca subsericea.*

　　Clypeus without notch. ....2.
2.—Posterior border of head broadly excised.—*F. exsectoides.* It occurs chiefly in the Alleghanies and nests in and under mounds which it constructs of earth and vegetable debris. Not only are these mounds often three or four feet in diameter and a foot or two high, but a single colony often extends over several mounds. A young queen establishes herself in a depauperate colony of *fusca subsericea.* The *fusca* workers rear her children and soon the colony is all hers. This species, like some of its relatives, eats many dead insects.

　　Posterior border of head not excised. ....3.
3.—Body rather stout; head of larger workers usually but little longer than broad; 2nd to 3rd funicular joints much more elongated than 6th to 8th; color red, with brown or black gaster. ....4.

　　Body more slender and graceful; head of larger workers distinctly longer than broad; 2nd to 3rd funicular joints but little more elongated than 6th to 8th; color rarely as in preceding. ....**5.**

4.—Petiole broad, with sharp upper border; body and lower surface of head without erect hairs.—*F. truncicola integra.* The nests are in piles of large stones or in old logs and stumps; they are stuffed with bits of grass and leaves. Like most other species of *Formica, integra* is much given to attending Aphids. It is most abundant in hilly regions, where it prefers clearings in the forests.

Petiole narrow, thick, and blunt above.—*F. difficilis consocians.* The queens are yellow and hardly larger than the largest workers. They are temporary parasites in the nests of *schaufussi* var. *incerta.* Soon after fertilization the queen seeks adoption in some depauperate and probably queenless colony of *incerta* and there permits her hosts to bring up her young. Later the *incerta* workers die off, leaving the *consocians* as a pure and independent colony, which grows rapidly in size and shows no evidence of its parasitic origin. The nests resemble those of *integra* but are smaller.

5.—Middle funicular joints more than 1.5 times as long as broad; scape very slender and nearly straight; petiole with convex anterior and posterior surfaces, and blunt upper margin; body smooth and rather shining. —*F. pallidefulva.* The subspecies *schaufussi* (Pl. 68) is yellowish- or reddish-brown, gaster but little darker; it has erect hairs on the lower surface of the head and on the petiolar border. It is one of the common species of *Formica* and nests in rather small colonies under stones or in small, obscure mound-nests in sunny, grassy fields. Its food consists largely of dead insects and the excrement of Aphids.

Middle funicular joints usually less than 1.5 times as long as broad; scape distinctly curved at base; posterior surface of petiole flat; body more densely pubescent.—*F. fusca.* The variety *subsericea* is extremely common. Its habits are much like those of *schaufussi* and, like it, *subsericea* is very timid. As the preceding notes show, it is a convenient creature for its relatives.

CHRYSIDOIDEA

See p. 391. The scientific name refers to the golden color of certain (European) species and "Ruby Wasps" to the color of others, but most American species are metallic green or blue. "Cuckoo Wasps" is a name that describes their habits, since they lay their eggs in the nests of other Hymenoptera and their larvæ deprive the rightful owner of food, even if they do not actually eat the owner first. Some students count these insects as Vespoidea. In any case, we have the family CHRYSIDIDÆ. The bee-like *Parnopes* has a tongue longer than its thorax. The type genus, *Chrysis* (Pl. 98), has grooves or pits near the margin of the third abdominal segment.

VESPOIDEA

See p. 391. Some authors place the ants, as well as Chrysididæ, here. However, it may be that the future will bring "splitting" instead of "lumping." Females of some parasitic or, better, "parasitoid" families are wingless. Some families of Serphoidea are included in the following key for fear those who use it may not have recognized them as such. They and usually rare families are troublesome in classification. Several have been omitted here. Amateurs are, for the most part, concerned with only three families: Mutillidæ (hairy; females wingless); Vespidæ (especially "social" species; wings at rest folded longitudinally); and Psammocharidæ, also called Pompilidæ.

1.—Wingless or wings much reduced. ....2.
  Winged. ....5.
2.—Top of thorax in one piece or with merely the pronotum separated by a suture; no scutellum.—Chiefly MUTILLIDÆ (p. 411). If the pronotum is separated by a suture and ocelli are present it is one of the MYRMOSIDÆ, considered by some to be a subfamily of Tiphiidæ.
  Top of thorax clearly divided into three parts by constrictions or at least the pronotum distinct; scutellum usually present.—If more than 20 antennal joints, the rare SCLEROGIBBIDÆ of uncertain position; otherwise. 3.
3.—Either antennæ on a frontal shelf or marked prominence (rare EMBOLEMIDÆ, no distinct abdominal petiole; some DIAPRIIDÆ, 12-jointed antennæ; and some BELYTIDÆ, 15-jointed antennæ), or side of abdomen acute or sharply margined (a few female SCELIONIDÆ and male PLATYGASTRIDÆ), or antennæ on the middle of the face far above the clypeus (a few SERPHIDÆ).—Except Embolemidæ, usually put in Serphoidea, p. 399.
  None of these. ....4.
4.—Antennæ 10- or 11-jointed.—Some DRYINIDÆ (Front tarsi of female pincers-shaped. Considered by some as a subfamily of Bethylidæ, p. 410; possibly better in Sphecoidea. They are parasitic on Homoptera) and some CALLICERATIDÆ (See Serphoidea).

Antennæ 12- or 13-jointed.—A few male Mutillidæ (antennæ 13-jointed) and a very few female
Psammocharidæ (antennæ 12-jointed) come here.
They have greatly reduced wings but tegulæ are normally developed. The following have no wings and
their tegulæ are reduced to minute tubercles: female
Methocidæ (mesosternum without plates that overlie
or project between the bases of the middle coxæ);
some Mutillidæ (abdomen with a distinct cylindrical
petiole); and Thynnidæ (abdomen not petiolate;
femora flattened).

5.—Hind wings without distinct venation and with no
closed cells. Usually small insects and chiefly Serphoidea (p. 399) or Chrysidoidea (p. 407) but also
Embolemidæ, Sclerogibbidæ, Dryinidæ, Bethylidæ, Clep-
tidæ and Calliceratidæ.

Hind wings with at least one distinct closed cell. ..6.
6.—Antennæ with 14 or more joints.—Trigonalidæ
(Mandibles with 4 teeth; antennæ at least 16-jointed.
This rare family may belong in Ichneumonoidea. They
are parasitic, possibly only on Hymenoptera including
other parasites and wasps. See p. 397) and Belytidæ
(Mandibles with 3 or fewer teeth; antennæ with less
than 16 joints. See Serphoidea.)

Antennæ no more than 13-jointed (usually 13 in
male, 12 in female).—What might be called the True
Vespoidea. ....7.
7.—First discoidal cell (See p. 442) very long, usually
much longer than the submedian cell. Front wing
usually folded lengthwise when at rest.—Vespidæ,
p. 412.

First discoidal cell shorter than the submedian.
Front wings rarely folded. "Solitary" (not living in
colonies with one or more "queens") species. ....8.
8.—Legs, including coxæ, very long; hind femora unusually long. Middle tibiæ with 2 spurs. Mesopleura
(the space between the wings and the middle coxæ)
divided by an oblique suture.—Psammocharidæ, p. 411.

Hind femora usually not reaching to apex of abdomen. Mesopleura not divided by an oblique suture. 9.
9.—Meso- and metasternum forming together a flat
plate overlying the bases of middle and hind coxæ.
Wing-membrane with fine longitudinal wrinkles beyond
the closed cells. Last ventral abdominal plate of males
spined.—Scoliidæ, p. 410.

Not so. Sometimes with a pair of thin plates overlying the bases of middle coxæ. ....10.
10.—Joints of antennal flagellum spined. Tarsal joints
of female broad and lobed.—A small family, Rhopalo-
somatidæ. At least one species is nocturnal. Its
larvæ are external parasites on crickets.

Not so. ....11.

11.—Mesosternum with two plates that overlie or project between the bases of middle coxæ. If ocelli are very large, the nocturnal males of Brachycistinæ of Mutillidæ; otherwise. ....12.

Mesosternum simple, without appendages behind, or with the plates reduced to a pair of small teeth. ....13.

12.—Females winged; with a deep constriction between the first and second ventral abdominal segments. Male abdomen ending in a single upcurved spine.—TIPHIIDÆ, p. 410.

Females wingless. Male abdomen usually not ending in a single upcurved spine in our American genus, *Glyptometopa* of California.—THYNNIDÆ.

13.—Hind wing with a prominent lobe at the anal angle. ....14.

Hind wing without such lobe. Body very hairy (If not and the first abdominal segment separated from the second by a strong constriction above and below: the rare *Sierolomorpha*).—MUTILLIDÆ, p. 411.

14.—Abdominal segments separated by strong constrictions. Males.—METHOCIDÆ (last ventral plate with a strong, upcurved spine) and MYRMOSIDÆ (not so).

No such constrictions except between the first and second segments.—SAPYGIDÆ.

BETHYLIDÆ.—The head is usually quite elongate. In contrast with Dryinidæ (sometimes classed as a subfamily) the front tarsi are not modified into "pincers." The species are parasitic on larvæ of beetles and Lepidoptera.

SAPYGIDÆ.—Larvæ live in nests of solitary bees, apparently eating the food of their hosts, not the hosts themselves except incidentally. In other words, they are "inquilines," not "parasites."

As limited here, our principal genera of TIPHIIDÆ are *Tiphia* and *Elis* (See Pl. 98), the larvæ living on beetle (chiefly *Phyllophaga*) larvæ. METHOCIDÆ (Our common *Methoca stygia* preys on Tiger Beetle larvæ) and MYRMOSIDÆ (At least our principal genus, *Myrmosa*, probably lives at the expense of solitary wasps and bees) are often classed as subfamilies of Tiphiidæ.

Although formerly considered to include Tiphiidæ and others, SCOLIIDÆ is now limited chiefly to *Scolia* and *Campsomeris*. Females dig into the ground to find beetle larvæ, especially of *Phyllophaga*, "white grubs." If successful, the wasp makes a cell around its prey and lays an egg from which a wasp larva hatches to feed on the grub.

MUTILLIDÆ

These are the Velvet-ants, pretty but the females certainly can sting. As far as the amateur is concerned, the Methocidæ and Myrmosidæ might as well be grouped with them; they formerly were. The common name is well given. The wingless females of these wasps, scurrying about in open, especially sandy, places, look like ants covered with black, yellow, or red velvet. In the Southwest some of the species have long, white hair. The winged males can not sting. Those of some species are often found about flowers; others are nocturnal. The two sexes of a given species usually have dissimilar markings. Most of these insects are unkind guests in the nests of other wasps and of bees.

The old genus *Mutilla* has been split up so that *occidentalis* (Pl. 98) had now better be given the generic name *Dasymutilla*. For at least the East the following notes on females, the sex most often seen, will help with the principal genera.

Mutilla and *Pseudomethoca* have their petiole greatly enlarged toward the apex and usually they have a ridge between the eyes and the antennal bases. The eyes of *Mutilla* are elongate and there are no spines on the lower angles of the temples. *Dasymutilla* has a definite, roughened area on the last dorsal abdominal segment. *Sphærophthalma* (bases of antennæ not touching each other) and *Ephuta* (antennal bases touching; first segment of abdomen entirely pubescent) have no such area.

PSAMMOCHARIDÆ

These are rather slender, long-legged, solitary wasps; usually black or blue, often with orange bands. The wings are usually black and kept jerking while the insect is running about. They prey chiefly upon spiders, the big *Pepsis* of the Southwest not stopping short of "tarantulas." Most of our species burrow in the ground to form their nests but others, such as *Pseudagenia*, make cells out of mud, placing them under stones, etc., while the larvæ of some live in the nests of other diggers. *Ceropales* has the last-named habit, *Pseudagenia* being its host. *Ceropales* may be recognized by the claws of the hind tarsi being bent at a right angle. Unfortunately, others of the numerous genera do not have such good "catch" characters. Plate 99 shows *Psammochares atrox*.

VESPIDÆ

Usually the trend in classification has been toward splitting large groups into smaller ones but here what were families are now subfamilies. Possibly the next step will be to make them families once more and limit the name Vespoidea to these. Euparagiinæ, with two species of *Euparagia* in the Southwest preying upon beetle larvæ, is omitted from the following key.

1.—Front wings with only 2 submarginal cells. Antennæ club-shaped.—Masaridinæ, "solitary" wasps represented in the West and Southwest by *Pseudomasaris*. *P. vespoides* makes a mud nest on twigs and stocks it with pollen. We know very little about the habits of our other species.
Front wings with 3 submarginal cells. . . . . .2.
2.—Tarsal claws cleft. Middle tibiæ with one apical spur. Solitary wasps. . . . . .3.
Tarsal claws simple. Middle tibiæ with one apical spur. Usually social.—Polybiinæ (also called Epiponinæ), Polistinæ (See below. Clypeus ending in a point. First abdominal segment gradually narrowed in front), and Vespinæ (See below. Clypeus ending in a broad free margin, often with two widely separated teeth. First abdominal segment very broad and sharply truncate in front). Of the Polybiinæ we apparently have only two species of *Mischocyttarus* (Southern and Western. First abdominal segment distinctly petiolate. Make open paper nests like those of *Polistes*) and *Nectarina* (or *Brachygastra*) *lecheguana* (Southern). The latter makes a closed paper nest somewhat like those of *Vespa* but the combs are attached to the nest's walls instead of being hung from a central support. Although a wasp, it stores honey in its paper combs, possibly (but by no means certainly) as food for adults and not for larvæ.
3.—Mandibles short and broad; the apex obliquely truncate and toothed. Apex of petiole globose and strongly constricted before the second abdominal seg-

PLATE 69

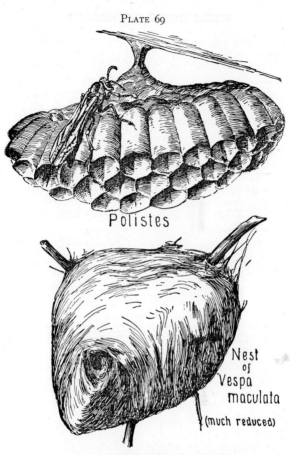

Polistes

Nest
of
Vespa
maculata

(much reduced)

Mud-dauber's nest

ment.—Zethinæ, of which we have several species of
Zethus.

Mandibles elongate, knife-like.—Eumeninæ, p. 415.

POLISTINÆ

Polistes is our only genus and probably we have very
few species, but there is so much variability that it
seems well not to attempt their differentiation here.
The nests are all much like the one shown on Pl. 69.
The wasps themselves are relatively gentle, not objecting
to close observation if the student moves slowly. The
queen does not differ much in appearance from the
worker.

VESPINÆ

Unlike *Polistes,* these wasps make paper coverings for
their nests and the workers resent too close observation.

There is still a dispute about it, but apparently *Vespa
crabro* is our only species entitled to the name *Vespa.*
It was introduced from Europe to New York about
1850 and has not yet spread far. Some individuals are
over an inch long. The color is reddish brown with
dull yellow markings. Head swollen behind eyes; upper
ocelli placed well below the level of the tops of the
eyes. Since it uses living wood and bark for making its
paper nest it is injurious to trees and shrubs. The
paper is brown and very brittle. The nests are usually
in sheltered places in buildings, hollow trees, or under
overhanging rocks. Strictly speaking, this is our only
"Hornet."

Vespula, then, includes the remainder of our Vespinæ, but there are two subgenera: *Vespula* proper (the
space between eye and mandible short) and *Dolichovespula* (that space longer, at least nearly as long as the
next to the last antennal joint). Most of these are
Yellow-jackets, only some of the jackets are not yellow.
Many people call them, especially *V. D. maculata,*
Hornets.

In each of these subgenera we have at least one not
very common species, *austriaca* in *Vespula* and *adulterina* in *Dolichovespula,* that has no workers. The
mother simply lays her eggs in the nest of a related

species and the daughters of that nest feed her children. These lazy, if you please, mothers may be recognized in its subgenus as follows. *V. V. austriaca:* black, marked with yellow; long, erect hairs scattered over the whole length of the upper side of the hind tibiæ. *V. D. adulterina* and its variety *arctica:* the clypeus about as wide as long, with strongly projecting anterior margin, the edges of which form strong, triangular blunt teeth, and the antennal flagellum is entirely black.

Of *V. Dolichovespula, maculata* is conspicuous for its own rather large size and for the often very large size of its nest (Pl. 69). It is black with white markings but the queens and workers have no white on the first two abdominal segments (The male has a narrow white margin on the first segment). Nests that are just being started usually have a long, slim entrance tube. The nest is usually placed well above the ground, whereas the nests of other *Vespula* are usually near to or under ground.

EUMENINÆ

The nest of *Eumenes fraternus* (Pl. 98) justifies the common name, Potter Wasps, given to the group; but all of the species seem to use clay, even when their nests are burrows in the pith of plant-stems. The many species are, from an economic standpoint, of great importance to our farmers and fruit-growers; very few of whom know about the great benefit they are deriving from these brightly marked wasps. The prey of these wasps is Lepidopterous and Coleopterous larvæ, of which they kill many thousands every year. As with most solitary wasps, the prey is first paralyzed by stinging and is then packed in the nest as food for the larvæ that will hatch from the egg laid before the nest is sealed. Certain genera may be separated as follows:

1.—Abdomen with much narrowed and elongate first segment, forming a long petiole.—*Eumenes.*
  First abdominal segment not forming a long petiole. ....2.
2.—First abdominal segment funnel-shaped, narrower

than the second.—*Pachymenes* (Former American records of *Nortonia* belong here).

First and second abdominal segments of about the same width. ....3.

3.—Labial palpi with a comb of conspicuous long hairs.—*Pterochilus.*

Labial palpi without a comb of hairs. ....4.

4.—First abdominal segment with transverse ridge.— *Ancistrocerus.*

First abdominal segment without such a ridge...5.

5.—Maxillary palpi 6-jointed.—*Odynerus.*

Maxillary palpi 5-jointed.—*Monobia* (Pl. 98).

Odynerus was our largest genus. Now authors divide it into a number of genera and subgenera. In that case *birenimaculatus* (Pl. 98) belongs to the genus *Ancistrocerus.* Some species nest in the ground, others in plant stems, and others make exposed nests of mud or tuck their mud nests in such crevices as keyholes.

SPHECOIDEA

See p. 391. There are, apparently, no truly social species in this subfamily, although in some cases the mother feeds her larvæ from day to day instead of merely laying her eggs on full supplies of food and leaving them. This food, usually but by no means always buried at the ends of underground tunnels, consists of other insects or of spiders, sometimes killed by the mothers, sometimes only paralyzed by her sting. Even when killed, the prey does not decay as quickly as might be supposed. Possibly the sting's venom is an antiseptic also. The Peckhams called Philanthidæ "Grave Diggers." The name was probably not intended to be distinctive of the family. Its appropriateness in any case depends on the viewpoint, because the grave of the victims is the nursery of the wasps.

Some authors have classed all of the following as one family, Sphecidæ, but this seems unwise. The key given here is that of Brues and Melander slightly modified.

1.—Middle tibiæ with two apical spurs, both well developed. ....2.

Usually no or only one well-developed apical spur on each middle tibia. If there are two well developed, either the hind femora are widened at the tip (as in *Alyson*) or the mandibles are emarginate externally ..8.

2.—Pronotum usually long, conically produced in front, usually with a median groove, its hind lobes often rather close to the tegulæ. Mesosternum (middle part of under side of thorax) produced into a forked process behind.—AMPULICIDÆ. Very rare. *Ampulex canaliculatus* stocks its nests with roaches.

Not so. ....3.

3.—Abdomen with a distinct, usually long, cylindrical petiole, which, at least at the base, consists only of sternite (the usually entirely ventral part of the segment).—SPHECIDÆ, p. 419.

Not so. ....4.

4.—Labrum well developed, wider than long, triangular or semitriangular, extending beyond the clypeus.—STIZIDÆ. In the East we have only *Sphecius speciosus* (Pl. 99). It is our largest Sphecoid and, because of the food with which it stocks its underground burrow, it is called the Cicada-killer. The Western *Stizus unicinctus* lays its eggs in the nests of another wasp, *Chlorion*.

Labrum short, not or barely extending beyond the clypeus. ....5.

5.—Antennæ inserted near the clypeus. Eyes of male usually very large and touching each other above. Radial cell broadly truncate at apex and prolonged as a small, weakly defined cell.—DIMORPHIDÆ. When *Dimorpha* is called *Astata,* the family is called Astatidæ. It is sometimes lumped with Larridæ. In the East we have *Dimorpha.* The flattened abdomen is black in *D. unicolor* and red in *D. bicolor.* They provision their nests with Pentatomid bugs.

Not this combination of characters. ....6.

6.—Antennæ inserted very near the clypeus. First abdominal segment usually long, slender, swollen at the apex and separated from the second by a distinct constriction. Second submarginal cell not receiving a recurrent vein.—MELLINIDÆ. *Mellinus* preys on Diptera.

Not so. ....7.

7.—Propodeum rounded. Thorax smooth, not coarsely punctuate.—GORYTIDÆ, usually classed with Nyssonidæ. Our genus *Gorytes* stocks its nest with Homoptera such as Leaf-hoppers.

Propodeum with the upper hind angles acute. Thorax coarsely punctuate.—NYSSONIDÆ. *Nysson* may be our only genus. It lays its eggs in nests of Gorytidæ.

8.—Eyes with one margin deeply indented.—TRYPOXYLIDÆ, p. 420.

Eye-margin not deeply indented or, if so, there are 3 submarginal cells the second of which is not narrowed into a "petiole." ....9.

9.—Front wings with more than one submarginal cell, their bounding veins distinct. ....10.

Not so. ....15.

10.—Labrum large, triangularly elongated beyond the clypeus, much longer than wide. Ocelli more or less aborted.—BEMBICIDÆ, p. 421.

Labrum small, usually entirely concealed by the clypeus. At least the front ocellus well formed. ....11.

11.—A deep constriction, both above and below, between the first two abdominal segments.—According to one arrangement this is the family PHILANTHIDÆ. Others split off *Cerceris* (Basal segment of abdomen narrower than the second; all the segments more or less constricted at the edges. Second submarginal cell petiolate. Marginal cell rather obtuse at apex. Hind femora with a projection at the apex below) and its relatives as the family CERCERIDÆ. Some *Cerceris* (Pl. 99) store up beetles; others use solitary bees, particularly *Halictus*. *Eucerceris* (third submarginal cell very large, scarcely or not at all narrowed toward the marginal cell) is a largely Western genus. The sexes differ in venation, especially the shapes of the marginal and second submarginal cells. In Philanthidæ proper (hind femora usually simple at the apex) *Philanthus* (inner margins of eyes indented; apex of marginal cell touching the wing margin) is the principal genus. The numerous species prey upon bees, including the Hive Bee. *Aphilanthops* (eyes not indented; marginal cell apex not touching the wing margin) uses queen or worker ants as larval food.

Not so. ....12.

12.—Hind femora produced below at apex and overlapping the base of the tibia. First abdominal segment not narrowed.—ALYSONIDÆ.

Not so. ....13.

13.—Marginal cell not appendiculate. Mandibles without an emargination externally. Inner margin of eyes not indented.—PEMPHREDONIDÆ, p. 421.

Not this combination of characters. ....14.

14.—Second submarginal cell present and not petiolate above. Upper ocelli usually aborted or deformed.— LARRIDÆ, p. 422.

Second submarginal cell petiolate or, rarely, absent. Three perfect ocelli. Small wasps.—MISCOPHIDÆ.

15.—Postscutellum with two scale-like processes which project back. Propodeum with a projection. Eyes not divergent above.—OXYBELIDÆ. *Oxybelus,* our principal genus, has the propodeal projection acute at the tip. In *Notoglossa emarginata* it is broad and slightly forked at the tip. The family food is Diptera. It is said that some species crush their prey; others sting it. Of these others, some are said to carry their prey home on their stings.

Not so.—Chiefly CRABRONIDÆ (Black, usually with yellow markings. Head large and rather square-cut.

Radial cell appendiculate. Hind wings with distinct cells. See p. 422 but also a few Pemphredonidæ.

SPHECIDÆ

These are the Thread-waisted Wasps. There have been a number of very confusing, but apparently necessary, changes of names. Four groups, treated here as subfamilies, have been recognized. They and our principal genera may be separated as follows.

1.—Second and third submarginal ("cubital") cells each receiving a recurrent vein. ....2.
    Not so. ....4.
2.—Antennæ inserted at the middle of the face. Claws with 1 to 6 teeth near the base. Tibiæ spiny. Except in *Isodontia* the females have a tarsal comb.—Chlorioninæ (Sphecinæ of older books). We have the following subgenera of *Chlorion.* ....3.
    Antennæ inserted below the middle of the face. Claws with at most one tooth near the middle. Tibiæ not spiny. Females without tarsal comb.—Podiinæ, of which *Podium* occurs as far north as Maryland and Illinois.
3.—Second submarginal cell wider than long.—*Chlorion* (tarsal claws with only 1 inner tooth) and *Priononyx* (these with 3 to 6 teeth). The common bluish *C. cyaneum* provisions its nest with crickets. *P. atratum* (abdomen dark brown or black) uses grasshoppers. The abdomen of *P. bifoveolatum* is reddish or yellowish.
    Second submarginal cell longer than wide.—*Isodontia* has the abdominal petiole more than twice as long as the hind coxæ; the marginal cell does not extend beyond the third submarginal cell. In *Ammobia* (formerly called *Sphex*) the marginal cell is relatively longer and the abdominal petiole tends to be relatively shorter. Pl. 99 shows *C. A. ichneumoneum;* the abdomen and legs of *A. pennsylvanicum* are black. Both species store up grasshoppers.
4.—Abdomen rather elongate; petiole of one or 2 segments. No U-shaped area on propodeum. Tarsal claws usually without teeth. Tibiæ somewhat spiny. Females with tarsal combs.—Sphecinæ (Ammophilini of older books). ....5.
    Abdominal petiole of one segment. Females with no tarsal combs. ....6.
5.—Both the 1st and 2nd abdominal segments in the petiole.—*Sphex* (formerly called *Ammophila*). Unfortunately, it was discovered too late that the generic name of *urnaria* on Pl. 99 is mispelled "Spex."

Petiole including only the 1st segment.—*Psammophila*. Two of our species are *luctuosa* (body black) and *violaceipennis* (abdomen partly reddish).

6.—Antennæ inserted at the middle of the face. Disk of propodeum U-shaped. Mesopleuron not longer than the height of the thorax.—Sceliphroninæ: *Chalybion* (metallic blue; Pl. 99) and *Sceliphron* (yellow and black; also called *Pelopœus*).

Antennæ inserted far below the middle of the face. Propodial disk not U-shaped.—Podiinæ. See **2**.

Much has been written about the caterpillar hunts of the Sphecinæ. One of the most interesting points is that certain *Sphex,* after having stocked the nest, laid an egg, and filled up the entrance to the tunnel, pick up a pebble and, using it as a tool, pat down the loose earth.

Sceliphroninæ are Mud-daubers (Pl. 69). *Sceliphron cementarium* (Pl. 99) is often seen nervously gathering mud for its nests, which are now usually placed in or on our buildings. *Chalybion cyaneum* (*cæruleum* on Pl. 99 and older books) appears to be either lazy or efficient or both. Rau has shown that at least some of the individuals of *Chalybion* let *Sceliphron* carry the mud and build the nest. Then they carry water and soften the hardened mud of the nest so that they can get in and use it for their own purposes. Both species use spiders for larval food.

TRYPOXYLIDÆ

Formerly called Trypoxylonidæ. Our principal genus is *Trypoxylon* (only one clearly defined submarginal cell; abdomen narrow, enlarged apically and longer than the head and thorax). The species are either all black, or marked with red. Some of the large species make mud nests consisting of parallel tubes like a pipe-organ. Small species use the hollows of cut straws, wood-boring beetles' burrows and chinks in masonry. If the chinks are too large, they may be made smaller by plastering them with mud, and the partitions between the cells, each containing an egg and sufficient food for one larva, are made of mud. Some may repair and use "second-hand" nests of their own or of another species. The nests are provisioned with spiders; the reported use of Aphids is doubtful. The males of at least some species are exceptional among Hymenoptera in the interest they take in household affairs. They stand guard at the nest while the female is out hunting food. *Pison* and *Pisonopsis* have more than one submarginal cell.

BEMBICIDÆ

The females of *Bembix* (or *Bembex*) often nest close to each other in populous "villages." Since each comes frequently to open its underground burrow for the purpose of giving a larva another fly to eat, there is much activity in such a village.

1.—Each mandible with a tooth on the inner side. ....**2**.

Not so.—*Microbembex*. *M. monodonta* is black, with greenish-white markings. It is particularly abundant on the seashore. Preys on dead or dying insects.

2.—Propodeum indented behind.—*Bicyrtes* (= *Bembidula*). It departs from family tradition by preferring Hemiptera for larval food and by completely stocking each nest before egg-laying. Two species are *B. quadrifasciata* (About 0.75 in. long. Metanotum black. Abdominal spots much wider at the sides) and *B. ventralis* (About 0.5 in. Metanotum with yellow spots. Abdominal spots little, if any, wider at the sides).

Propodeum not indented behind. ....**3**.

3.—Front ocellus round or kidney-shaped.—*Stictia carolina* is about an inch long, marked with black and yellow. Its habit of hunting flies around horses has given it the name "Horse Guard."

Front ocellus narrow.—*Bembix,* of which *spinolæ* (Pl. 99) is common.

PEMPHREDONIDÆ

1.—Three complete submarginal cells.—Pseninæ. Our principal genus is *Psen.* They nest either in sand or in twigs and provision their nests with Homoptera.

Two complete submarginal cells.—Pemphredoninæ. **2**.

2.—Eyes large, their inner margins converging above.—*Plenoculus.* Nests in sand.

Eyes small, inner margins not converging above; head well developed behind the eyes. ....**3**.

3.—Only one recurrent vein in front wings. ....**4**.

Two recurrent veins. ....**5**.

4.—Abdomen with a distinct petiole.—*Stigmus. S. ameri-*

canus provisions its nests in branches or stumps with Aphids.

Abdomen without a petiole.—*Spilomena.* Our principal species is *pusilla.*

5.—Abdomen with a petiole; head and thorax rather hairy.—*Pemphredon.* As far as known, the species prefer to make their nests in decaying wood, provisioning with Aphids.

Abdomen without a petiole; head and thorax not hairy.—*Passalœcus.* They nest in rotten wood, galleries of wood-boring insects and hollow plant-stems, provisioning with Aphids and other small insects.

LARRIDÆ

While fairly numerous, these wasps are not very showy. They usually take Orthoptera for larval food.

1.—Hind ocelli perfect; inner margins of eyes nearly parallel; pronotum trilobed.—*Lyroda triloba* (wings dark all over) and *subita* (wings dark at tips). Larval food, *Nemobius.*

Hind ocelli imperfect, flattened; inner margins of eyes converging above; pronotum simple. ....2.

2.—Front of head strongly raised so that there is a transverse ridge below front ocellus; mandibles toothed (in *Larra* there are no teeth); hind ocelli narrow; tip of abdomen with silver pile.—*Notogonidea argentata.* Larval food, immature crickets.

Front not strongly raised. ....3.

3.—Hind ("side") ocelli oval or elongate-oval in outline; front not raised along inner margins of eyes; tip of abdomen without pile.—*Tachysphex.*

Hind ocelli larger dorsally so that they appear hooked. ....4.

4.—Front slightly raised along inner margins of eyes; pygidium without pile.—*Larropsis distincta.*

Front not raised along inner margins of eyes; pygidium clothed with pile.—*Tachytes.* All of the numerous species probably stock their nests with grasshoppers.

CRABRONIDÆ

These wasps are usually much less than half an inch long and black, often marked with yellow. The head is large and rather square-cut. *Anacrabro* has the abdomen depressed, flat beneath; the second discoidal cell is much longer than the first and pointed at the tip. Our only species, *ocellatus,* nests in sand banks and provisions with bugs of the genus *Lygus*. Our other genus is *Crabro* (Pl. 99). It is much split up in the recent classifications, but some of the distinctions are rather technical. If "Crabro" is accepted as the name of the Sawfly genus *Cimbex* the wasps here called *Crabro* must be known as *Solenius* and the family name be changed accordingly. Different groups of species have different habits; nesting in wood, stems, and soil; provisioning with flies, bugs, Aphids (?), and moths.

APOIDEA

See p. 391. Although wasps visit flowers, they usually do so in their individual interest: to secure food for themselves and not to provide for their offspring. Bees, on the other hand, not only eat pollen and nectar themselves but, except for the "cuckoos" which lay their eggs in other bees' nests, store their nests with pollen and honey (modified nectar) for their young to eat. Although they thus take, in the aggregate, large quantities of pollen, they are of great benefit to the plants because they, incidentally and unconsciously, transfer pollen from one flower to another, thus fertilizing the plant's ova so that the ova may develop into seeds. Certain rare bees with large ocelli fly at night.

It has long been known that bumblebees (*Bombus*) and the honeybee (*Apis*) are "social" in the sense that some of the daughters ("workers") of a family do not mate but spend their lives attending to the affairs of the family. Now, however, see *Halictus* and Ceratinidæ. The social Meliponidæ of the Tropics are not known to occur in our area.

Male bees typically have 13-jointed antennæ and 7 visible dorsal abdominal segments; females, one less of each.

Some authors have classed the bees as a family or families of Sphecoid wasps. It is true that there are fair intergrades between wasps and bees but so are there between most related groups. Among the bees some large groups of species seem certainly deserving of family rank; others are very doubtful. In what follows the figures to which references are made are those on p. 425.

1.—Less than 2 closed submarginal cells.—The Tropical Meliponidæ, social Stingless Bees, have pollen-collecting apparatus or at least considerable hair on hind legs. *Phileremulus* (small Western Nomadidæ, p. 435) has no pollen-collecting apparatus.

Two closed submarginal cells. ....2.
Three closed submarginal cells. ....5.

2.—See Fig. 17. Small; almost hairless; face usually with light markings. Second submarginal cell usually nearly quadrate; only slightly, if any, longer than high and conspicuously smaller than the first. First recurrent vein often uniting with the first transverse cubital. Second recurrent vein bent or directed outward before joining the first portion of the subdiscoidal vein. Marginal cell elongate and not square-cut at the tip. Clypeus usually longer than broad. Tongue flat and bilobed. No flat triangular area on the apical dorsal abdominal segment.—PROSOPIDIDÆ, p. 427.

See Fig. 18; details differ in different genera. Second submarginal cell much longer than high and usually not conspicuously shorter than the first. Second recurrent vein not strongly bent or directed outward before joining the first portion of the subdiscoidal vein. Marginal cell not truncate at the tip. Tongue long, rather thread-like. Pollen-collecting apparatus, if any, chiefly specialized hairs on the under side of the abdomen. No flat triangular area on the apical dorsal abdominal segment.—MEGACHILIDÆ, p. 432.

See Figs. 2 and 19; details differ in different genera.

EXPLANATION OF FIGURES ON PAGE 425

These figures are merely more or less typical examples. In some genera there are considerable variations from species to species (and sometimes even within a species) from the condition illustrated.

1. *Apis mellifera,* the ordinary Hive-bee. 2. A diagram of a side view of the head of a bee in which the posterior angle of the mandible is not farther forward (toward the left) than the posterior margin of the eye. 3. A similar diagram showing this angle farther forward than the posterior margin of the eyes. 4. *Bombus.* 5. *Xylocopa.* 6. *Anthophora.* 7. *Melissodes.* 8. *Exomalopsis.* 9. A diagram of tarsal claws with a pad, called pulvillus or epodium, between them. 10. A diagram of tarsal claws without such a pad. 11. *Epeolus.* 12. *Nomada.* 13. *Ceratina.* 14. *Halictus.* 15. *Andrena.* 16. *Colletes.* 17. *Prosopis.* 18. *Megachile.* 19. *Perdita.*

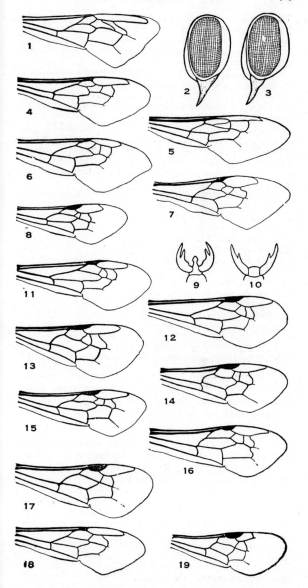

Usually the apex of the marginal cell is somewhat truncate, often distinctly so but in *Halictoides,* for example, this cell is pointed. Females and most males with a flat triangular area on the apical dorsal abdominal segment.—PANURGIDÆ, p. 431.

None of these. Forms that, although having two submarginal cells, are placed in families that typically have three. ....3.

3.—Except for submarginal cells, having the general characteristics of Halictidæ (9), including the arching of the basal vein.—*Dialictus,* p. 428.

Not so. ....4.

4.—Sparsely hairy or bare, with little or no pollen-collecting apparatus. First portion of subdiscoidal vein shorter than third portion of discoidal vein.—NOMADIDÆ, p. 435.

At least somewhat hairy, pollen-collecting bees. First portion of subdiscoidal vein distinctly longer than the third portion of the discoidal.—ANTHOPHORIDÆ, p. 434.

5.—Marginal cell very long, almost reaching the apex of the wing (Fig. 1). No apical spurs on the hind tibiæ. Eyes with hair visible under a strong lens.—APIDÆ, p. 441.

See Fig. 4. Submarginal cells all of about the same size but the second somewhat the longest and strongly produced toward the body; the first usually divided by a delicate, rather indistinct oblique nervure. Stigma not well developed. First discoidal cell not much longer than the marginal cell, which is pointed at the tip and extends far beyond the apex of the third submarginal cell. Rather large and densely hairy bees.—BOMBIDÆ, p. 436.

See Fig. 5. Third submarginal cell almost as long as the 1st and 2nd combined; the 2nd wedge-shaped, narrowed and pointed toward the body; the 3rd scarcely narrowed toward the marginal cell, which is long and narrow. First recurrent vein uniting with the second transverse cubital. Stigma well developed. First discoidal cell not much longer than the marginal cell. Large bees.—XYLOCOPIDÆ, p. 431.

None of these. ....6.

6.—Females and most males with flat, triangular area on the top of the apical abdominal segment. ....7.

Not so. Stigma well developed. ....11.

7.—Posterior angle of mandible not in front of posterior margin of eye (Fig. 2). ....8.

Posterior angle of mandible in front of posterior margin of eye (Fig. 3). Clypeus protuberant or mandibles so beveled as to show most or all of labrum. Tongue rather thread-like. Eyes usually extending to, or nearly to, the mandibles. Marginal cell rarely longer than the first two submarginal cells united. First recurrent vein not meeting the first transverse cubital. ..10.

8.—First recurrent vein meeting the 1st transverse cubital: *Caupolicana*. Marginal cell narrow and longer than the first discoidal; first recurrent vein meeting the 2nd transverse cubital: *Protoxæa*. These are large, Southern bees of somewhat doubtful relationships. Possibly they are Andrenidæ.

Neither of these. ....**9.**

9.—Basal vein forming more or less perfectly an arc of a circle (Fig. 14). Face with no pubescent depressions or foveæ.—HALICTIDÆ, p. 428.

Basal vein forming a more or less straight line (Fig. 15). Face, at least of females, with pubescent depressions or foveæ.—ANDRENIDÆ, p. 428, except that *Protandrena* (apex of the marginal cell truncated) is put in Panurgidæ.

10.—Rather hairy bees; the hind legs of females with pollen-collecting hairs. First portion of subdiscoidal vein distinctly longer than the third portion of the discoidal vein (Figs. 6, 7, 8). Male antennæ often very long. Stigma not well developed.—ANTHOPHORIDÆ, p. 434.

Almost hairless; no pollen-collecting apparatus. First portion of subdiscoidal vein shorter than the third portion of the discoidal.—NOMADIDÆ, p. 435.

11.—Second recurrent vein strongly sinuose, the lower half bulging towards the apex of wing (Fig. 16). Second and 3rd submarginal cells about equal in length. Stigma well developed. Tongue flat and bilobed. Face pitted. Hairy bees. Head and thorax not metallic.—COLLETIDÆ, p. 428.

Small bees; usually more or less metallic blue-green. First submarginal cell about as long as the 3rd; longer than the 2nd, which is much narrowed towards the marginal (Fig. 13).—CERATINIDÆ, p. 430.

PROSOPIDIDÆ

See p. 424. *Prosopis* (Pl. 70) is our only genus. Perhaps we should use the names Hylæidæ and *Hylæus*. In any case, they are considered to be very primitive bees. They almost or quite lack bee-like hair although a few such branched hairs can usually be found on the thorax. Unlike other industrious bees, they do not carry pollen on the outside of their bodies. They swallow it and then, having reached their nest, regurgitate it, mixed with nectar, to prepare food for the babies they never live to see. They nest in plant stalks and other cavities, including those made by other insects, lining the burrow with a very thin layer of some glistening substance, probably saliva.

COLLETIDÆ

See p. 427. Possibly *Colletes* (Pl. 70) is our only genus, although others have been put here. The Colletidæ are believed by some to be so closely related to Prosopididæ as to be merely a subfamily. The species are black, often with light hairs but no yellow markings on the body itself. They nest in holes made in the ground or in loose masonry; and often a number of females nest close to each other. They plaster the sides of these holes, and the cells which they make in them, with a secretion that dries rapidly to form "a membrane more delicate than the thinnest goldbeater's skin, and more lustrous than the most beautiful satin." This secretion, like that used by *Prosopis,* may be saliva.

HALICTIDÆ AND ANDRENIDÆ

Some good authorities unite these two groups, each of which contains an exceedingly large number of species so nearly alike that none but the specialist can successfully identify them and relatively few generally accepted genera have been made. For the most part they nest in underground burrows. Some species make simple tunnels; others, branched. They smooth the sides, stock with a pill of pollen the cells connected with the tunnel, lay an egg in each cell, and then fill the tunnel's opening with loose dirt. In some cases mated females hibernate in the burrows where they were born. Although many individuals may nest close together, each mother typically attends to all of her own work. Recently, however, it has been discovered that at least some European *Halictus* are truly social: the overwintered female lays eggs from which develop daughters that do not mate but help their mother to rear younger daughters and sons. Since the Halictidæ are otherwise rather primitive bees this is very interesting and would repay investigation in America as well.

Our Halictidæ can conveniently be divided into at least three genera: *Dialictus* (only 2 submarginal cells), *Sphecodes* (red or black or both; 5th segment of female's abdomen without a furrow) and *Halictus* (abdomen

PLATE 70

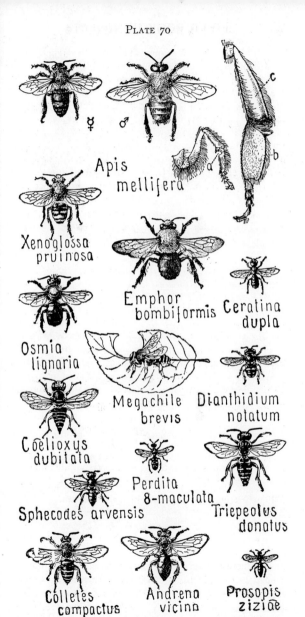

Apis
mellifera

Xenoglossa
pruinosa

Emphor
bombiformis

Ceratina
dupla

Osmia
lignaria

Megachile
brevis

Dianthidium
notatum

Coelioxys
dubitata

Perdita
8-maculata

Triepeolus
donatus

Sphecodes arvensis

Colletes
compactus

Andrena
vicina

Prosopis
ziziae

usually not shiny; 5th segment of female's abdomen with a median longitudinal furrow). *Halictus* can then be split into a number of subgenera. Of these, *Halictus* in a limited sense, *Augochlora* (body entirely metallic blue or green; first recurrent vein usually ending at or near the apex of the 2nd submarginal cell) and *Agapostemon* (Pl. 100; males and some females have only the head and thorax metallic colored; first recurrent vein received by the 2nd submarginal cell near the middle) are the more important.

Sphecodes, the Wasp Bees (so-called from their resemblance to small wasps, Pl. 70), have had champions who opposed the charge that they lay their eggs in nests prepared by others, their young devouring the food and doubtless the young of their hosts, but there is strong evidence that they are supported by their relatives, *Halictus,* and possibly by also other bees.

Some species of *Halictus,* in the limited sense, are very small and are called Sweat Bees because they seem fond of alighting on perspiring humanity. Some of the species are among the first bees to appear in the spring. The pupæ are enclosed in transparent, skin-like cocoons.

The large and confusing genus *Andrena* (Pl. 70) is by far the principal one in Andrenidæ, although *Nomia* sometimes attracts attention because literally thousands of individuals may nest in a very small patch of ground. Three genera may be separated as follows.

1.—The 1st and 3rd submarginal cells of about the same length.—*Nomia.*
    The 1st conspicuously longer than the 3rd. ......2.
2.—Ocelli arranged in a triangle. Apical joint of antenna not obliquely truncate.—*Andrena.*
    Ocelli arranged in a curve. Apical antennal joint obliquely truncate.—*Melitta,* chiefly *americana.*

CERATINIDÆ

See p. 427. We have only one genus, *Ceratina* (Pl. 70). There are several species, making nests in tunnels which they dig in the pith of plants such as sumac and raspberry. A probably related genus, *Allodape,* in South Africa has been found to have somewhat of a social mode of life. It might be well to study the habits of *Ceratina* more carefully.

XYLOCOPIDÆ

See p. 426. In this family also we have only one genus, *Xylocopa*. The only Northeastern species is *virginica* (Pl. 100), both males and females hibernating as adults. Species of *Xylocopa* are large Carpenter Bees that nest in tunnels which they make in rather solid wood, such as porch-posts. Like some bumblebees, they are given to biting through the base of a flower instead of getting at the nectar in a more legitimate way.

PANURGIDÆ

See p. 426. This "family" seems to be more nearly an orphan asylum containing unrelated genera that can not conveniently be put elsewhere. Further study is needed before a generally accepted system can be made. The following are the more usual genera with us.

1.—Two submarginal cells. ....**2.**
    Three submarginal cells.—*Protandrena* (second submarginal cell the same height as the other submarginal cells) and the rare night-flying *Xerophasma* (the ocelli very large and the second submarginal cell stunted and petiolate above).
2.—Apex of marginal cell rather pointed and at the costa. ....**3.**
    Apex of marginal cell either broadly, obliquely truncate or not touching the costa. ....**4.**
3.—The second joint of the hind tarsi attached to the anterior tip of the apex of the metatarsus. The hind metatarsi very broad; in females as broad or even broader than the hind tibiæ. The hind femur of males short and stout, shorter than the hind tibia.—*Macropis*, sometimes put in a separate family, Macropidæ.
    The hind metatarsi narrow in both sexes; the second tarsal joint attached more nearly at the middle of the apex of the metatarsus.—Have been put in a separate family, Dufouridæ (represented in U. S. by two closely related genera *Halictoides* and *Parandrena*).
4.—Marginal cell about equal to or shorter than the long and usually well developed stigma. The head and thorax usually more or less metallic green but sometimes yellow

or even black. Abdomen partly or wholly maculated, rarely all black.—*Perdita* (Pl. 70) and subgenera.

Marginal cell much longer than stigma. . . . . .5.

5.—Abdomen with conspicuous light spots or bands in the "skin" (not produced by hairs).—*Spinoliella.*

Abdomen without such ornamentation, usually all black.—*Panurginus, Calliopsis* (hair bands, often more or less interrupted, on the abdomen), *Greeleyella* (first recurrent vein meeting, or nearly so, the first transverse cubital), and *Pseudopanurgus* (the first recurrent vein meeting the second submarginal cell toward the middle of the cell; wings in some of the species very dark).

MEGACHILIDÆ

See p. 424. This large and very interesting family may be divided on the bases of both habits and structure into several subfamilies or, if desired, families. In many cases the males differ markedly from the females, particularly as to the front legs and abdomen.

1.—The female makes a nest, provisioning it with pollen carried home on a brush of plumose hairs (scopa) covering much of the under side of the abdomen. Abdomen narrow and conical. . . . . .2.

Females have no pollen-collecting hairs on the under side of the abdomen or, at most, not a definite scopa. Either the tarsal claws are cleft and the tooth is near the apex or the abdomen is conical. In the former case the body usually has pale markings not due to hairs...4.

2.—Body with pale markings not entirely due to hairs, these markings often yellowish or red. Last dorsal abdominal segment of males and of some females toothed, lobed, or otherwise different from the preceding segments.—Anthidiinæ: *Dianthidium* (Pl. 70; a pad between tarsal claws) and *Anthidium* (no such pads). Each has been further divided into subgenera and even genera.

Pale markings, if any, not in the "skin" but due to hairs. . . . . .3.

3.—Usually of medium or large size and with the thorax rather hairy. Not metallic colored. Apex of marginal cell more or less distinctly separated from the costal margin: 2nd submarginal cell receiving both recurrent veins (Fig. 18).—Megachilinæ: *Megachile* (No pad between the tarsal claws. Apex of marginal cell obtuse) and *Lithurgus* (Male with a pad between tarsal claws but female without such pad. Apex of marginal cell sharply pointed. Female's face with an elevation across the middle. Southern and Western).

Frequently metallic blue or green; when black, usually

rather small. Abdomen strongly convex. A pad between tarsal claws.—Osmiinæ. ....5.

4.—Claws cleft. A pad between the tarsal claws.— Stelidinæ: *Stelis* (Second recurrent vein received beyond the tip of the 2nd submarginal cell. Usually black with whitish or yellowish markings on the abdomen not entirely due to hairs) and *Chelynia* (Second recurrent vein received at or a little before the 2nd transverse cubital. Some species dark green or blue. Western).

Abdomen conical, pointed in female, armed with teeth or spines in male. Pale markings, if any, due to hairs. No pad between tarsal claws.—Cœlioxiinæ: *Cœlioxys* (Pl. 70. Fine hair, visible only with a lens, on the eyes. Axillæ produced into spines on each side of the scutellum) and *Dioxys* (Eyes not hairy. Post-scutellum with a median tooth. Western).

5.—Usually metallic green, bluish, or purplish. Apex of marginal cell more or less distinctly separated from costal margin; 2nd submarginal cell not more than half narrowed on the side of the marginal. Stigma not well developed. Abdomen globose or nearly so.—*Osmia* (Pl. 70. Antennæ similar in both sexes) and the relatively rare *Monumetha* (Rather large. Black. Abdomen long, parallel sided. Male antennæ somewhat as in *Alcidamea* but without an apical hook).

Stigma well developed; lanceolate. Head quadrate, considerably extended behind the eyes. Vein separating the stigma from the 1st submarginal cell not longer than that between stigma and marginal cell. Base of first abdominal segment with flattened or concave, smooth, shining plate or basin, the edge of which is well defined.— *Heriades.* (Abdomen of male *Ashmeadiella* ends with 4 projections.)

None of these. Marginal cell more or less distinctly separated from the costal margin. Vein separating the stigma from the 1st submarginal cell longer than that between stigma and marginal cell. First dorsal abdominal segment rounded and with a narrow longitudinal groove. —*Andronicus* (flagellum of male antenna broad at first but abruptly narrowed at the 6th joint; the apical joints distinctly longer than the basal), *Alcidamea* (male flagellum usually thickened, the basal joints the longer, the terminal one abruptly narrowed into a slender, curved spine) and *Robertsonella* (flagellum long and threadlike). The rare Southern and Western *Chelostoma* has the 2nd submarginal cell much narrowed at the marginal.

Note that the Stelidinæ and Cœlioxiinæ have no pollen-collecting apparatus. They lay their eggs in the nests of their relatives: the Stelidinæ chiefly in those of Anthidiinæ and some Osmiinæ; and the Cœlioxiinæ chiefly in those of Megachilinæ (*Dioxys* in those of Osmiinæ). *Dianthidium* makes nests of resin, sometimes mixed with small pebbles, on rocks and other surfaces, and *Anthidium* uses down off of woolly-leaved plants for nests in burrows or other cavities. The Osmiinæ, particularly *Osmia,* are called Mason Bees because they construct small, earthen cells on or under stones, in burrows dug in earth, twigs or decaying wood, in plant-galls, and elsewhere. The many species of *Megachile* are called Leaf-cutters because the females snip more or less circular pieces out of leaves or petals (Pl. 70). Then they fit these pieces together so skillfully that they form tight, thimble-shaped cells snugly filling some suitable space in wood or earth. Putnam estimated that thirty cells, arranged in nine rows under a board in his porch, contained at least 1000 pieces of leaves.

ANTHOPHORIDÆ

See p. 427. One interpretation of taxonomic rules changes the name to Podaliriidæ. The Anthophoridæ usually make burrows in the ground, furnishing them with a paste of pollen and honey for larval food. Our principal genera may be recognized as follows.

1.—Two submarginal cells.—See *Exomalopsis.* ......4.
 Three submarginal cells. ....2.
2.—First discoidal cell much longer than the marginal cell (Fig. 6). ....3.
 First discoidal cell scarcely, if any, longer than the marginal (Figs. 7 and 8). ....4.
3.—Third submarginal cell almost quadrate; about as wide above as beneath. Marginal cell obtuse at the tip, which extends beyond the apex of the 3rd submarginal cell only about as far as the marginal cell is wide.—*Anthophora* (Fig. 6. Mandibles with not more than 2 teeth) and *Clisodon terminalis* (Mandibles tridentate. Female has yellowish red hair on the apex of the abdomen. Nests in dead wood).
 Third submarginal cell narrower above than beneath. Tip of marginal cell far beyond the apex of the 3rd submarginal cell and touching the costal margin. First recurrent vein reaching the apical corner of the 2nd submarginal cell.—*Emphoropsis.* Largely Western but *E. floridana* is common in the East.
4.—Apical part of marginal cell sharply diverging from

wing-margin. First submarginal cell about as long as the 3rd. Fig. 8. Southern and Western.—*Exomalopsis*. (*Anthophorula*: possibly merely *Exomalopsis* with only 2 submarginal cells.)

Second submarginal cell rather longer than either the 1st or 3rd; not narrowed above. Marginal cell obtuse at tip; not extending more than its width beyond the apex of the 3rd submarginal, which is much narrowed at the marginal. Hind legs of female with long dense pubescence. Southern.—*Centris*.

Neither of these. ....**5.**

5.—Vertex raised in the middle at the ocelli. Male antennæ usually conspicuously longer than female's and his clypeus with yellow markings. ....**6.**

Not so. ....**7.**

6.—Clypeus nearly touching the eyes. Maxillary palpi often less than 5-jointed.—*Melissodes*.

Clypeus separated from the eyes by a fairly large triangular area.—*Tetralonia* (Max. palpi 6-jointed), *Xenoglossa* (Max. palpi 5-jointed. Tarsal claws cleft. *X. pruinosa*, Pl. 70, has "frosted" bands on abdomen), and *Cemolobus* (Max. palpi 5-jointed. Claws toothed but not cleft).

7.—Pulvilli (pads between tarsal claws; Fig. 9) present. —*Melitoma* (Proboscis, when folded, extending as far as the base of the abdomen. Our *M. taurea* has the abdomen cross-banded with white) and *Diadasia* (Proboscis shorter. Western).

No pulvilli (Fig. 10).—*Emphor* (Pl. 70).

NOMADIDÆ

See p. 427. All appear to have "cuckoo" habits, laying their eggs in the nests of other bees. They are largely hairless and rather wasp-like in appearance. Quite probably the genera included here are not all properly put in one family. Our principal ones may be separated as follows.

1.—Less than 2 submarginal cells. Western.—*Phileremulus*.

Two submarginal cells. ....**2.**

Three submarginal cells. ....**3.**

2.—Thorax and head black. Abdomen red, with white markings due to hair. Marginal cell long; obtuse or very slightly truncate at its tip. Size small. Maxillary palpi 6-jointed.—*Neopasites*.

Marginal cell extremely small. Very small bees.—*Neolarra*.

Neither of these.—*"Phileremus."* Possibly not a good genus, and its species may not belong here.

3.—Apex of marginal cell touching the costa (Fig. 12). Color usually either mainly red or a combination of black with yellow or red (Pl. 100). Light marks, if any, on abdomen not due to hairs. Maxillary palpi 6-jointed. —*Nomada.*

Not this combination of characters. . . . . .4.

4.—Marginal cell scarcely or not half the length of the first discoidal cell and not or scarcely extending beyond the apex of the 3rd submarginal cell. Abdomen with hairs, and the light markings, if any, due to them. Western.—*Bombomelecta* (Scutellum with two spines. Abdomen usually without pale hair-spots) and *Pseudomelecta* (Scutellum sometimes with merely two lobes or tubercles. Usually spots of white pubescence on abdomen).

Neither of these.—*Viereckella* (Max. palpi 5-jointed. Our common species, *pilosula,* looks like a black *Nomada* with hair on its abdomen), *Epeolus* (Fig. 11. Max. palpi 2-jointed) and *Triepeolus* (Max. palpi 3-jointed. Pl. 70).

BOMBIDÆ

See p. 426. The burly Bumblebees (Humblebees in the speech of England) are so conspicuous, abundant, interesting and important that I am giving them considerable space. *Bombus* is the industrious genus. Some nomenclaturists—they are often called worse names than that by those nature-lovers who do not like to have familiar names changed—say that we should call the genus *Bremus* and the family Bremidæ. *Bumblebees and Their Ways* by O. E. Plath is a recent, reliable account of American species.

Young queens of *Bombus* mate in the autumn and pass the winter in some snug retreat in the ground or elsewhere. Their husbands, brothers, old-maid sisters and mothers die before winter sets in. Next year each queen starts housekeeping by herself. The nest is usually in some ready-made hollow such as a deserted mouse-nest, some species preferring under-ground ones. After arranging a mat of dried grass or the like, she builds an egg-cell, primes it with honey-moistened pollen, lays her first eggs, and then closes the cell. She also makes a waxen honey-pot and fills it with rather liquid honey, which she uses during inclement weather, meanwhile incubating and guarding her eggs.

When the larvæ hatch they feed on the honey-moistened

pollen supplemented with special meals furnished by their mother. In about ten days the larvæ reach their full size and each makes a thin, papery but tough cocoon, in which it pupates. The queen still broods her young and sips from her honey-pot. A week or two later the first young, all small-sized daughters, emerge and take up their duties as workers. These workers do not mate. Males and mating females are born later in the season.

Perhaps you wondered why I called these bees important. Of course, like other wild things, they are important because they are a definite part of the world in which we live, but they are more directly important to us because they carry pollen from one flower to another. This enables the plants to set seed and fruit. Red clover depends almost entirely upon them. Remember the famous defense of the thesis that old maids are the support of the British Empire: "Old maids keep cats; cats catch field mice that otherwise would destroy humblebee nests; humblebees enable red clover to set seed; red clover is good food for cattle; and roast beef gives strength to men who are the support of the British Empire."

Psithyrus is a lazy genus that goes to live with its relatives and does not help with the work. *Bombus* must feed the mother *Psithyrus* as well as the latter's children, none of which is a worker. What is worse, the female *Psithyrus* may even kill the *Bombus* queen.

The following key is to the species of the Atlantic Coast, omitting the extremely variable *rufocinctus* and other Western species. *P.* stands for *Psithyrus;* *B.* for *Bombus;* and *B. B.* for *Bombias,* a subgenus of *Bombus.* "Occiput" is the top of the head. "Pleura" refers to the side of the thorax especially in front, below the front wings. "Scutellum" is the triangular hind part of the top of the thorax. "Interalar band" is on the top of the thorax between the wings. The "malar space" is between the eyes and the jaws. The "supra-orbital line" is an imaginary line from the top of one compound eye to the top of the other. The notes on color refer to the color of the hairs; and the upper side of the abdomen is all that is considered when stating its color.

1.—Divisions of tarsal claws very unequal; 12 antennal joints; 6 visible, abdominal segments (Females). ......2.

Divisions of tarsal claws subequal; 13 antennal joints; 7 visible, abdominal segments (Males). ....15.

Females

(The female of *P. tricolor* is unknown unless *fernaldæ* be it.)

2.—Outer face of hind tibiæ convex and hairy.—*Psithyrus*. ....3.

Outer face of hind tibiæ concave and bare, except at margins.—*Bombus*. ....5.

3.—Occiput black with little or no yellow; lower portion of pleura with dark hairs.—*P. ashtoni*.

Occiput with much yellow. ....4.

4.—Thorax without interalar black hairs but disk bare; pleura light; little or no yellow on fourth abdominal segment; face largely dark.—*P. laboriosus*.

Thorax with interalar black hairs; pleura mostly light; no reddish on fifth abdominal segment but yellow, at least on the sides, on the fourth.—*P. insularis*.

Thorax with or without interalar black hairs; lower pleura yellow or dark; fourth abdominal segment almost entirely covered with yellow; often with reddish on sides of fifth; apical, abdominal segment very pointed and strongly recurved.—*P. fernaldæ*.

5.—No distinct interalar black band. ....6.

Black interalar band. ....9.

6.—First to fourth abdominal segments largely yellow.—*B. fervidus dorsalis*.

Third and fourth segments largely black. ....7.

7.—Ocelli large, the lateral ones farther from each other than from the margins of the eyes and below the supraorbital line; occiput and face largely black; first abdominal segment yellow, the others black except for (usually) brownish at the middle of the base of the second.—*B. B. separatus*.

Ocelli small. ....8.

8.—First abdominal segment yellow, second and following segments without yellow; occiput largely yellow; face wide and largely black.—*B. impatiens* (Pl. 100).

First abdominal segment yellow, some yellow at basal middle of the second, otherwise the abdomen black; occiput largely yellow; face long, triangular, black.—*B. bimaculatus*.

First abdominal segment largely yellow; the yellow which largely covers the second segment is notched in the middle behind and, in the workers, usually mixed with red; third to fifth black; frequently considerable interalar black; occiput largely black; face wide and black; pleura yellow.—*B. affinis*.

First and second segments largely yellow and remainder of abdomen largely black; disk of thorax not nude and without black; pleura usually black; occiput largely yellow; face largely black.—*B. perplexus.*

First and usually the second abdominal segments yellow, the remainder usually largely black; pleura yellow; disk nude and with scattered, black hairs; occiput largely yellow in queens and usually so in workers; face long and largely black.—*B. vagans.*

9.—Second and third abdominal segments red, first and fourth largely yellow, the remainder black.—*B. ternarius* (Pl. 100).

Third and following segments black, the first two largely yellow. ....10.

Third segment yellow. ....11.

10.—Ocelli large, separated from each other, and below the supra-orbital line; yellow on second segment neither notched nor mixed with red; face and occiput black.—*B. B. fraternus.*

Otherwise.—See *B. affinis* (8).

11.—First to fourth segments yellow, the remainder largely black. ....12.

Fourth segment black, also pleura and often the scutellum. ....13.

12.—Pleura black; face and occiput largely light.—*B. borealis.*

Pleura largely yellow; face (largely) and occiput black.—*B. fervidus.*

13.—Ocelli large, separated, and below the supra-orbital line; first abdominal segment largely black, second largely yellow, third yellow, the remainder black; occiput either black or yellow; face black.—*B. B. auricomus.*

Otherwise. ....14.

14.—Second and third abdominal segments yellow, the remainder black except that there is often considerable yellow on the fifth and sixth; face (largely) and occiput black.—*B. terricola.*

First (largely), second, and third abdominal segments yellow, otherwise black; face and occiput black.—*B. pennsylvanicus* (Pl. 100. Possibly the name should be *americanorum*).

Males

15.—Ocelli large, the lateral ones not much, if any, more than their diameter from the margins of the eyes, and below the supra-orbital line; eyes bulging. ....16.

Ocelli otherwise. ....18.

16.—First (usually), second, and third abdominal segments yellow, the remainder largely black; sometimes interalar black; third antennal segment as long as the fourth and fifth combined.—*B. B. auricomus.*

Otherwise colored and third antennal segment at most not much longer than the fifth. ....**17.**

17.—First abdominal segment yellow, the remainder black except for brownish on basal middle of the second and, sometimes, yellow at sides of third; face largely yellow.— *B. B. separatus.*

First and second abdominal segments yellow, the remainder largely black; face largely black.—*B. B. fraternus.*

18.—Second and third abdominal segments red; first (largely) and fourth yellow; fifth and sixth black; interalar black; pleura, face, and occiput, yellow.—*B. ternarius.*

Third segment not red. ....**19.**

19.—Sixth and seventh abdominal segments largely red, the others variable; face largely black; occiput yellow.— *P. tricolor.*

Sixth segment not largely red. ....**20.**

20.—First and fourth abdominal segments black; second and third yellow; the remainder variable; interalar black; pleura black; face largely yellow.—*B. terricola.*

First abdominal segment largely yellow. ....**21.**

21.—First to fourth, inclusive, abdominal segments largely yellow. ....**22.**

Not so. ....**23** (and also *B. perplexus,* **22**).

22.—First abdominal segment usually with some black, fifth usually black; interalar, pleura usually, and scutellum sometimes, black; occiput black; 0.6 to 1 in. long. —*B. pennsylvanicus* (See **14**).

No black on first or fifth abdominal segments; interalar sometimes, and scutellum, yellow; interalar usually, and occiput black; 0.4 to 0.7 in. long.—*B. fervidus.*

No black on the first but usually on the fifth abdominal segments; interalar and usually the pleura black; occiput and sometimes the pleura yellow.—*B. borealis.*

No black on the first abdominal segment, but the fourth and fifth usually black although the whole abdomen may be yellow; interalar, occiput, and usually the face and pleura, yellow; face triangular, not long (as in *fervidus* and *borealis*).—*B. perplexus.*

23.—Second abdominal segment with little or no black. **24.**

This segment with considerable black. ....**25.**

24.—Occiput, interalar, and pleura, largely yellow; face largely black; first abdominal segment, usually the second, and sometimes the third, yellow; abdomen otherwise black.—*P. laboriosus.*

Occiput (usually largely) and face black; interalar often with much black; pleura, and most of the first abdominal segment, yellow; yellow of the second segment usually mixed with red and notched behind; remainder of the abdomen without yellow.—*B. affinis.*

Occiput, pleura, and face (largely) yellow; very

little, if any interalar black; first two abdominal segments yellow, the remainder usually black.—*B. vagans.*

25.—Face, occiput (usually), and pleura black; first (usually) and fourth abdominal segments yellow, the remainder largely black.—*P. ashtoni.*

Face (largely), occiput, and pleura, yellow; first and part of the second abdominal segments yellow, the remainder black.—*B. bimaculatus.*

Face (usually), occiput (largely), pleura, and first abdominal segment yellow; remainder of abdomen black. —*B. impatiens.*

APIDÆ

See p. 426. Our only species is the Asiatic *Apis mellifera.* It is the cultivated Honey- or Hive-bee. The color of the abdomen is variable. It is probably the most written-about insect. Maeterlinck's *Life of the Bee* is a classic. *Beekeeping* by Phillips and *How to Keep Bees* by Mrs. Comstock are both excellent. The individuals usually seen are workers, almost sexless females. As in other bees, and many other insects as well, the legs are not concerned solely with walking. Pl. 70 shows the device (*a*) on the front legs for cleaning antennæ, and a part of the pollen-gathering apparatus on the hind legs. The basitarsus (*b*) has pollen combs on the inner side which scrape the pollen from the abdomen and the second pair of legs. Pollen is removed from these pollen combs by a row of stiff hairs at the end of the tibia and then is pushed upward into the corbicula (*c*), or pollen basket, by means of the projection which is just below the tibial comb, shown at the base of the basitarsus. The long hairs on each side of the corbicula prevent the load from slipping side-ways. The notch between the tibia and tarsus has been called the wax-shears, but it has nothing to do with the manipulation of wax.

The swarming of the honeybee brings about an increase in the number of colonies but it is the queen of the old colony, and not one of her daughters, which goes out to form the new colony. The stimulus to the act of swarming is not understood. Since a swarm sometimes starts without a queen, she cannot be the instigator. In fact, if she is detained by a trap or in some other way, the bees may destroy her and swarm with a young queen.

The swarming bees usually cluster on a branch or some other support before going to a cavity, such as a hollow tree, in which to start the new colony. The old-fashioned idea that ringing bells or beating tin pans hastens this clustering is a mistaken one. If there be a delay in finding a suitable cavity, an unprotected comb will be made on the branch where the bees have clustered.

Shortly after the swarm has departed, a young queen which has been left behind in her sealed-up cradle eats her way out, takes her mating flight several days later, and settles down to her work at the old stand with the help of such of her unmarriageable sisters as have remained.

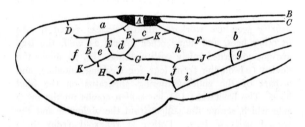

A, stigma; *B*, costal vein; *C*, subcostal vein; *D*, marginal vein; *E*, transverse cubital veins; *F*, basal vein; *G* and *H*, first and second recurrent veins; *I*, subdiscoidal vein; *J*, discoidal vein; *K*, cubital vein; *a*, marginal cell; *b*, median cell; *c*, *d*, *e*, and *f*, first, second, third, and fourth submarginal or cubital cells; *g*, submedian cell; *h*, *i*, *j*, first, second, and third discoidal cells.

NOTES ON SOME OF THE GALLS MADE ON PLANTS BY INSECTS AND THEIR RELATIVES

Plant galls are interesting to the zoologist because most of them are made by animals; to the botanist because of the unsolved problems of abnormal plant growth they present; and to all of us, not only because ornamental and useful plants are frequently damaged thereby, but also because much of our food is dependent upon them. The bacterial root-galls of legumes are Nature's principal agents in making atmospheric nitrogen available for plant use. It has also been said—and denied—that potatoes are fungal root-galls. Of the galls caused by insects, oak galls have been used in dyeing, tanning, and the manufacture of ink. Note also the fig insect, p. 398.

As is the case with so many things in natural history, we must go back to Pliny for the first ideas concerning plant galls. This philosopher knew that a "fly" was produced in them, but he did not associate this "fly" with the cause of the gall growth. He thought that galls sprang up in a night and that the larvæ merely devoured this growth. However, the interest of the early observers was not always entirely biological. Important prophecies were deduced as to the events of the coming year by observing whether galls contained spiders, worms, or "flies."

The constant occurrence of certain larvæ within certain galls at length aroused the suspicion that galls were formed by the larvæ. To account for the presence of the egg and larvæ, it was supposed that the female insect laid the egg in the ground and thence it was drawn up with the sap and carried to the outer parts of the plant, where it lodged and gall formation ensued. This theory soon met with opposition. Redi, a poet and physician of the Seventeenth Century, not having seen the eggs laid, assumed that the plant had a "vegetable soul" which produced galls with their eggs, larvæ, etc., while, at the same time, it gave birth to flowers, fruits and seeds.

Sprengel, 1793, is credited with having been the first to point out cross-fertilization in plants, but this is a mistake. Thirty years before, Filippo Arena, an Italian, wrote rather fully on the subject and, noting the cross-pollination by insects, stated that galls were developed by the plants for the express purpose of having insects ready at hand for the sake of pollination.

Malpighi, late in the Seventeenth Century, was the first to record the fact that the producion of galls followed the puncture of vegetable tissues by insects, and he came to the conclusion that the insects inject a substance into the plant tissue which produces a swelling similar to that which the sting of a bee causes in animal tissue. His idea is now rather generally accepted but, even so, there is almost certainly more to the story and it will be interesting. Possibly insects are merely carriers of bacteria that are the real gall-makers.

If the galls are inhabited, a clue to the makers may be gained by a study of the inhabitants. Mites have four pairs of legs, at least when full-grown; no wings; and are very small. Aphids have three pairs of legs and they sometimes have wings. Galls made by both of these groups are usually open. Saw-fly larvæ have thoracic, and usually distinct abdominal, legs; their galls usually have a large hollow on the inside. Gall-making Lepidopterous larvæ have thoracic but no abdominal legs. It is not so easy to distinguish Hymenopterous and Dipterous larvæ; and it should always be remembered that galls may be inhabited by creatures which did not make them —parasites of the maker and also inquilines, the latter being "guests" which avail themselves of the abundant food but do not directly injure the maker of the gall. Some galls are complicated communities. We speak of creatures "making" the galls; the plants really do this, acting on some (not understood) stimulus furnished by the animals. It is exceedingly curious that insects which are so similar that they may be distinguished only with difficulty cause such different and distinctive galls. In addition to the unknown chemics of the process, the gall-causing instinct is one of the most mysterious things in entomology.

The number of different galls caused by animal para-

PLATE 71

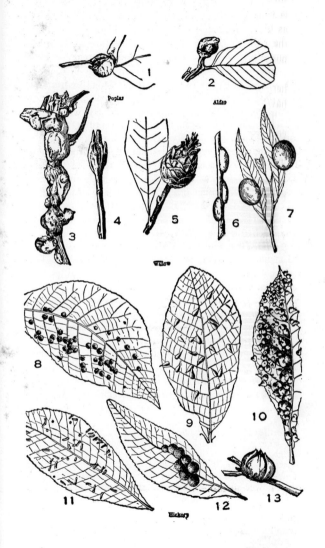

Poplar

Alder

Willow

Hickory

sites runs into thousands. Almost no form of plant life is exempt. Although certain of the higher plants, such as the oak, willow, rose, and goldenrod, are preeminently the gall-bearing plants, still algæ, fungi, ferns, and gymnosperms come in for their share.

Many of the galls of woody plants have been omitted here, but those of herbaceous plants, including grasses, have been, necessarily, almost ignored.

The notes and illustrations given here are arranged according to the plants on which the galls occur and with but little reference to the relationships of the makers. The illustrations are, for the most part, about half-size and are of Northeastern species. The following list of genera will help to make the relationships clear.

MITES.—*Acarus, Eriophyes, Phyllocoptes.*

HOMOPTERA.—Aphididæ: *Chermes, Colopha, Gobaishia, Hamamelistes, Hormaphis, Melaphis, Mordwilkoja, Pachypsylla, Pemphigus, Phylloxera.*

LEPIDOPTERA.—Tortricidæ: *Eucosma.* Gelechiidæ: *Gnorimoschema.*

DIPTERA.—Cecidomyiidæ: *Asteromyia, Caryomyia, Cecidomyia, Cincticornia, Contarinia, Dasyneura, Itonida, Lasioptera, Oligotrophus, Retinodiplosis, Rhabdophaga, Rhopalomyia, Schizomyia, Thecodiplosis, Trishormomyia.* Trypetidæ: *Eurosta, Œdaspis.* Agromyzidæ: *Agromyza.*

HYMENOPTERA.—Saw-flies: *Euura, Potania.* Cynipidæ: *Amphibolips, Andricus, Aulacidea, Biorhiza, Callirhytis, Cynips, Diastrophus, Diplolepis, Disholcaspis, Dryophanta, Gonaspis, Neuroterus, Xystoteras.* Chalcidoidea: *Hemadas.*

Conifers.—The orange-colored larva of *Cecidomyia pini-rigidæ* lives in a basal enlargement of shortened, deformed needles of pitch pine; and *C. balsamicola,* of balsam. *Thecodiplosis ananassi* makes a brown, pineapple-like gall on cypress. *Itonida anthici* makes a whitish, flower-shaped, fungus-like growth on cypress. *Retinodiplosis resinicola* larvæ are orange "grubs" living in clear or whitish masses of pitch on the under side of pitch-pine branches; *R. inopis,* in resinous masses on scrub-pine leaves.

Poplar and Cottonwood.—*Pemphigus populicaulis* makes globular galls at the base of leaves (Pl. 71, Fig. 1); *P. populi-transversus,* oval, somewhat elongated galls on the petioles; *P. populi-venæ,* yellow galls on midrib of

PLATE 72

Oak

leaf. *Mordwilkoja vagabundus* folds and crinkles the foliage. *Agromyza schineri* causes irregular, somewhat globular enlargements of young twigs.

Willow.—Many kinds have been described. See Pl. 71. The following are samples of those on twigs. *Phytophaga* (also put in *Rhabdophaga*) *rigidæ* (Fig. 4). *Rhabdophaga batatus* (Fig. 3) and *strobiloides* (Fig. 5). *R. strobiliscus* is like *strobiloides* but all the leaves are pointed at the tip. *R. rhodoides* and others make more open growths, resembling small, double flowers. *R. brassicoides:* bunches of oval, single-celled, sessile galls, each three-fourths to two and a fourth inches, "like the sprouts of a cabbage stump," usually not near tips of branches. *R. triticoides:* many-celled and resemble a wheat-head. *R. nodulas:* like *batatus* but smaller, more solitary, and only single-celled. For *Euura ovum* see Fig. 6; *E. nodus,* a smooth twig enlargement, one-fourth to twice normal diameter; *E. orbitalis,* enlarged bud-gall.

The following are on willow leaves. *Trishormomyia verruca:* about 0.1 inch in diameter, on veins; about evenly divided by the leaf; the upper side flattish or with a minute nipple, the lower side wart-like. *Pontania pomum,* Fig. 7, on midrib. *P. pisum:* pea-like, yellowish, on under-side of leaves. *P. desmodioides:* smooth, flattish, sessile, yellowish-green, about equally divided by the leaf. *P. hyalina:* fleshy, reddish, in parallel rows on either side of the midrib. *P. borealis:* solitary, smooth, reddish, pear-shaped, about one-third above the leaf. *P. consors:* gregarious, hairy, rather spherical, near leaf-base, about one-third above the leaf. *P. gracilis:* spherical, smooth, near petiole to one side of midrib, about equally divided by leaf. *P. terminalis:* green swelling on upper surface; the leaf eventually rolls.

Hickory.—Plate 71. The principal twig-gall is *Phylloxera caryæcaulis* (Fig. 13). Numerous other species of *Phylloxera* make galls on the leaves. Of these the petiole bears *caryæren,* kidney-shaped; *subelliptica,* elongate, nut-like; and *spinosa,* irregular, spiny galls. On the leaves, those of *caryæyenæ* are keel-like pleats along the leaf-veins; *caryæfallax* crowded, conical, on upper surface; *deplanata,* reddish- or greenish-yellow, conical below; *depressa,* depressed, fringed; *pilosula,* hairy, light green, flattened above, below convex and with a nipple. The galls of *Caryomyia holotricha* (Fig. 8) are pubescent; *caryæcola* (Fig. 9), smooth; *sanguinolenta* (Fig. 10), red; *tubicola* (Fig. 11); and *persicoides* (Fig. 12), brownish, downy. *C. cynipsea* makes a round, hard, midrib gall, about half an inch across. *C. nucicola* deforms the husks.

Alder.—*Dasyneura serrulatæ* causes deformations, with whitish "bloom," of terminal buds (Pl. 71, Fig. 2).

PLATE 73

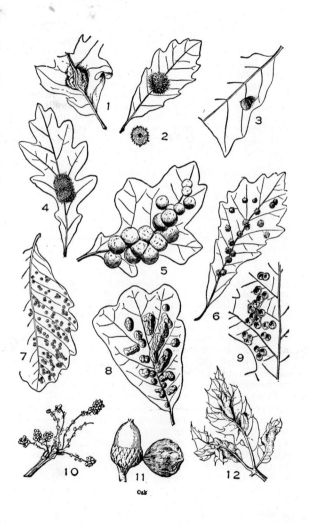

Oak

Oak.—More than three hundred different galls have been listed.

Plate 72 shows *Amphibolips confluentus* (Fig. 1), spongy inside; *A. inanis* (Fig. 2), merely larval cell and radiating threads inside; *A. ilicifoliæ* (Fig. 3); *A. cœlebs* (Fig. 5). *Callirhytis futilis* (Fig. 4) is somewhat flattened, projecting on both sides of the leaf; inside are kernels kept in position by white filaments (Alternate generation is in a woody gall on the roots). *C. papillatus* (Fig. 7), somewhat nipple-shaped, projects on both sides, surrounded by a reddish areola (Alternate generation is in a woody gall on the roots). *C. capsulus* (Fig. 9). *C. palustris* (Fig. 11), hollow inside except for a loose kernel (Alternate generation is in a small seed-like gall on leaves). *Andricus singularis* (Fig. 6), something like a small *inanis; flocci,* also called *lana* (Fig. 8), like a mass of wool with brown kernels; *petiolicola* (Fig. 10), many celled.

Plate 73.—*Andricus piger* (Fig. 1), under side of midrib. *Cynips prinoides* (Fig. 2), shiny, single-celled, under side of leaf. *C. pezomachoides* (Fig. 3), surface finely netted, two cavities, and *C. erinacei* (Fig. 4), spines red when young (Alternate generations of these two in small seed-like cells in the buds in spring). *Dryophanta polita* (Fig. 5) sometimes grows singly. *Neuroterus pernotus* (Fig. 6), with white hairs, under side of leaf; *N. umbilicatus* (Fig. 7), small nipple in deep, central depression, under side of leaf; *Cincticornia pilulæ* (Fig. 8), upper side of leaf; *Xystoteras poculum* (Fig. 9), pale red to light lavender, under side of leaf (not a Cecidomyid gall as formerly believed); *Cecidomyia niveipila* (Fig. 12), fold lined with white pubescence. *Dryocosmus deciduus* makes galls about the size of wheat-grains on the under side of midrib, often 30 on a leaf. Fig. 10 shows the white, shot-like catkin gall of *Andricus pulcher* and Fig. 11 the acorn gall of *Amphibolips prunus.*

Plate 74.—*Callirhytis cornigerus* (Fig. 1). *C. punctatus* (Fig. 2) resembles *cornigerus* but without "horns." These two often damage black oak and pin oak respectively. *C. seminator* (Fig. 3), white or pinkish, woolly; *C. similis* (Fig. 4), usually on scrub-oak; *C. clavula* (Fig. 5), usually on white oak. *Cynips* (given thus but should be in some other genus) *strobilana* (Fig. 6), hard and corky, with a single cell in each division. *Disholcaspis globulus* (the gall usually more hollow than shown by Fig. 7); *D. duricaria* (Fig. 9), with sharp point at apex. *Biorhiza forticornis* (Fig. 10), pale yelllow with reddish tinge when fresh, kernel of each division held by radiating fibers (Alternate generation is in a fleshy root-gall). *Neuroterus batatus* (Fig. 8), pale bluish bloom, corky, many larval cells; *N. noxiosus* (Fig. 11), hard, woody,

PLATE 74

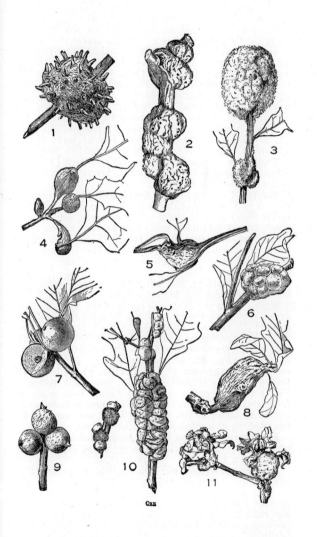

Oak

many larval cells (The alternate generations of these two are in similar galls on the leaves in the spring).

Elm.—Plate 75, Fig. 1, shows galls of *Colopha ulmicola*. *Gobaishia ulmifusus* makes solitary, spindle-shaped galls on the upper surface of red elm leaves.

Hackberry.—Plate 75: *Pachypsylla cucurbitæ* (Fig. 4) on under side of leaf, concave in the middle, with a small nipple; *P. vesiculum* (Fig. 5), flat, blister-like, convex with a small nipple; *P. mamma* (Fig. 6), nearly cylindrical, apex rounded bluntly; *P. gemma* (Fig. 7), variable in shape and size, woody, numerous cells; *P. venusta* (Fig. 8), on petioles, several compartments.

Witch-hazel.—Plate 75: *Hormaphis hamamelidis* (Fig. 2), greenish or reddish, on upper side of leaf; *Hamamelistes spinosus* (Fig. 3), green or reddish bud-galls.

Tulip-tree.—Plate 75: *Cecidomyia tulipifera* (Fig. 9); *Thecodiplosis liriodendri* (Fig. 10), brown spots with a yellow or greenish areola.

Maple.—Plate 75, Fig. 11: *Cecidomyia* (?); incorrectly classed in *Sciara;* probably not a Mycetophilid according to Dr. Felt) *ocellaris,* light yellow or green, usually with a red, central dot; it has never been reared. *Phyllocoptes aceris-crumena* makes slender, spindle-shaped galls on the upper surface of sugar-maple leaves; and *P. quadripes,* small, bladder-like galls on the upper surface of soft-maple leaves.

Sumac.—Plate 75, Fig. 12: *Melaphis rhois,* yellowish-green tinged with red, hollow, on under side of leaf.

Rose.—Plate 76: *Diplolepis bicolor* (Fig. 1), yellowish-green sometimes tinged with red in summer, brown in winter; *D. radicum* (Fig. 2), on root; *D. dichlocerus* (Fig. 4), tapering at ends, reddish; *D. rosæ* (Fig. 5), mossy mass containing hard cells (an imported species); *D. ignota* (Fig. 8), white-mealy surface, rather round, sometimes coalescing; *D. vernæ* (Fig. 7), reddish; *D. lenticularis* or *rosæfolii* (Fig. 6), somewhat flattened. Fig. 3 shows a gall described as having been made by *Diplolepis* (or *Rhodites*) *globulus* but now believed to be started by some, as yet, unknown insect and modified by the presence of a guest-fly, *Periclistis pirata.*

Raspberry.—Plate 76, Fig. 9: *Diastrophus radicum,* especially on roots of black raspberry; varies from size of a pea to 2 x 1 inches.

Blackberry.—Plate 76: *Diastrophus bassettii* (Fig. 10), on the stems of trailing blackberry close to the ground; greenish, tinged with red, pithy with many rounded cells; *D. nebulosus* (Fig. 11), dark green, turning reddish; *D. cuscutæformis* (Fig. 12). *Lasioptera farinosa* makes an irregularly ridged, warty, light brown swelling, about half an inch long, on the under side of leaf-veins; *L. nodulosa,* an irregular, elongate swelling about an inch long on the smaller branches.

PLATE 75

1

Elm

2

Witch Hazel

3

4

5

6

Hackberry

7

8

9

10

Tulip-tree

11

Maple

12

Sumac

453

Cratægus.—*Cecidomyia bedeguar* makes a tufted, nearly globular gall, about half an inch in diameter, on midribs; and *Trishormomyia cratægifolia,* a cockscomb gall on the leaves.

Cinquefoil.—Plate 76, Fig. 13: *Gonaspis potentillæ,* on axils of leaves, single-celled. Two species of *Diastrophus, niger* and *minimus,* make galls on the stems.

Wild Cherry.—Plate 76: *Eriophyes padi,* also called *Acarus serotinæ* (Fig. 14), hollow, stemmed pouches, opening on under side of leaf; *Cecidomyia serotinæ* (Fig. 15), bright red in spring.

Grape.—Plate 77: *Schizomyia pomum* (Fig. 1), variable, with 8 or 9 ridges when mature, numerous longitudinal cells each divided by a partition; *Cecidomyia viticola* (Fig. 2), green or red; *Lasioptera vitis* (Fig. 3), yellowish-green or reddish, on stems and leaf-stalks. *S. coryloides* makes a rounded mass, about 2 inches in diameter, of from 10 to 50 opaque, woolly, rather spindle-shaped, green galls. *Asteromyia petiolicola* makes spindle-shaped dwellings on the petioles. For *Phylloxera* or *Peritymbia vitifoliæ* (*vastatrix*) see page 83; the leaf-galls are hollow, fleshy swellings, which are rather wrinkled and hairy, on the under surface of leaves, opening above.

Touch-me-not.—Plate 77, Fig. 4: *Cecidomyia impatientis,* succulent, semi-transparent, containing a number of cells, at base of flower of *Impatiens.* *Lasioptera impatientifolia* causes a swelling of the base of leaves.

Linden and Basswood.—Plate 77, Fig. 5: *Cecidomyia verrucicola,* wart-like, about 0.2 inch in diameter, usually formed in July. *Cecidomyia citrina* deforms young terminal buds; *Eriophyes abnormis,* top-shaped galls on the under side of leaves.

Dogwood.—Plate 77, Fig. 6: *Lasioptera clavula,* contains an elongated channel inhabited by a single larva.

Huckleberry.—Plate 77, Fig. 7: *Hemadas nubilipennis* (*Solenozopheria vaccinii* is a guest fly) on stems of *Vaccinium.* The illustration shows an old gall with exit holes.

Wild Lettuce.—Plate 77, Fig. 8: *Aulacidea tumida* varies greatly, on main stalk of *Lactuca canadensis,* often involving the flower-panicle.

Goldenrod.—Plate 77: *Eurosta solidaginis* (Fig. 10 shows galls from which the flies have emerged), pithy inside with a rounded cell in the center on the main stalk; *Rhopalomyia solidaginis* (Fig. 11), caused by the arrest of stalk; *Œdaspis polita* (Fig. 12), caused by the arrest of side branches. *Lasioptera solidaginis* makes a gall much like that of *Eurosta.* Galls made by two genera of moths are often confused with these but, if the larvæ are present, one can at least determine whether or not they are Lepidopterous. To mention two species: the

PLATE 76

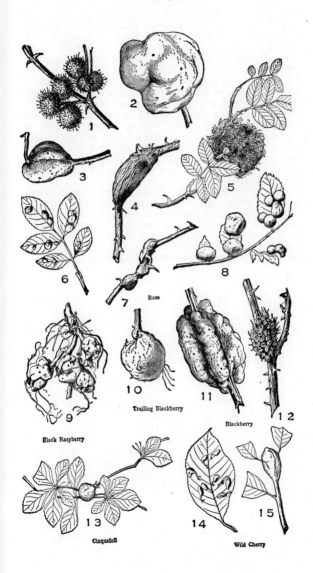

1

2

3

4

5

6

7 Rose

8

9
Black Raspberry

10
Trailing Blackberry

11

12
Blackberry

13
Cinquefoil

14

15
Wild Cherry

gall of *Gnorimoschema gallæsolidaginis* is about the size of *Eurosta* but is more tapering (Adults emerge in September and hibernate), that of *Eucosma scudderiana* is merely an elongate thickening of the stem near the flower head (Adults are found from June to August, larvæ or pupæ hibernating). The aerial gall of *Rhopalomyia hirtipes* is a large swelling of a bud "resembling a dried prune in texture; hard center"; it also makes a subterranean root-stalk swelling. *R. fusiformia* causes a ribbed, elongate structure, about 0.25 inch in length, which occurs singly or in masses on the stem or foliage. Species of *Asteromyia* live mostly in galls which are apparently affected with fungus; *carbonifera* causes a black blister and *rosæ* a rosy one; similar galls occur also on asters. About 150 kinds of galls have been recorded from American Compositæ.

Ash.—Plate 77, Fig. 9: *Contarinia canadensis,* succulent, pale green and sometimes tinged with red, formed in May or June. *Eriophyes fraxiniflora* deforms the catkins; and *E. fraxini* makes numerous galls on a single leaf, wart-like, subdivided by irregular, hairy curtains within. *Dasyneura tumidosæ* causes a gall on the base of the midrib and apical part of the petiole.

PLATE 77

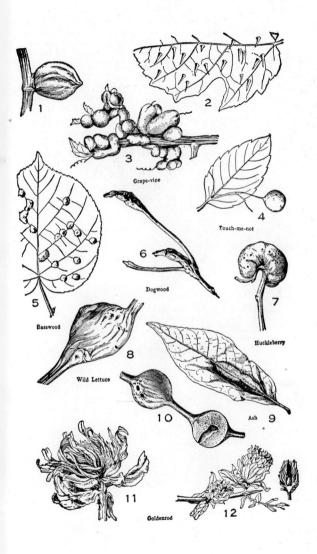

1

2

3

Grape-vine

4

Touch-me-not

5

Basswood

6

Dogwood

7

Huckleberry

8

Wild Lettuce

9

Ash

10

11

Goldenrod

12

COLORED ILLUSTRATIONS

PLATE 78

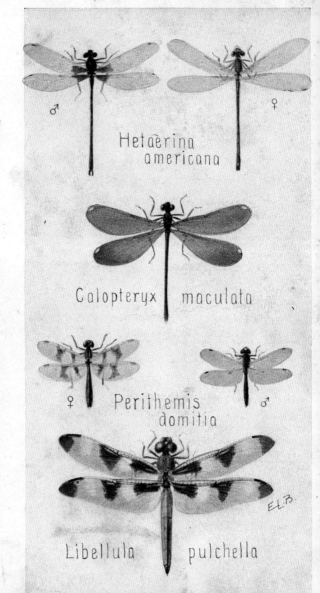

Hetaerina
americana

Calopteryx maculata

Perithemis
domitia

Libellula pulchella

PLATE 79

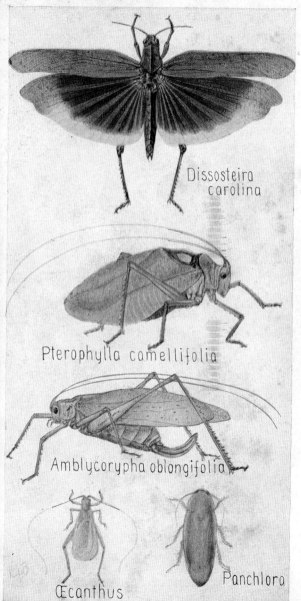

Dissosteira
carolina

Pterophylla camellifolia

Amblycorypha oblongifolia

Œcanthus

Panchlora

PLATE 80

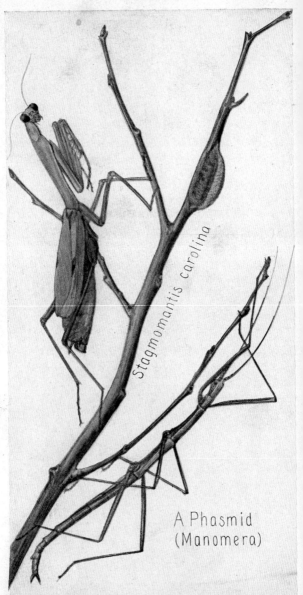

Stagmomantis carolina

A Phasmid
(Manomera)

PLATE 81

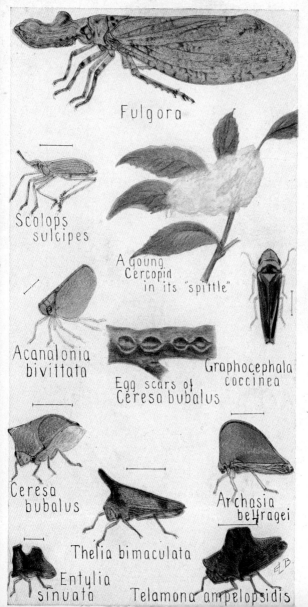

Fulgora

Scolops
sulcipes

A young
Cercopid
in its "spittle"

Acanalonia
bivittata

Egg scars of
Ceresa bubalus

Graphocephala
coccinea

Ceresa
bubalus

Thelia bimaculata

Archasia
belfragei

Entylia
sinuata

Telamona ampelopsidis

PLATE 82

Anosia plexippus

E.L.B.
arthemis

Basilarchia

archippus

PLATE 83

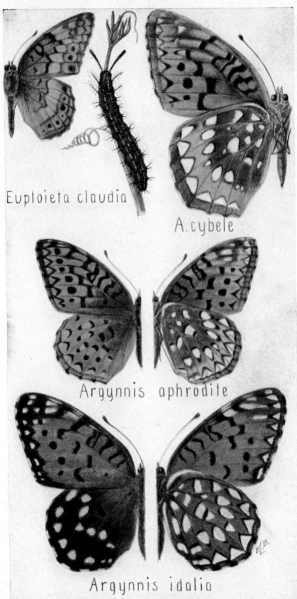

Euptoieta claudia

A. cybele

Argynnis aphrodite

Argynnis idalia

PLATE 84

Lycaena
comyntas

Lycaena ladon

pupa

Chrysophanus
hypophlaeus

Feniseca tarquinius

Thecla melinus

Thecla damon

Libythea
bachmani

Calephelis
borealis

Plate 85

Papilio

turnus   glaucus

troilus   polyxenes

philenor

PLATE 86

Deilephila lineata

Hemaris thysbe

Ampelophagus myron

Pholus pandorus

PLATE 87

Actias Luna

Plate 88

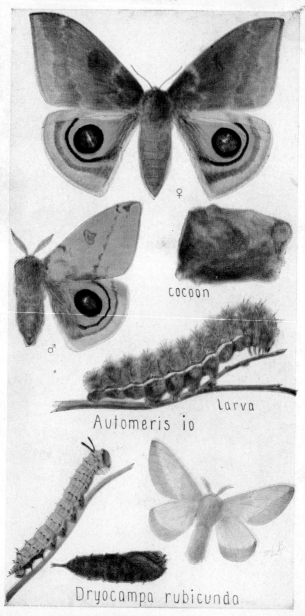

cocoon

larva

Automeris io

Dryocampa rubicunda

PLATE 89

Haploa clymene

Utetheisa bella

Isia isabella

Estigmene acraea

Diacrisia virginica

Apantesis nais

Euchaetias egle

PLATE 90

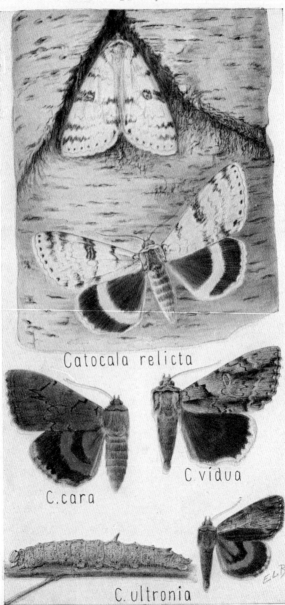

Catocala relicta

C. cara

C. vidua

C. ultronia

PLATE 91

Euclea
chloris

Thyridopteryx ephemeraeformis

Sibine stimulea

Harrisina americana

PLATE 92

Odontomyia
cincta

Tabanus
nigrovittatus

Chrysopila
thoracica

Anthrax
lateralis

Bombylius
major

Psilopodinus
patibulatus

Syrphus americanus

Volucella
evecta

Bombyliomyia
abrupta

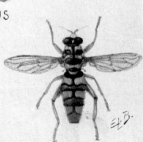

Milesia
virginiensis

PLATE 93

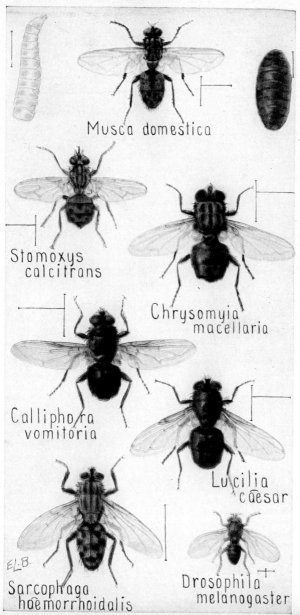

Musca domestica

Stomoxys calcitrans

Chrysomyia macellaria

Calliphora vomitoria

Lucilia caesar

Sarcophaga haemorrhoidalis

Drosophila melanogaster

PLATE 94

Lebia
grandis

Cicindela

sexgultata   generosa

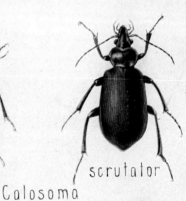

calidum   scrutator

Calosoma

Agonoderus
pallipes

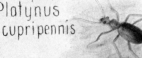

Platynus
cupripennis

Brachinus fumans

PLATE 95

Silpha noveboracensis

Necrophorus
marginatus

Staphylinid larva

Tachinus
fimbriatus

Creophilus
villosus

Coccinella 9-notata

Megilla
fuscilabris

Adalia
bipunctata Hippodamia
convergens

Anatis 15-punctata

Epilachne
borealis

Plate 96

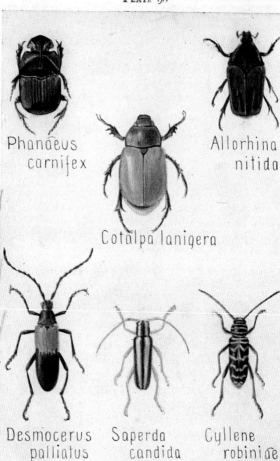

Phanaeus
carnifex

Cotalpa lanigera

Allorhina
nitida

Desmocerus
palliatus

Saperda
candida

Cyllene
robiniae

Chrysochus
auratus

Galerucella
luteola

PLATE 97

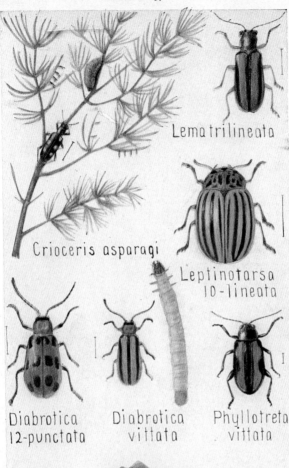

Lema trilineata

Crioceris asparagi

Leptinotarsa 10-lineata

Diabrotica 12-punctata

Diabrotica vittata

Phyllotreta vittata

Chalepus rubra

Larva of Cassida bivittata

Coptocycla bicolor

PLATE 98

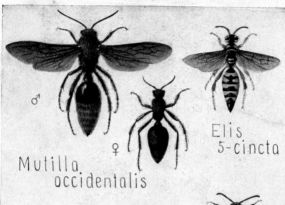

♂

♀

Mutilla
occidentalis

Elis
5-cincta

Chrysis
coeruleans

Eumenes fraternus

Odynerus birenimaculatus

Monobia
quadridens

Vespa communis

V. crabro

V. maculata

PLATE 99

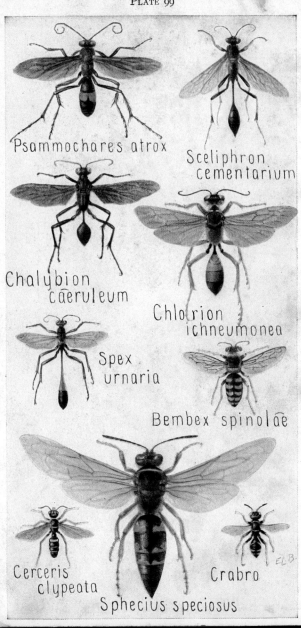

Psammochares atrox

Sceliphron cementarium

Chalybion caeruleum

Chlorion ichneumonea

Spex urnaria

Bembex spinolae

Cerceris clypeata

Sphecius speciosus

Crabro

PLATE 100

Bombus

impatiens   ternarius

♀

☿   ♂

pennsylvanicus

Xylocopa virginica

Nomada luteola   Agapostemon radiatus
♂   ♀

INDEX

In addition to listing the technical names down to subgenus, this index includes the "common" names and also a selection of technical specific ones. Indirectly it is a GLOSSARY by reason of references to definitions throughout the text. Since an insect's FOOD is often an indication of its identity, principal food-plants are included in this index. However, this hint is of little value in the case of "general feeders."